JOURNEY TO GORAKHPUR

JOURNEY TO

GORAKHPUR

AN ENCOUNTER WITH
CHRIST BEYOND CHRISTIANITY

JOHN MOFFITT

△ HOLT, RINEHART AND WINSTON
New York   Chicago   San Francisco

ISBN: 0-03-086577-8
Library of Congress Catalog Card Number: 70-155525
First Edition

Printed in the United States of America

ACKNOWLEDGMENTS

THE SCRIPTURE QUOTATIONS in this publication are from the
Revised Standard Version of the Bible, copyright 1946 and
1952, by the Division of Christian Education of the National
Council of the Churches of Christ in the U.S.A., and are used
by permission.   Quotations from the Upanishads are from
Swami Nikhilananda (trans., ed.), *The Upanishads* (Abridged
Edition), © 1963 by George Allen & Unwin Ltd., and are re-
printed from the 1964 Harper Torchbook edition by permission
of George Allen & Unwin, Ltd., London, and Harper & Row,
Publishers, New York.   Quotations from the Dhammapada
are from Buddha, *The Dhammapada*, translated by Irving
Babbitt, copyright 1936 by Edward S. Babbitt and Esther B.
Howe, and are reprinted by permission of New Directions Pub-
lishing Corporation, New York.   Quotations from the Bhaga-
vad Gita are from Swami Nikhilananda (trans., ed.), *The
Bhagavad Gita*, with Commentary, copyright 1944 by Swami
Nikhilananda, and are reprinted by permission of the Rama-
krishna-Vivekananda Center, Inc., New York.   The poem
"A Word to the Wise" by John Moffitt is from his volume

This Narrow World, © 1956, 1957, 1958, by John Moffitt, and is reprinted by permission of Dodd, Mead & Company, New York.   Quotations from the poem "Sorrows and Joys of the Buddha" by John Moffitt are from his volume *Adam's Choice,* © 1967 by John Moffitt, and are reprinted by permission of the Golden Quill Press, Francestown, N.H.   The poems "Dance of the God," "Heard in the Night," "Presence," and "Spirit of the Land" by John Moffitt are from his volume *The Living Seed,* © 1961, 1962, by John Moffitt, and are reprinted by permission of Harcourt Brace Jovanovich, Inc., New York.

The author also gratefully acknowledges permission from the following publishers to quote from works published by them: Advaita Ashrama, Mayavati India, for quotations from Swami Nityaswarupananda (trans.), *Ashtavakra Samhita,* copyright 1940; Ramakrishna, *Teachings of Sri Ramakrishna,* copyright 1934; *Life of Sri Ramakrishna,* copyright 1929; and *The Complete Works of Swami Vivekananda,* in 8 volumes, copyright 1921, 1922, 1935, 1936, and after; all rights reserved.

Alba House, Staten Island, N.Y., for quotations from Paul Garvin (trans., ed.), *The Life and Sayings of St. Catherine of Genoa,* © 1964 by Society of St. Paul.   America Press, New York, for a quotation from a letter to the editor by Ellen Weaver, Princeton University, in *America,* April 3, 1971 (revised by the writer), and quotations from John C. Haughey, "From Proclamation to Dialogue," in *America,* May 8, 1971; all rights reserved, © 1971, America Press, Inc., New York.

Burns & Oates Ltd., London, for quotations from Justin McCann (ed.), *The Cloud of Unknowing,* 1943, and J. P. de Caussade, *Self-Abandonment to Divine Providence,* 1952, not copyrighted.   Centre Védantique Ramakrichna, Gretz, France, for a quotation from Swami Siddheswarananda, "Le Yoga de St.-Jean de la Croix." 1949, not copyrighted. Doubleday & Company, Garden City, N.Y., for a quotation from Robert McAfee Brown and Gustave Weigel, S.J., *An American Dialogue,* © 1960 by Robert McAfee Brown and Gustave Weigel, S.J.   Helicon Press, Inc., Baltimore, Md., for a quotation from James Kritzeck, *Sons of Abraham,* © 1965 by James Kritzeck.   Longmans Group Limited, Harlow, Essex, England, for quotations from E. T. Sturdy (trans., ed.), *Narada Sutra: An Inquiry Into Love,* copyright 1896, all rights reserved. New Directions Publishing Corporation, New York, for quotations from Thomas Merton, *Zen and the Birds of Appetite,* © 1968 by The Abbey of Gethsemani, Inc.   Navajivan Trust,

Ahmedabad, India, for quotations from *The Collected Works of Mahatma Gandhi,* Publications Division of the Government of India, New Delhi, 1958ff., all rights reserved, and *Gandhi's Autobiography,* copyright 1948 by Public Affairs Press, Washington, D.C.   Ramakrishna-Vivekananda Center, Inc., New York, for quotations from Swami Nikhilananda (trans.), *The Gospel of Sri Ramakrishna,* copyright 1942 by Swami Nikhilananda; Swami Nikhilananda, *Holy Mother,* © 1962 by Swami Nikhilananda; Swami Nikhilananda (ed.), *Vivekananda: The Yogas and Other Works,* copyright 1953 by Swami Nikhilananda.   Schocken Books Inc., New York, for quotation from Philippe Devillers, *Mao,* © 1969 by Macdonald & Company, London.   Sri Aurobindo International Centre of Education, Pondicherry, India, for a quotation from Sri Aurobindo, *The Synthesis of Yoga,* © 1957 by Sri Aurobindo International University Centre.   Sri Ramakrishna Math, Madras, India, for quotations from Swami Ramakrishnananda, *Life of Sri Ramanuja,* © 1959 by Sri Ramakrishna Math; and Swami Saradananda, *Sri Ramakrishna the Great Master,* copyright 1952 by Sri Ramakrishna Math.   Sri Ramanasramam, Tiruvannamalai, India, for quotations from *Sri Maharshi,* © 1965 by Sri Ramanasramam, and *The Mountain Path* (a periodical, no date). Charles E. Tuttle Co., Tokyo, Japan, and Rutland, Vt., for quotations from Zenkei Shibayama, *A Flower Does Not Talk,* © 1970 by Charles E. Tuttle Co.   All these sources and several others that need not be formally listed here are acknowledged in detail in the reference notes at the end of the volume.

Those individuals who have in one way or another contributed to this study are far too many to list in full. I want them to know I am deeply grateful to each of them. Especially valuable help has been extended to me by several friends in the United States, to whom I express heartfelt thanks. Philip Scharper, of Stamford, Connecticut, first urged me to write the book and has shown consistent interest ever since. Kenneth W. Morgan, of Colgate University, made possible through the Fund for the Study of the Great Religions of the World a trip to better prepare myself for its writing. Joseph Cunneen, of New York, had faith enough in the project to find me a contract and has provided patient and discerning editorial assistance. Brother Patrick Hart, of Gethsemani Abbey, read the entire manuscript at the halfway mark and offered valuable encouragement. K. L. Seshagiri Rao, of Punjabi University and the University of Virginia, painstakingly went through the completed manuscript and made many useful suggestions. Richard Martin and Martin Davis, of the University of Virginia, introduced me to and guided me through the extensive South Asian Collection of the Alderman Library. William H. Dodd, Librarian of America Press, gave ungrudging help in checking numerous references. Doris Kellogg Neale, of Gordonsville, Virginia, not only offered pertinent comments throughout the writing but graciously allowed me the use of her library and of a charming cottage in which to write. Finally, it was Swami Nikhilananda, of the Ramakrishna Order, who taught me in New York almost everything I know about Hinduism.

The number of those who provided inspiration and assistance in India and the Far East is even larger. I mention only Nirmal Kumar Bose, of New Delhi and Calcutta, India; Krishna B. Bajpai and Major T. Ramachandra, of New Delhi; Sri Pran Kishore Goswami, Captain Shibdas Bhattacharyya, and Father Robert Antoine, of Calcutta; Dr. U. Dhammaratana, of Nalanda, Patna; Bhagwan B. Singh, of Gorakhpur; Dom Bede Griffiths, of Kulittalai; C. S. Ramakrishnan, K. Ramalingam, Father Ignatius Hirudayam, and Swami Kailasananda, of Madras; Nyanaponika Thera, of Kandy, Ceylon; Masao Abe, of Kyoto, Japan; and Father William Johnston, of Tokyo. Without their and a great many others' encouragement this book could not have been written.

I should fail in my duty if I did not express my appreciation, as well, to five chauffeurs in the East, who by their unfailing cooperation enabled me to visit, and in some instances make contact with, many of the monks and scholars from whom I gained important insights. Their names are: Atmaprasad Dubey, of Banaras, India; C. S. Rangaswamy Iyengar, of Bangalore; C. Subrahmanians, of Madras; Piyaratna Wanigatunga, of Colombo, Ceylon; and Anupol Apichatsokol, of Bangkok, Thailand. From each of them I learned much, in addition, about the cultures that helped make them the fine persons they are.

J. M.

CONTENTS

INTRODUCTION

"I am a Christian," I said, "but I can no longer say I am *not* a Hindu or a Buddhist."

It was early December in Tokyo. I had been talking with a genial and most unclerical looking Roman Catholic priest who shared with me a lively interest in Eastern spirituality. The words came out unexpectedly, as they occasionally do when some hidden area of the mind wants to make a self-revelation. What I said seemed to cause my friend the priest no surprise. But I confess it startled me.

Twenty-five years as a monastic member of an important modern Indian religious order had led me to expect to end my days a Hindu. Then in 1963 some inner necessity cut me loose from my Eastern moorings and piloted me back to the Christian sphere of influence. In becoming a Roman Catholic, however, I was not led to forget or deny the profundities of my earlier faith. After the first flush of convert zeal subsided, I realized there was a deeper kinship between Hinduism and the teachings of Jesus Christ than most Westerners had up to now perceived. Oddly enough, during this same period, between 1963 and the present, a new interest has arisen—first among Roman Catholics and then among Protestants—in hearing what the non-Christian religions are saying.

Early in 1970 I was invited to write the present book on evidences of Christ beyond Christianity. I accepted the suggestion because of my continuing interest in the subject. Perhaps, I began to see, the real meaning of my becoming a Christian after so many years of dedication to another religious ideal lay in something more than a mere turning from an insufficient to a sufficient faith. As a result of what happened to me, a meeting of Hindu and Christian beliefs had taken place in my mind that had slowly transformed my religious outlook. It might be my task, now, to share whatever slender insights I had gained in the process—allowing others to undergo, as it were, the confrontation I myself had undergone.

For the past half-dozen years or so I have pondered the relationship between Christian and Hindu beliefs. In 1966 and in 1969 I published papers on this relationship as I saw it at the time. First, as a good convert, I was concerned with how Hinduism could be fulfilled by accepting Jesus Christ as the sole mediator between God and man. Later I explored the situation more in terms of dialogue, urging Christians to beware of condescension toward other faiths. I even suggested their looking into the possibility that Christ was speaking to men through more than one revelation. What Christians must guard against, I said, was a premature assumption that God intended everyone in the East to become a professing Christian.

During the late summer and fall of 1970, preparatory to writing this book, I traveled in India and the Far East. In this way I renewed my acquaintance with modern Hinduism by making contact with men who knew it through practical experience as well as study, and was thus able to see its truths in clearer perspective. I was also able to become more familiar with Buddhism in several of its forms as they are practiced today.

As my trip progressed and the scope of my task began to dawn on me, I sometimes wondered if I was equipped to fulfill it. I am essentially a poet rather than a scholar—let alone a theologian. It was my twenty-five years' experience of modern Hinduism at first hand, I realized, that had prompted the suggestion to write the book. But something my teacher in musical composition at the Curtis Institute of Music, Rosario Scalero, had told me many years before reassured me. In speaking of writing for solo instruments with orchestra, Maestro Scalero said, "You know, it doesn't always hurt if a composer is not too familiar with the instrument he is writing for. Brahms was not a violinist. When he wrote his concerto for violin, people thought certain passages were impossible to play as he intended them. Still, violinists learned to play them, and the art of the violin was advanced."

Possibly there was a value in my writing on a subject usually dealt with by theologians. Were I a professional theologian I should know there were some things I simply could not say. As a poet, I might stumble on a few ideas that an expert would never allow himself to entertain—ideas that might advance the prospects of a true meeting between Christians and believers of other faiths. I recalled, too, the advice I had received from Jean Leclercq about an earlier project: "Yes, make it a poetic book. We're dying of scholarship."

This book, then, records my search for evidences of Christ's working beyond the bounds of organized Christianity. To put it differently, it is the product of an attempt to see the truths of non-Christian religions in terms of Christian truth. If at all successful, it should serve as a sort of telescope to provide inquiring and open-minded readers with an unbiased view of what goes on outside their own island universe. The non-Christian religion I know best is Hinduism, and with this complex of living faiths I am chiefly concerned.

In dealing with the various points where Hindu beliefs—and, so far as they are known to me, Buddhist and other beliefs— seem to relate to Christ, the volume is faithful, I think, to its original aim. I confess, though, that it has turned into something more than it set out to be. For it also records an uncharted journey of exploration on its author's part toward a destination whose promise he can only dimly surmise. This aspect of the work may interest other than Christian readers.

A very real danger is built into the present subject. The detailing of evidences of Christ's working outside Christianity could easily become a vehicle for a decidedly imperialistic notion: whatever is good in other religions is simply the working of Jesus Christ, through the Holy Spirit, in ways we have yet to recognize so everybody else should with all deliberate speed come over to Christianity. I nevertheless took up the subject because I felt I could see it from a rather different angle. Everything depends, of course, on one's point of view. Readers from East or West who are not Christians should understand that this volume is intended primarily for Western Christians with no knowledge of Hindu or Buddhist thought. They will sense that its frame of reference is quite different from what it would be were I writing about, say, "Vishnu Beyond Vaishnavism" or "Buddha-consciousness Beyond Buddhism."

Christians, for their part, should realize that if they want to enter into the spirit of Hinduism or Buddhism, they face no small challenge. The great majority of people in the West have largely misunderstood both religions. Up till now these ancient faiths have been devoutly misrepresented by most scholars who are professing Christians. (A notable exception is the brochure *Towards the Meeting With Buddhism*, by Étienne Lamotte, published in 1970 by the Secretariat for Non-Christians, in Rome.)

To such unconsciously slanted scholarly interpretation is to be traced the almost totally negative view of them held by very many Christians. The average person reading these pages might do well to study them as if he were hearing about Hinduism and Buddhism for the first time. He should also keep in mind that our purpose here is to understand religious experiences and concepts, not to judge the societies that have fostered them in terms of how well they have adhered to them—a risky business in any case.

One thing more. When I speak of writing for Christians or exposing Christians to the truths of another religion, I mean to include all those who accept Jesus Christ as their Savior and who have received baptism in witness to that acceptance. So as to speak to as many as possible, I shall confine myself to comparisons of Hindu dogma with the words of Jesus and the apostles. These, after all, convey the body of teaching from which the various dogmas of the separated denominations have sprung. If occasionally I include references to the words of a few saints or other members of the Christian Church—Orthodox, Protestant, or Roman Catholic—it is because I feel that what they have to say does not go counter to the original teachings.

During my first few weeks in India I had the first hint of how to tackle the subject I had so enthusiastically agreed to explore. I had set out with no definite plan—trusting that inspiration would furnish what forethought had neglected. But in mid-September some friends and I took an automobile ride in Northern India. In the course of that one journey we met with a series of happenings that summed up for me—not very precisely, perhaps, but vividly enough to stir my own imagination—what it is that Hindu spirituality, and by extension non-Christian spirituality in general, has to offer the Christian.

It was only near the end of the whole trip that I surprised myself by telling my priest friend in Tokyo about no longer being able to say I was not a Hindu or a Buddhist. How I came to make the statement should be clearer at the end of the volume.

"Behold, I stand at the door and knock."

JOURNEY
TO GORAKHPUR

It was shortly after graduating from college that I came in contact with Buddhist and then with Hindu thought. Unfortunately—or was it the reverse?—I had not received an adequate schooling in the Protestant Christianity into which I was born. Hinduism's doctrines of the "divinity" of the soul, the nonduality of the Godhead, the unity of existence, and the harmony of religions were strongly appealing, and I ultimately joined the Ramakrishna Order of India, working at the Ramakrishna-Vivekananda Center of New York under the direction of Swami Nikhilananda.

My family was in many ways a free-thinking one, but even for them the situation must have been uncomfortable. They lived in a conservative, self-contained Pennsylvania town. It could not have been easy to admit to a son who had entered a Hindu religious order with a strange name and eventually answered to the title Swami Atmaghanananda. What was my surprise, then, after my return to Christianity, to learn that a married brother of mine had become seriously interested in Hindu philosophy and especially Yoga.

The teacher he studied with had impeccable credentials. He taught philosophy in a university in the north of India and had come to the United States to obtain a Ph.D. His name was B. B. Singh. I met him one evening at a party at my brother's house and found him lively and personable. Tall and vivacious, he expressed an easy confidence and openness that had endeared him to my brother's friends. Finding that a number of people at the university he attended were interested in serious study of Yoga, he had undertaken to conduct a course, and my brother and a number of his friends attended. Dr. Singh finally left for India after several years' stay, not long before my own recent trip. On taking leave of my brother, he had said that when I came to India he would go anywhere to meet me and would be of such help as he could. Most Singhs are followers of the Sikh religion, but his family, I learned, was Hindu.

1

When after a few weeks' travel I reached Banaras, Dr. Singh was waiting for me at the airport. We went directly to Clark's Hotel, a holdover in style from the days of the British regime, on the outskirts of the holy city. We planned to stay only two nights and two full days before leaving for Gorakhpur, Dr. Singh's home town.

Banaras is unique even among sacred places in India. The river Ganges flows in a huge crescent past a fantastic collection of temples of all descriptions, crowding the East Bank. There are big temples and small temples, mostly of a gray stone, their spires often tipped with a gold trident. Here and there a larger structure stands out, sometimes with whitewashed walls. Houseboats crowd in various places along the river's edge. During winter and spring, the graceful flights of shallow steps leading down to the bathing areas, or *ghats*, are in constant use. Holy men sit there under great umbrellas, while teachers give religious instruction. In certain places are cremation grounds. But just now the river was swollen as a result of the monsoon, and the steps were almost completely submerged. Nevertheless people from all parts of India were here to bathe in the Ganges' turbid waters, which are believed to cleanse men of sin. There is an ancient legend that anyone who leaves the body in Banaras will instantly be liberated from ignorance of truth. As a result, many elderly people cherish a desire to spend their last days here. So even now the lanes leading to the river made a colorful scene.

The river is only one of the many elements that go to make Banaras the unique place it is. For a Westerner one of the gratifying sights is the famed hospital, or "Home of Service," conducted by the Ramakrishna Order, to which I once belonged. Its charitable work goes on day and night, most of it being done by monks and novices. The wards, small one-storied buildings, are set among flower beds filled with brightly colored flowers. Again, there is the famous Banaras Hindu University, one of the main seats of learning in India. It spreads out on a vast campus, bringing into this haven of orthodoxy the breath of a modern India half in tune, half out of tune, with the ancient way of life. Most important to the faithful is the gold-domed Temple of Vishwanath, or Shiva. The Deity has been worshiped here from time out of mind. Destroyed by Muslim invaders centuries ago to build a mosque, the shrine was rebuilt on a site nearby, and the worship has continued.

Dr. Singh knew I was on the lookout for new insights into Hindu spirituality that would make it easier to relate the essential dogmas of Hinduism to those of Christian belief. He took me to meet several professors of philosophy and religion at the university. But his special desire was that I should meet a prestigious "holy man" or *sadhu,* Gopinath Kaviraj, who was an adept in Yoga. The *sadhu* was very old, and not at all well, so we could only pay our respects. It was no doubt a privilege to see him, but I received no distinct impression of his sanctity. Dr. Singh hoped that in Gorakhpur we could meet a scholar who could tell me all about Gopinath's extraordinary life. As it was, I had merely seen an old man, his mind withdrawn within himself, lying on one of the table-like beds typical of India. I thought of the reply an elderly monk had once given me, on an earlier visit to India, when I asked him how one recognized a "realized soul," that is, a man who had seen God. "I don't know who is a realized soul," he said, "but I know who I like."

We had train reservations for the next evening, but at the end of this our first full day at Banaras we decided to cancel them and drive to Gorakhpur by taxi. We were assured that the drive would take no more than four hours—five at the very most. In view of the consequences of this decision, it might be considered part of a divine conspiracy. But the fact is that I cannot sleep on trains and hardly relished the thought of arriving at 7 A.M. for a busy day of visits to philosophers and devotees of God after a sleepless night. What was more, a drive through the countryside would give me an intimate picture of this part of India, with which I was not very familiar.

From a line of taxis outside Clark's Hotel we chose one with a stocky, round-faced, capable-looking driver, Atmaprasad Dubey. As nearly every Indian would recognize, his family name meant that he was a brahmin descended from ancestors who had been scholars in two of the four Vedas, which are, of course, the Hindu scriptures. In India, after all, religion is like the air you breathe, and almost every Hindu's given name—in our driver's case, even his family name—has a religious association. But it is not just a matter of conventions. Even villagers who practice what look to Westerners like grossly superstitious forms of worship are not unfamiliar with many of the subtleties of what we in the West would call scholastic philosophy. And almost every Hindu I have met (except for a few from Westernized families, who probably are ashamed to admit it) shows complete familiarity with the stories contained in the ancient epics and other mythological chronicles.

Dr. Singh explained to me the significance of Dubey's name.

The fact of our choosing this special driver *does* seem more than chance.

Dubey asked if he could take along his helper, Pande, a not very robust, not very tall young man with a nice smile and—strangely for an Indian—dull brownish rather than black hair. We agreed to his coming along. Dr. Singh decided, on the spur of the moment, to take the son of a friend of his from Gorakhpur. The young man, Ramprasad Shukla, of a quiet and pleasing nature, was a graduate student in Banaras Hindu University. Since almost no one who stops at Banaras leaves without visiting Sarnath, where the Lord Buddha preached his first sermon, we set out about noon for that place of pilgrimage, just across the Ganges, in Dubey's time-scarred but not too rattly taxi.

Many Westerners know something of the life of the Buddha. Born the son of a petty prince in Northern India about 566 B.C., he is the first great spiritual luminary of the post-legendary period of Indian history. Prince Siddhartha was the name given him at birth; he is also known by his family name, Gautama. (These are the Sanskrit spellings used some centuries later when Buddhists began to use that language instead of Pali; in the original Pali scriptures, first recorded in Ceylon, the names were spelled Siddhattha and Gotama.) Luxury surrounded the prince throughout his youth, but gradually he became aware that life was not all pleasure. The facts of old age, of sickness, of death, convinced him that the world was wanting in true happiness. He began to question the values of the society of his day.

In a poem, "The Sorrows and Joys of the Buddha," I have tried to express the feelings in the young Siddhartha's mind:

> Did you sigh, my Lord,
> As a slim young prince
> At the promise denied
> Your proud innocence
> When you newly described,
> With sight opened fresh,
> How heavily age
> Hung its yoke on the flesh;
> How the rancor and shame
> Of the lame and the ill
> Spelled as sure defeat
> For the high as the small?
> Did you sigh, my Lord,

When you saw in surprise
How the hand of decay
Warped the world to its wish;
How the rigors of death
Waited silent beneath
To confound your conceit
And deprive you of faith,
When desiring was done
—Compassionate One?

The sight of a monk with a serene and happy face, it is said, showed him there might be another way of life than the life followed at his father's court.

Siddhartha was brought up a follower of the Vedic religion, and when at the age of twenty-nine he decided he must renounce his wife and newborn son in quest of spiritual understanding that would yield true happiness, he started his search in traditional fashion. He went first to the forest for solitude. Later he sought guidance from renowned teachers. But he finally became disillusioned by the sterile asceticism of the monks of his day— just as he had been earlier, no doubt, by the dogmatism of many brahmin priests. After six years of searching, during which for a time he underwent extreme self-denial, he set out in a novel direction. Sitting under a great tree, known as the Bodhi Tree or Bo Tree (the "Tree of Enlightenment"), at a place now called Buddha-Gaya, he resolved not to rise till he had found what he was seeking. After a heroic struggle to gain, through meditation, a decisive insight into the truth behind the appearances of the world, and so find a way out of bondage, he achieved —by his own unaided efforts, he insisted—a state of transcendental awareness, or realization, he named Nirvana (in Pali, Nibbana). The word indicates the "blowing out" of the flame of desire. Thus he became Gautama Buddha, Gautama the Enlightened. So ineffable was this experience that he never spoke of it except to say what it was not.

The Buddha revealed to his disciples the content of his meditation prior to attaining Nirvana. He told them that he had regained the memory of all his former lives, that he had fathomed the secret of the causal origination and cessation of all things, and that he had understood that with his present birth he had reached his last life. He had also discovered in the course of his meditation a new type of spiritual discipline, which avoided both extreme sensual indulgence and extreme self-mortification. This he called the "Middle Way." In the canonical Pali scripture *Samyutta Nikaya,* he described the extreme of sensual indulgence as "base, common, vulgar, unholy, and unprofitable," and the extreme of self-mortification as "painful, unholy, and unprofitable."

In my poem on the Buddha I also tried to suggest something of Siddhartha's inexpressible experience. Here is the passage:

>Did you smile, my Lord,
>In Nirvana's dawn,
>As the daystar of truth
>Rose higher and higher,
>And obedient in will
>To your mind's intent
>You traced the design
>Of the subtle laws
>That dispose the flow
>Of effect from cause;
>When your mind and your heart
>And your life and your hope
>Fused all in one
>In a quick, new shape
>As the thrust of your sure
>Sharp questionings
>Pierced straight down
>To the deep of things?

The most fruitful aspect of the Buddha's illumination was his discovery of what he called the "Four Noble Truths." These are as follows: Life in the world is unsatisfactory and full of suffering. Defiling taints or cravings are the cause of its unsatisfactory character. There is such a thing as cessation of these defiling taints and cravings that cause suffering. There is a path to the cessation of suffering. This path, as we noted, lies between sensual gratification on the one hand and sterile asceticism on the other. The Buddha called it the "Noble Eightfold Path." It consists of the following elements: correct understanding, correct thought, correct speech, correct action, correct livelihood, correct effort, correct mindfulness, and correct concentration of mind. The path falls into three sections: wisdom (the first two elements), virtue (the next three), and concentration (the final three). The sections are not separate but really interdependent.

Out of compassion for men, Gautama Buddha renounced the bliss of Nirvana and began to preach the Four Noble Truths. In his sermons he discouraged discussions of the nature of ultimate reality as of no service in freeing men from suffering. This much he said: that all things are impermanent (*anichcha*), full of suffering (*dukkha*), and without individual identity (*anatta*).

At the beginning of his ministry the Buddha had only a handful of disciples. When they increased to about sixty, he said to them, "Go forth now and wander, for the welfare of the many, for the happiness of the many, out of compassion for the world. No two of you should go the same way. Proclaim the excellent law." During the eighty years of his life, this wise and merciful man wandered on foot in Northern India, preaching a basically practical message: the nature of life in the world is unsatisfactory; overcome the suffering caused by this unsatisfactory character of the world by following the Noble Eightfold Path.

When the Buddha spoke of the universality of suffering, he never meant to deny the fact of happiness in life, but he saw that it must always come to an end. His aim was to enable men to view the world with a dispassionate discernment as they pursued their search for true happiness.

In time a great band of disciples, known as the *Sangha*, gathered about him. Into his monastic order he received both his wife and his son. As he lay on his deathbed he said to his sorrowing followers: "All things in this world are subject to constant change. Be mindful and strive on."

Here is how my poem on the Buddha concludes:

> And so, as I lay,
> On the day that I died,
> The thrice-blessed day,
> With my friends at my side,
> On the low-spread couch,
> Fully quit of pride,
> I asked them to shun
> Deluding tears
> Lest fondness swerve
> Their purposes,
> And I bade them honor
> My going hence,
> In faithful witness

To my peace,
By striving in strength
And with diligence
For the working out
Of their own release.

-2-

We arrived at Sarnath, a place dominated by a huge brick reliquary mound, or *stupa*, beside which extend the ruins of an ancient monastery that flourished here. The well-kept lawns, punctuated here and there with formal flower beds, are a far cry from the divine confusion of Banaras. In a nearby museum are many excellent pieces of sculpture unearthed in the neighborhood. These include the Sarnath Buddha, one of the supreme examples of Indian art, and the famous Lion Capital, now the emblem of India. This capital once crowned one of the Buddhist emperor Ashoka's polished stone columns which he had had set up in the third century B.C. in many places sacred to Buddhists. It consists of four stylized lion's heads above an ornate band circled with animals and representations of the "Wheel of the Law," the symbol of the Buddha's teaching. Not far from the great *stupa* is a modern temple with colorful frescoes of Buddha's life by a Japanese artist. In addition, within the area are a number of modern monasteries of the different branches of Buddhism to be found in the East.

Holy places of pilgrimage—whether in India or elsewhere—always hold an atmosphere of peace. It was very evident here at Sarnath: a gentle, strangely this-worldly peace in complete harmony with the clear, sunny September weather that had begun after the rainy season. To convey this atmosphere is not easy. Most people feel the aesthetic impact of beautifully designed buildings, such as the best Gothic cathedrals, or the harmonious contours of an arresting landscape, and they frequently produce a frame of mind that we vaguely think of as spiritual. The majestic serenity of a great cathedral—like that of St. Ouen in Rouen, for instance—is undeniable. But how do you explain the quality of Charles de Foucauld's simple chapel in the old buildings of the Poor Clares in Jerusalem, or of the dark, unaesthetic cave of the Nativity underneath St. Helena's church in Bethlehem, or of the rather heavy church

over the rock where Jesus is said to have endured his agony in
the Garden of Gethsemane? There is nothing notably artistic
in any of these places. In the last two instances, the atmosphere
is possibly the result of the association with the memory of
Christ. But what of a simple Quaker meeting house or the
plainest of plain Protestant chapels? At Sarnath, the modern
temple is not of such quality, aesthetically, as to elicit anything
like the awe one feels before the Buddhist frescoes in the Ajanta
caves. And yet the peace is palpable here, as well.

Hindus add a further suggestion: years of worship or of
reverential thought cause a spiritual atmosphere that is tangible
to those with genuine sensibility. And it is different in different
holy places. Now it is intensely otherworldly, now this-worldly,
as here at Sarnath. Since the Buddha was one who refused to
allow speculation about the nature of ultimate reality, the effect
here seemed perfectly right.

The pervading peace of Sarnath I had experienced on
previous visits. What I had not experienced was the interior of
a modern monastery enclosure. Had I not been with an Indian
I should probably have hesitated to enter one of the monasteries.
But Indians are entirely matter-of-fact and quite free from
shyness in such matters. Dr. Singh simply chose the nearest
one—it happened to be the Chinese monastery—and walked
through the front gate. Surrounding an impressive square
temple was a garden space with shrubs and small flowering
trees. Beyond this, on three sides of the temple (all but the
front), were rows of rooms for monks. As we skirted the temple,
we dimly glimpsed a tranquil image of the Buddha in the
shrine.

No one was about. Passing to the rear, we found in one of
the rooms a quiet, somewhat reserved Indian Buddhist monk,
or *bhikshu,* who bade us come in. The room, a spacious one,
was very plain. There were a table, a chair, a bed, and several
bookcases stood against the walls. The monk communicated a
feeling of inwardness and calm, a smoothness as of velvet. His
voice, too, was soft, and his eyes, not large, but deeply veiled,
gave evidence of much practice of meditation. I told him I was
trying to meet people from whom I could gain ideas for a book
for Christians about "the truth outside Christianity." (That
seemed a courteous way to explain something that might have
sounded a bit presumptuous to one who was not a Christian.)

Suddenly we became aware of the presence of another monk
—a slight, sweet-faced, elderly man, very plainly dressed in

faded yellow garments. He was obviously Chinese. The Indian
monk, whose name was Bhikshu Shashanarasi, introduced him
to us as the abbot. We never learned his name. Though he
smiled very kindly and made us know we were welcome, he could
speak no English. As the abbot left, Bhikshu Shashanarasi asked
the three of us—Dr. Singh, Shukla, and myself—to sit down.
Even when he spoke, nothing seemed to disturb his inner attention to something else. We sat on the bed and the *bhikshu*
sat facing us.

At the very start of our visit I became discouraged. This was
my first talk on the present trip with a Buddhist monk, and
an Indian Buddhist at that, which is something of a rarity.
Here, if anywhere, I should be finding points of contact. But
Bhikshu Shashanarasi seemed politely inscrutable. I had been
warned that often in the East, on a trip like this, unless one
asks the right questions one gets only stock replies. So instead
of inquiring about the principles of Buddhism, I told him I had
belonged to a Hindu monastic order for twenty-five years and
stressed my desire to make Hinduism and Buddhism understandable to Westerns. The monk, however, began by talking
about the great number of books in the world and the uselessness
of depending on them! You could understand Buddhism, he
said, only by leading the life.

I then asked about any personal experiences he might have
had. Again he failed to respond as I hoped. He said he had
"realized" nothing, that is to say, had had no deep spiritual
experiences. (I was to learn later that many Buddhist monks
consider it improper to speak of their inner life.) But when I
asked if any one idea had inspired him to take up the monastic
life, his reserve melted just a little. As a Hindu, he told us, he
had read many works of scholastic philosophers. There was
Shankaracharya, with his theory of Nondualism. There was
Ramanujacharya, with his theory of Modal Nondualism. There
was Madhvacharya with his theory of Dualism. And so on. Each
one differed with the others. Their hairsplitting was hard for
him to follow. (I recalled an Indian saying I had heard many
years before: "A philosopher is someone who differs with everyone else.") But the Buddha, he found, spoke simply and clearly.
There could be no doubt about his meaning. He had thus decided
to become a Buddhist monk.

As we continued talking, Bhikshu Shashanarasi began to
open up. Though he himself had had no personal experience,
he said, the Buddha's words had impressed him. The Buddha

taught that monks should work "for the welfare of the many, for the happiness of the many." So it was his desire to help others by starting a school for boys. For this purpose his monastery had recently acquired a plot of land near the museum that cost Rupees 1,400,000 (or about $186,000).

The goal of life, for Bhikshu Shashanarasi, was to see the Buddha in all. To help one come to this understanding there were the Four Noble Truths. He quoted a number of texts from the Dhammapada, the great scripture supposed to be a collection of the Buddha's memorable sayings—all of them relating, in one way or another, to the four pillars of the Buddhist Law, or *Dhamma*. Early in this collection occurs what might be termed the Buddhist Golden Rule, and so far as I recall that is the verse Bhikshu Shashanarasi quoted first. "Never does hatred cease by hatred here below: hatred ceases by love. This is an eternal law," he half chanted in a soft but sonorous tone. "The world does not know that we must all come to an end here; but those who know, their quarrels cease at once."

I made no note of all the verses the monk quoted. Here are two more relating to the virtue aspect of the Noble Eightfold Path: "The fault of others is easily perceived, but that of one's self is difficult to perceive; a man winnows his neighbors' faults like chaff, but hides his own, even as a dishonest gambler hides a losing throw." And again: "As a solid rock is not shaken by the wind, wise people falter not amidst praise and blame."

Another well-known verse that Bhikshu Shashanarasi quoted was the following: "How is there laughter, how is there joy, as this world is always burning? Why do ye not seek a light, ye who are shrouded in darkness?" This verse, of course, relates to the wisdom aspect of the Noble Eightfold Path.

One of the most famous of all the verses in the Dhammapada is this one: "Looking for the maker of this tabernacle [of the body] I ran to no avail through a round of many births; and wearisome is birth again and again. But now, maker of the tabernacle, thou hast been seen; thou shalt not rear this tabernacle again. All thy rafters are broken, thy ridge-pole is shattered; the mind approaching the Eternal has attained the extinction of all desires."

Several verses related to the concentration aspect of the Path are: "Let the wise man guard his thoughts, which are difficult to perceive, very artful, and rushing wherever they list: thoughts well guarded bring happiness." Another in the same vein: "As a fletcher makes straight his arrow, a wise man

makes straight his trembling and unsteady thought, which
is difficult to guard, difficult to hold back.'' How is this to
be accomplished? The Buddha's prescription: ''Cut off the
stream valiantly, drive away the desires, O Brahmin! When
you have understood the dissolution of all that is made, you
will understand that which is not made.''

In praise of the man of enlightenment, the Buddha says,
''Him I call indeed a brahmin who calls nothing his own,
whether it pertains to past, present, or future, who is poor and
free from grasping. Him I call indeed a brahmin—the manly,
the noble, the hero, the great seer, the conqueror, the impassible,
the sinless, the awakened.''

When we asked about any belief among Buddhists in the
existence of God, Bhikshu Shashanarasi began, ''If there is a
God . . .'' At once Dr. Singh interrupted, ''What does that 'if'
imply?'' The monk then gently and good-humoredly said that
the Buddha had avoided the question as a waste of time. He
had taught all that was needed for enlightenment. When the
Buddha was asked if he had taught his disciples everything he
knew, he had picked up a handful of grass from where he was
sitting. Pointing to all the grass around them, he said that so
much as was in his hand was all that was necessary.

''Come and see''—this was his challenge. In other words,
make the effort by following the path he prescribed. The goal,
Nirvana, is the destroying of all craving, all attachment—the
''maker of the tabernacle.'' But disciplines are by no means all.
Once you have crossed a stream by a raft, you don't carry the
raft on your head for the rest of your life. You finally give up
attachment even to the moral law, the *Dhamma*. (Such a state
comes only, I reflected, with a very high degree of spiritual
development. For the ''stream'' here stands for the worldly
man's state of ignorance about reality.)

To my question whether one could attain enlightenment, or
Nirvana, through religions other than Buddhism, disciplines
other than the Noble Eightfold Path, Bhikshu Shashanarasi replied quietly, ''All that is needed is the extinction of craving.''
The monk paused. Perhaps he thought we had talked enough. I
myself was well satisfied. Though we had heard for the most
part ''stock replies'' I was already familiar with, somehow they
came alive for me in a way I had never experienced when
reading them on the printed page. I laid this effect principally
to the influence of the man's spiritual inwardness. It was all
of a piece with the serenity of the locality.

We were ready to take our leave. As if by magic the Chinese abbot reappeared, and we paid him our respects by saluting in the Indian fashion with joined palms. But now, on an impulse, Dr. Singh asked the two monks if they would mind having their pictures taken. At once the abbot disappeared. In a few minutes he reappeared in a handsome, stiff ceremonial robe, looking quite impressive. Noting that the place seemed rather deserted, one of us asked if they had many visitors. "Not many come to inquire," said Bhikshu Shashanarasi. We left with expressions of good will on both sides, and the two monks stood watching till we passed out of sight around the large square temple at the front.

By now we were ravenously hungry. Clark's Hotel in Banaras had prepared us three box lunches, each containing cold chicken, boiled eggs, rather forbiddingly dry ham and cheese sandwiches, an apple, and two short and fat bananas. The driver bought soft drinks at a refreshment stand, and in what seemed to me a rather feudal manner we shared with him and his young helper Pande what we couldn't eat. Both men, standing a little to one side, finished off the food as if this was the most natural thing in the world.

About 4:30 P.M. we left Sarnath for Gorakhpur, hoping to reach it in four hours. Dr. Singh said he planned to take me and the driver to separate hotels there, and we would meet again in the morning for further adventures with Indian spirituality. Dubey, despite his long years as a taxi man, had never driven to Gorakhpur.

-3-

Traveling by automobile in India is a fascinating business. Short of living with a family in a town or village, one never comes in more direct contact with the everyday, down-to-earth life of average Indians. And that means the 80 percent of India's people who live outside the cities. This trip was no exception. Flat though the countryside is in most parts, it is nevertheless constantly varied. In this section of Northern India, small, compact villages of mud huts give way to broad stretches of green paddy fields, divided into varied patterns by the ridges separating the surprisingly small holdings of individual owners. (It is these fractional holdings, made even more minute when divided up at an owner's death, that make it difficult for farmers to achieve the efficient production of grain and other foods that is possible in Western countries, where larger fields are the rule.) Now and again in the distance a stretch of gray-green sugar cane contrasts with the intense green of the paddy, or a field of what looks likes yellow mustard asserts itself against the blue sky, dotted at this time of year with large white clouds. Slim snowy egrets course in the lower air; ominous-looking dark vultures circle above.

Here and there by the roadside a family of light gray monkeys with small heads, delicate hands, and black, intelligent faces play fearlessly in a great tree or rest motionless as if to ponder some diverting mischief. Heavy, curved-horn water buffaloes pull archaic plows or wallow happily in cool mudholes. Dreamy-eyed Brahmani cattle along the road gaze at you with more than human pensiveness. It is easier to understand the unwillingness of Hindus to eat beef when one realizes how much love and affection is lavished on cattle by their owners. Even in many poverty-stricken households they are treated as Westerners treat household pets, and on festive occasions their necks are encircled with garlands or, in the south of India, their horns painted red and blue.

From time to time, as one speeds by, the graceful top of a small temple—shaped like two intersecting Gothic arches—rises from a grove of trees. These are usually temples either to the Lord Shiva or the Lord Vishnu in one of his many aspects. But sometimes they are dedicated to lesser manifestations of the divine as well.

Along the road, *ashvattha* trees, the variety of Indian fig under which the Buddha attained enlightenment, stand out by their great size and the elephant gray of their smooth bark. The graceful shape of their leaves is much like that of Carolina poplars, but with a longer pointed end. Even more stately are the tremendous, wide-spreading banyans, whose horizontal branches send down secondary roots which after a time create what amounts to a whole grove of smaller trees. The ends of these roots, as they hang at varying distances, seem visibly yearning for the touch of the life-giving earth.

Beneath certain roadside trees held sacred according to local custom rest a few stones daubed red in honor of some village deity. These relics of ancient animistic religion have endured into the modern age alongside one of the most refined metaphysical religions in the world. Though unable to fully understand the sentiments of those who follow such customs, I hesitate to say they represent mere superstitions and cannot bring solace or reassurance to many souls by helping them reach a level of consciousness tapped by the more sophisticated through other means.

Plentiful, too, are rows of thick-leaved mango trees, sometimes planted by a thoughtful rich man to provide fruit in season for the poor. Though most of these have long since reached maturity, even now one sees small saplings, recently planted, their thin stems protected by a circling wall of bricks laid with spaces between each brick to let the air through. It was just such protective walls that the saint Ramakrishna in the last century likened to moral and spiritual disciplines. A young tree, he said, must first be fenced round so that goats and cattle—the distractions and temptations of worldly life—may not feed on its tender bark. But once it has become full grown the fencing may be removed, and both animals and men may take shelter under it. His parables, like those of Jesus, were drawn from the everyday events and objects of life.

At long intervals one comes to larger towns. These, like many in every part of the world, have grown up along old travel routes, and their main streets are often narrow and sometimes not very straight. Both sides of these streets are lined with shops and eating places of all descriptions, often consisting of only one room.

It was here that the skill of our driver Dubey first became evident. Even in driving through the open country he was constantly giving four short warning taps on the horn—whenever, in fact, any creature or conveyance came in sight. As a result, all the users of the road—people, hungry looking dogs, goats, herds of sheep or cattle, wagons, bullock carts, bicycles, automobiles, even the long two-wheeled contrivances piled high with bamboo poles or some other construction material and pulled by a single, wiry man—were well to the side of the road before we came near. (All, that is, but the domineering buses and trucks, whose drivers seemed to pay no attention to our horn but went unheeding on their obstinate way.) But in the towns, as Dubey wove in and out among the multitude of vehicles and living creatures, he showed an uncanny ability to "flow with the stream." His skill was abetted, of course, by everyone else's seemingly equal ability to move aside just before a fender brushed him. I learned to have complete faith in both driver and occupants of the road, who seemed possessed of a sixth sense—

as in so many other situations in India. Only the children constantly caused me concern lest, whimsically, they should decide to run into the road just as we passed.

Another, quite different, problem was posed by villagers who chose the convenient surface of the road to thresh their grain. One could see neatly arranged piles at the road's edge. But occasionally the grain (I never learned to identify the varieties) was spread thin over the road as if to allow it to dry out. At times there was nothing to do but run right through it. At other times, which I myself was unable to recognize, it seemed that farmers welcomed the help from the automobile's tires in removing the husks. No doubt only the driver's familiarity with the look of the grain told him when to try to swerve around the grain and when to plow straight through.

Shortly after we left Banaras, Dubey revealed something about himself that was to characterize this second phase of our journey. He began to sing. Like so many other Hindus, he was a "devotee," a lover of God, and the association of the region we were driving through brought his feelings into the open. This was the country of Rama, legendary king of Ayodhya, and we were on a road that passed through the town of Ayodhya. It was fitting that he chose to sing songs about King Rama, who to most Hindus is the paragon of righteousness. This noble character, as many readers are aware, is counted one of the divine descents, or *avataras*, of the all-pervading Godhead, Vishnu. The Lord Krishna says in the great Hindu scripture, the Bhagavad Gita, "Whenever there is a decline of righteousness [*dharma*] and a rise of unrighteousness, I incarnate myself. For the protection of the good, for the destruction of the wicked, and for the establishment of righteousness, I am born in every age." As if to emphasize this particular *avatara*'s importance, Krishna says elsewhere in the same scripture, "Of warriors I am Rama."

The story of Rama's exploits is told in the *Ramayana*, one of India's two major epics, which took form probably between the fourth century before Christ and the second century after. The purpose of Vishnu's manifestation as Prince Rama was to destroy the demon king Ravana. By dint of extremely austere disciplines the demon had obtained from two of the greatest deities, Brahma and Shiva, the boon of invulnerability. He had asked for assurance that he could not be killed by any of the gods or other supernatural beings, and it had been granted; since he had a great contempt for men, he had not thought to mention them. After obtaining his wish, he began to harass both gods and men unmercifully. To put an end to his wickedness, Vishnu was thus impelled to be born as a man—the son of King Dasaratha of Ayodhya.

The king had three wives, and by them he had several sons. Rama was the son of his favorite, Kausalya, and was the crown prince. When Rama came of age, the king, seeing that he was growing old, determined to turn over the rule of his kingdom to his beloved son. But through the machinations of an evil-minded servant, one of the other wives was persuaded that her own son, Bharata, was entitled to rule. Having beguiled the old king, in an unguarded moment, to grant her any wish she might desire, she unexpectedly demanded that he banish Rama to a life in the forest for fourteen years and place her own son on the throne. According to the code of the time, Dasaratha could not go back on his word. Thus he sent away his son, who obediently acquiesced to his father's command. Out of grief at what he had had to do, the old king fell ill and died. The second queen's son, however, deeply revered his half brother Rama, and refused to rule. On the throne he placed Rama's sandals to show that he remained only as his steward till the rightful king should return.

Immediately upon his banishment Rama went to the forest. He was accompanied by his lovely wife, Sita, and his loyal brother Lakshmana. One morning when the two brothers were absent from their cottage, Sita was abducted by Ravana, the mighty king of the demons. In an aerial conveyance, he took her to his sumptuous palace in Ceylon, then known as Lanka. There he wooed her with all manner of enticements, but Sita always scornfully rebuffed him. To help Rama rescue Sita and destroy Ravana, various friends and allies came to his aid—most notably the monkey chieftain Hanuman, the embodiment for all time of devoted service. The long campaign was waged with varying fortunes on both sides. At last Rama took up the most powerful weapon in his arsenal, the redoubtable Brahma weapon, and slew Ravana.

When Sita was brought safely back, much to her chagrin her husband refused to receive her. He implied that he had no way of knowing she had remained faithful to him while staying so many years in Ravana's palace. To prove her chastity she asked to be allowed to pass through an ordeal by fire. The ordeal meant that the person tested should submit himself to the flames of a blazing fire: the truth of his claim would be proved by his emerging unscathed. Sita asked that a funeral pyre be erected. She leaped into the flames, and being the very embodiment of purity, emerged unharmed. Then Rama told her there had never been any doubt in his own mind about her, but as king he had felt the measure was necessary. As protector of morality, he could only retain the trust of his subjects if they were convinced that his queen was spotless.

The fourteen years assigned for Rama's banishment had come to an end. Rama and Sita therefore returned to Ayodhya, where he was crowned king and assumed the throne amid general rejoicing.

Peace was thus restored to the kingdom and everything seemed to be proceeding harmoniously. But one day it was reported to Rama, by one of his inspectors, that a washerman had been heard beating and berating his wife because he suspected she had been unfaithful. He was not so foolish, he was heard to say, as to believe like Rama that a wife who had lived long years in the house of another man was pure. Apprehending danger to society if he kept Sita with him, to his deep shame and sorrow Rama sent her to a hermitage. Beside him, in the throne room, he kept a representation of her made of gold.

When, after some years, Sita finally returned, people once more clamored for an ordeal by fire. This was too much even for the long-suffering Sita. Tradition had it that as a child she was found by a farmer in a furrow of the field he was plowing, and it was thus said that the earth was her mother. In her extremity the queen now prayed to the Goddess of Earth to take her back, asking that if she had never been untrue to Rama in thought, word, or deed, the earth might open and receive her. The earth opened and she sank forever from sight.

All these, and innumerable other dramatic details, have been repeated for untold centuries—by religious teachers to their disciples, by poets in new interpretations, by storytellers to village audiences, by grandmothers to their grandchildren—in illustration of the ideals of love, loyalty, service, courage, and above all righteousness. The story of Rama is woven into the very fiber of Hindu civilization. It, like the other stories from Hindu mythology, is as real to people as their everyday lives. Even if a man knows little of religious philosophy, he knows these tales of the exploits and the virtues of his religious heroes, often illustrating many of the conclusions of that philosophy. (But sometimes a villager who piously observes the rites of popular Hindu devotional religion may have mastered the fundamental doctrines of his particular denomination to a degree unknown among more educated persons in the West.)

It was the "Ram-nam kirtan," a highly simplified form of this ancient tale, that Dubey began to sing.

The songs about Rama, largely of a healthy, joyous, rhythmical, masculine type, are among the most invigorating in all Hindu devotional music. As the beautiful, strong melody continued, in Dubey's untutored but expressive tenor voice, unexpectedly my friend the professor revealed that he, too, had a devotional side. He joined in the singing lustily, and with a voice almost professional in quality. Finally Shukla, the university student, and the driver's helper, Pande, added their voices. Since I too knew the tune, I hummed along with them, managing to repeat not only the word "Ram" (a modern form of the word "Rama"), which is stressed at the end of each line, but also a phrase or two that I remembered from my Hindu days. Such a nondescript taxi, its five occupants singing of Rama at the top of their voices as it sped through the gathering dusk, would have created a sensation in a Western country. Here in India it was just another fact—and no one even turned his head.

Now and then, when Dr. Singh sensed it was advisable, we stopped at a small village for a cup of tea, but more often to buy something called *pan* (pronounced with a long "a") for Dubey and Dr. Singh. *Pan* is a unique preparation relished by very many Indians. It is a combination of crushed betel nut, spices, and lime, neatly folded in an aromatic, shiny betel leaf. Though it is said to be mildly intoxicating, I myself have never felt any effect at all. One of its ingredients colors the saliva of the user a deep red, and a confirmed user always has rust-like stains on his teeth. Dubey's teeth betrayed his devotion to *pan*, and that no doubt is why Dr. Singh stopped for it so often. Once the *pan* had been consumed, the singing would continue —as it did all evening.

From time to time Pande, emboldened by our growing spirit of camaraderie, offered a solo performance. To me his voice sounded like that of a very simple man with a decided village patois. But at the conclusion of each of his offerings, sung with great fervor, my Indian companions always encouraged him with expressions of approval. At one point I myself ventured to sing a Bengali song about Ramakrishna that I had learned many years earlier, and this performance was similarly commended, though no doubt my own pronunciation sounded far stranger than the accent of the driver's helper.

At supper time we had an Indian meal at a wayside eating place: several kinds of curry, *chapattis* or unleavened bread, *dal* (a delicious sauce made from Indian lentils), and sweet curds. When we were about to start out again, B. B. Singh casually remarked that there must have been some slight miscalculation, for though we had not yet reached Ayodhya, we had already spent almost three hours on the journey. But he encouraged us by saying it would not take very much longer.

After supper, as we continued our songful way, I remarked to Dr. Singh how beautifully right the farmers' simple mud huts looked, with their pinpoints of lamplight enlivening the dusk. His answer pulled me up short. "We must never cease to feel for the poverty *inside* those romantic looking houses," he said. I had always prided myself on being able to accept conditions in India as I found them and not to feel critical of the lack of modern progress. Now I realized that I had somehow to go beyond mere willingness to enjoy appearances. What I valued, even felt at home with, for its artistic appeal was a bare simplicity that could only be legitimately enjoyed if willingly adopted—as, for instance, by a monk. Dr. Singh was right to stress the desperate need to make more food and education and basic comforts available to villagers. And this had been one of the consuming drives behind Mahatma Gandhi's life. But somehow, I felt, it was equally necessary, as these basic human necessities became available, to preserve the inimitable combination of simplicity and dignity—yes, and culture in the profoundest sense—so often evidenced in rural India. That it could be managed, I felt certain. Was it not proved by the way educated and uneducated alike could join in singing devotional songs about Rama, paragon of righteousness, while speeding along in a modern, Western-made, but Indian-assembled car?

-4-

Several times during our trip Dr. Singh had spoken of a saintly man, known to his family, who lived in Ayodhya. His name was Bhagwan Dasji, and he was one of the four priests of the Temple of Hanuman. (The suffix "-ji" is added to Indian names to show respect and also affection.) Gradually it dawned on me that the professor hoped to take us to meet him. But as the hours passed, I wondered if we would ever reach the town. In fact, it seemed to me that B. B. Singh himself was becoming a bit doubtful if we were on the right road. After a few more vicissitudes we finally reached Ayodhya about 10:30 P.M. and began to search out the holy man's ashram, or retreat.

At last Dr. Singh located what he thought must be the place. Though it was now dark, he made his way down a narrow path to the gate, which was set back quite a distance from the main road. It all looked very unpromising. But suddenly the gate opened and a white-robed student, or *brahmachari*, let him in. Soon all the lights went on, and B. B. Singh motioned us to follow him. It turned out that the *brahmachari*, recognizing him, had told him Bhagwan Dasji had just retired after returning from the temple. Since he would not yet have gone to sleep, he could be informed we were there.

We passed under a great tree with hanging roots and went toward a small alcove-like room at the center of the one-storied main building, in which stood a low wooden platform. This shallow room, which had no front wall, was evidently Bhagwan Dasji's only reception room. As we entered through the front yard we glimpsed several young students, wrapped in white sheets, sleeping to one side on the ground.

Very soon the old man appeared. He was spare and wiry, with graying, short-clipped hair, and wore the ocher-colored garb of a man of renunciation. His motions were quick; his small piercing eyes were gray-blue—not dark, like the average Indian's. The first impression I had was of utter candor and sincerity. Obviously glad to see B. B. Singh, the old man asked us to come in. He spoke in Hindi, the language of this part of the country.

B. B. Singh explained to me that, like many priests of Hanuman, Bhagwan Dasji had been renowned for his strength and had been a champion at wielding the huge clubs that devotees of Hanuman employ to develop their strength. Even now, though about seventy-five years old, he could still manipulate them handily. As we entered we saw one of them—it looked like a bowling pin with an exaggerated head and was at least four feet high—standing in a corner. Since Hanuman was the loyal servitor of Rama, I knew the old priest was a worshiper of the all-pervading Vishnu, of whom Rama is believed to be a manifestation.

The professor, Shukla, and I seated ourselves on the platform, facing Bhagwan Dasji, who sat with his back to the road. Outside was the intensely dark Indian night. Though the priest could speak no English, he smiled at me to make me know I was welcome. There were no formalities, since older Indians usually waste little time on formal politeness. Indeed, many Indians of the old school, when they feel something deeply, make a point of saying exactly what they think, without dissembling to save hurting people's feelings.

The student who had let us in now brought a plate piled high with a sweetmeat called *laddu*, made of sugar and strained curds of fresh milk, deep-fried in oil. They had been offered to God in the temple and thus were consecrated food, or *prasad*. At this juncture Dubey, either instructed by B. B. Singh or emboldened by our fraternal spirit, entered and was given a stool beside the priest and just in front of the sweets. (These were passed back and forth during the ensuing conversation and with the driver's help soon disappeared.)

I myself was sitting directly before Bhagwan Dasji. B. B. Singh and Shukla were at my right. Immediately the old man began to talk, using forceful gestures to bring his points home. I do not know whether Dr. Singh told him the reason for my coming, but very likely he did. Now and then he translated in capsule form what Bhagwan Dasji was saying. Finally, though, my translator became so absorbed that he forgot to translate. I myself was completely oblivious of the fact, happily watching this transparently honest soul. Perhaps others judge differently; but my way of divining who is a saint is not through what he says but through what he transmits without words.

B. B. Singh must have asked him, for my sake, something about his personal experiences, for he first launched into the story of his life. It had been predicted, he said, that his father's line would be preserved only through his daughters. This prediction seemed to have been set at naught by Bhagwan Dasji's being born to his third wife. But the son early renounced the world to become a servant of Hanuman, the legendary monkey chieftain. In later years, though the head of his family, he refused to enter into their quarrels over what appeared to have been a rather large estate. He added that this had been his way, also, with regard to politicians who sought his favor.

In India, as elsewhere, politicians often seek to associate themselves with "holy men," or *sadhus* as they are called, and sometimes have their pictures taken with them. These are duly published in the newspapers. But Bhagwan Dasji had steadfastly refused to cooperate with politicians in any way. That, he felt, was not his responsibility. It was the duty of politicians and military men, he said, who represent the second, or *kshatriya*, caste, to rule society and protect the moral and spiritual order, represented by the priestly and intellectual caste, the *brahmins*. It was obvious that the ancient system of caste still governed his attitude toward society.

The old man then cited copious texts from the *Mahabharata*, the second of India's two major epics, in support of his thesis, invariably accompanying them with his quick, forceful gestures. One could understand he was a man of independent views. It was at this point that B. B. Singh forgot to keep on translating, while I contented myself with savoring all I could of his personal presence. (This experience is what Hindus refer to as "having *darshan*." The word *darshan* means, literally, "a seeing," but it connotes something deeper; it is analogous to the attitude of Roman Catholics when having an audience with —or simply getting a close view of—the Pope.) My renewal of contact with traditional Indian spirituality was making me increasingly aware of a relationship with India that was still very much alive though seven years had passed since I had embraced Christianity.

It was time to go and we all rose. Each took his leave of the saint either by saluting with joined palms or by touching his feet with the right hand and then placing it on the head— "taking the dust of the feet," it is called. (Since the head is the most respected part of the body, and the feet are the least, the gesture is one calculated to show deep reverence. Sometimes one places one's head on the holy man's feet.) I waited till last. As I rose after touching his feet the old man embraced me and began stroking my head and neck repeatedly in blessing. As he did so, I bent my head so that it touched his chest and his bare right arm. It felt utterly natural and right, and I was pervaded by a sense of warmth. To show my responsiveness I remained in that position for some seconds. An infusion of strength seemed to pass from the saint to me.

Bhagwan Dasji followed us to the gate. As I looked back at him and joined my palms in salutation, he nodded and raised his hand. Now I was aware of his age as I had not been when seated before him. More than once I looked back. Indeed, it was hard for me to go. I felt enlarged, strengthened, in a way that cannot be put into words—and the memory of the experience stayed with me. From then on, I could remember the old man whenever I wanted. For some weeks I made a practice of thinking of his lively and guileless presence whenever a mood of doubt or weakness invaded me, and invariably it passed off.

-5-

After we left Bhagwan Dasji, though the songs began almost immediately, I was for a time abstracted and could not join in. More than two hours had passed when B. B. Singh said cheerfully, "In fifteen minutes we shall be in Gorakhpur unless God wills otherwise." Soon we stopped to ask our way at a crossroads village that served as a check point for trucks. (This place was fairly near the Nepalese border, and the state government wanted to see that no goods were smuggled across.) It was now 1:30 A.M. Finding we were on the right road, we were about to proceed when Dubey announced, "The clutch must be broken. I can't make the car move."

What to do? A policeman on duty, and several others standing about, were understandably guarded, no doubt thinking we might mean mischief. At last they accepted our story as B. B. Singh unfolded it. They referred us to a brahmin schoolteacher who, because the night was warm, was sleeping outside his school, just a few yards from where we were stalled, on a bed made of loosely interwoven ropes. By happy coincidence he was an automobile mechanic as well as a teacher. Also by coincidence his name was Dubey.

The schoolteacher got up without the slightest trace of annoyance. I noted that, in the old-fashioned way, his hair was tied in a small knot behind, near the top of his head. On his lips was a smile of quiet contentment that never left him. His young son, who was lying on a bed nearby, was allowed to go on sleeping.

We pushed the car to the side of the road. The driver explained our predicament. Without a word, the schoolteacher went inside his house, which was a long, low cottage with a thatched roof, and brought out a metal box crammed with all manner of nuts, bolts, nails, pieces of wire, and what not. Our driver now lay on his back under the car and by means of a flashlight tried to find out precisely what had happened. His legs stretched, it seemed to me, dangerously far out in the road. I suggested that he cross them to keep them out of the way of the great trucks that now and again passed after being checked, and he complied. For a few minutes he fiddled around and then emerged with a thin, four-sided piece of metal three or four inches long, bent at right angles at both ends. Part of one of these ends had broken off.

Now began a long process of trial and error. At first Dubey looked nonplussed. But soon he decided just what he wanted to do and went over to the schoolteacher's metal box and began digging around in it. Taking a few nuts and pieces of wire, he returned to his position under the motor. From time to time he would send his helper back to have the schoolteacher make some sort of adjustment. There would be hammering of metal, fitting on of nuts. Then Dubey would start the motor and try to make the car move—but all to no avail. Finally the flashlight gave out and a small kerosene lamp was substituted. Again more experimenting, again more hammering when the part was returned to the schoolteacher.

I myself, on a hunch, began to look for the broken part, which must have dropped near where we had stalled. Our driver now had the same impulse, and he joined me. After a few moments he bent down and picked up out of the gravel a piece of metal about an inch long. It was the part that had broken off. With this as a guide, the two Dubeys began to fashion a substitute piece just the right length. Again there was much hammering, bending of metal, fitting of nuts. It all seemed so hit-or-miss that I wondered if they knew what they were doing.

During one period of waiting, when the driver had sent his helper back to the schoolteacher mechanic for further adjustments on the part, the kerosene lamp went out. Dubey was lying under the car. Suddenly I heard snores emanating from beneath the motor. Our plump Dubey, his legs still obediently folded as before, was fast asleep! (He had enough good humor to be amused when I woke him and told him.)

The minutes began to stretch into hours. After the experimenting had gone on for perhaps a half hour, B. B. Singh had very sensibly stretched out on the schoolteacher's rope bed and gone to sleep. Shukla, too, had arranged himself as best he could on the back seat of the car. Though rather tired myself, I was much too engrossed in what was going on to try to sleep. And so, at last, I was able to savor Dubey's cautious satisfaction when, upon once more sitting in the driver's seat and starting the motor, the car began to move as he put it in gear.

Thereupon B. B. Singh awoke and, accepting the situation as he found it, was ready to start off. I looked at my watch and found it was now 5 A.M. The job had taken over three hours.

When the work had been successfully completed, Dubey's namesake quietly withdrew toward his cottage, the same contented smile on his face. I watched him bend down and shake his son awake and send him to wash before beginning his religious duties and starting his studies. After our driver and Pande had gathered up the few tools scattered about, and the professor and Shukla were getting into the car, it occurred to me we should ask the schoolteacher-mechanic what we owed him. But when I spoke to our Dubey about paying him, I found that he had already asked how much we should pay, and the schoolteacher had replied, "Oh, nothing." He had done it out of good will. So far as he was concerned, we were all part of one family. He assumed we would have done the same for him in a similar situation. This seemed the more remarkable since three of us were obviously "educated," and one of us—with the white skin—obviously came from that land of limitless wealth, the United States.

All during the journey I had felt strangely at home with things as I was finding them in India. Now, even more than before, there was an identification with the people, the customs, the very atmosphere of the country. Obviously all Indian villagers are not as uncalculating and generous as the schoolteacher, but I was reminded that when one finds goodness in India, it is of a quality one seldom finds elsewhere—effortless as the shining of the sun, artless as the falling of rain.

It took us another two hours, over bumpy country roads, to reach B. B. Singh's house in Gorakhpur. By that time we had become so much a unit that all thought of hotels was forgotten. Dubey and Pande were given two of the couches in the small parlor to sleep on. I was put in the professor's own bed. Not counting the time out for the repair work (and a twenty-minute stop at a doctor's in a village on the way, to get medicine for a huge blister on B. B. Singh's thigh caused by a small green insect that had somehow got squashed under his clothes), our journey had consumed eleven hours.

-6-

Later, consulting my diary entry covering our journey to Gorakhpur, I found I had immediately sensed a special meaning in it. This trip, with its four distinct episodes, seemed to symbolize the various types of spirituality to be met with in India. At Sarnath, in the person of the quiet monk Shashanarasi, it had brought us face to face with a sort of intuitive wisdom. During the evening's ride to Ayodhya, thanks to everyone's uninhibited singing, we had lost ourselves in a mood of devotion to God. At Ayodhya we had sat spellbound before a guileless saint, who called to mind the disciplined, meditative life. And when the taxi was being put back—astonishingly—into running order by our undaunted companions, we had known at first hand the spirit of human community.

It was what I already knew of Hindu thought that suggested to me in these four episodes the basic types of Hindu religious aspiration. Modern Hinduism's analysis is a realistic and practical one. Every man, whether he knows it or not, is on his way to self-fulfillment through communion with ultimate reality —what we in the West call God. Since each possesses a unique temperament he must find his own special way to that goal. Nevertheless religious seekers—even, in fact, persons not consciously religious—may be roughly divided into four basic types. These are the intellectually intuitive, the emotionally dedicated, the mentally disciplined, and the physically active.

The qualities that make for the first two of these types are present, in widely varying degrees, in all human beings except the least developed. Frequently one of the two sets of qualities predominates, and the person is called either intellectual or emotional. Those that make for the third type, the mentally disciplined, predominate far less frequently. Since this type embodies purposive will, it is decisive when combined with either of the first two. Without its help, no man can hope for any form of achievement: he will remain an aimless idealistic dreamer or a prey to uncoordinated sensitivity. It is indispensable for spiritual seekers who want to know God in the present life rather than wait for some kind of revelation after death. The qualities that make for the fourth type, the physically active, include those of the third, as well. They predominate in the majority of men, sometimes in combination with one of the first two. Among spiritual seekers, just as the basic temperaments differ, so the disciplines appropriate to them vary. In India the four disciplines are known as *yogas*, ways of union.

In the fourfold Hindu discipline lay the basis of the design I needed to present to Christians what was most vital in Hindu religious life. It was not until perhaps a month later, in Calcutta, that I understood how I could tie this design in with the search for Christ beyond Christianity.

Almost all my religious training, before my return to the Christian Church, was received under the aegis of that rarest of Bengali spiritual geniuses, Ramakrishna Paramahamsa Culturally speaking, I am almost as much a Bengali as an American. Whenever I visit Calcutta, friends and favorite haunts claim much of my time. Somehow, even after becoming a Christian, just about the last thing that occurs to me there is to look up fellow Christians. Consequently, during my trip in 1970 I never thought of paying a call on the Belgian priest Robert Antoine till a few days before I was to leave, even though he had been recommended as someone I should not fail to see.

Father Antoine received me in a big, plainly decorated room that I took to be his study and bedroom. Books lined the walls, and the father sat on the bed, a rather wide one, behind a short-legged work table that had been placed upon it. I paid him only two visits in his house tucked away in one of the innumerable by-lanes of South Calcutta, with the grandiloquent name Prince Golam Muhammad Road. It was my loss, for he turned out to be a warm, perceptive, good-humored, truly open-minded follower of Christ. Our conversations ranged over a wide variety of subjects, mostly dealing with the relation of Hindu and Christian beliefs. We found ourselves in complete agreement. Through long years of teaching at Jadavpur University, Father Antoine had acquired an intimate knowledge of Indians and Indian culture. "Isn't it odd," he said to me with a smile, "it took you twenty-five years to learn to appreciate Christianity. It has taken me thirty to learn to appreciate Hinduism!" He told me he was engaged, along with a Bengali poet, in translating the *Aeneid* into the Bengali tongue. In the house a number of white-clad students were moving about, so I presumed he had accommodations for a few Indian Christians from the university.

During my second visit Father Antoine served me coffee which he made himself. I was explaining to him my difficulties in planning a book on the evidences of Christ's working outside the limits of organized Christianity. I mentioned the possibility of beginning with the story of the automobile trip, but I was not quite sure how it fit in with the idea of the book. After I had briefly sketched the story of my adventures, Father Antoine at once broke in, "Why don't you think about treating your trip as another journey to Emmaus? You can then develop it, as you had planned, around the episodes of your trip."

Here was the spark that set my imagination on fire. The priest had put his finger on what my mind was trying to tell me all these weeks. One can hardly call oneself a modern Hindu, I knew, without acknowledging the four aspects of the spiritual life symbolized by our journey to Gorakhpur. But one can hardly call oneself a Christian, either, without acknowledging and following them. Their significance for Christians, I began to see (perhaps I had unknowingly felt this for years), lay in the fact that all these ways of union with God are pointed to, in their teaching and example, by both Jesus and the apostles. I had not before thought of Christianity in just these terms. But the presence of the four ways in Hinduism did not make them any less authentically Christian. In purely Christian terms, I came to see these four aspects of the spiritual life as the several "voices" of Christ, through which he calls Christians to his presence and his likeness.

In the modern Christian these approaches, flowing naturally from his faith in Christ, are seldom if ever manifested in isolation. It may nevertheless be helpful to study the voices as if they could be separated. This is what the Hindus have done: in fact, they have often temporarily separated them in practice. As a result, even the average Hindu has a lively appreciation of nuances and subtleties in the spiritual life that Christians often miss. In the chapters that follow, I shall examine the four approaches in Hinduism separately, as Hindus would explain them. It may clarify things for the reader to point out here that a distinction is maintained throughout between a mere "hearing" of the theoretical message of the voices—especially of the first two—and the "heeding" or following of that message through practice of spiritual discipline. Ordinary believers in any religion may hear the message, but it is saints and mystics (known or unknown) who strive to make the message an integral part of their lives.

Hints of these various approaches to God are supplied not only by Jesus and the apostles. Down through the centuries there have been Christian saints and mystics who, depending on individual temperament, have taken up the suggestions found in the New Testament (and in the Old Testament, too) for spiritual practice. And they have stressed either intuitive wisdom, devotional self-giving, dedicated service in the spirit of human community, or a combination of several of these, always implemented by conscious discipline. (It should be noted that in Christian practice, unlike Hindu, there has never been a *yoga,* or way of union, based predominantly on this last voice.) These Christians, no less than Jesus and the apostles, represent the spirit of Christ. In later Christian practice, except for the disciplines used by Christian monks or hermits, the devotional and active approaches have been generally combined. With these has always gone a certain amount of prayer. The way of intuitive wisdom, referred to more explicitly by two of the apostles—John and Paul—than by Jesus himself, has most often been followed by practicing mystics.

For some years, in the West, the more purely spiritual aspects of religious life have been suspect among most thoughtful Christians other than monks and nuns. Protestants, indeed, have long looked askance at them. More recently, among Roman Catholics too, a justifiable concern with human values and social justice has superseded the old preoccupation with theology and private devotions. Serious concern for ways of union with God began to seem beside the point when millions of human beings were deprived of the most elementary human rights. Now, however, the pendulum has begun to swing back. Many religiously inclined Westerners are ready to learn once again—in a more chastened mood—from the experience of mystical witnesses. Finding few such competent witnesses among their fellow Christians, some have turned to Hinduism and Buddhism for inspiration.

In India, on the other hand, the pendulum is still continuing to swing in the direction of greater concern for human values. But things move more deliberately in the East. What Westerners now want to know about spiritual discipline is still abundantly available. It is a fortunate situation, because though all that is necessary for Christians in the way of discipline can be found in their own tradition, sometimes the same or related teachings become more convincing when spoken by outsiders.

THE VOICE OF
INTUITIVE WISDOM

It WAS A HAPPY coincidence that the first of the four episodes
in our journey to Gorakhpur had to do with a follower of the
Lord Buddha. What the Buddha experienced when he attained enlightenment is one of the purest examples of intuitive
wisdom the world has seen. True, by the year 1000 A.D. Buddhism had almost completely died out in India. But many Buddhists hold that modern Hinduism has been deeply colored by
the Buddha's experience and example and by the philosophies
that grew out of them, a tacit admission that there is a more
than casual resemblance between Buddhism's and Hinduism's
expressions of the voice of intuitive wisdom.

Our aim, however, is to search out the best evidences of the
several voices of Christ wherever they are found in the East
outside the Christian Church. It happens that I know more
examples of the voices and more important ones—in Hinduism than in Buddhism. We shall therefore be dealing here
chiefly with Hindu experience and doctrine. The first episode
of our journey must stand for more than Buddhist mysticism.

In Christian terms, the voice of intuitive wisdom bears witness to God's dwelling in the depths of the human soul,
where he is to be known. It tells a man to know God as the
foundation of his own existence. This voice harks back to a
passage early in Genesis: "Then God said, 'Let us make man
in our image, after our likeness.' " It suggests that there can
be an intellectual search for God as well as the better known
devotional type of search that predominates in most Christian
saints. If men are created in God's image, something can be
known of him through more than one of the essential elements
in their makeup.

In the four Gospels there are few overt references to this
approach, no doubt because Jesus was speaking mostly to
crowds of uncomplicated people who needed a more intimate
and understandable relationship with God. Without the concept
of a loving Father, and an emotional approach to him through

faith and love, men in Palestine in Jesus' time, like men in the West in later ages, might never have appreciated what he offered them. In Jesus' flat statement "I and the Father are one," many Hindus see a perfect expression of this voice. But the oneness of Jesus Christ with the Father does not refer to the presence of God in the human soul. In the Acts and Epistles, however, one finds clear references to the search for the God within. St. Paul strongly hints of it when he says, "Yet he is not far from each one of us." (Where can that "not far" be if not within the individual consciousness? Note the emphasis on the words "each one," as if to make it clear that the search is a matter of individual concern to every Christian.)

The translation of Jesus' saying "For behold, the kingdom of God is in the midst of you," was earlier worded "For behold, the kingdom of God is within you." The newer version adds meaning to this saying. But the old version suggested, accurately, to those of an intellectually mystical temperament that they could validly seek direct knowledge of God through their own souls. A most vivid expression of this knowledge is found in the fourteenth-century work *The Cloud of Unknowing*. "Sometimes peradventure," the unknown author says, God sends out a "beam of ghostly light" that pierces the cloud between himself and the one who seeks him. These "beams" are what intuitive mystics down through the ages have reflected in their writings.

Early echoes of intuitive wisdom are found not only in St. Paul. St. John the apostle was certainly aware of its role, and it was not unknown to Origen and St. Gregory of Nyssa later. Another important mystic largely of this type is an unidentified writer of the fourth century who called himself Dionysius the Areopagite and is therefore now known as the Pseudo-Dionysius; no doubt he took the name of the early Christian to assure his works a wide readership. Outstanding witness to intuitive wisdom is later found in the sermons of Meister Eckhart and in the writings of his pupil Jan van Ruysbroeck. The small treatise *Theologia Germanica*, a product of fourteenth-century Rhineland mystics, gives striking expression to it; much of the work sounds as if it were written by a follower of the Hindu Nondualistic Vedanta philosophy. A certain echo of the voice is to be found, in more recent times, in the writings of the Quakers. George Fox, their founder, asked men to seek the "inner light."

The voice of intuitive wisdom, as it is hinted at in the New

Testament and more clearly expressed by some of the Church
Fathers and later Christian mystics, is not a voice congenial
to all minds. Of the four voices of Christ, this one is the most
removed from the human scene. It is of the very essence of
intellect, of the reasoning faculty in man. The uneasiness it
causes in many persons stems, no doubt, from the fact that
reason is a late development in man's evolution. In one sense,
of course, it is that very fact that makes it most truly human—
not, however, when taken in isolation, but rather when combined with the other faculties in the human makeup: emotion,
will, and activity.

When this faculty is manifested as pure reason, and shorn of
all connection with those other faculties, it appears so austere
as to repel the average man—in theoretical research, for instance, and in speculative philosophy, or in scholarship, including theology. This appearance of austerity may explain, also,
why the pursuit of intuitive wisdom by certain mystics has
seemed alien to most religiously inclined persons, even in Hinduism; and why, unless it was carefully related in its expression to
the Bible and the concept of the Trinity, it has sometimes been
condemned by the Roman Church. We know, however, that
without scientific thought or philosophical inquiry, without
scholarly investigation or theological studies—divorced from
the slightest suspicion of personal prejudice—there would be
little material or intellectual or spiritual progress in human
society. Just so, without dedicated pursuit of intuitive wisdom
within the self or soul of man, men's spiritual development
would be the poorer. It is in the early sacred literature of
India that we find its clearest expression as an isolated voice.
I confess that it was this aspect of Hindu mysticism that first
attracted my own interest.

I begin our search for Christ with the voice of intuitive
wisdom in Hinduism not simply because of the chance order
of the episodes in our journey to Gorakhpur. Not even because
it was this aspect of Hindu philosophy that first interested me
personally. I give it first place because through it the Vedic
seers broke out of the confines of the original Aryan myth-
centered religion and brought their religious tradition in touch
with a universal truth. Historically it deserves to come first.
What is more, it is this voice in Hinduism that speaks most
directly to thoughtful modern men and women in the West.
This is, in fact, the aspect of Indian spirituality that most
Westerners refer to when they speak of "Hinduism."

Before we take up some of the basic elements of Hindu belief and experience that yield positive evidence of the voice of intuitive wisdom, however, we should have a look at the canonical Hindu scriptures as a whole.

-2-

The Hindu scriptures, the Vedas, are four in number. They are a treasure house of early Indo-Aryan religious beliefs and of exalted and timeless spiritual insights. Begun, according to most scholars today, at least as early as 1500 B.C., their original sections probably came into being before the time of Moses. They reached their final form, in which they have come down to the present, during a period of at least a thousand years. In terms of intuitive wisdom, the part of the Hindu scriptures that means most for Western Christians is certainly the Upanishads.

Hindus, like most religious believers (here Buddhists are the exception), hold that their scriptures are revealed by God. The Hindu scriptures, which are as old as and perhaps older than any others, advance an additional claim not found elsewhere among the great religions. They state that what they contain is not revealed for the first time. The truths of scripture have appeared in exactly the same form in each of an unending series of cosmic cycles of creation, which they liken to the breathing out and breathing in of the Creator. This dogma orthodox Hindus still accept.

So highly did the ancient Hindus revere the Vedas that the celebrated "six systems" of orthodox Hindu scholastic philosophy accepted them as their authority. These systems were probably elaborated in the early centuries of the Christian era from aphoristic treatises composed much earlier. Several of the systems, including that of the Vedanta, were constructed on the basis of the Vedic teachings. An even later scholastic philosophy, the Shaiva Siddhanta, though it does not accept the Vedas as infallible, claims to express their true import.

On what authority, it may be asked, do the Hindus substantiate their belief that the Vedas are divinely revealed? The reply of a believing Hindu to this question is: on the authority of scripture itself. In the scriptures, he will say, are found the teachings and descriptions of the experiences of ancient sages, or *rishis*. (The word *rishi* is a Sanskrit term meaning "seer of truth," that is to say, one who has not merely known the truth, but *seen* it, experienced it by participation.) The test that applies here is that of competent witness. Hindus believe that the teachings and the religious experiences their scriptures embody are attested to by sages whose word cannot be doubted. In the purified minds of the *rishis* were revealed, first, instructions about ritualistic worship of the various gods of the Vedic dispensation, and subsequently the truth about the transcendent Godhead that was understood to endow the gods themselves with their being and power.

Modern Hindu thinkers do not hold the revelations in the Vedas as something final or incapable of growth. God is constantly revealing himself in every age. Moreover, when a man experiences God the Vedas are transcended. The Bhagavad Gita, a later scripture, says, "To the enlightened brahmin [knower of ultimate reality] all the Vedas are of as much use as a pond when there is everywhere a flood."

Each of the four Vedas is made up of two disproportionate sections: a longer section known as the "ritual part," and a much shorter section known as the "wisdom part." In the first is also included a section known as the "meditation part." The ritual part preserves the immemorial hymns to the Aryan gods, to be recited during the Vedic fire sacrifices. (Agni, god of fire, is the mediator between men and the gods.) These hymns were handed down for untold centuries simply through oral transmission; it was one of the duties of students to commit them to memory. The ritual part includes, as well, detailed descriptions of rites to be performed, always with the help of brahmin priests, for meeting the various situations of daily life or for attaining certain religious or material ends.

The meditation part included in this section prescribes mental variations of the ritual sacrifices. These were intended for persons who had retired after fulfilling their worldly duties and to whom the numerous items required for the actual rituals were unavailable. It amounts to a kind of instruction in mental ritualistic worship.

In contrast to the Old Testament, whatever racial history is to be found in this longer section of the Vedas can be gleaned only from hints in the hymns or instructions for the rituals. We find here, not the record of a unique God's continuing relations with a special people, but rather an elaborate liturgy by which the Indo-Aryan gods might be propitiated and the contingencies of daily life successfully dealt with.

The wisdom part of the Vedas preserves the Upanishads, or

books of spiritual instruction, placed at the end of each of the four original scriptures. Their teachings embody the spiritual experiences of the later Vedic sages. Another name for the Upanishads is "Vedanta," which means "ends of the Vedas," also their conclusions.

Many of the sages lived in forest retreats. They taught students who came to them for instruction—but only after putting them through certain tests of fitness. In one instance the test consisted simply in the young man's tending the teacher's herd of cattle, in solitude, over a long period of time. (Since this particular student was already of an introspective turn of mind, he actually began to have inner experiences even before returning to the teacher for regular instruction.)

Some of the important Upanishads appear to have reached their final form slightly before the time of Gautama Buddha, who, as we noted, was born in the sixth century before Christ. Others may have been completed slightly after his time. These scriptures amount to a kind of instruction in meditation and a preparation for deeper contemplation. They mark a distinct advance in spiritual understanding over the ritualism of the original Indo-Aryan scriptures.

-3-

Unlike the New Testament, to which in certain respects they may be likened, the Upanishads do not announce the advent of a personal Savior. What they announce is, rather, the advent of a new consciousness of the nature of ultimate reality. Even among the earlier hymns of the Vedas we find one or two that contain speculations about the first cause of the universe. But with the Upanishads we have a new and liberating revelation. We turn to this revelation, which took place sometime before 500 B.C., to trace out clear evidences of the voice of intuitive wisdom.

The advent of the new consciousness comes in compelling form. The Upanishads record the efforts of the later Vedic sages to communicate to qualified pupils what they had found as a result of their quest for the True Self of man and the Divine Ground of the universe. These treatises, though they still reflect some of the earlier beliefs, offer a profound insight into the nature of ultimate reality and of the soul. Traditional

Christian thought would no doubt brand the Upanishadic
record as heretical. Yet, from the point of view of intuitive
wisdom, it is far more explicit about the soul's relationship to
God than any of the books of the New Testament.

In many passages the Upanishads identify the soul's essential
nature, which they call "Atman," with the essential nature of
God, which they call "Brahman." "This Atman is Brahman"
is the classic formulation of the doctrine. Along with it, three
other texts make up the four "great statements" accepted as
the core of the Upanishadic teaching by the several schools of
philosophy that go by the name of Vedanta. The first of these
three is the statement "You are that [Brahman]." The
second is "I am Brahman." The third statement is "Consciousness is Brahman." What all these terms meant to the
Vedic sages who first used them, and whether all the early
Upanishads taught an identical truth, is not certain. For
the purposes of this chapter we shall rely on the interpretation
advanced by the mystical philosopher Shankara in his system of
Nondualistic Vedanta philosophy. Shankara lived in the ninth
century of the Christian era, but he believed he had experienced
the ultimate reality spoken of by the Upanishads.

What is this ultimate reality, this Brahman? Brahman,
according to the Upanishads, is being itself—the only being
that is unchangingly real. It is that which gives temporary
being to all things in this changing universe. One of the
earliest of the eleven major Upanishads commented on by
Shankara, the *Brihadaranyaka Upanishad,* begins with an
invocation: "That is full; this is full. This fullness has been
projected from that fullness. When this fullness merges in that
fullness, all that remains is fullness." This arresting passage
is not only a generalized allusion to the creation and to the
bestowal of being upon all created things. It amounts also to
a sophisticated description of the Godhead—so far as the
Godhead can be described.

If we accept the interpretation by Shankara we may render
the passage this way: Ultimate reality is infinite; this relative
world is infinite. The infinity of the relative world has proceeded
from the infinity of ultimate reality. When the infinity of
the relative world merges in the infinity of ultimate reality,
all that remains is the Infinite. Hindu commentators say the
word "merges" can refer to the individual's attainment of
communion with reality as well as to a merging of the creation
in God at the end of a cosmic cycle. In passing, one may note

that in the later development of Buddhism, the Mahayana
Buddhism, there is a maxim: "*Samsara* is Nirvana"—the
world of becoming is not other than the world of ultimate
reality. The passage quoted above provides an interesting
parallel to this latter statement, made perhaps eight hundred
years afterward.

To show that Brahman, ultimate reality, is not to be known
as an object, the *Brihadaranyaka Upanishad* gives the following
instruction: "Now, therefore, the description of Brahman:
'Not this, not this.' " Brahman does not correspond to this
definition or that definition, the Upanishad is saying; it cannot be described by this quality or that quality. In the last
analysis nothing can be stated about ultimate reality. It is not,
after all, an object. Here the Upanishad anticipates the statements of later Christian mystics following in the footsteps of
the Pseudo-Dionysius, who said that God can only be known
through "unknowing." The helpless "Nothing, nothing"
(*"Nada, nada"*) that St. John of the Cross offers as his only
description of the Godhead seems almost a direct echo of the
Upanishadic "Not this, not this" (*"Neti, neti"*).

Very close to the time of the early Upanishads, Lao-tzu was
saying much the same thing: "The Tao that is described is not
the eternal Tao: names that can be named do not name the
Eternal. All is nameless at the beginning of creation; with the
origin of everything comes naming." Emphasizing the indescribability of ultimate reality, he said elsewhere, "It is the form
of formlessness, the picture of nothing. It is called infinitesimal. Face it and you cannot see its face; follow it and you
cannot see its back."

Shankara speaks of the indescribable and indivisible "unconditioned Brahman." The second century Mahayana Buddhist philosopher Nagarjuna refers always to "the Void," and
the later Zen masters of China and Japan to "Emptiness." All
these terms signify intuitive realizations that ultimate reality
is not a conceivable object. The experiences, despite all the difficulties raised by faithful Christian and other dogmatists and
literalists, sound tantalizingly alike. We can understand better,
now, the Buddha's refusal to make any direct statements about
God or the soul.

Immediately following the passage in the Upanishad giving
the negative "description" of Brahman occurs the sentence
"Now the designation of Brahman: 'The truth of truth.' " This
phrase "the truth of truth" is meant to emphasize the supreme
worth of Brahman, despite its indescribability, to anyone who

needs a positive affirmation of ultimate reality. The Upanishad
has made sure that the hearer knows there is no adequate way
to describe Brahman, because it is in essence not different from
either speaker or listener. It then proceeds in this fashion to
offer a "designation" of Brahman to show it is not something
nonexistent. It is that without which truth itself could not be,
hence "the truth of truth."

A passage in the Old Testament is called to mind by these
two approaches, positive and negative, to God. In Exodus it
is written: "Then Moses went up on the mountain, and the
cloud covered the mountain. The glory of the Lord settled on
Mount Sinai, and the cloud covered it six days; and on the
seventh day he called to Moses out of the midst of the cloud."
The cloud reminds one of the "cloud of unknowing" between
the worshiper and the Lord. Within it is the inexpressible
glory of the Lord, who had already told Moses his name: "I
AM WHO I AM"—and, as if to explain the unexplainable, had
added, "Say this to the people of Israel, 'I AM has sent me to
you.' "

The use of the phrase "the truth of truth" has a peculiar
fitness in the Hindu context. In India men have from time
immemorial emphasized the centrality of truth. The Rig-Veda,
the earliest of Indian scriptures, declares, "It is truth that
bears up this earth." The *Taittiriya Upanishad,* a source book
for Shankara's Vedanta philosophy, says, "The Satya [the
True] became all this: whatever there is." And this veneration
of truth has continued into modern times. It is well known
that Mahatma Gandhi, though for many years in the habit of
saying, "God is Truth," at a certain point in his life began
to say, "Truth is God." Perhaps without knowing it, he had
gone back to the Vedas. The great Ramakrishna Paramahamsa, who lived in the nineteenth century, might even be
called a bondslave of truth. Once he had given his word to do
something, he could not rest till it was fulfilled. If a man
follows truth perfectly for twelve years, he would say, whatever that man states will come to pass. The word "truth"
here includes truth in thought, word, and deed. When a man
can bring such a happening to pass, he performs what is known
as an "act of truth." The Hindu scriptures abound with references to such acts. When the earth opened at Queen Sita's
bidding, in the *Ramayana* story, and when she passed through
the flames unscathed, what happened bore witness to her perfection in truth.

What seems an even more positive "designation" of Brahman was advanced some centuries after the *Brihadaranyaka Upanishad* was completed. In a late Upanishad the Godhead is given the name Satchidananda. The word is a combination of three terms indicating absolute being (*sat*), absolute awareness (*chit*), and absolute joy (*ananda*). Here we find a striking parallel with the Christian Trinity, a concept implicit in the words of Jesus and carefully elaborated by the Fathers of the Church. As Christians familiar with scholastic philosophy are aware, the Trinity consists of three "Persons": the eternally existing Father; his eternally existing perfect image, the Son, "eternally begotten" of him as a necessary result of his perfect self-awareness; and the eternally existing Spirit, who "proceeds from the Father and the Son," out of their mutual relationship of love. God, though triune as to Persons, is nevertheless one as to nature.

In the Hindu conception, *sat*, absolute being, would suggest the eternally existent Father. Similarly *chit*, absolute awareness, would suggest the Son, the eternally existent image of the Father, "begotten of the Father." And finally *ananda*, absolute joy, would suggest the Holy Spirit, who "proceeds from the Father and the Son." Each rests in and is intimately united with the others. It is not necessary to affirm an identity in the concepts to see a curious similarity.

As we shall discover on proceeding farther, it almost seems as if in Hinduism God has revealed, in their naked, pure splendor, the various elements of his revelation, which, in Christianity, are united in an indissoluble whole. If they were to be joined in a slightly different arrangement, by a Hindu prophet, how much less valid would they be?

To modern minds the Trinity sounds like a speculation. Before disregarding it, one should remember that it is strongly indicated by the words of Jesus and the apostles, all of whom experienced an intimate relation with God. The attributing of three Persons to him should not mislead anyone into thinking that the Godhead is not a unity. The simple statement that he embodies three Persons is no more complete than would be the statement that, as the image of the Father, a man embodies a reflection of pure being, awareness, and joy. As the elements of a man's personality are inseparable in his one self, so the three Persons are inseparable in God's one nature.

The three aspects of Brahman we have been discussing—*sat, chit*, and *ananda*—are likewise based on spiritual experience. The mystics who spoke of them were not indulging in mere speculation. In Shankara's interpretation they are no less eternal, and no more separate, than they are in Christian doctrine: each and all are inseparable from the indivisible ultimate reality. Yet, strictly speaking, the term "Satchidananda" is not a positive description of Brahman for a nondualist Hindu. It is said to indicate only this much: that Brahman is not nonexistence, not absence of awareness, not the opposite of joy. Just so, one may conjecture that the Trinity is after all simply a means of "designating" the indefinable and unthinkable Godhead, which the Pseudo-Dionysius pointed out could only be known by "unknowing." Christians may have something to learn from Hindu followers of the path of intuitive wisdom about not taking their own Trinity too literally.

Can the three aspects by which the Upanishad designates Brahman be said to be Persons in the Christian sense? This is certainly open to question—especially in view of the fact that so many Hindus speak of Brahman as "impersonal" and refer to it by the pronoun "it." And yet Satchidananda can hardly be said *not* to be personal, at least in the everyday, nontheological sense of the word. Without the presence of personhood, that which makes a person the unique and undivided whole he is, even Satchidananda cannot be experienced by participation. Ultimate reality may thus be thought of as a new dimension of personality. If the three aspects of Brahman may be said to be joined in one nature, that one nature may also be said to be "suprapersonal" rather than merely "impersonal."

-4-

We turn now to the other term of central importance in the Upanishads: Atman. What is this Atman? It is the unchanging reality that confers being on the changing conscious self of man. It is the "witness," of the states of waking, dreaming, and dreamless sleep. In teaching about Atman, the True Self, the *Brihadaranyaka Upanishad* tells a delightful and yet profound story about a sage and his wife. The sage, whose name is Yajnavalkya, is one of the very first exponents of the way of intuitive wisdom identified by name. Yajnavalkya has told his two wives he is planning to renounce worldly life for the final stage of life, that of monkhood. He wants to make a settlement between them. But the thought of possessions does not appeal to his younger wife, Maitreyi. She asks him, "Venerable Sir, if indeed the whole earth, full of wealth, belonged to me, would I be immortal through that?" "No," her husband replies, perhaps a little surprised at her question. "Your life would be just like that of people who have plenty. Of immortality, however, there is no hope through wealth." "Tell me, venerable Sir," she says, "of that alone which you know to be the only means of attaining immortality." Yajnavalkya is highly pleased. "My dear," he says, "you have been my beloved even before, and now you say what is after my heart." Then he explains to her what he knows, asking her to meditate on what he tells her.

First the sage impresses on her the fact of Atman's existence. "Truly," he says, "not for the sake of the husband, my dear, is the husband loved, but he is loved for the sake of the Self. Not for the sake of the wife is the wife loved, but she is loved for the sake of the Self. Not for the sake of the All is the All loved, but it is loved for the sake of the Self. My dear Maitreyi, it is the Self that should be realized—should be heard about, reflected on, and meditated upon. By the realization of the Self, my dear—through hearing, reflection, and meditation —all this is known." For the sage Yajnavalkya, Atman is in a real sense "the true light that enlightens every man."

More than this, each man is himself the true light. Yajnavalkya continues, "The brahmin rejects one who knows him as different from the Self. The warrior rejects one who knows him as different from the Self. . . . The All rejects one who knows it as different from the Self. This brahmin, this warrior . . . and this All are that Self." The sage is trying to explain to his wife that the real nature of every creature is Atman, which is not different from Brahman, or ultimate reality. Do we catch here a foreshadowing of the haunting words "Truly, I say to you, as you did it to one of the least of these my brethren, you did it to me"?

Finally, speaking of the realization, the experience, of Atman, which like Brahman is "the truth of truth," Yajnavalkya tells Maitreyi, "When there is duality, as it were, then . . . one sees another, one hears another, one speaks to another. . . . one knows another. But when everything has become the Self, then . . . what should one see, what should one hear, what should one speak . . . what should one know—and through what [means]? Through what should one know That owing to which all this is known? Through what, my dear, should one know the Knower?'' Here we are once more confronted with the impossibility of describing ultimate reality—simply because no one can ever separate himself from it. In these last two sentences Yajnavalkya is repeating about Atman what the Upanishad has already said about Brahman: '' [It is] not this, not this.''

How utterly indescribable Atman is in itself is also indicated in a passage from the *Shvetashvatara Upanishad*: ''Grasping without hands, hasting without feet, it sees without eyes, it hears without ears. It knows what is to be known, but no one knows it.'' We find a striking parallel in a statement of St. Catherine of Genoa, uttered almost two thousand years later, in an attempt to convey the experience of her soul: ''I see without eyes, I understand without mind, I feel without feeling, and I taste without taste. . . . When the creature finds himself cleansed and purified and transformed in God, then he sees what is pure and clean. This sight, which is not seen, cannot be spoken of or thought of.'' St. Catherine, like St. John of the Cross, is an outstanding illustration of the way of devotional self-giving. That both of them on occasion were able to speak in terms of intuitive wisdom shows how closely intertwined these two ways can be in the experience of a Christian.

It is the Upanishads that first taught the essential identity of the individual soul and God—of Atman and Brahman. This concept of nondifference does not, in Shankara's interpretation, assert that the individual soul is the equal of the Creator. The creative aspect of the Godhead, known as Ishvara, and the individual soul, the *jiva*, though both involved in the world of becoming, are poles asunder. It is the Atman, or True Self, of each of these that is identical with the other. The one nature of the Godhead, as it were, is identical with the one nature of the image of God. In this sense only is Atman, the essential self of the *jiva*, said to be one with Brahman, the essential self of Ishvara the Creator, by followers of the way of intuitive wisdom.

In the introduction to his translation of the *Brihadaranyaka Upanishad*, Swami Nikhilananda sums up the implications, from Shankara's point of view, of the doctrine of the identity of Brahman and Atman. ''Though the reality underlying the universe may be unlimited,'' he writes, ''it may appear to be something vague; it may also appear to be material in nature. The self, conversely, is clear, directly perceived, and spiritual in nature, though it may appear to be limited by other selves.

The realization of the identity of the self and Brahman in a mystical experience establishes the existence of a reality which is infinite, directly perceived, unlimited, and spiritual." In this passage we have a succinct statement of what the doctrine of the "divinity" of the soul implies for a nondualist.

How is one to know the Self, or Atman, and when will one know it? Here is what the *Katha Upanishad* says: "This Atman cannot be attained by the study of the Vedas, or by intelligence, or by much hearing of sacred books. It is attained by him alone whom it chooses. To such a one Atman reveals its own form." Ramakrishna's disciple Vivekananda pointed out that this sounds like a doctrine of election. "Election is true," he said, "but explain it as an inner experience." In the Upanishadic passage one finds an anticipation of the four maxims said to embody the characteristics and ideals of Zen: "Transmission outside scriptures; not relying on letters; pointing directly to one's Mind; attainment of Buddhahood (enlightenment) by seeing into one's Nature."

Though nothing can cause the realization of Atman, certain preconditions are to be fulfilled. "He who has not first turned away from wickedness," says the Upanishad, "who is not tranquil and subdued, and whose mind is not at peace, cannot attain Atman. It is known only through the knowledge of Reality." Here the passage just quoted from St. Catherine of Genoa again comes to mind: "When the creature finds himself cleansed and purified and transformed in God, then he sees what is pure and clean." Atman, it would seem, does not "choose" itself unless the limited self, or phenomenal ego, has been purified and transformed in God.

In a commentary on this passage in his translation of the *Katha Upanishad,* Swami Nikhilananda explains: "Both self-effort and divine grace are necessary for the realization of Atman. Through self-effort the seeker removes obstacles and prepares the ground; next there is the spontaneous revelation of Atman." Here, then, is the equivalent for the man of intuitive wisdom of what the devotionally-minded call the Lord's grace. It is not generally something that comes without effort. As if to emphasize the need for emptying oneself of ego, the Upanishad says later, "When all the desires that dwell in the heart fall away, then the mortal becomes immortal and here attains Brahman."

The disciplines for realizing Atman (which is one with Brahman)—"turning away from wickedness," becoming "tranquil and subdued," and putting the mind "at peace"—we shall examine in detail in a later chapter. It is enough to note here what the *Katha Upanishad* has to say about the experience: "By the mind alone is Brahman to be realized; then one does not see in it any multiplicity whatsoever." The direct approach detailed in the Zen passage quoted above is indicated here, rather than the approach of speculative thought.

Despite the indescribability of Atman, the Upanishadic seers cannot resist trying to convey what it is like. The *Mundaka Upanishad* thus speaks of Brahman in the form, as it were, of Atman: "The radiant Brahman dwells in the cave of the heart. . . . It is the great support of all; for in it is centered everything that moves, breathes, and blinks. O disciples, know that to be your Self." Of that Brahman it declares, "It is pure; it is the light of lights; it is that which they know who know the Self. The sun does not shine there, nor the moon and the stars, nor these lightnings, not to speak of fire. When he shines, everything shines after him; by his light everything is lighted." One is reminded vividly of what is written in Revelation of the holy city Jerusalem: "And the city has no need of sun or moon to shine upon it, for the glory of God is its light, and its lamp is the Lamb. By its light shall the nations walk . . . and there shall be no night there."

I am tempted to apply in a special way to the unnamed sage who spoke the prophetic words of the *Mundaka Upanishad* these words from the Gospel of St. John: "He came for testimony, to bear witness to the light, that all might believe through him. He was not the light, but came to bear witness to the light." Of that light John said, in words that to a Hindu nondualist might well seem to express his own belief, "The true light that enlightens every man was coming into the world. He was in the world, and the world was made through him, yet the world knew him not." Can that light which was Christ also have been coming into the world through Upanishadic seers whose names are lost to history?

-5-

Originally the Upanishadic teachings were not given to all men. In Vedic times many were not ready for their difficult doctrine. Hence the prolonged tests of character imposed on students from the three upper castes (who, being Aryans, were alone entitled to hear the Vedas) before they were given the instruction. A man might easily assume, on hearing it, that he was farther advanced than he actually was. Or he might make it an excuse for lack of personal effort or even for amorality. "Do not give dogs what is holy," is the way Jesus expressed the same precautionary attitude five hundred years later.

Not many centuries after the closely guarded teachings had been collected in the Upanishads, that is to say, about 200 B.C., the mystical doctrine—possibly in response to the challenge of Buddhism, whose doctrines were taught in the language of the people—became more available. The change was effected through their inclusion in that highly important source of moral and spiritual instruction, the epic *Mahabharata*. Though the teachings appear, in less organized form, in various parts of the vast work, they are found in definitive form in a treatise embedded in it, the Bhagavad Gita, now looked upon as a canonical scripture.

The Bhagavad Gita not only illuminates but carries forward the teachings of the Upanishads in a grand synthesis whose potentialities were only fully realized in India over two millenniums later. In the colophon at the end of each chapter, this scripture actually calls itself an Upanishad. Perhaps the most popular and influential Hindu scripture among all classes of people in India, it has appeared in any number of translations in the present and the preceding century. Though it deals with a great variety of spiritual matters, we shall concern ourselves here simply with its expression of the voice of intuitive wisdom.

In the Bhagavad Gita the Lord Krishna—total embodiment of the all-pervading Sustainer of the universe, Vishnu—instructs his friend and disciple Arjuna. A warrior and aristocrat, Arjuna nevertheless hesitates in his duty to join battle with his enemies. Many of his cherished relatives and even friends are ranged against him in support of his evil cousin Duryodhana. His cousin's cause is an unrighteous one, and in opposing him Arjuna would be fighting for the vindication of justice. But his human sentiments overpower his judgment. (The theme may be interpreted subjectively, as well: what we have to oppose in ourselves is often what is dearest to our own hearts.) In his instruction, Krishna defines not only what Arjuna's duty is as dictated by his position in society, but also the basis of belief for those who by nature emphasize the voice of intuitive wisdom. Followers of this voice speak of the Bhagavad Gita as a dialogue between the Supreme Self and the individual self.

"The unreal never is," Krishna says. "The Real never ceases to be. . . . That by which all this is pervaded know to be imperishable. . . . [The Self] is never born, nor does it ever die, nor, having once been, does it again cease to be. Unborn, eternal, permanent, and primeval, it is not slain when the body is slain." The "Real" is synonymous with Atman. It is the sole unchanging reality in a man: "Weapons cut it not, fire burns it not, water wets it not, the wind does not wither it." The "unreal" is not, however, something illusory; it is simply whatever is subject to change. We have here the Upanishadic doctrine of Atman, spelled out in slightly greater detail.

After discussing many other aspects of spirituality, Krishna speaks of the complementary Upanishadic doctrine, that of Brahman. From what he says it is clear, just as it was in the Vedas, that ultimate reality is both immanent and transcendent: God dwells in the universe, as it were, and yet is not limited by it. Identifying himself with the Godhead, Krishna explains what he calls his lower and higher natures. He first describes the totality of the material universe, gross and fine. It includes mind as well as matter, Creator as well as creatures. "This is my lower nature," he says. "But different from it, know, mighty Arjuna, my higher nature—the indwelling Spirit by which the universe is sustained. Know that these two natures form the womb of all beings. I am the origin of the entire universe and its dissolution. There exists nothing whatever higher than I am, Arjuna. All is strung on me as a row of gems on a thread."

Krishna does not leave matters there, but goes beyond the explanations of the Upanishads. Proceeding from this conception of the "Indwelling Spirit" that sustains the universe, he declares, "By me, in my unmanifested form, are all things in this universe pervaded. All beings exist in me, but I do not exist in them. And yet the beings do not dwell in me—behold, that is my divine mystery. My Spirit, which is the support of all beings and the source of all things, does not dwell in them." From the point of view, as it were, of God, the objects and beings of the universe, being ultimately nondifferent from God, cannot be said to dwell, as such, in him at all. Here is the germ of a thought on which a school of extreme nondualism is based. Its implications are worked out in another treatise, the *Ashtavakra Samhita*.

These few quotations from the Bhagavad Gita, like those from the Upanishads, offer only an infinitesimal hint of the rich variety of experience in the form of intuitive wisdom to be found in the Hindu canonical scriptures. They show the kind of thinking and experience that preoccupied the later Vedic seers. Those who followed them in the post-Vedic age, by weaving their findings into the stories of legendary heroes, made these available to the average man. They also provided future generations with their first detailed, though perhaps partly idealized, view of everyday life in ancient India.

As I have mentioned, there has been more than one interpretation of the Upanishadic teachings. The nondualists of Shankara's school have consistently seen these teachings in terms of the voice of intuitive wisdom. They appear not to have noted that with the Bhagavad Gita a new advance was made. While Krishna speaks in this work of Atman and Brahman as they are spoken of in the Upanishads, he also goes beyond these scriptures. He constantly presents himself, a living and breathing person, as the supreme Godhead. From the point of view of Brahman, as it were, Krishna is Brahman. But he is something more—a something that includes both Atman and Brahman. Had Christian mystics tending toward the way of intuitive wisdom not perceived that there was something more to God than the "one nature," they too might have built a system of thought like that of the Vedantic nondualists.

The *Ashtavakra Samhita*, the more extreme treatise just referred to, reproduces what may well be a picture of the final instruction imparted by one of the forest sages to a qualified student. This work is thought by some, because of its literary style, to be from the same period as the Bhagavad Gita. Others place it many centuries later. It purports to be a conversation between the sage Ashtavakra and his pupil, King Janaka of Videha, a highly advanced spiritual seeker who figures prominently in the *Brihadaranyaka Upanishad*.

In the course of his preliminary instruction, Ashtavakra says to Janaka, "You are the one seer of all and really ever free. Truly, this alone is your bondage, that you see the seer as other than that. . . . You are unattached, actionless, self-effulgent, and without blemish. This alone is your bondage, that you practice *samadhi* [concentration of mind leading to spiritual ecstasy]." Janaka, having attained a realization of the True Self through his teacher's instruction, makes a startling pronouncement: "As I alone reveal this body, even so do I reveal this universe. Therefore mine is all this universe, or truly nothing is mine." His "I" is now identified with Atman. "Wonderful am I!" he exclaims. "Adoration to myself, who know no decay from Brahma, the

Creator, down to a clump of grass. . . . Wonderful am I! Adoration to myself, who have nothing—or have all that is thought of and spoken of.''

During the ensuing discussion Ashtavakra tests and seeks to strengthen the pupil's realization of Atman. The teacher says, ''Rare is the man who knows the Self as one and without a second and as the Lord of the universe, as well. He does what he knows [is to be done] and has no fear from any quarter.'' Atman is fearless, there being no other whom it might fear. (Here we have the Upanishadic doctrine that Atman includes the Lord rather than is included by him.)

When Janaka finally gives expression to his mature realization, he says, ''Thinking about the unthinkable, one betakes oneself only to a form of thought. Therefore giving up that thought, thus truly do I abide.'' He adds, ''The tranquillity that springs up in one who is thus without anything is rare even when one possesses only a loincloth. Therefore, giving up renunciation and acceptance, I live happily.'' Janaka does not exchange his life in the world for that of a monk, for he is serene in the knowledge that nothing is his.

This is not a form of Quietism. Janaka is the ruler of a great kingdom. He has reached this state of awareness through attenuation of his ego after having completed a long moral and mental discipline.

Ashtavakra makes a subtle distinction: ''He who has seen the supreme Brahman [the Godhead] meditates, 'I am Brahman.' What would he who has transcended all thought think, when he sees no second thing?'' So long as one is conscious of being anything, even Brahman, one has not reached the goal of intuitive wisdom. At the very conclusion of this transcendental dialogue Janaka exclaims, ''What is existence or nonexistence? What more is there to say? Nothing emanates from me.'' We have gone as far as the voice of intuitive wisdom as taught in the forest retreats can go.

The experience recorded in the Upanishads and carried to its extreme in works like the *Ashtavakra Samhita* is a very real experience. Yet it certainly represents only one aspect of Hindu, just as of Christian, experience. It required, perhaps, the infusion of another strand of thought—from Mahayana Buddhism, the Bhagavad Gita, and later Hindu doctrine, especially Tantra—to make fully clear the need to return, like Moses from Mount Sinai, from the Presence on the mountain to the Presence in the valleys, to appreciate the need for a personal God and the

importance of his creation. We see here a new application for
Isaiah's luminous words: "Every valley shall be lifted up, and
every mountain and hill be made low."

Yet who can say with certainty that the knower of Brahman
(or Atman) does not finally enjoy the experience the worshiper
of a personal God enjoys? Perhaps he simply fails to think
it needs to be or can be talked about. As the sage Yajnavalkya
said to his wife Maitreyi, "When everything has become the
Self . . . what should one speak . . . and through what
[means] ?"

-6-

The forest retreats where much of the later Vedic wisdom
evolved were in the nature of schools. No more of them is known
than the hints to be found in the scriptures. Such schools
formed around one or another sage renowned for his knowledge
of spirituality or of social law and morality. Perhaps in some
of them all the elements necessary for a young man's education
were available. What they were like need not remain a complete
mystery, however. Today, in India, one sees plows in use in
the fields that preserve the shape and build of those used
thousands of years ago. Perhaps, by observing some of the
smaller traditional retreats, or ashrams, still to be found in
out-of-the-way places in India, one can obtain some notion of
what those Vedic schools, or *gurukulas*, were like. On my recent
visit I spent a few hours in one of these, a simple retreat at
Rishikesh in the foothills of the Himalayas. In 1959 I had
the good fortune to see an ashram of another type, near Puri
in Orissa state, under the direction of a holy man, a *sadhu*,
who wore no clothes. Each contrasts sharply with the other.
From visits to both I thought I had more than an inkling of
what the forest retreats were like in Upanishadic times.

It was in September 1970 that I visited the first of these two
retreats in the company of a close friend, Krishna Bajpai,
whom I have known for many years. Krishna, a professor of
political theory in a large Indian university, is a devout Hindu.
To reach the town of Rishikesh, a traveler has to pass through
Hardwar, an important Hindu place of pilgrimage. Hardwar is
situated on the Ganges, which at this season, just after the rains,
is—as it was at Banaras, to the south—swollen and muddy.
Along the river bank are a number of small temples to various

gods, their arched and pointed domes making an uneven line against the steeply rising land behind. Though in many parts of India the wandering holy men are now not very numerous, in Hardwar they were almost as plentiful as in earlier times. Those I saw here, I felt, were not mere idle beggars but men sincerely seeking God.

The most sacred place of all in Hardwar is a wide, walled-off channel of the river, known as the Brahmakunda; a bath in its waters is held to be especially auspicious. It is believed that by bathing in the Ganges anywhere one's sins are washed away, but at Banaras or Hardwar there is an added blessedness. Despite modernization in many fields of activity in India, many "Western-educated" people, including university teachers and students, retain the old beliefs.

Since Krishna and I were at Hardwar, we naturally took a plunge. For me, a Westerner, and now a Christian, its meaning was not the same as for my friend. Nevertheless I cannot say it was all "play-acting" on my part: to join in observing customs that mean a great deal to the people around one is in some measure, however small, to share their exaltation.

The outer containing wall of the sacred bathing place is actually a broad promenade. Here many pilgrims leave their clothes in the care of a priest, or *panda*, who usually sits under a large canvas umbrella overshadowing a small platform. Often the same *panda* serves a family through many years, whenever they come to the holy place. Choosing one of these men, we removed all but our undershorts and, after soaping ourselves and washing in the swiftly flowing Ganges outside, along with many others immersed ourselves in the holy waters of the Brahmakunda. The waters were not only very cold, but even swifter here, and one had to hold to iron chains set at intervals in the steps so as not to lose one's footing. I myself, never having been taught the sacred formulas, or *mantras*, to be repeated on such an occasion, came out shivering as quickly as I could. But Krishna, obviously moved with intense feeling, immersed himself the prescribed three times, sprinkling his head with the water also. All the while his lips were moving as he silently repeated the prayers to be said on such an occasion, which he had learned as a child, as all brahmins do. Around us were other Indians, some in family groups, some alone. No one seemed to take particular notice of the white-skinned stranger. The one important duty for everyone who had come to the Brahmakunda was to receive the purifying grace of the river.

After visiting various temples and ashrams in and about

Hardwar, we left early the next morning by taxi for Rishikesh. The countryside was lush and vivid green after the rains. When we had gone some way through varied scenes and across a few streams, small mountains appeared, deep blue-green against the lighter green of the paddy and other vegetation near the road. As we drove along we met with the usual heterogeneous collection of creatures and vehicles, which after the long ride to Gorakhpur no longer claimed my attention as before.

Rishikesh is a large village scattered on two sides of the Ganges. Here the river is even swifter than at Hardwar, having narrowed to about one-third its width there. Joining these two not very crowded settlements is a famous bridge, the Lakshman Jhula. Up through the last century it had been made of ropes, and to cross it was an adventure. Now it consists of a graceful single span of cables, supported by two pylons. The locality is famous as a place where many holy men have performed spiritual practice in the past; even now they are to be found in considerable numbers. We were told that at the top of the small mountain just beyond the bridge a German girl lived in a cave. She had taken a vow of silence, and animals were said to have no fear of her. There are also some monasteries of certain rather well-advertised Hindu organizations on both sides of the river at Rishikesh.

We had been advised the day before, by a *pandit* in Hardwar who taught Sanskrit, that while we were in Rishikesh it would be profitable to visit the ashram of a swami named Vedavyasananda. After crossing the bridge on foot, we inquired about his place at one of the larger ashrams. We found it, at last, about a quarter of a mile away, down a lane shaded by mango trees. On all sides stretched sunlit vegetable gardens divided up in small plots by low hedges. The main building, a bungalow-like, one-storied affair, was located some distance from the gate that opened off the lane.

We were welcomed by a brahmin scholar, well over middle age, who appeared to be connected with the ashram in an official capacity. He informed us that the head of the ashram was about to make a trip to the city of Simla. After consulting the swami, he found that he would see us in a half hour. Meanwhile we were accommodated in a small cottage with two rooms and a simple bath. We reached it by passing through more gardens.

Behind our cottage was a field of sugar cane, above which

spread the intense blue sky, made even more intense by the presence of several great, dazzling, sun-bathed clouds. Fruit trees grew in the hedgerows, and goats and cattle grazed at a distance. Overhead flew the ever present gray-headed crows. Other sober-colored birds hopped about in the trees. Since no one kills them in India, they are much tamer there than in the West. From time to time we could see a white-robed student, or *brahmachari*, passing by as if on an urgent errand.

Swami Vedavyasananda lived in a simple thatched building, practically a hut. We were called to see him not long after we had settled ourselves in our new accommodations. He was seated on a small table bed, of the style found in average Indian homes, on which had been thrown a leopard skin. Around him on the walls were pictures of Hindu deities. His face covered with innumerable shallow pockmarks, the swami was not handsome, but he immediately inspired confidence and respect by his unassuming and straightforward manner. We sat in front of him on the floor, and the brahmin scholar stood at one side.

Krishna asked him in Hindi, for my sake, about his early experiences, and translated for me what he replied. We learned that the swami was the son of a rich landowner, or *zamindar*, but even at the age of ten he had resolved to give up the world in quest of ultimate reality. This he finally did, but only after obtaining a B.A. degree in a university and becoming a qualified teacher, or *acharya*, in Sanskrit. For a time he had felt inspired by the example of Gandhi to join the nationalist movement for independence, but for the past seventeen years —after spending a considerable period of time in spiritual discipline, or *sadhana*, in the important places of pilgrimage— he had made his headquarters here in Rishikesh, conducting a school for young men where Sanskrit, English, and academic subjects were taught. Perhaps, I thought, the brahmin scholar helped teach Sanskrit. At the present time about a dozen students were enrolled. The place was supported by donations.

As the leader, or *mahamandaleshvar*, of the Niranjani Akhada, a special subsect of monks, Swami Vedavyasananda attends the all-India convocation of monks, the *kumbhamela*, held every twelve years, in rotation, in each of several holy places. When at the opening of the convocation the monks, in their various garbs, walk in procession, their *mahamandaleshvars* precede them, each at the head of his group of monks. Usually they ride on elephants furnished by rich followers. The swami, who was an exponent of Nondualistic Vedanta, had, as leader of the sect, a very large number of disciples whom he had initiated into the spiritual life. Yet his headquarters remained in this simple place, where instruction was provided to young men who wished to learn the ancient Indian culture along with that of modern times.

In response to Krishna's questioning, he said he had had no startling spiritual revelations, but had experienced a gradual deepening of insight. What he stressed particularly was formation of a good character, and for this purpose he impressed on us the importance of studying and living by the Bhagavad Gita. He made the following observation, which I have kept in mind ever since: "Every smallest incident of life can be a help on the way, if you have an inner desire for spiritual advancement. If you don't have the inner desire, even happenings of major importance cannot lead you on." Before leaving, we saluted him with joined palms, and he blessed us as we departed.

The existence of small retreats like this one throughout India is an indication that despite appearances an undercurrent of spirituality still flows strong within Hindu society. The simplicity in this school-retreat near the Himalayas gave me a hint of what some of the Vedic retreats must have been like. Not all retreats are organized on the same plan, and this must also have been the case in ancient times. I was aware of this fact from an experience I had had more than ten years earlier, at an ashram where more stress was placed on the meditative life than on study.

In February 1959, when I went to India with my teacher to take the vows of monkhood, I was able to visit the ashram of Langa Baba, the "Naked Father." We were in the sacred town of Puri, in Orissa, and a friend of ours in the state government told us we should not miss seeing the monk. He had lived in this one spot so long that no one remembered when he first came. It was said he was a hundred and seventeen, a hundred and twenty-five, even a hundred and fifty years old. There was a rumor that he was in fact the famous monk Tota Puri, who had initiated Ramakrishna into the Nondualistic Vedanta discipline and to whom Ramakrishna had given the name Nangta ("Langa" is a dialect version of the same word). At one time he was supposed to have been able to make gold, but he no longer practiced this art, people said.

Langa Baba's retreat, our friend told us, was on a sand dune near Puri—two or three miles outside town. There he lived with a number of disciples, young and old. Early one evening a party of us, including several senior monks of the Ramakrishna Order and two American women and myself, drove out with our friend to see him. Twilight had deepened into night before we reached the village from which the retreat was most easily approached. As soon as the automobile stopped, villagers clustered round. One was found who had a lantern and would lead us to the ashram. Soon we were trudging some distance behind him over an indistinct roadway of deep sand.

The moonless sky was heavy with stars of all degrees of brilliance. After walking about a mile in silence, we came to the "sand dune," which was really only a hill of sand. The villager opened a small gate and led us up a long and narrow concrete walk (with here and there a step to lessen the incline) toward a few low buildings, just discernible in the darkness. On a sign by the main gate, we could just make out the notice: "Hours of Darshan Till Five O'Clock." (*Darshan*, as explained earlier, means something like "audience": both the seeing of a holy person and the blessing derived from seeing him.) Since it was well past six, it seemed we would have to go back disappointed.

Undaunted, our Indian friend, who had visited the ashram several times before, disappeared around one side of the indistinct group of low buildings. Five minutes later he reappeared with the secretary, who let us through an iron gate into a small walled courtyard. In the middle of it stood a one-room, porch-like building with canvas screens hanging in the arched openings along its front. As we waited, a light appeared behind the screens and we saw the shadow of a tall figure move across from right to left.

We were called into Langa Baba's presence. As we entered the room, which was lighted by a single kerosene lamp, we saw him seated cross-legged on a four-poster bed over which hung a white canopy edged with red. His hands were folded in his lap. He was naked.

The Baba's large and commanding figure was somewhat in contrast to his smooth, round face and gentle features. His cheeks were full, and his eyes bloodshot as if from prolonged meditation. The eyeballs, which seemed to be covered by an opaque film, rolled free as if not under complete muscular control. The Baba had a fairly long whitish beard, and on his head was what I took to be a turban—but later decided was probably his own hair wound around in a tight coil. I noted that the hair of the beard was extremely fine.

After "taking the dust of his feet"—that is, touching his feet to show our reverence—we sat in front of him in a semicircle on the floor. The several monks were at one end, the two women and I in the middle, and the villager who had brought us at the other end. Several young men, not disciples but visitors who had followed us from the village, stood near the secretary, who was at the footboard. (I was told later that Langa Baba's disciples, who look upon their teacher, or *guru*, as the embodiment of God, performed ritual worship before him at stated intervals each day, as in a temple.)

For a time our little group sat in silence, gazing at the splendid figure, which grew more and more distinct as we became accustomed to the dim light of the lamp. The Baba's face wore an expression of gentle contentment. Gradually I became aware of a delicate joy emanating, much as reflected light moves through water, from the kindly and untroubled face and the rock-like torso. Finally, one of the monks asked him a question: "What is the way?" (That is to say, "What is the most efficacious way to pursue the spiritual ideal?" It is a traditional question to ask of holy men in India.) Though I could not understand much Hindi, the response of the holy man was crystal clear: "What do *you* say?" "Devotion to the Lord," replied the monk. The Baba then said a few words, in a gentle voice, about *prapatti*, self-surrender to God. It was odd to hear one who followed the austere way of intuitive wisdom express a devotional precept—but in India the two ways sometimes blend, as in Christianity.

Langa Baba's voice, though natural and soft, seemed to come from an interior distance. Sometimes, when he became engaged in talk, he became rather spirited. To one question, as to whether he was praying for the welfare of India, he replied with animation, "Why India alone? The whole universe. All is one."

Another question, as to whether he had met the saint Tota Puri, he parried nicely (as I was told afterward), saying, "I have met many people. Sometimes I see them, sometimes I do not." The matter of his identity remained unresolved. When he was told that several of our party had come from America, he showed special interest.

Much of the time we were with Langa Baba—perhaps a half hour—we sat without speaking, just looking at him. The pregnant pauses between questions made the questions seem rather irrelevant. Merely to sit in the presence of one who has given his life to knowing God was enough. During our whole stay, Langa Baba's body did not move.

It was time to go. Each of us, in turn, "took the dust" of the Naked Father's feet. I was last. When I bowed before him, I thought intensely about the life I was embarking upon—the life of a monk. He seemed to return a look of recognition and encouragement.

As we went out into the still night, under the canopy of brilliant stars, and walked slowly through the deep sand to our waiting vehicles, this visit seemed more dream than reality. All were sobered by having sat with this man of God. We had been in contact with a tradition between two and three thousand years old—as living, perhaps, as it had ever been. An elderly monk of the Ramakrishna Order, usually very taciturn, suddenly spoke as we trudged back side by side. "This is what I like," he said. His voice had become that of a young man. He told me of certain holy men he had met in the early days of his life as a monk, one of them in Tibet. This latter had reminded him vividly of one of the great disciples of Ramakrishna with whom he had been intimately acquainted.

The atmosphere created in this ashram by the aged Langa Baba must have been more than a little like that created by the Vedic knowers of Brahman in their forest retreats, teaching the truths that became embodied, finally, in the Upanishads. "All this is Brahman. From it the universe comes forth, into it the universe merges, and in it the universe breathes," says the *Chhandogya Upanishad*.

-7-

The body of doctrine drawn from the mystical experiences of the Upanishadic seers represented an almost complete break with the original Indo-Aryan tradition. Nevertheless the earlier sections of the Vedas, the ritual part (including the meditation part), were not completely disregarded. They were still held sacred, even though their prescriptions for worship were slowly superseded. Perhaps from the devotional element in the original scriptures evolved the next revelation, that of the personal God. Even with this new development, the Upanishadic wisdom was not forgotten. The tradition of intuitive wisdom continued to appeal to those temperamentally suited to its message. It was not till about thirteen hundred years after the Upanishadic revelation that a notable resurgence of this tradition took place with the appearance of the school of Nondualistic Vedanta philosophy. This school, like several others that followed it, accepted the Vedas in their entirety as authoritative and sought to accommodate its tenets to them. The development of the various systems of religious philosophy fulfilled a further need of the Hindu mind. Like many medieval Christians, inquiring Hindus of the first thousand years of the Christian era, besides cherishing a desire for communion with God, felt a need to think about what the experiences of their sages implied. It was not that they or the great philosophers who founded the scholastic schools wanted to make thinking a substitute for experience. The philosophers were also men of realization. Having personally experienced communion with ultimate reality, they felt no hesitation in using their rational faculties to convey their understanding to others. Though the aim of the intellectual or devotional Hindu was still to pierce beyond the insufficiencies of the world of change, it was not considered illogical for him to try to understand that world and its relation to ultimate reality. To support their contentions, the philosophers of opposing schools made use of the same Vedic texts. Sometimes they seem to have twisted the textual meanings. Since they merely used them to corroborate their own mystical experiences, whether their interpretations of scripture are literally correct is hardly important so far as we are concerned.

Systems of scholastic philosophy may appear irrelevant to the voice of intuitive wisdom, just as they do to that of devotional self-giving. We shall nevertheless consider the most important of them in this and the following chapter. Not only in the Hindu expression of the two voices, but in the systems built up around them, one finds many striking similarities to Christian belief and practice.

It is the Nondualistic Vedanta philosophy of Shankara that expresses most clearly the voice of intuitive wisdom. This spiritual genius, whose full name was Shankaracharya, and who is thought to have lived from A.D. 788 to 820, developed a comprehensive system out of the Upanishads, the Bhagavad Gita, and an aphoristic work known as the *Brahma Sutras* which systematizes the teachings of the Upanishads. What Westerners usually think of as "Hinduism" is largely the result of his work. Hinduism, however, is far more complex than this; actually less than 10 percent of Hindus profess the Nondualistic or Advaita philosophy.

A great deal in the existing accounts of Shankara's life is

legendary. This much can possibly be accepted: He was born of brahmin parents in Kaladi, a town in Southern India. By the time he was ten years old he had become a prodigy of learning. He had memorized the scriptures and written commentaries on them. Shankara held, even at this age, discussions with famous scholars from various parts of the country. (Though India was then ruled by a number of different princes, there seems to have been no interference with travel between kingdoms.) Observing that his teachers failed to practice what they taught, he became disgusted with learning for its own sake. He resolved to make his own life an example for men and thus help stem the tide of spiritual decadence he found all around him.

Upon the death of his father, Shankara began to ponder the question of life and death. Eager to find out the meaning of existence, he resolved to renounce a worldly career and become a monk. His mother, naturally reluctant to part with her son, finally yielded to his persuasion. He promised to return to see her before she died.

At once Shankara went in search of a worthy teacher. Perhaps the greatest sage then living in his part of India was Gaudapada, who was known to have attained the knowledge of ultimate reality, or Brahman. It was he who had written an illuminating commentary, or *karika*, on the *Mandukya Upanishad*. The young lad sought out the old man, but Gaudapada refused to accept him as a disciple. He had taken a vow to remain absorbed in Brahman. Instead, he sent him to his chief disciple, Govindapada, who initiated Shankara into the spiritual life and instructed him in Vedantic meditation and also in the disciplines of Yoga. In a short time Shankara personally realized the highest truth of this school of Vedanta and himself became a teacher.

One morning, it is said, as Shankara was on his way to bathe he found an untouchable with four dogs blocking his path. Momentarily forgetting all about his Vedantic knowledge, he yielded to caste prejudice and ordered the untouchable out of his way. (The fact of the man's having dogs with him made the situation, from the orthodox point of view, even more reprehensible. Dogs, never having become pets in India to the extent they have in the West, were considered unclean.) But the man, instead of obeying, said to him, ''If God, as you say, is one and without a second, how can there be any distinctions among men?'' Shankara was overwhelmed with shame.

It was the custom in Shankara's time, as it was later, for scholars to debate with rival scholars. The one who could find no fitting or convincing reply to his opponent's arguments would acknowledge his defeat by adopting the philosophical position of the scholar who defeated him. On a certain occasion Shankara, who had heretofore defeated all his opponents with ease, discussed with a famous scholar named Mandana Misra the relative value of the monk's and the householder's life. Mandana Misra, who was married, was arguing in support of the married life. The referee in this debate was Bharati, Mandana's wife, a woman quite as learned as her husband.

Shankara seemed to be getting the best of his opponent, when at last Mandana asked him a question involving knowledge that only a married man could possess. Pleading that this was unfair, Shankara obtained Bharati's permission for several days' leave. Making use of the powers he had acquired in his study of Yoga with Govindapada, he entered the dead body of a man that was being carried on a litter to the cremation ground. The man, much to everyone's astonishment, seemingly revived. He returned home to his wife. Through this man's body Shankara found out the answer to the intimate question Mandana Misra had asked him. When Shankara left the body and returned to his own, the man again fell down dead. Returning to the debate he was able to defeat Mandana, who thereupon renounced the world and became his follower.

Shankara died at the age of thirty-two at Kedarnath, a holy shrine in the Himalayas, having completed detailed commentaries on the principal Upanishads, the Bhagavad Gita, and the *Brahma Sutras*. These have had an immense impact on Hindu thought. He also founded, during his short life, an order of Vedantic monks, with ten subdivisions, dedicated to realizing and teaching the truths he had personally experienced or arrived at through his study of scripture. In the course of his wanderings he traveled on foot over much of the Indian peninsula. Four important monasteries at the four cardinal points of India, in existence to this day, are said to have been founded by him.

Certain Buddhists claim that Shankara was strongly influenced by their own later philosophers. However that may be, this gifted man was probably one of several contributing causes of the almost complete disappearance of Buddhism in the land of its origin after the first millennium of the Christian era. In the scope and profundity of his thought he is comparable to

Thomas Aquinas. His chief concern was certainly the "God beyond God," yet he did more than anyone else in India, in his time, to counter the Buddhist-inspired attitude that whether God existed or not was of no great importance. Our survey of his system will begin with the question of the nature of God.

-8-

Shankara's conception of ultimate reality derives not only from what he judged to be the Upanishadic teaching about Brahman, but from personal experience. He maintained that all distinctions in the world, even the distinction between Creator and creature, are "unreal" (that is, impermanent). They are appearances that disappear when a man experiences communion with ultimate reality, at which time one sees that Brahman alone exists. So long as that realization has not occurred, however, the Creator and the creature are quite as real as they are conceived to be in Christian thinking. Ultimate reality, declares Shankara along with the Bhagavad Gita, is both immanent and transcendent. But the meaning of those terms is not something that can be grasped by faith alone; it can be grasped only through knowledge of reality.

When most Christians hear the word "God," probably the first thought that flashes in their minds is that of creatorship. In the Hindu scriptures, especially as interpreted by Shankara, the equivalent of the Christian concept of creation is what is called the "projection" of the universe out of an already existing primordial rudimentary matter. This phenomenon is accomplished by the fiat of the Creator God, often referred to as Ishvara, and not by Brahman itself.

Theologians concerned with a transcendental reality have been hard put to explain the fact of the universe. Why should an eternally existent, intelligent, and blissful reality, unborn and self-sufficient, ever want—indeed, ever be in a position to want—to create anything "outside" itself? Here Shankara advances his famous theory of *maya,* one of his most characteristic concepts. He uses the term *maya* to indicate an inexplicable power inherent in the very nature of Brahman, which veils Brahman and creates the delusion that there is a world of becoming separate from Brahman. God does not create the universe, nor does he become the universe; either of these acts would, in Shankara's view, limit him. God appears as the universe, living souls, and the Creator God through the "superimposition" of the mysterious veil of *maya*.

One school of nondualistic thought, following a rigorous logic, holds that there is indeed no such thing as *maya*: there never was a world separate from reality itself or anyone in "bondage" to seek release from ignorance about ultimate reality. But Shankara avoids this rarefied sort of thinking. He makes an allowance for human limitations and admits the contingent reality of the world of phenomena. He speaks of two levels of reality, as it were: reality unconditioned by any humanly conceivable limitations, and the conditioned reality of the changing world of becoming. For him, the concept of *maya* explains not only the appearance of the world but our seeing the world as something absolute in itself—instead of as the changing thing it is, dependent entirely for its reality on the reality of God. *Maya* is responsible for the delusive superimposition on the Divine Ground of ultimate reality of both the personal Creator God and the individual soul. It is on the basis of his concept of *maya* that Shankara proceeds to build an elaborate philosophical system, which at times seems far removed from the simplicity of the Upanishadic vision. Yet he never allows the student of his philosophy to forget the sole reality of Brahman-Atman.

The appearance of the universe and the individual soul through *maya*, it seems to me, is suggestive of the familiar Christian idea of "creation out of nothing." Most Christians will find difficulty with the idea that the personal Creator God is the result, as it were, of this same *maya*. Theologians may prefer the way the Tantra philosophy resolves the problem, as outlined in the next chapter. Jan van Ruysbroeck might resolve it, however, by appealing to the apparent distinction between the trinity of Persons and the unity of nature in God. We grasp God intellectually in the "qualified mode" represented by the Trinity. We know him—*see* him, as the Indian sages would have said—only in the impenetrable dark abyss, the naked namelessness, that is the unqualified Unity. In his essential nakedness he can be known, as the Pseudo-Dionysius indicated, only through "unknowing." The Creator God of Shankara's philosophy would thus be on the same level as the Trinity, while the Nirguna Brahman, the "unqualified" reality of which all that can be said is "Not this, not this," would be on the level of God's Unity. And yet, somehow, these two—Creator and divine ground—are not different.

The Hindu scriptures supply another detail about the personal Creator God, one also not unrelated to Christian belief. It is the theory of cosmic cycles, a theory accepted and elaborated by Shankara. According to both the Vedas and the Bhagavad Gita, the material world has no beginning. The world process is not a simple progress from unique creation to unique consummation. The material universe continuously appears and disappears—after tremendously long periods of time —in relation to the lifetime of the first-born Deity, known also as Ishvara and the Cosmic Mind. God as Creator does not create the universe out of "nothing," since the material of the universe is indestructible and already available in rudimentary form. At the beginning of each cycle of creation, he "projects" the material world in accordance with the order of the preceding cycle. It is for the liberation of souls from ignorance that the universe is manifested again and again for all time.

Different as this conception may seem from the Christian dogma of unique creation at the beginning of time, there are more similarities than would at first appear. In the cyclic projections of the universe by the Creator's will, we may see approximations—though on a vaster scale—of Christianity's creation of the world by God's act of will. There are thus, so to speak, two sorts of "creation" in Hindu dogma: first, the extra-temporal phenomenon of *maya*, or superimposition, by which the indefinable and nondual Godhead appears as the material universe (including its Creator), and second, the time-related phenomenon by which the personal God projects the cosmos again and again out of unmanifest rudimentary matter.

Shankara's doctrine of *maya* seems to be another way of saying that "before" God's creative act there was neither matter nor time—time and matter coming into existence at one and the same instant. In the same way, in a dream, both time and matter are created by the human mind out of a previous "nonexistence," though once begun they seem to be beginningless. The infinite duration of time and matter, once the world of *maya* is seen to have appeared, is real while the phenomenal world endures. But on the dawning of God-consciousness, it is discovered, from a point of view as it were outside time, to have had a "beginning." The *maya* doctrine here supplies the element of "creation out of nothing" missing from the cyclic doctrine. All attempts at illustration of the meaning of *maya* are necessarily shot through with contradiction. None can be taken completely literally.

Involved in the question of creation is the origin of the human soul. Shankara, like the Upanishads, speaks of the True Self, or Atman, as being in its essence one with ultimate reality, or Brahman. A Christian may imagine that this concept of the Self constitutes Shankara's full definition of the soul. But here he would be mistaken. True, as the universe and the Creator God have their being in ultimate reality, souls, too, derive their being from the True Self. But from the point of view of "relative" existence in *maya,* the world of becoming, the individual soul, or *jiva,* is a very real person with an exceedingly complex makeup.

According to a teaching that can be traced back at least as far as the *Taittiriya Upanishad,* the individual Atman of the human person is encased in five "sheaths." These are known as the sheaths of flesh and blood, nervous energy, memory, discriminatory power, and joy. Through them, Atman in a man carries on its daily activities in the world. According to later Vedantists, when it passes from this life to another, it carries with it the "subtle body," which consists of all but the physical sheath of flesh and blood.

In his first letter to the Corinthians, St. Paul writes of the resurrection of the dead, "What is sown is perishable, what is raised is imperishable. . . . It is sown a physical body, it is raised a spiritual body." Strictly speaking, the concept of bodily resurrection in Christianity is closer to that of communion with God in Hinduism than it is to the Hindu concept of reincarnation of the soul. One wonders, nevertheless, if this "spiritual body" has any connection with the subtle body that is said by Hindus to transmigrate and be reborn.

Closely related to the nature of the individual soul and to the theory of cosmic cycles is the doctrine of *karma* (action and the fruits of action) and rebirth. Souls in this contingent physical world, Shankara teaches and most Hindus believe, are born after death into higher and lower bodies as a result of their actions—virtuous, indifferent, or wicked—caused by desire. The doctrine is a sort of extension of the thought "Whatever a man sows, that he will also reap." In the Bhagavad Gita, Krishna describes the phenomenon this way: "Even as a person casts off worn-out clothes and puts on others that are new, so the embodied Self casts off worn-out bodies and enters into others that are new." Later he elaborates on this statement: "An eternal portion of myself, having become a living soul in a world of living beings, draws to itself the five senses, with the mind for the sixth, which abide in *Prakriti* [Krishna's lower nature]. When the lord [of the body and senses, i.e., the individual soul] acquires a body, and when he leaves it, he takes these with him and goes on his way, as the wind carries away the scents of flowers from their places.''

Various theories about rebirth are mentioned in the Hindu scriptures and commentaries, but they are conflicting and need not be discussed here. Shankara stresses some of the disadvantages of being born again and again, enforcing his point with graphic descriptions of the soul's wanderings through all sorts of bodies—animal, marine, insect, and even inorganic.

What should be remembered is this: in the Hindu view the soul is not entirely the victim of an inexorable law of cause and effect in the present life. In the first place, the results of a man's own actions in a previous human life have determined the general design of his life in his present existence. He can undo many of these results, and those to come, by what he does now; for the soul, within certain limits, possesses free will. Free in its essential nature, it has a glimpse now and then of the True Self. This is what gives a man the sense of free will, even though his bodily and mental inclinations have been determined by his previous desires and actions. Thus Atman breaks through, so to speak, the limits imposed upon it by the individual *maya*, or deluding ignorance, that limits it. It is also said that through spiritual discipline and sincere repentance one can weaken the force of past unfavorable *karma*. A holy person's prayer and blessings, too, can help.

The doctrine of *karma* and rebirth, like that of cosmic cycles, is said by Hindus to give men an incentive for seeking God in the present life rather than suffering the uncertainty, ignominy, and pain of choosing (by indecisive action) a life separated from God in a seemingly endless series of limited physical or angelic bodies.

It should thus be clear that the goal of the individual soul, according to Shankara's Hinduism, is to become conscious that its true nature is Satchidananda—absolute being, absolute awareness, absolute joy. Such consciousness is to be attained through exercise of discrimination and through long and constant study of the revealed truths of scripture and meditation on them. Only thus can the soul effect its escape from ignorance about its true nature. Nor should the word ''escape'' be interpreted here as a retreat from reality. Nondualist Hindus would insist that in finding their identity with the Godhead they neither escape from anything real nor become absorbed into a vague impersonal abstraction, but instead rediscover their own spiritual identity.

The one who has attained this state is said to be "liberated while living," *jivanmukta*. Some such persons remain immersed —like Gaudapada, teacher of Shankara's teacher—in their identity with the being-awareness-joy that is their True Self. Others, seeing "themselves in all beings and all beings in themselves," return from that state, as it were, to help mankind. In his acknowledging of the importance of the "relative" world, Shankara reveals an understanding that places him on a level with the most integral mystics.

These two types of "realized" souls remind one of the two kinds of perfected souls in Buddhism. The earlier school, Theravada Buddhism, conceived as its ideal the perfected *Arhat,* who on attaining the goal enters Nirvana. The later school, Mahayana Buddhism, developed the ideal of the *Bodhisattva,* who takes a vow not to enter the bliss of Nirvana till everyone else has attained it. Only those who have attained that state know the real difference between these two types.

In developing the system of religious philosophy that embodies these ideas, Shankara gave an ordered explanation of the statements of Upanishadic seers who lived more than a thousand years before him. Not only that: he provided an intellectual approach to a realization of the state he believed, in the light of his own mystical experiences, those seers were talking about. In addition to his commentaries on scripture, a further work of his deserves mention. A Western reader interested in the way of intuitive wisdom as expressed in Hinduism will derive enjoyment and benefit from his great philosophical and mystical poem *The Crest-Jewel of Discrimination,* or *Vivekachudamani.* In this long and eloquent composition his ideas are presented in less forbidding form than in his commentaries on the Upanishads, the Bhagavad Gita, and the *Brahma Sutras.* Shankara claims our respect for his ability to keep a balance between the demands of the mystical experience of the way of intuitive wisdom and the demands of the everyday world that most men experience throughout their lives.

In further witness to Shankara's catholicity it may be noted that many of his followers, today, give his goal of communion with the nondual suprapersonal reality their intellectual assent, but meanwhile devote themselves to worship of Shiva, a form of the personal God, as a means to this goal—without, however, according Shiva the status of ultimate reality that his devotional worshipers accord him.

In the present century, the great thinker and mystic Sri Aurobindo conceived a system of his own, in which, it is claimed, he has not only satisfactorily explained the relationship of the Godhead to the phenomenal world but opened a way to the "divinization" of the universe. His magnum opus, entitled *The Life Divine*, would appear to have made certain of Shankara's ideas more understandable for modern minds. Indeed, his followers claim he has gone beyond Shankara. There is no doubt that his approach is much closer than Shankara's to modern Christian thinking, especially to that of Pierre Teilhard de Chardin. In Aurobindo's system have been incorporated the best concepts of Tantra and Vaishnavism—which we shall encounter in the next chapter—as well as the best of traditional Nondualistic Vedanta.

-9-

The goal of the voice of intuitive wisdom as heard in Hinduism is the state of freedom known as *jivanmukti*, "liberation in life." It is a state that recalls St. Paul's phrase "the glorious liberty of the children of God." That liberty is achieved, Hindu nondualists say, by a man's removing the layers of ignorance that cover the True Self and thus revealing that Self in all its simplicity. Christians have sometimes argued that the idea of gradually removing layers of ignorance encrusting an already perfect soul is static compared to the dynamic concept of a soul that is to be perfected by degrees up to its full capacity. Perhaps the disagreement here is merely a matter of terms. In speaking of the soul, Christians are not always talking about the same thing that Hindu Vedantists are. What corresponds in Shankara's Hinduism to the Christian soul is, as we have noted, the Atman somehow deluded by *maya*, ignorance or misapprehension, into believing it is a separate entity, to all intents and purposes independent of God. That soul may indeed be spoken of as becoming perfected by degrees up to its full capacity. But do these words faithfully express, even for Christians, what happens in the process?

The Christian soul, which is a complex of reason, emotion, will, and ego, does not receive the grace of God unless by degrees the limited ego is dissolved and Christ allowed to enter into it. Does he really enter in, a Hindu may ask, or, as the "true light that enlightens every man," is he there already—only waiting, like the germ in the grain of wheat, to grow and bear fruit? Is there any place where Christ is not? Perhaps, then, there is not so much difference between the Christian experience of emptying oneself for the sake of Christ and the Hindu experience of emptying oneself of ignorance for the sake of the True Self. Perhaps we may begin to grasp what the Benedictine monk Dom Bede Griffiths was driving at when, in a talk he gave in New York some years ago, he said, "Christ is the Atman." Though followers of the way of devotional self-giving may have their reservations about such a remark, those who stress the way of intuitive wisdom should find it suggestive.

It is a Buddhist doctrine that there is no permanent self. This teaching, known as the "*anatta* doctrine," has been taken by many Hindus (and Christians, too) as a denial of the existence of the True Self, or Atman, as well as of the individual self. (*Atta* is a word in the Pali language related to the Sanskrit *atman*.) Even where the individual self is concerned, however, Buddhists allow themselves to speak as if a permanent individual self existed; they talk of a person's doing this or that, wanting this or that, even of dying and being reborn. They are only following, as I have heard many times from Thai Buddhist monks and laymen, "conventional usage." What, one wonders, are Christians and Hindus really doing when they speak of "I"?

St. Catherine of Genoa provides a strange parallel with this way of speaking when she says, "God is my being, my *me*, my strength, my happiness, my good, my delight. I have to say *my*, otherwise I cannot speak. But I do not know what is *me* or *my* . . . and I am ashamed to say so many words so far from the truth and from what I feel it to be." The parallel becomes even more pronounced when she says, "Inside me I can see nothing else but God, for I allow no one else to enter, myself even less than others. . . . Yet it is necessary for me to name this *me*, according to the usage of the world." As if to explain these startling declarations, she also said, "When the soul has become annihilated by divine action, it abides wholly transformed in God, and it is he who moves it and fills it in his own way, without any action on man's part." Perhaps in Buddhism, too, there is at least a parallel with the Hindu idea of an individual self that has to be emptied of ignorance and with the Christian idea of a soul that has to be emptied of the ego-bound self.

Out of all this emerges another problem for one who follows the way of intuitive wisdom, be he Christian or Hindu. It is the riddle of liberation or salvation. If the soul is to be emptied of selfwardness in order to know Christ, who is it— what recognizable entity—that realizes the True Self, enjoys the beatific vision? Before I started on my world trip, I had the privilege of talking with the learned Cambodian Buddhist Khim Tit, in New York. When I asked him who it was (if there was no permanent self) that experienced Nirvana, he unhesitatingly replied, ''Nirvana.'' Must a Christian follower of the voice of intuitive wisdom say, then, that there is only one enjoyer of God: Christ himself? In the next chapter we shall see how certain concepts of the more devotionally-minded nondualists may manage to save the soul, Christian as well as Hindu, from being totally swallowed up in ultimate reality.

The nondualist conception of communion with God through intuitive wisdom—whether Hindu, Buddhist, or Islamic Sufi seems far removed from most Christian experience. This situation reflects a sad ignorance on the part of most Christians about many central figures in their own mystical tradition. Inquiring Christians should feel a challenge here to become better acquainted with the message of intuitive wisdom and to find out whether it has been sufficiently stressed by Christian writers. There may also be elements of mysticism in the East that are wanting in Christian tradition, but that could complement the ''deposit of faith'' without in any way compromising what is essential to Christian belief.

The reader should remember that the way of intuitive wisdom is by no means the sole way toward sanctity to be found in Hinduism. In fact, only a small percentage of believing Hindus follow this austere voice. In Buddhism, though the nondevotional nature of intuitive wisdom seems to satisfy the needs of most Theravada Buddhists (excepting the simpler followers of this denomination), it does not appear to satisfy all the adherents of the Mahayana schools. And yet to the true votary of this voice, it is not austere at all. There is an intellectual beauty in pure reason that he would not exchange for all the passing beauty of the world. For such a person, intuitive wisdom is his shining way of fulfillment. It delivers him from a ceaseless round of fruitless, ego-centered working and hoping, of weaving of plans and waiting for plans to succeed.

A hint of that vision may be found in a poem I wrote while still a practicing Hindu:

A WORD TO THE WISE

Watching the weaver,
Time's contriving
Web-worm, weaving
Blindly the clouded
Webs; watching the
Waiter, time's slow-
Turning sunflower
Counting deafly the
Daylong sunsteps—
Hear me, I hollo,
Weaver and waiter,
Hear me, you two, my
Ageless henchmen:
Though forever you
Toil and torture,
Never staying the
Beat of the shuttle,
Staying the sight that
Stiffly follows the
Sun's slow stepping,
How will your webs be
Utterly woven,
How your counting be
Ended, ever?

Weaver, cease from the
Restless weaving:
Naked you came and
Naked your lonely
Going onward;
Light for your garment,
Banish the busy
Shuttle, robed in the
Light of unwed
Being. Waiter,
Cease from the barren
Waiting: empty you
Came and empty your
Lonely going
Onward; flame for your
Garment, stand in the
Stepless sun at the
Source of flaming.

O you two, my
Sole delights, my
Sole companions,
Clean unweave me
Out of this robing,
Out of this waiting
Safe unwind me.
Now is fulfillment
And arrival;
Now is an end of
Webs and a fruitful
End of counting:
Here in the living
Lull at the core of
Unwed being,
Here where the ancient
Sun-quick fountain
Flows and flames, where
Sight stands still and the
Shuttle ceases.

Self-awareness, the knowledge of Atman, is a state that, once
fully attained, never permanently leaves the saint. Forever
after he is aware of his union with ultimate reality, even while
he speaks and acts like an ordinary human being. With Meister
Eckhart he lives in the knowledge that God is born anew in him
each moment. Though probably no one man exemplifies any one
of the voices we are tracing, to the exclusion of the others, a few
mystics show such a preponderance of the characteristic qualities of intuitive wisdom as to make it more real for others. An
Indian saint who, by universal agreement, attained to and lived
in this state of self-awareness within the present century is
Ramana Maharshi.

-10-

The man now known as Sri Ramana was born on December 30, 1879, in the town of Tiruchuzhi, near Madurai, in South
India, to Sundaram Aiyar, a lawyer, and his wife Alaggamal.
His parents gave him the name Venkataraman. In his early
years the boy received a normal education, proceeding fairly far

in high school. Not at all industrious at school, he was given more to sports than to study. A spirit of independence marked him as different from his fellow students; he resented injustice and always retaliated when it was directed toward himself. Like any well-trained brahmin, he was fastidious about the purity of his food, about the kinds of food he ate, and so on. Since he was not particularly religious, if he ever visited the famous Meenakshi Temple of the Divine Mother, in Madurai, it was to keep company with friends or to while away the time.

When Venkataraman was sixteen years old a startling transformation took place in his character. He was sitting alone in a room when for no apparent reason a fear of death seized his mind—a fear that was terrifying and almost overpowering. Illness had nothing to do with it, for he had a robust constitution. Even as he experienced the fear, however, he was able to observe quite clearly what was going on within himself, and he was deeply puzzled. A curiosity was aroused in his mind about the problem of life and death, now so vividly forced upon him, and he at once set out to find the answer.

Venkataraman imagined he had died. As he examined his state, the symptoms of death appeared in his body. Already inert, it gradually became rigid; breathing stopped. Nevertheless he remained conscious of his body's condition as well as of an "I" quite apart from it. He realized that with the body's death the true "I" did not die. He could feel the full force of his personality, completely separate from the inert body. All this was not something that simply went on in the intellect, he said later. It flashed before him as living truth, a matter of direct, indubitable experience.

The episode lasted hardly more than a half hour, and the fear of death left him as unexpectedly as it had come. From then on, he was completely engrossed in the true "I" or Atman, of which the Upanishads speak. There was a marked effect on his everyday life; an unforced humility and a sort of holy indifference took the place of his former tendency toward resentment. He lost all interest in relatives, friends, studies. Forgetting his fastidiousness about food, he now accepted anything that was offered. Most noticeable, however, was his new attitude toward the Meenakshi Temple. No longer aloof, he would go to the great place of worship daily, alone, spending long hours in adoration before the images. For the most part, lost in the Self within, he would not pray at all. Tears of neither pleasure nor pain, he said afterward, marked the overflow of his soul.

Venkataraman's family, to whom the change in his nature had become obvious, were distressed. He paid even less attention to his studies than before, and they were resentful. Things went on in this way for about two months, when as the result of a critical remark by his older brother, he suddenly asked himself, "What business have I here?" Immediately rose in his mind the thought of the sacred hill of Arunachala, near Tiruvannamalai. A few months earlier, its mention by a relative of his had roused in him an unexplained feeling of wonder and joy. At once he left home, never to return. With him he took three rupees for his train fare.

The young man left a note for his family, which read in part: "In search of my 'Father' and in obedience to his command, I have started from here. This person is only embarking on a virtuous enterprise, so no one should grieve over the matter. No money need be spent in tracing this person out." The use of the impersonal "this person" is significant; he no longer identified himself with the body. The letter was left unsigned.

Venkataraman reached Tiruvannamalai three days later. He made his way to the Temple of Sri Arunachala, with its four huge entrance gates, or *gopurams*. No one was in sight and all the gates were open. He went directly to the innermost shrine to greet Arunachaleshvar, the Lord of Arunachala. Leaving the temple he had his head shaved like a monk and discarded both his brahmin's sacred thread and the little money he had left. From his clothes he tore two strips to make a loincloth, and he threw the rest away. He then returned to the temple and sat in silent meditation. Thereafter for some years he spoke no word.

Without formal initiation into monkhood, or *sannyasa,* the young man had become a swami. The fact of his youth and of his silence roused everyone's curiosity. Pious people came to see him; mischievous children made him a target for their pranks. The young swami now retreated to a small, unlighted underground room beneath a great hall in the temple, the Hall of a Thousand Pillars. Though it was held sacred, few had courage to enter the place—the Patala Lingam, it was called.

No one knows how many days Venkataraman remained there, alone and without physical nourishment. Lost in the state he now continously lived in, the young monk was completely unaware of what was happening to his body. When he was finally discovered he was a shocking sight. The lower part of his thighs had been eaten away by the vermin that infested the place, and blood and pus discolored the spot where he sat. Completely unconscious of the body, however, he had felt no discomfort, no pain.

Once he had been rediscovered, people immediately recognized the intensity of his spiritual austerity. From this time on he was cared for by the local holy man, or *sadhu*, although he constantly changed the place where he stayed in order to escape attention. A regular attendant soon joined him, and pilgrims, too, began to pay visits. So he moved to another temple, outside town, where he spent eighteen months rapt in constant communion with the Self.

Another regular attendant one day performed ritualistic worship before him, as to the Deity. The next day he found written in charcoal on the wall the words: "Food alone is the service for this body." When it was thus revealed that he knew how to write and might be persuaded to reply to questions, another visitor, who came every morning, decided to find out who he was. The visitor stubbornly refused to leave, even at the risk of losing his job, until the swami revealed his identity. Finally he found a slip of paper beside the young monk on which were the words: "Venkataraman, Tiruchuzhi."

When the news reached Venkataraman's home, an uncle visited Tiruvannamalai. He found his nephew seated in a mango grove, his body covered with dirt, his nails long and curved, his hair matted. The uncle, expressing regard for his sanctity, implored his nephew to return home. But the swami kept silent. Finally his mother Alaggamal came with her oldest son. They, too, had to leave disappointed. After they had gone away, the swami left the town and began to stay in a cave on the hill of Arunachala, known as Virupaksha Cave.

During the more than three years Venkataraman had remained at Tiruvannamalai he had preserved absolute silence. As a result, hardly anyone understood the depth of his spiritual attainments. Nevertheless, sincere worshipers of God, seeing his indifference to the world and his tremendous austerity, were drawn to his presence, and some now made their way to Virupaksha Cave. Out of compassion for them, the swami began writing down answers to questions on small slips of paper. Several of his disciples, recognizing the rare worth of his practical instructions, preserved these replies, and the manuscripts they thus kept have been published under the titles *Self-Enquiry* and *Who Am I?*

Here are some of the teachings the young swami wrote down in this way:

"By incessantly pursuing within yourself the inquiry 'Who am I?' you will know your True Self and thereby attain salvation." "The mind can find rest only when it has found the answer to the query 'Who am I?' " "In this body, what asserts itself as 'I' is only the mind. So if you inquire what the 'I'-thought arises from, it will plainly be seen that the heart is the source."

The swami also, at the request of the increasing number of devotees gathering around him, composed several stirring hymns, giving expression to both the sweetness and the power of divine love and grace. From the beginning of his stay in Tiruvannamalai he had manifested the greatest reverence for the hill of Arunachala. More than one hymn identifies the hill with the Supreme Being. The only religious book he is known to have read before the experience leading to his "conversion" was the *Periapuranam*, containing the lives of sixty-three famous Tamil saints. Perhaps he read there that in the *Skanda Purana*, a Hindu mythological work, it is written: "Meditate on the fact that in the heart of the hill surges the spiritual glory in which is contained the whole world." Thus, like the nondualist Shankara, who also wrote hymns to the personal God, he exhibited throughout his life a harmony between the ways of intuitive wisdom and devotional self-giving, though he stressed the former. The several mendicant monks who now stayed with him used to sing many of his hymns when they went daily to beg food in the town.

It was in November 1907, about eleven years after his arrival in Tiruvannamalai, that the swami acquired the name he has been known by ever since. A well-known Sanskrit scholar and poet, Ganapathi Muni, one midday climbed the hill of Arunachala at the bidding of an inner call and went straight to Virupaksha Cave. He found the swami alone. Falling on his face before him, he said, "I have read everything that has to be read. I have studied the whole of the Vedanta. I have repeated the Lord's name to my heart's satisfaction. And yet I have not understood what real spiritual discipline is. So I am seeking refuge at your feet."

The swami was now speaking with those who sought him out, and he explained to the scholar that the real spiritual discipline was to watch where the notion of "I" springs from till the mind becomes absorbed there. Satisfied with the instruction, Ganapathi Muni spent the afternoon at the cave. He then suggested to some devotees who were present that their swami be called

Bhagavan Sri Ramana Maharshi, that is to say Blessed Lord Ramana, the Great Sage. From that day he has been known by this name.

Ganapathi and his own pupils collected the more important of the replies they had received to their questions, and these were published as *Sri Ramana Gita*. In this volume are described the state of God-consciousness, the relation between the mind and the heart, how to control the mind, and various other topics. The scholar has recorded that once, in the year 1908, while he was in a temple far from Tiruvannamalai, he had a longing to see his teacher. Suddenly the Maharshi, though still at Arunachala, appeared before him and blessed him. Ganapathi felt a strange influx of spiritual power. The Maharshi himself confirmed the experience afterward. (I myself heard from a devotee in Ceylon of another incident bearing witness to the Maharshi's supernormal powers.)

During the years, the Maharshi's mother visited him on numerous occasions. After many members of her family had died, she came in 1916 to live near him permanently. Finally, when he moved to a more commodious retreat, she began cooking the meals for the considerable number of persons who by now stayed with him. But the Maharshi treated her just as he did any of the others at the ashram, thus helping her to turn more actively toward the spiritual life. She died in 1922. On the last day Ramana Maharshi sat by her throughout the morning and afternoon. Thereafter he visited almost daily the place at the foot of the hill where her ashes were buried. After six months he remained there, and that is where his final ashram was built.

As time passed, more and more visitors—some of them persons of national prominence—came to see him. But amid all the comings and goings he remained undisturbed. On festival days sometimes thousands of visitors gathered. For all who came he showed a kindly concern. Everyone was deeply impressed by his utter tranquillity and lovingkindness, even if sometimes he spoke no word. Many have written about the unusual quality of his eyes, which shone with an inner glow. Animals and all living things were objects of his devoted concern. At the ashram on the hill, the dogs, cats, squirrels, monkeys, and cows were treated as if they were human beings. The Maharshi had the same attitude even toward reptiles and insects. Once, passing through some trees on the hillside, his thigh grazed a hornets' nest. In a moment all the hornets settled on it and began stinging. "Yes, yes," he said. "That is the leg that disturbed your nest. Let it suffer." He stood there unmoving till they finally flew away.

Ramana Maharshi rose before 3 A.M., and most of the members of the ashram rose with him. In the main hall they gathered for silent meditation or to sing religious songs. Then he generally went to the kitchen and could be found nearby, cutting vegetables for the noon meal. The Maharshi felt that each should do his share of necessary work, which included gardening, tending the cows, cooking, office work, and temple worship. After breakfast visitors began coming to see him. In his later years, during most of the day he sat on a couch in the meditation hall, correcting proofs of future publications, reading correspondence and dictating replies, or answering visitors' questions. A Sanskrit school had been started for boys, and after the early evening meditation they would chant the Vedas in company with the devotees of the ashram. As the years passed, an increasing number of details had to be attended to. The infinite care and regularity with which the Maharshi performed each duty provided an example for everyone. Nothing was too insignificant to receive his complete attention.

At the end of 1948 a small growth was noticed on the Maharshi's left elbow. Though it was removed after two months, a new growth appeared above it. This too was removed. It was diagnosed as a kind of malignancy. Since a fresh growth appeared almost at once, physicians suggested amputation of the arm in the hope of saving the Maharshi's life. He said, smiling, "There is no need for alarm. The body itself is a disease. Let it have its natural end. Why mutilate it? A simple dressing is enough." A third operation was performed, however, by a team of physicians and surgeons. By the end of November there was another growth, necessitating a fourth operation. When an additional growth appeared by the left armpit, it was clear that death was not far away.

The malignancy from which Ramana Maharshi suffered was of a particularly painful sort. Through all this time of suffering and growing weakness, he remained unconcerned. When devotees asked him, in December 1949, what treatment to try next, he said, "Have I ever asked for any treatment? It is you who want this for me; so it is you who must decide. If I were asked, I should always say, as I have said from the beginning, that no treatment is necessary. Let things take their course."

During the next four months the Maharshi grew slowly weaker. Yet he remained always serene and never lost his sense of humor. Up to the last he continued to see visitors. Though he was extremely exhausted, his mind was clear. "Everything will be all right in two days," he said. The day before he died he refused the medicine a doctor had brought to relieve congestion in the lungs.

On the evening of April 14, 1950, a vast gathering of devotees came to see the sage. About sunset he asked his attendants to help him sit up in bed. He motioned away a doctor who had begun to administer oxygen. Outside the hut where he was staying, a group of devotees began chanting a hymn to the hill of Arunachala—one he had composed many years before. The Maharshi's eyes opened a little, and to those near him they seemed to flash. Tears of ecstasy rolled down from their outer corners. His breaths followed softly, smoothly, one after another. Then the breathing stopped. An extraordinary hush of peace descended.

When, twenty years later, I visited the ashram, it was my privilege to take lunch in the refectory where the Maharshi ate, sit in the modest hall where he used to sit, climb up to Virupaksha Cave, and visit the room where he died. The peace I sensed everywhere—that same peace he left with his devoted followers on the day he died—is, like that at the Buddhist holy place Sarnath, something that cannot be conveyed in words. In it is a power to still the mind, almost to lift one for the time being out of the web of imaginings and plannings constantly being woven by the time-bound ego. It is the fruit both of the life that was lived there and of the devotion of untold numbers of faithful men and women to the great soul whose presence inhabits the ashram.

THE VOICE OF
DEVOTIONAL
SELF-GIVING

THE SECOND EPISODE OF OUR journey to Gorakhpur evoked
for me the devotional side of religion: love inspired by a personal God or a personal Savior. What our driver, Dubey, and
his helper were bearing witness to in singing songs about Rama
was the need most men and women feel—in countries where
a spiritual tradition has persisted—for belief in something
beyond themselves, a power they can relate themselves to and
go to in times of distress and of thanksgiving. (Even in countries that are officially nonreligious, something of this need is
felt; a part of it is filled by the State itself.) Whether the driver
and his helper, Pande, knew some of the finer points of Hindu
teaching about the personal God, I cannot say. It is not impossible. Probably what they knew best were stories and beliefs
that form the basis of popular devotion. Still, the episode
symbolizes for us the devotional approach as a whole; the
wellsprings of Hindu spirituality include devotionally inclined
systems of philosophy.

I confess that it was a long time before I realized, as a professing Hindu, the importance of devotional self-giving in the
spiritual life. Becoming more realistic about my own limitations,
however, I found that temperamentally I was not made to pursue intuitive wisdom in isolation. This awareness undoubtedly
made me ready, when the time came, to recognize the validity
for myself of the Christian combining of these two voices.

For Christians, the voice of devotional self-giving bears witness to God as the soul's loving Creator and as the Creator of
the universe. It tells a man to love God as the source of his own
being—but as a reality apart from himself. For very many
Christians this has been the most persuasive voice of all, as in
Jesus' first and great commandment: "You shall love the Lord
your God with all your heart, and with all your soul, and with all

your mind, and with all your strength." The centrality of love and faith is stressed by St. John in the often quoted declaration: "God so loved the world that he gave his only Son, that whoever believes in him should not perish but have eternal life." John wants to make it clear that God is manifested in love of men for one another. "As the Father has loved me," he tells us that Jesus said, "so have I loved you; abide in my love. If you keep my commandments, you will abide in my love, just as I have kept my Father's commandments and abide in his love." Again, Jesus said, "Greater love has no man than this, that a man lay down his life for his friends." And he proved that he meant literally what he said by sacrificing himself for his disciples and for all mankind. But this love must be practiced daily by one who would follow him. "A new commandment I give to you," Jesus said, "that you love one another; even as I have loved you, that you also love one another."

Jesus himself is the supreme example of devotional self-giving in Christianity—non-Christians will pardon his followers for extending the statement to the whole world. Because we lack sufficient information, we do not know if the same claim can be made for him with regard to intuitive wisdom. But there can be no doubt in the Christian's mind that through Jesus' relationship with God a love flowed through him to men that in a preeminent degree manifested the Father, who is love, in the world. And this love has passed from Jesus Christ to his true followers throughout the ages.

Perhaps, if this love were understood rightly, it would be seen not to differ essentially from the sort of wisdom we considered in the last chapter. Indeed, in St. John's interpretation of God's manifesation in the love men bear each other, a parallel has recently been seen with the idea in Mahayana Buddhism of the *prajna*, or pure wisdom of enlightenment, that imbues all beings and needs only to be called forth.

Outstanding examples of this predominantly loving approach in Christian history are, in addition to Christ's own disciples and his faithful women helpers, St. Francis of Assisi, St. Catherine of Genoa, St. Teresa of Avila, St. Thérèse of Lisieux—to mention only a few of a host of saintly persons in all denominations. There are, as well, innumerable others who have, less spectacularly but nonetheless effectively, followed this voice.

In the Roman and Orthodox traditions a great deal of prominence has always been given to the popular devotional approach. In Protestant denominations, with only a few exceptions, less stress has been laid on external manifestations of piety; at the same time, the devotional mood has always been given first importance. Recently, after the "updating" of the Roman Church, there was a marked turning away from external devotional practices, but the devotional approach appears to be making a comeback among Catholic Pentecostals and, for Protestants, among the "Jesus people."

The voice of devotional self-giving has been most often heard, in both Hinduism and Christianity, simply because it speaks to the most readily available aspect of most men's nature: their personal and sensuous feelings and their emotional reactions to these feelings. This aspect is bound up both with men's sexual and other physical appetites and with their aesthetic needs. Outside the religious experience, perhaps it is in the aesthetic sphere that it has found its most delicate play. Had we the space, I could cite a world of examples in Indian art. Often enough the aesthetic and the religious have been partly confused.

Though in one sense closely identified with the more self-centering aspects of human nature, devotion is paradoxically capable, in as great a degree as any of the other voices, of raising the self or soul above the small concerns of the ego to an almost sublime self-forgetfulness. The love of husbands and wives, of parents for children, of friend for chosen friend, can on occasion become the vehicle for a spirit of sacrifice that through its spontaneity rises beyond sacrifice. Even those without conscious religious commitment are able, in response to an inner urge very like a blending of this voice and the sense of human community, to devote their entire mature lives to serving their fellow men and women.

When the voice of devotional self-giving is expressed through worship of the personal God, its capacity to free the individual from his own narrower interests reveals itself most clearly. In Christianity, though it is always predominant, it is usually expressed along with one or two other approaches. Only in post-Vedic Hinduism have we an opportunity to study it in isolation and estimate its intrinsic power to lift a man above himself into communion with his highest ideal.

-2-

Even in the ritual part of the Vedas there are references to God in more or less the sense in which Christians think of him today. In the earliest of them all, the Rig-Veda, occurs an extraordinary composition, the "Hymn of the Supreme Person," or "Purushashukta," which describes not only the Person himself, but the details of his sacrifice, out of which the creation originated.

Here are a few of the verses most meaningful for Christians:

> Thousands of heads had the Supreme Person, thousands of eyes, thousands of feet.
> He encompassed the earth on all sides and reached immeasurably beyond.
> That Supreme Person is all that has ever been and all that is yet to be;
> He is the Lord of immortality, who grows still greater through offerings of food.
> So glorious is his greatness—yes, even greater is that Supreme Person.
> All creatures are but a quarter part of him; three-quarters of him is eternity in heaven.

* * *

> When the gods made ready the sacrifice with the Person as their offering,
> The oil was springtime, autumn the sacred gift, and summer the sacrificial firewood.
> They anointed on the grass, as victim, the Person born in the earliest time;
> Through him the deities and angels of old, and the sages, performed their sacrifice.
> From that sacrifice they, as celebrants, caught the dripping fat.
> He formed the birds of the air, the wild beasts and the tame.

* * *

> When they divided up the Person, into how many parts did they separate him?
> What do they say was his mouth, what his arms? What his thighs and his feet?
> The priests were his mouth, his two strong arms the warriors,
> The farmers were his thighs, his two feet those who perform works of service.

* * *

Seven were the logs that fenced him round, seven the
layers of fuel made ready,
When the gods bound as victim the Supreme Person
and of him made sacrifice.

As early as 1000 B.C., such was the Vedic conception of a
Supreme Person, offered in sacrifice for the creation of the world.
For Christians, the image may symbolize either the sacrifice
involved in the Supreme Person's creation of the world, even
while remaining immeasurably beyond it, or the sacrifice we as
individuals impose on him in ignoring the life-giving principle
in the universe.

Again, the *Shvetashvatara Upanishad*, one of the authoritative (though not one of the earliest) Upanishads, exhibits in
contrast to most of the others a strongly theistic strain. Here
is a celebrated passage, ending with a luminous petition:

"Rudra, the Lord, is truly one; for the knowers of Brahman
[ultimate reality] do not admit the existence of a second being.
He alone rules all the worlds by his powers. He dwells as the
inner self of every living thing. After having created all the
worlds, he, their protector, takes them back into himself at the
end of time.

"His eyes are everywhere, his faces everywhere, his arms
everywhere, everywhere his feet. He it is who endows men with
arms, birds with feet and wings—and men, too, with feet. Having produced heaven and earth, he remains as their nondual
manifestor.

"He, the all-knowing Rudra, creator of the gods and bestower
of their powers, the support of the universe, he who in the beginning gave birth to the Golden Egg, Hiranyagarbha—may
he endow us with clear intellect."

Here Rudra, who has been identified with the god Shiva, is
conceived, somewhere before 500 B.C., as the Godhead. He is
the spirit that dwells in all living beings, one and without a
second, omnipresent, all-knowing. Through the creative principle Hiranyagarbha, begotten of his own substance, he is also
the all-powerful Creator; and having created the world, he
remains, as Sustainer of the universe, its manifesting principle.
Again, as Dissolver of the universe, a role assigned in later
mythology to Shiva, he takes the world back to himself at the
end of a cosmic cycle. (This conception of a suprapersonal and

yet personal God, included as it was in one of the Upanishads on which he was commenting, must have exerted a powerful influence on Shankara's picture of the world of *maya*, or becoming, superimposed through *maya* on Brahman. The passage graphically shows that Shankara drew the central ideas of his theory of the cosmos not from his own imagination but from scripture: even the concept of *maya* is a logical deduction from this passage and others like it.)

The Golden Egg or creative principle referred to above was supposed to have been "formed from the seed deposited in the primordial waters by the self-existent Brahman on the eve of creation." The seed, as Swami Nikhilananda has explained, "took the form of a golden egg, out of which Brahman was born as Brahma, the Creator God." Immediately one recalls the passage in Genesis: "The Spirit of God was moving over the face of the waters." The ancient image is evoked, too, by Jesus' statement as recorded by St. John: "Unless one is born of water and the Spirit, he cannot enter the kingdom of God." (There seems, as well, to be a hint of the male-female relationship of the Spirit and the waters, as Robert Antoine, of Calcutta, pointed out to me, in the lowering of the Paschal candle into the baptismal waters in the Roman Catholic vigil of Easter.)

From the beginning, the Vedic sages understood that personality provides an important clue to the understanding of ultimate reality. Witness the innumerable hymns to the gods in the Rig-Veda. And this understanding obviously continued into the age of the Upanishads—though in general the mysticism that characterizes most of them is distinctly slanted toward intuitive wisdom. Yet something seems to have been wanting in these conceptions of the personal God. Even the theistic revelation found in the *Shvetashvatara Upanishad* may not, with the passage of time and the growth of men's self-understanding, have proved any more congenial to the ordinary Indian of its time than the intuitive revelations of the earlier Upanishads. Not only in the Vedic hymns, but even in the theistic passages of the Upanishads, there is often a lack of warmth in God's relationship to man—a lack noticeable at times in the Old Testament, too. Perhaps largely in response to a need for human intimacy with God, a new devotional revelation occurred. It is from this time that what is known as popular Hinduism began to take shape.

-3-

Devotionally oriented Hindus, who make up perhaps 90 percent of those professing Hinduism, are influenced by the teachings of a number of scriptures that developed in all likelihood in the eight hundred years between 400 B.C. and A.D. 400. They possess practically as much authority, for most of these Hindus, as the Vedas themselves. The epics *Ramayana* and *Mahabharata*, of the pre-Christian era, and mythological chronicles such as the *Vishnu Purana*, the *Bhagavata Purana*, and the *Skanda Purana* (to mention only a few) arc often called the "fifth Veda." They acquired this title because they made the truths of the Vedas available to Hindus otherwise unable to receive them—either because they could not understand them or because their social position barred them from reading or hearing them. Though adapted to mass enlightenment, the epics and Puranas yield expressions of spiritual insight that even sophisticated minds study with profit. They are part of the psychological background of almost every modern Hindu, educated or uneducated.

The two epics, written around the lives of Rama and Krishna and the heroes associated with them, though not without plentiful theological overtones, concern themselves mainly with the doings of human beings. It is through the legends and fragments of history they contain that we obtain our first detailed glimpse of life in early India. The Puranas, mythological chronicles about Brahma, Vishnu, Shiva, and other aspects of the personal God, achieved their present form after the epics. This places them, in all probability, within the first four hundred years of the Christian era. (Some scholars would date a few of them even later.) The legends they contain, however, date from as early as the time when the epics were reaching their final form.

The mythological world revealed in these noncanonical but still influential scriptures is one of almost inexhaustible variety. Each of the Puranas introduces elaborate mythical tales in celebration of the glories and exploits of several personal Gods, most of whom, as distinguished from most of the early Vedic gods, are still worshiped in India. And each of them offers a self-contained picture of the world under the rule of an all-knowing, all-powerful, all-merciful God in one or another manifestation. These aspects of God worshiped by devotional Hindus are personal not exactly in the Christian sense, but simply in the sense that, no matter in what form the divine being is depicted, he always takes the form of a person, acts like a person, and can be worshiped as a person. (It should be noted that the Deity is worshiped in each sect in a twofold form: as male and female. Each male manifestation has his consort or female complement; and it is this twofold Deity that sustains the universe, as Divine Ground and Creative Power.)

The Hindu devotional tradition achieved its first major expression in one of the epics, the *Mahabharata*, through the Bhagavad Gita, or "Song of the Lord." We have already seen that this scripture, which forms an integral part of the epic, includes a highly refined statement about intuitive wisdom. In the chapters that follow, we shall find that it contains important information about meditative discipline and motiveless service, too. But its presentation of devotional self-giving is especially congenial to Christian thinking. Here the Brahman of the Upanishads is presented, at its climax, not as something beyond the reach of human experience, but as a reality with whom man can enjoy an intimate personal relationship.

I shall quote a few passages from various chapters. It is, as before, the Lord Krishna who speaks to his friend and disciple Arjuna. From the devotional point of view, the work may be looked upon as a conversation between the soul and God.

"In whatsoever way men approach me," Krishna says, "even so do I reward them; for it is my path, Arjuna, that men follow in all things." This idea he later elaborates in the following passage: "Those persons who worship me, meditating on their identity with me and ever devoted to me—to them I carry what they lack and for them I preserve what they already have. Even those devotees who, endowed with faith, worship other gods, worship me alone, though in a wrong way. For I alone am the Enjoyer and the Lord of all sacrifices. But these men do not know me in reality; hence they fall." Krishna is the Supreme Lord. A Hindu theologian might even say that those who are worshiping "other gods" are actually worshiping him through what Christian theologians call "implicit faith."

How may a man show his love? "Whoever offers me, with devotion," Krishna tells his disciple, "a leaf, a flower, a fruit, or water—that I accept, the pious offering of the pure in heart. Whatever you do, whatever you eat, whatever you offer in sacrifice, whatever you give away, and whatever you practice in the form of austerities—do it, Arjuna, as an offering to me."

Repeatedly one hears the devotional refrain: "On those who

are ever devoted to me and worship me with love, I bestow the understanding by which they come to me.'' In his commentary on this verse, based on Shankara's commentary, Swami Nikhilananda says: ''Realization of the Lord is possible only through his grace, which he bestows on those who worship him with whole-souled love. As a result of his grace, their hearts become pure, and being pure in heart they see God. Men can never know the true essence of the Lord through their worldly minds or their power of reasoning. The attainment of true understanding, by which the Lord can be known and which comes through his grace alone, is the purpose of all spiritual endeavor and discipline.''

Faith unaccompanied by experience, however, is no more sufficient for the Hindu eager for a vision of the Lord than it is for the Christian mystic. Krishna, at his disciple's plea, grants the warrior Arjuna the staggering vision of his universal form, reminding one of the several Vedic passages quoted earlier in this chapter. ''Behold here today, Arjuna,'' he says, ''the whole universe, of the moving and the unmoving, and whatever else you desire to see, all concentrated in my body.'' It is a terrifying experience, for the disciple is granted a glimpse of God's omnipotence. ''In an ineffable oneness are revealed,'' Swami Nikhilananda adds in his commentary, ''all the facets of the Godhead—spirit and matter, being and becoming, creation and destruction, infinite and finite, space and time, past and future.''

Arjuna experiences the Lord not as his innermost Self, but as the sovereign of the cosmos. In one of the most powerful outbursts in Hindu scripture, he exclaims, ''Thou art the first of gods, the ancient Soul; thou art the supreme Resting-place of the universe; thou art the Knower and That which is to be known and the Ultimate Goal. And by thee is the world pervaded, O thou of infinite form! Thou art Wind and Death and Fire and the Lord of water. Thou art Prajapati, Father of mankind, and their Great-grandsire, Father of Brahma, the Creator, as well. Salutations, salutations to thee a thousand times, and again and yet again salutations, salutations to thee!''

For the average soul, not privileged to have walked with the Lord, such a vision—like the Transfiguration of Jesus—is not available simply for the asking. The Lord Krishna says, ''Neither by the Vedas, nor by penances, nor by almsgiving, nor yet by sacrifice, am I to be seen in the form in which you have now beheld me. But by devotion to me alone may I be known in this form, Arjuna, realized truly, and entered into.''

What then is the way for a worshiper? Immediately Krishna launches into a practical discourse on devotion to God. "He who never hates any being," he tells Arjuna, "and is friendly and compassionate to all, who is free from the feelings of 'I' and 'mine' and even-minded in pain and pleasure, who is forbearing, ever content, and steady in contemplation, who is self-controlled and possessed of firm conviction, and who has consecrated his mind and understanding to me—dear to me is the one who is thus devoted to me. . . . Exceedingly dear to me are they who regard me as the Supreme Goal and, endowed with faith and devotion, follow this immortal *dharma* [law of life]." Faith and devotion, strengthened by practice of self-discipline and good works, constitute the way to approach the Lord.

Finally, as if to sum up all his teaching on devotion, the Lord Krishna says, in the last chapter of the Bhagavad Gita, "Again listen to my supreme word, the profoundest of all. . . . Fix your heart on me, give your love to me, worship me, bow down before me; so shall you come to me. This is my pledge to you, for you are dear to me. Abandon all duties and come to me alone for shelter. I will deliver you from all sins." It is a striking anticipation, indeed, of those compassion-laden words, "Come to me, all who labor and are heavy-laden, and I will give you rest."

The Bhagavad Gita offers a highly refined and well-balanced exposition of love of God. Christians should ask themselves what they are hearing in lines such as those just quoted if not the voice of devotional self-giving. But one misses the central meaning of this scripture, I believe, if one fails to recognize what is suggested about this voice, namely that, like the other three voices, it is not the only one. Contrary to the claims of the different Hindu scholastic philosophers (as expressed in their philosophical systems, not in their practice), the Bhagavad Gita represents a synthesis of the four approaches—a synthesis quite as explicit as that found in the New Testament.

-4-

In telling the story of our trip to Gorakhpur, I included a brief sketch of the story of Rama, the great hero and king. I would also like to relate something of the legend of Krishna, as recounted in the *Bhagavata Purana* and the *Mahabharata*.

Whether Krishna ever existed as a historical person is not important to a Hindu devotee. What is crucial is that he is a spiritual reality. His life and example are as pivotal in the history of Hindus who worship him as Jesus' life and example are in the tradition of Christians. When Hindus use the word "myths" in connection with legends such as those of Rama and Krishna, as I see it, they use it in a special sense. They do not necessarily imply that certain sages or poets wrote stories about a central figure, and that then other legends grew up around him, and that finally men began worshiping an imaginary Deity. Possibly occasional details of the stories were added in this way, just as certain details are now held to have been added to the life of Jesus as presented in the New Testament. But the basic story is to be taken as revelation. The Deity in question was first experienced as a living reality by a man or group of men in a mood of spiritual rapture—much as Abraham or Moses or Isaiah or Job experienced God's presence in the Old Testament accounts—and along with that experience was revealed the spiritual history. If any of the great "historical" figures of Jewish religious history could be shown never to have existed, it would not detract, in the Hindu view, from the spiritual significance of what the stories about them transmit. Let us turn, then, to perhaps the most deeply cherished of Hindu myths.

The child who was to be known and worshiped as Krishna was born in the town of Mathura to parents of noble birth, Vasudeva and Devaki, attached to the court of King Kansha, a viciously cruel tyrant. Devaki was Kansha's sister. On the very day of their wedding, the king had heard a voice from heaven prophesying his death at the hands of the eighth child of the couple. At once he ordered the pair to be thrown into a dungeon in his palace, where he could make certain no child escaped alive. All but one of the first seven children born to Vasudeva and Devaki were slain by Kansha's order. (The child that escaped, a male child named Balarama, was the seventh. The parents reported that he was stillborn; but actually he had been miraculously transferred to the womb of another wife of Vasudeva.) It was at midnight during a violent storm that Devaki gave birth to her eighth child, another boy. Miraculous events attended the birth, convincing the parents that none other than Vishnu, Supreme Lord of the world, had been born as their son. But instantly their vision became clouded by delusion and they saw him as merely a human child.

Then Vasudeva heard a voice from heaven: "Arise and take this child to Nanda, chief of the cowherds. And bring here the girl just born to his wife Yashoda." The father took up the young child. As he did so, the bolts slipped back from the prison doors and they swung open on their heavy hinges. All the sentries lay overcome by deep slumber. Passing through the storm, Vasudeva reached the cowherds' village. Everyone was asleep. Finding the chieftain's house, he exchanged the children without being seen. Immediately upon his return to the dungeon with Nanda's daughter, the doors swung shut and the sentries awoke and resumed their watch.

In the morning, the cowherd chieftain, Nanda, was happy to learn he was the father of a boy. He named him Krishna, "the Dark One," for his complexion was the color of a rain cloud. Meanwhile in Mathura, the tyrant Kansha, learning of the birth of another child to Devaki, rushed to the dungeon. He was determined to kill it with his own hands—even when he found it was a girl. But as he tried to seize the child, who was in reality an appearance of the Divine Mother of the universe, she ascended into the air. "He who will slay you, vicious man," the child said, mockingly, "is born and is alive and well." Then she disappeared. Filled with fear and rage, Kansha ordered that all the young children in and about Mathura should be slaughtered. But having nothing to fear from Krishna's parents, the king now freed his sister and her husband. Vasudeva took his son Balarama to live with Nanda.

Soon Kansha learned of Krishna's whereabouts, and sent vicious demons who were under his command to entrap and slay the young child. Against him, one after another, they used all their wiles. But despite their great strength, the divine boy faced and destroyed each one—almost in play, it seemed to the wondering cowherds.

As Krishna grew older, he became the cowherds' favorite. Young and old alike were drawn to him. Full of mischief, he stole their cream, butter, and milk in order to feed his friends or his pet monkeys and birds. But the cowherd women always forgave him, for his pranks secretly delighted them. One day, however, while playing Krishna ate some earth. His foster mother, Yashoda, becoming distressed, made him open his mouth to wash it out—when suddenly she saw within it the whole universe: sun, moon and stars, heaven, earth, and the nether world. She recoiled in fright and wonder, and Krishna resumed his natural boyish form.

When Krishna was eight years old, Nanda moved his whole

village to the groves and glades of Vrindavan. Here the boy
spent long hours with the cowherd boys and girls in pastures
along the river Jamuna. Several of his friendships with the
young cowherds were especially intimate, but it was with the
cowherd girls that his relationship was most intense.

One of Krishna's accomplishments was his ability to play
the flute with great expressiveness. The sound of it would draw
the cowherd girls, even married women, away from their
homes and their worldly duties—just as the call of the Lord
may draw humans to leave their earthly ties and follow him.
Chief among the cowherd girls, or *gopis*, was the beautiful
Radha. It was she who realized the most exquisite delight in
Krishna's presence and suffered the most searing anguish
when separated from his presence—sometimes, it seemed to
her, through sheer willfulness on his part. For often, as they
were sporting in the groves, he would disappear, leaving her
inconsolable. The various moods of Radha and the *gopis* have
inspired countless Indian devotional songs.

One night, at the culmination of this love relationship, the
cowherd girls gathered in one of the groves and danced about
him in a ring. The youthful Krishna danced with them till
they were carried away in ecstasy. So intense was their identification with him that each girl thought he was dancing with
her alone, that she was the special object of his love. In later
centuries erotic details entered into the legend. During the
dance, in these versions, each of the cowherd girls enjoys sexual
union with the Lord. However the relationship is expressed,
Hindus accept it as symbolic of the soul's relationship to God.

While I was a Hindu I tried to express a worshiper's meditation on that scene:

DANCE OF THE GOD

Dance! Dance!
Krishna, dance!
Dance as you danced
That only night
By the glittering stream:
Dance again
With the lifting step,
With the airy turn
Sudden as thought.
Mukunda, dance!

Holding your flute
As you held it once,
High to your lips
In your upheld hands,
Dance me that same
Dance again:
Swirl and sway
Through my cloudy trance
As for the milkmaids
Ringed about:
Leap and float
As you floated then,
When your flute notes
Drew each one
From the dream of desire,
From the dream of home,
With smooth voice
Found out each one
And drew her, anguished
For love and shame,
To join you in your
Luminous dream.

And always the black eyes
And blue skin
Urging, urging them
Ever on
To the lonely bank
Of the glittering stream,
To the flowery grove
In fierce moonlight,
Where, garlanded
With yellow and white
Of jasmines and marigolds
Tightly twined,
You danced your dance
In wild moonlight,
And the maids whirled round
To your anklets' sound,
And with all you danced
Though you danced alone.

Till each knew at last
That her lover was

Not the sure lover
She left at home,
But the eight-years boy
With the piercing eyes,
With the night-black eyes
And storm-blue skin
And the gleaming hair
That tossed and fell
As you danced your dance
With the milkmaids there:
And the god in you
Was the god in them
As they joined in love
By the glittering stream.

High to your lips
In your upheld hands
Holding your flute
As you held it once,
Dance as you danced
That only night
By the silent stream
In fierce moonlight,
With the lifting stop,
With the airy turn:
Mukunda, dance
In my perilous dream,
Leap and float
As you floated then
While the milkmaids circled,
Clasping hands,
The dance of your naked
Innocence.

Dance! Dance!
Krishna, dance!

When he was twelve years old, Krishna left the groves of
Vrindavan. The tyrant Kansha, having thus far failed to
destroy him, arranged a great sacrifice to be accompanied by
games and feats of strength. To it he invited Krishna and
Balarama (who had grown up with his brother in Gokula and
Vrindavan). The king instructed the strongest of his court
wrestlers to challenge the two boys to a "mock contest" of
strength for the spectators' entertainment, and if they accepted

the challenge, at an opportune moment to slay Krishna. Nobles, officers, and all manner of other guests, including holy men, commoners, and the simple villagers of Vrindavan, crowded the galleries of the arena. Kansha was seated on a high throne where he could be seen by all.

As the two handsome brothers, Krishna and Balarama, entered the arena, dressed now as the noblemen they were, their bearing attracted everyone's attention. A tremor of amazement and awe passed through the assembly. The wrestlers saw in Krishna, as it were, a death-dealing thunderbolt; women saw him as the god of love; sages saw him as the Supreme Lord; the commoners of Mathura saw simply a nobleman, now once more recognized as the son of Vasudeva and Devaki. Nanda and the villagers of Vrindavan saw their beloved cowherd boy; his parents saw the helpess child born to them in the dungeon that stormy night so many years ago. Kansha saw before him, as it were, his inescapable doom.

The chief of the court wrestlers came forth as he had been ordered. But when, during the pretended exhibition of strength, he tried to kill Krishna, the lad destroyed him effortlessly—once again as if in play. Thereupon Kansha himself sprang in rage from his throne and threw himself upon the Lord. In a moment he lay dead on the sandy floor of the arena.

From now on Krishna's life changed. Destiny summoned him to the world of affairs, and he began to mix with kings and princes. When he failed to return to Vrindavan, the cowherd girls and boys were griefstricken. They sent a message by one of their number, imploring him to return. This he could not do, but he promised to reveal himself in their hearts, in his spiritual form, whenever they longed intensely to see him.

Here we turn to the *Mahabharata* for the conclusion of the legend. The epic gives us an account of Krishna's many-sided dealings in diplomacy, statecraft, and war. In treating with kings and princes he never imposed his own will. Because he was the Supreme Lord, his presence alone was sufficient to reveal what was right or wrong; but he left it to each man to decide what he should do. The tale, though fascinating, is far too involved to relate in its entirety here. To put it briefly, Krishna had become the friend and counselor of the noble and upright warrior Arjuna and his four brothers. When war broke out between them and their evil cousin Duryodhana over the possession of a kingdom, Krishna acted as Arjuna's charioteer. It was in the midst of the battlefield, while the two sides were waiting for the first engagement, that Krishna spoke to his doubt-ridden friend and disciple the instructions embodied in the Bhagavad Gita. Here it was, too, that he revealed to Arjuna his universal form.

In the end, the five brothers conquered their enemies and regained the kingdom wrongfully seized from them by Duryodhana. The name given to Kurukshetra, the field of the battle in the Bhagavad Gita, is, significantly, *Dharmakshetra*, the "Field of Righteousness."

What Krishna taught in the Bhagavad Gita is an illustration of what he was. As I have pointed out, in his teachings we hear, in urgent clarity, not only the voice of devotional self-giving, but Hindu versions of all those other voices that would later be heard in the teachings of Jesus. These teachings of Krishna's led the disciple Arjuna to the final understanding that utter self-surrender to God is the goal of spiritual life.

At last, retiring to Dwaraka, a city he had founded many years before in the western part of India for the clan he derived from, Krishna witnessed his own people's complete destruction through civil strife. Knowing his death was imminent, he went to the forest. There he controlled his mind and senses, as he had prescribed to Arjuna at Kurukshetra, and sat down in meditation by a river. As Krishna was thus communing with himself, a hunter, mistaking him for a deer, shot him with an iron-tipped arrow. He died with a blessing on his lips for the griefstricken hunter.

To their worshipers, all the myths about Vishnu and Shiva and other manifestations of Deity constitute spiritual history —a history of God's intervention from age to age in the affairs of men, to reestablish righteousness (*dharma*) and to destroy the wicked. In these legends, those with eyes to see have discovered, through the centuries, a way of liberation from the sin of disobedience to God's will—a disobedience born of ignorance about his nature and their own relation to him.

-5-

Somewhere near the end of the age of the Puranas—that is, very roughly about A.D. 400—the devotional tradition took another turn. In southern India, among the followers of Vishnu and Shiva, arose a succession of poet-saints known respectively as Alvars and Nayanmars. The intensely devotional songs they wrote to express their feelings and experiences show a strong Puranic influence. Full of subtle meanings, they were an important source from which the philosophers of Vaishnavism and Shaivism—the religions of the worshipers of Vishnu and of Shiva—drew ideas for their theological treatises known as Agamas.

The poetic tradition did not stop with these poet-saints. It is one of the arresting facts of Indian religious history that in the three hundred years between the birth of Kabir in A.D. 1380 and the death of Ramdas in 1680 occurred the most intense and sustained outburst of popular devotional fervor India has ever seen. The aspects of Deity the poet-saints of this period celebrated were Rama and Krishna. And while these singers were bearing their witness to the primacy of divine love, St. Catherine of Genoa, that grand apostle of Christian love and service who died in 1510, was sharing with her devoted followers confidences about love that any Vaishnavite or Shaivite could wholeheartedly accept.

"The longer I live," Catherine once said, "the greater is my awareness daily that the end for which man is created is to love, and to rejoice in this love. When a man reaches the desirable haven of pure love, even if he wished and tried his best not to, he can do nothing but love and be joyful. This grace God gives a man in so wonderful a measure, beyond all human desire and imagination, that while in this life he feels he is sharing in heavenly glory." On another occasion she said, "I will have nothing to do with a love that would be *for* God or *in* God. I cannot bear the word 'for' or the word 'in,' because they denote something that may be in between God and me. This is a love that pure love cannot bear, since pure love is God himself."

A century later in India, Mirabai, a princess persecuted for her love of Krishna (and like St. Catherine of Genoa, the unwilling wife of an unsympathetic husband), was singing in the role of Radha of her separation from Krishna. If Catherine spoke out of a mood of fulfillment, Mirabai usually expressed herself in terms of the unfulfilled yearning that is part of the Radha tradition:

O friend, I am mad with love: none knows my anguish. . . .
Only he who is wounded knows how the wounded feel,
Or he who has struck the blow. . . .
Physician I have found none.
Mira's pain will leave her, Lord, only when thou art her physician.

Again, she could sing:

> Whom shall I beseech for help?
> My Beloved has dealt me a deep wound.
> The Huntsman tracked me like a deer:
> His arrow pierced me through and through. . . .
> And yet this wound I cherish.
> Singing Lord Krishna's deeds
> I shall cross the round of birth and death.

Another song in the same tradition, of unknown authorship, was much appreciated by Ramakrishna in the nineteenth century:

> Listen! The flute has sounded in yonder wood.
> There I must fly, for Krishna waits on the path.
> Tell me, friends, will you come along or no?
> To you my Krishna is merely an empty name;
> To me he is the anguish of my heart. . . .
> I hear his flute calling, ''Radha, come out!
> Without you the grove is shorn of its loveliness.''

What Christian who knows the Bible is not immediately reminded by these fragments, chosen from hundreds of examples, of that exquisite love song from Jewish tradition, the Song of Solomon? Today, Christian scholars tend to stress the purely secular origin and connotation of this biblical masterpiece. Such a tendency is found, also, among certain students of Indian culture, who see in this sort of writing no more than eroticism. In a culture like India's, however, where everything is given a religious turn, a wholly secular interpretation is out of the question. The flesh is to be enjoyed, but the spirit need not be forgotten. And in a case like Mirabai's or St. Catherine of Genoa's, the flesh *was* forgotten. Though the contemporary consensus in regard to the Song of Solomon would tend to deemphasize its spiritual content, Christians have traditionally interpreted it as a dialogue between the Lord and his people, the Church, or between Christ and the individual soul. The latter interpretation would automatically come to a Hindu Vaishnavite's or an Islamic Sufi's mind on hearing these lines:

> O that he would kiss me with the kisses of his mouth!
> For your love is better than wine.

My beloved speaks and says to me:
"Arise my love, my fair one, and come away."

"I will rise now and go about the city, in the streets
    and in the squares;
I will seek him whom my soul loves."
I sought him but found him not.

The watchmen found me, as they went about in the city.
"Have you seen him whom my soul loves?"
Scarcely had I passed them, when I found him whom
    my soul loves.
I held him, and would not let him go.

My beloved put his hand to the latch. . . .
I opened to my beloved, but my beloved had turned
    and gone.
My soul failed me when he spoke.
I sought him but found him not;
I called him, but he gave no answer.

I adjure you, O daughters of Jerusalem, if you find my
    beloved,
That you tell him I am sick with love.

I am my beloved's and my beloved is mine;
He pastures his flock among the lilies.

O you who dwell in the gardens,
My companions are listening for your voice; let me
    hear it.
Make haste, my beloved, and be like a gazelle
Or a young stag upon the mountains of spices.

The songs of Mirabai and others of her tradition were
written long after the Christian Church placed its spiritual
interpretation on these perhaps originally wholly secular verses.
Nevertheless, the message it heard is a timeless one, and the
relationship between the two traditions is unmistakable.

Songs of this type are put to different uses in India by saints
and the faithful. The ordinary believer is deeply moved by them
and uses them to intensify his faith. But the mystic makes use
of them, as did no doubt the poets who wrote them, to commune
directly with God. Ramakrishna has spoken very revealingly

about his own experience when listening attentively to religious singing. "As I listen to the singer," he said, "the mind ascends, as it were, on a delicate thread toward God. If there is the slightest error in rhythm or pronunciation or intonation, it is as if the thread is shaken. The mind with a shock descends to the realm of normal consciousness. But if the singing goes on without error, the mind enters into ecstasy." We shall see later that the singing of devotional songs was one of the means this saint used to obtain his first vision of God.

For a highly developed mystic, then, the attentive hearing (or singing) of expressive music joined to expressive poetry, perfectly performed, is a way of union. This may have been true of a Christian poet-saint like John of the Cross as well as of Hindu saints. The Islamic Sufis no doubt also put their songs to the same use, and often write as if God is speaking to his lover. Here are a few lines of the great Arab mystical genius, Muhyi al-Din Ibn 'Arabi:

> Beloved, love me, love me only, love me for love alone.
> In me lose yourself, in me only.
> Bind yourself to me, take me in your embrace.
> None is more intimate than myself. . . .
> When you draw near me, it is simply I that have drawn
>   near to you.
> Nearer to you I am than your own self,
> Than your very soul, nearer than your breathing.

The extreme emotional sensitivity required for cultivating the devotional mood we have been considering in this section is far removed from the average thinking of today's Christian or Hindu. But there is no denying that this mood is an almost perfect example of the voice of devotional self-giving in isolation from the other voices.

-6-

Hindu scholastic philosophers differ noticeably from Christians in the variety of ways they have interpreted their "divinely revealed" scriptures. Even though Christian denominations hold divergent beliefs on certain isolated points of faith, they are generally agreed about the nature of God and of Jesus Christ, the nature of the soul, and a great number of the elements of the Christian plan of salvation. Hindu religious philosophers, on the contrary, have distilled out of the Vedas systems of thought of widely divergent meaning. In doing so, they have produced what some Christian observers have understandably seen as a tension in the Hindu religion between the devotional and the intellectual approach. Like the poet-saints, the devotional philosophers flourished after the Puranic age.

We have seen how, in southern India, Shankara in the ninth century interpreted the Vedic statements about the identity of Brahman and Atman, the ultimate reality behind the changing universe being identical with the True Self behind the flux of human consciousness. In much the same way, the great teacher Ramanuja—like Shankara, also from southern India—in the eleventh century sought to give his own interpretation of these same statements, explaining them in terms of a personal God and a soul intimately joined to him but never entirely identified with him.

Ramanuja was the finest flower of the long line of poet-saints known as Alvars. Ramanujacharya was his full name; he was born in 1017 and died in 1137 A.D. His life reveals one of the most lofty and noble devotional personalities in the annals of Indian sainthood. It was on the basis of the Alvars' hymns and his own understanding of the Vedas that Ramanuja developed his system of nondualism, known as Vishishtadvaita—what we may term "synthetic" or "modal" nondualism. (It is sometimes inaccurately called "Qualified Nondualism," but there is nothing "qualified" about God's nondualism in Ramanuja's system.) Something of the flavor of the Alvars may be gleaned from the story of one of them, Tiruppanalvar, who came of a family of *chandalas*, a mixed caste who were a sort of untouchables.

Tiruppanalvar used to pass his days singing of the glories of God and accompanying himself on the *vina*, a stringed instrument like a highly refined form of guitar. While singing he would become utterly oblivious of the world, and often appeared like a madman. Once he was singing in this way, sitting on the steps of the bathing place on the river Kaveri in front of the great temple of Sri Ranganatha, an aspect of the Lord Vishnu, at Srirangam. Overcome with emotion, he lay across the steps, unconscious of everything around him. One of the priests of the temple, Lokasaranga Muni, seeking to return from the river with a jar of water to bathe the image in the temple, found this man, obviously of a low station, blocking his way. After calling him to no avail, he threw a stone at him to rouse him. On coming to his senses and realizing he had been lying in the way of the brahmin priest of Ranganatha, Tiruppanalvar was abashed and begged a thousand pardons. He hurried away in fear.

On returning to the temple, Lokasaranga Muni to his surprise found the gates locked from within. Though he called, there was no response. The other priests, who also happened to be outside, were terrified to see the gates shut at this unusual hour. At last Lokasaranga realized that the Lord himself must have locked the doors. With joined palms he prayed earnestly for forgiveness for whatever sin he might have committed. Then a voice spoke from within the temple, "Muni, you hit me today with a stone, and I shall not allow you to serve me any more." "When did I strike you, Lord?" the startled priest inquired. From inside the voice replied, "The great soul who was chanting my name on the steps by the river is my other self. Only if you walk around the temple carrying him on your shoulders will the doors reopen."

The priest rushed to the river and, after finding the low-caste man, begged his forgiveness and repeated to him the Lord's command. With pain he noticed a cut on Tiruppanalvar's brow where the stone had hit him. Seeing the brahmin bowing before him, the saint was distressed and fearful. "Sir, it is I who have committed the offense," he said. "Punish me if you will by throwing more stones at me from a distance. Don't defile yourself by touching my body." But Lokasaranga Muni, seizing him by main force, placed the saint on his shoulders and carried him around the whole vast temple of Ranganatha. In performing this act of penance he had done something unthinkable for an orthodox brahmin. Thereupon the temple doors came open. When the priest stood before the Lord's shrine, he saw that a few drops of blood had trickled down from a cut in the brow of the image.

Such was the tradition into which Ramanuja was born. The story of his life, though no doubt also partly legendary, is preserved in greater detail than Shankara's. He was born in a brahmin family in a village not far from Madras, and from childhood showed signs of being highly gifted. Besides being extremely handsome, he was extraordinarily intelligent. After hearing his teacher's instruction only once, he could grasp its import, no matter how difficult it might be. His chief interest, however, was to associate with holy men, and in time Ramanuja became the disciple of a famous teacher of Nondualistic Vedanta, who followed the voice of intuitive wisdom according to Shankara's interpretation.

Dissatisfied with his teacher's explanation of certain Vedic passages, Ramanuja ventured to advance his own. After he had challenged the teacher several times, the latter decided he was a threat to the continued supremacy of his school of Nondualistic Vedanta. Deluded by a false sense of loyalty to his school of thought, he persuaded several of his most faithful disciples to put Ramanuja's life to an end by violent means. Before they could carry out the teacher's order, Ramanuja escaped, as he did later when another priest sought to poison him. During all these trials he retained his humble respect for whoever happened at the time to be his teacher. What is more, he never failed to show the greatest regard for saints, even if they came from an untouchable caste.

The caliber of Ramanuja's spirituality may be understood from the following incident. When, after many refusals, he finally received initiation from a famous teacher, the latter told him he must not repeat to anyone the sacred formula, or *mantra*, he had been given for repetition and meditation. It was most holy and would bestow on whoever repeated it the grace of illumination. What was the teacher's dismay, and then anger, when he found that immediately upon leaving him Ramanuja had called one and all—even members of the least respected caste—to receive from him what he described as a "priceless jewel." A great crowd assembled. In front of the temple of Srirangam he made all repeat, three times, the sacred formula *"Om, namo Narayanaya,"* that is to say, "Om, salutation to the Supreme Godhead." This they did, and were at once filled with spiritual joy. When confronted by his outraged teacher, Ramanuja said, "Revered Sir, I knew that to repeat this *mantra* was a great sin. I disobeyed your command only because I was ready to suffer the pangs of hell. If I go to hell and thousands of men and women are thereby able to go to heaven, what could be more fortunate?" The teacher, realizing his disciple's greatheartedness, clasped him in a warm embrace. Finally the humble saint became the acknowledged leader of the Vaishnava community.

Another story illustrates the extraordinarily loving reverence in which Ramanuja's disciples held him. Varadacharya and his wife Lakshmi Devi were poor brahmin devotees of the Lord Vishnu. They had once received spiritual initiation from the saint when he visited their locality. Daily the husband went out in the morning to beg food, and with what he received Lakshmi Devi prepared dishes which they offered to Vishnu in their household shrine. They then partook of the offering as consecrated food. Lakshmi Devi was not only pure-souled and pious like her husband, but also exquisitely lovely. Near the couple's house lived a very rich merchant who had become infatuated with her beauty. In the mornings, when Varadacharya was out begging, he would now and then send a woman servant to Lakshmi to offer her money if she would satisfy his sexual desire. Lakshmi Devi, of course, paid no attention to his advances.

Once Ramanuja happened to be on a walking tour with some of his disciples. When he reached the village where Varadacharya lived, he decided to be a guest in his house. This was the highest honor a disciple could receive from his teacher. Lakshmi's husband was out begging when the teacher and his disciples arrived. Overjoyed to see them, she saluted her teacher "Revered Sir," she said, "my husband is begging. Please sit down and make yourselves at home." She offered them water to wash their feet, which had become dusty after their long walk from a distant town, and asked them to bathe in the pond nearby. Meanwhile, she said, she would prepare the offering for Lord Vishnu and they could all eat.

On entering the kitchen, Lakshmi Devi found to her dismay that there was no rice at all, nor any fresh vegetables. What could she do? She and her husband would be deprived of the blessing of serving their *guru* if she could not feed him. Suddenly Lakshmi had an inspiration. She remembered the merchant. "Why should I not serve my teacher at the sacrifice of this worthless body of mine?" she thought. "Let me go to the merchant and promise to fulfill his desire tonight in exchange for food to entertain our guests." Through the rear door of their small house she hurried down a lane till she reached the merchant's house. Passing through many sumptuous rooms, she reached his private apartments, where she found him. "Merchant," she said, "tonight I will fulfill your desire. My *guru* and his disciples have honored us by coming to our house as guests. Please send at once all I shall need to entertain them." Amazed and delighted, the merchant sent all sorts of delicious food to Varadacharya's house.

After preparing the offerings for the Lord Vishnu, Lakshmi invited Ramanuja and the others to sit down and eat. Some time after, Varadacharya returned from his begging with only a few morsels of food. Finding his revered teacher and the disciples there, he was overjoyed. When he learned that his wife had offered them many delicious dishes, he was startled. Where could she have obtained all these things? He went inside to ask Lakshmi about it. At once, with joined palms and eyes downcast, she told him about the merchant and about what she had done. Instead of showing anger, Varadacharya was delighted. "I am blessed!" he cried. Then he said to his wife Lakshmi, "Faithful woman, today you have given the highest possible testimony to your chastity. Lord Vishnu in the form of the teacher is the Supreme Person, the husband of all creation. What greater good fortune than to serve him in exchange for this wretched body of flesh and bones?" Holding her hands in his own, he led her to Ramanuja and humbly told him what had happened.

The saint and his disciples were astounded. At Ramanuja's request, the husband and wife ate some of the food that was left over, as consecrated food. Then, taking up the remainder, both went to the merchant's house. Varadacharya waited outside while Lakshmi went in and urged the merchant to eat some of it. This he gladly did. But on his partaking of it, a strange transformation came over him. All sensual desire disappeared from his mind, and he burst into tears. Looking at Lakshmi as if she were his mother, he said, "What a shameful thing I was prepared to do! It is through your compassion that I am saved. Forgive me, I beg you, for my many sins and make a man out of me instead of the animal I have been." The merchant then asked Lakshmi to take him to her teacher.

Hearing the news, Varadacharya was as astonished and gratified as his wife. Together the three went to Ramanuja. Prostrating themselves before him, they told him about the merchant's change of heart. The saint blessed them all. Later, at the merchant's earnest entreaty, he initiated him as a disciple. For the customary fee a disciple offered his teacher, the merchant had presented him with a large sum of money. This Ramanuja wanted to give to the poverty-stricken couple so they would no longer have to lead a wretched life. But Varadacharya said to him, with joined palms, "Revered Sir, through your grace we want for nothing. We are easily able to live on what I get by begging. Money only helps delight the senses

and draws the mind from the thought of God. Please do not
order your servant to accept this sum.''

Ramanuja, highly pleased, embraced Varadacharya. ''Today
I have been made pure,'' the teacher said, ''by touching a
great soul like you—so utterly free from craving, so full of
peace.''

Ramanuja's life overflows with evidences of his complete
dedication to the Lord Vishnu. Not the least of these was his
promise to write a commentary on the semi-canonical work, the
Brahma Sutras, which he fulfilled brilliantly. In it he undertook
to refute all the arguments of Shankara about the meaning of
the Upanishadic revelation. It is on this commentary that his
fame as a scholastic philosopher rests. Some of his contentions
are said to be unanswerable. Ramanuja died in A.D. 1137—if
the records can be believed—at the age of one hundred and
twenty years.

-7-

In his great commentary, Ramanuja opposed Shankara in
maintaining that the Supreme Being is a personal God possessed
of attributes. In his view, God, the universe, and souls constitute an interrelated, indivisible whole: all of them are
equally real. The illustration is given of a mango fruit. Though
the skin, flesh, seed, color, and taste differ, it is the aggregate
of all these elements that is regarded as a mango. For
Ramanuja, souls and the physical universe are ''modes'' of
God, who is the indwelling presence, the Inner Controller. As
it is declared in the *Brihadaranyaka Upanishad*: ''He who
inhabits the intellect, yet is within the intellect, whom the
intellect does not know, whose body the intellect is, and who
controls the intellect from within—he is your Self, the Inner
Controller, the Immortal. . . . He is never seen, but is the Seer;
he is never heard, but is the Hearer; he is never thought of,
but is the Thinker; he is never known, but is the Knower. . . .
He is your Self, the Inner Controller, the Immortal. Everything
else . . . is perishable.''

God is, as it were, the Cosmic Soul, and the universe and
individual souls make up his body. Though matter and souls are
intimately related to him, even in the final state of liberation

from ignorance the distinction between God and the worshiper remains. There is no state where the distinction disappears. This is not to say that the relationship is not an extremely close one; but it is a relationship of "identity and difference." Individual souls, too, remain eternally distinct from each other. The ignorance of the soul about its relation to God is due to a contraction of consciousness, and its final communion with him results from expansion of this same consciousness. Thus, though the soul ultimately enjoys intimate communion with God, it is not merely Atman within him—or Christ within him, as certain Christians might be tempted to say—that enjoys the communion. The mysterious "difference" that accompanies his identity with the Lord saves the soul from being swallowed up in him.

According to Ramanuja, God appears in five aspects. He is the Supreme Lord, Satchidananda, whose nature is absolute being, awareness, and joy. He assumes various forms for the sake of creation, worship on the part of his devotees, and so on. He descends in the form of *avataras*, manifestations of himself in human or other forms. He lives in a man's heart as his most intimate friend. And he abides, too, in consecrated images. The direct means of attaining communion with God are whole-souled love and complete self-surrender, *prapatti*.

Since Ramanuja, like Shankara before him, started with the Vedas as his infallible authority, he believed in the cyclic evolution and involution of the universe and accepted the idea of *karma* (cause and effect) and rebirth for the individual soul. The physical creation comes into being, through the will of God, out of a preexisting rudimentary, unmanifested matter. Matter in this state is considered the "potency" of God. Ramanuja's answer to the question of why God thus creates the universe is that it is created in sport, *lila*, since he obviously needs nothing besides himself for self-fulfillment.

In the Bhagavad Gita, after speaking of the cosmic cycles of evolution and involution as the "day" and "night" of the Creator, or Brahma (to be distinguished from Brahman, ultimate reality), the Lord Krishna speaks of himself as ultimate reality. "Beyond this unmanifested [night of Brahma]," he says, "there is yet another unmanifested Eternal Being, who does not perish when all beings perish. This Unmanifested is called the Imperishable; it is said to be the Ultimate Goal, from which those who reach it never come back. That is my Supreme Abode." Here the obvious meaning of the text strongly supports the view of Ramanuja, and of Chaitanya later, that ultimate reality is a personal God. In view of this fact, I think we can safely say that these two great saints and thinkers came as close to the Christian experience of ultimate reality as any Hindu mystic before the modern period.

Another important theistic philosopher, Madhva, went a step farther. Madhvacharya is his full name, and he lived from A.D. 1199 to 1278. He held that the distinction between God, soul, and universe is eternally real. In his view, God alone exists, absolutely and independently; the physical universe and souls completely depend on him. Madhva, like Shankara and Ramanuja, believed the Vedas were divinely revealed. Though he therefore spoke of God as one and without a second (in the sense of his being without parallel), his school is generally known as Dualistic Vedanta. The founders of all three schools, in using the phrase "one and without a second," *ekamadvitiyam*, indicate that the oneness of God is not a numerical oneness. By calling him "one," scholastic philosophers do not imply anything quantitative about him. For devotional mystics, the phrase indicates that God is unique.

In every sect where a personal God is worshiped, he is conceived as Lord of the universe. He may be formless yet endowed with attributes (as in the theological conception of the Cosmic Mind, or Ishvara) or may possess form as well as attributes (as in such aspects of Deity as Vishnu, Shiva, Kali, Rama, Krishna, and so on). Besides being the basis of existence, present everywhere and full of compassion, God is said by worshipers of Vishnu to be possessed of six "treasures": infinite riches, glory, power, splendor, knowledge, and renunciation. Through his grace the soul is eventually joined to him in loving, eternal relationship.

A work that embodies the inner spirit of the Hindu version of the voice of devotional self-giving is the *Aphorisms on Divine Love*, or *Bhakti Sutras*, of Narada. Among the many personages mentioned in the epics and the Puranas, Narada is one of the more conspicuous. He is there designated a "divine sage," or *devarshi*. In all likelihood this treatise is the work of an author who, wishing to give his work greater authority, ascribed it to the renowned sage. (We observed the same phenomenon in the works of the Pseudo-Dionysius.) The treatise contains eighty-four terse sayings written in the spare style chosen by Indian authors of *sutras* so they might be easily memorized. Out of the Puranic stories of Krishna, the author who calls himself Narada has derived some of the basic principles of the voice of devotional self-giving. The work appears to have had a profound influence on subsequent thinking in India about devotion to God.

Here are some of the key aphorisms:

"The nature of divine love is that of extreme devotion to someone. It is undying. Obtaining it a man becomes perfect, immortal, and perfectly satisfied. And after obtaining it he desires nothing else, never grieves or feels hatred, takes no delight in the objects of the senses, and makes no effort [on his own behalf]. . . . The sage Vyasa says that love means devotion to ritual worship. Garga says it means devotion to hearing [about Atman]. Sandilya says it means an unbroken awareness of the Universal Self in [one's own self]. But Narada says it means surrendering all activities to God and feeling the greatest misery in forgetting God. It is indeed so—as with the cowherd girls of Vrindavan. . . .

"Love is superior to activity, knowledge, or Yoga. This is because love is its own end. . . . Love alone, therefore, is to be embraced by those who seek liberation. . . . Here is how teachers list the means to attain love: You must give up sense objects and the company of the worldly, cultivate unbroken devotion to the Lord, repeat and listen to praise of the Lord. But most important, you must obtain the compassion of a great soul or the gift of a spark of the divine mercy. . . .

"The nature of the highest love is inexpressible—as is the taste of something a dumb man has eaten. . . . Having obtained love, a man sees that alone, hears that alone, speaks of that alone, thinks of that alone. . . . The way of love is easier than other methods. Being self-evident, love does not depend on any other truths. . . . One should surrender all activities to the Lord, turning even one's passion, wrath, and pride toward him. . . .

"Among [lovers of God] no distinction is to be made of caste, learning, beauty, birth, wealth, occupation. For they are his alone. . . . Noninjury, truthfulness, purity, mercy, affirming of the truths of scripture—these are virtues to be observed. The Lord is to be worshiped with full concentration and without anxiety. . . . The one love assumes eleven modes: attachment to the Lord through his glory, through beauty, through worship, [through remembrance,] as a servant, as a friend, as a child, as a beloved, through self-sacrifice, through identification, through misery in separation. . . .

"He who believes and reveres this teaching given by Narada, at the command of Shiva, becomes possessed of love; he wins the Most Beloved."

We find here not only the gist of much of the later devotional tradition, but an attempt to reconcile sectarian differences through attribution to Shiva of the command to transmit a teaching couched in terms characteristic of the worship of Vishnu. The work may thus be a product of the period when the two great sects of Shaivites and Vaishnavites had reached their greatest influence.

-8-

The devotional aspect of Hinduism is not confined to the examples of Ramanuja, Madhva, and the poet-saints we have considered. Highly significant also are the theistic schools of Shaiva Siddhanta and Tantra, which probably reached their full development slightly after the time of Ramanuja.

The school of the Shaiva Siddhanta centers around Shiva as ultimate reality. Though it produced its own scriptures, or Agamas, it finds its roots in ancient beliefs. Immediately derived from the tradition growing out of the hymns of the saintly Nayanmars, all of whom worshiped Shiva, this school appears to have become consolidated between the eleventh and fifteenth centuries. Professing to embody the true meaning of the Vedas, it claims to be the "absolute intellectual finality." That is to say, it considers itself the final goal of religious striving, to which other schools are preliminary, if sometimes necessary steps. In making this claim, it comes close to the Nondualistic Vedanta of Shankara, as it does in a number of other respects. But it differs decisively from the latter in finding its ultimate reality in a personal God.

In the Puranas, the concept of sacrifice is associated with Shiva, as it was in the Vedas with the Supreme Person, the Purusha. It is told that, at the churning of the primeval ocean of milk by the gods, the various deities appropriated the nectar of immortality and other beautiful and desirable objects that emerged from the churning. But when, suddenly, a dreadful mass of blue-black poison appeared, the only one who was willing to drink it and save the others was Shiva. As he was swallowing it, his wife, Parvati, seized his throat to keep it from reaching his stomach. As a result his throat became blue, and hence he is called Nilakantha, the "Blue-Throated One."

The various categories the Shaiva Siddhanta philosophy distinguishes are not unlike those in the other devotional schools. They include a Supreme Being, Shiva; an individual soul; a primordial rudimentary matter as the basis of the phenomenal world; an ignorance that hinders the soul from realizing communion with the Supreme Being. Like the others, this philosophy presumes the existence of an accumulation of merits and demerits (i.e., the results of *karma*) in this and previous lives, which brings about future births and future pleasure and suffering. The material world and the human body are means for purifying the soul. Shiva's nature is love, and through his grace the soul is released by stages from its bondage to ignorance. Finally, purified and enlightened, it enters into communion with Shiva, sharing his nature and yet distinct from him.

In many ways similar to Shaiva Siddhanta is the system of Tantra, another great devotional school, which also developed fully, in all likelihood, after the period of the Puranas. The Tantra scriptures, or Agamas, refer to their Vedic origin. Central to Tantra is worship of the Divine Mother, or Shakti.

Tantra conceives ultimate reality to be Satchidananda, being-awareness-joy absolute, just as Shankara's Nondualistic Vedanta does. But its teachings enlarge on the austere position of this school and in many ways approach not only those of the Shaiva system (which finally absorbed much of the sect) but those of Vaishnavism. For Tantra the Creative Power of God, which in Shankara's system is called *maya* and given a secondary position, is inseparable from God. It thus celebrates the Deity as Shiva-Shakti. For this school, too, the individual soul is real, and here it approaches the teaching of the other devotional schools. Yet it differs from them in holding, with Shankara, that ultimately the soul becomes indistinguishably one with God.

In becoming one with God, however, the soul does not escape from an "unreal" world, for, as we have just seen, Tantra makes the positive statement that Shakti, the Creative Power of God, and God himself, that is to say, Shiva, are indistinguishable. Here the realization of Tantra parallels that of the profoundest mysticism in all religions. Mature saints and mystics in all parts of the world—Christians, Buddhists, Hindus, Jews, Muslim Sufis, original Taoists, followers of Zen—in devoting their lives to others bear witness, through their apparent sacrifice of "truth," that there is a truth beyond truth. And that truth beyond, it seems to me, is that it is the very nature of the Father, Nirvana, Brahman, Vishnu, Shiva, Yahweh, Allah, and of the Void, to be neither part of time nor apart from time. As the great Sufi Jalal al-Din Rumi said: "I have put duality away. I have seen that the two worlds are one." But this truth beyond truth is to be realized through seeking first the knowledge of reality as one's own tradition conceives it.

While the soul remains in the worldly state, Tantra says, it is turned away from reality, being bound to the objects of sense by the "fetters" of attachment. The purpose of Tantric discipline is to convert these very fetters into a means for the soul's release from the ignorance that veils reality. This release is effected not by asking the soul to avoid sense pleasures, but once it is sufficiently disciplined, to gradually sublimate desire through relating it in every instance to Shiva-Shakti, the Deity. At a certain stage in the soul's training, it is allowed the controlled use of wine and sexual enjoyment. Aspirants of the highest type rise above the use of external aids to stimulating their devotion to God. The ritual of this sect has strongly influenced modern devotional worship in Bengal and several other parts of India, and its practices have had a strong influence on Tibetan Buddhism.

One of the positive results of Tantric practice (when it is carried out as originally designed) is a profound respect for woman as the embodiment of the Divine Shakti. Another is ability to face the terrible in life as a manifestation of Deity—somewhat as the Old Testament prophets understood it. Its significance in stressing the concept of God as Mother can hardly be overestimated. The system of Tantra actually represents a grand synthesis of the ideas of all the various Hindu schools, nondualistic as well as devotional and Yogic.

An ardent worshiper of the Divine Mother Kali was the remarkable Bengali poet-saint Ramprasad, who lived from 1718 to 1775. To Kali he poured out his heart in songs that, at least in translation, equal in intensity and expressiveness those of the great South Indian Alvars and Nayanmars, devotees of Vishnu and Shiva, and of the lovers of Krishna and Rama who followed them. It was through Ramprasad's songs that Ramakrishna, during his devotional disciplines a century later, gave vent to his own superabundant feelings. Here is a song in his tradition:

In dense darkness, O Mother, sparkles thy formless beauty;
Therefore the yogis meditate in a dark mountain cave.
On the lap of boundless dark, by Mahanirvana's waves
  upborne,
Peace flows, serene and inexhaustible.

Taking the form of the Void, in the robe of darkness
  wrapped,
Who art thou, Mother, seated alone in the shrine of *samadhi?*
From the lotus of thy fear-scattering feet flash thy love's
  lightnings;
Thy spirit face shines forth with laughter terrible and loud.

After the various devotional movements we have been discussing, the most notable spiritual development in India was the
appearance in Bengal and Orissa, during the early sixteenth
century, of a new type of worship of Krishna. This school formed
about Krishna Chaitanya, a saint who lived from A.D. 1486 to
1534 and in some respects resembles St. Francis of Assisi.
Chaitanya, like Ramanuja before him, argued persuasively
against the philosophical conclusions of Shankara. So far as I
can judge, his thinking is a logical extension of Ramanuja's,
but his mission of spreading the message of love gave him no
time to construct a philosophical system. It was his disciples
who recorded his thoughts in systematic form—perhaps in
consultation with him. We shall take note of them later on.

The attitude of the followers of all these Hindu devotional
schools toward each other's beliefs is an oddly familiar one.
Christians schooled in the conviction that theirs is a unique
revelation, fulfilling and including whatever is true in the
aspiration of other faiths, draw strength from that conviction.
They are not alone in their certainty.

According to worshipers of Shiva, it is through the Lord
Shiva's grace alone that the individual attains salvation. Their
philosophers have called their school of religious philosophy the
Shaiva Siddhanta, which, as we saw, means the ''complete intellectual finality.'' They, quite as much as the followers of
Shankara's Nondualistic Vedanta, hold their dogma to be the
fulfillment of all other schools—some of which, however, may
be necessary steps toward the goal they envisage. Again, worshipers of the Lord Vishnu through the medium of Chaitanya
have declared that the Brahman, or ultimate reality, spoken of
in the Upanishads is nothing but the ''dazzling halo of the

divine body" of their Lord Krishna Chaitanya, whose presence as the Self in the hearts of human beings is only a partial manifestation of his reality. Followers of Tantra, devoted to Shakti, the Divine Mother of the universe, have declared that in her womb is enfolded the Brahman of the Vedantic non-dualists. In a sixteenth-century version of the *Ramayana,* by the poet-saint Tulsidas, is found the story of a crow who, having displeased the Lord Rama, flees from him throughout the universe—only to discover, when at last caught and swallowed by Rama, that he is back again at his own nest.

Perhaps the Hindu devotional scholastic philosophers have been partly responsible for this self-assurance; perhaps the tendency is strengthened by an emotional approach to reality. Whatever the case, sectarianism seems to flourish most among those who stress the voice of devotional self-giving over the other voices. Not all such persons, however, succumb to the temptation to exalt their own belief. If Ramanuja and Chaitanya appear to have stressed the supremacy of their own approach over that of the nondualist Shankara, throughout the history of the Hindu devotional sects saints have been at pains to show that there was really no difference between Vishnu and Shiva.

Speaking generally, we may hazard a guess that those Hindus who have merely inherited a devotional faith by accident of birth are more prone to claim theirs to be a unique revelation. Those who have actually experienced communion with the personal God, on the other hand, may be willing to grant, when they come to know of the revelations of other devotional sects, that the source of those revelations, wherever they are true, is one and the same. Such an attitude would be in complete harmony with the declaration in the Rig-Veda, first made perhaps in advance of 1000 B.C., "Truth is one: the sages give it differing names."

-9-

We have noted that the devotional schools include ritualistic worship of the Deity in images as one of the means available to the devout to achieve communion with God. Such worship is generally referred to when people speak of "popular Hinduism." Yet those adept in the philosophy of the various schools, devotional and even nondevotional, accept the validity of such rituals in a spirit unknown to Christians outside the Orthodox and Roman communions. In Hinduism, old sacraments are not discarded simply because of the advent of new trends. Hindus seem to have realized that there must be a way for every type of individual; even intellectuals may have moods in which the devotional approach best meets their needs. Hindu ritualism, in its several forms, preserves many ancient elements.

In temple rituals God is even today treated, literally, as a cherished guest or (in the larger temples) as a great king or queen, and is offered all the devoted service that would normally be tendered such a personage. Ceremonies are generally performed three times a day—at dawn, midday, and dusk—and are infinitely more complicated than even a Roman Catholic high mass in the days before simplicity became the rule. The rites include (among other details too numerous to list) the sprinkling of water by the priest to remove obstacles; thinking of being surrounded by a wall of fire to keep off evil influences; practice of breath control; offering of the priest's heart as a seat for the Deity; invocation of the Deity's presence in the image; offering of water for rinsing the mouth, water for bathing, fragrant sandalwood paste, flowers, incense, a flame (all these last six items being waved before the image); fanning with a yak-tail fan; making fruit offerings (sometimes cooked food as well); again offering water for drinking and rinsing the mouth. Along with all this go frequent repetition of sacred formulas, or *mantras,* periods of meditation, and at stated times the ringing of a bell. There are many variations for special occasions.

At the conclusion of the ceremony the priest surrenders to God the merits earned through the worship. He then withdraws into his heart the Spirit he has invoked in the image. Sometimes, at the end of a special worship, the image, if made of clay, is cast into a stream or a pond to indicate that after the worship it is no more sacred than any other material object.

Worshipers of Vishnu or of the Divine Mother perform the rituals before one of the many forms of those expressions of Deity. (In temples, the god is wakened in the morning, given a siesta in the afternoon, and put to bed at night.) Worshipers of Shiva perform their ritual before the usual emblem of Shiva, sometimes phallic in design, though often—as originally, some claim—of a purely abstract oval shape. It should be noted that there is no rule requiring Hindus to attend the worship in temples. Whether they attend or not, worship continues at stated times, and devotees may participate according as they feel the need.

Some years ago, I myself experienced the power of images and image worship in an unexpected way. With a few friends I was allowed to worship, as a Hindu, in a temple, perhaps the most sacred in all India, where no non-Indian had been permitted to worship before.

Because of painful memories of disrespect and desecration during the thousand years of alien rule, Hindu priests up till then had been unwilling to risk admitting foreigners into the innermost shrines of their most sacred places of worship, even if they professed the Hindu faith. Westerners had, it is true, been smuggled into shrines on occasion in disguise. But it is impossible to entertain a devotional mood—without which one cannot absorb what Hindu temples have to offer—when liable any moment to be discovered and given a thrashing. Now, happily, several American friends and I were officially admitted into that last refuge of orthodoxy, the Temple of Jagannath at Puri.

The Lord Jagannath is an aspect of Vishnu, Sustainer of the universe. Some hold that he is Vishnu in his totality. The representation on the altar is actually three images, identified, from right to left, as Krishna, his sister Subhadra, and his brother Balarama. The image said to be that of Krishna is the one spoken of as Lord Jagannath.

The temple constructed for his worship in Puri is of the style of architecture typical in Orissa state: a large prayer hall is backed by a giant tower, which rises over the shrine and is topped by a disk-like horizontal slab of stone suggestive of the discus, or *chakra,* one of the emblems of Vishnu. (Since this part of the country was conquered several centuries before the Christian era by the Emperor Ashoka, who after the slaughter was converted to Buddhism and thereafter never took the life of any living thing, one is also reminded of the Wheel of the Law, the *dhammachakra,* of Buddhism.) About this central group are many shrines to other gods and goddesses, making the place a true city of the gods.

The main temple is adorned on the outside with all manner of sculptures, many of them depicting the physical union of male and female figures. Such temples, built in the eleventh or twelfth century, are said to represent the world: on the material level, symbolized by the outer structure, are to be found innumerable sensual enjoyments, but at the core, represented by the innermost shrine, all is bare—since nothing can be said of the ineffable Godhead, at the heart of the world. Others hold that the frankly sexual images are themselves symbolic of the union of the soul with God.

The temple as it now stands has been in continuous use since about the eleventh century. It is said to have been erected on the site of a still earlier structure. Some believe the original temple was Buddhist because of the unusual fact that in the present one caste rules are not recognized. It is customary here for the pious to purchase food offered to the Deity in the prayer hall. A brahmin preparing to eat of this sanctified food may not object even if a low-caste man takes and eats something from his plate. Every three years, moreover, the three images are completely renewed. At this time, it is said, certain objects contained within them are transferred to the new images. There are scholars who have conjectured that these are relics of the Buddha. They surmise that the images once represented the Buddha, the *Dhamma* (*the Law*), and the *Sangha* (the Brotherhood)— the "Triple Gem" of Buddhism.

Our entry into the temple on February 4, 1959, marked a milestone in the religious annals of orthodox Hinduism. The *Amrita Bazar Patrika,* a Calcutta newspaper, announced the event with large headlines: "RIGID TRADITION OF PURI JAGAN-NATH TEMPLE BROKEN—3 U.S. Devotees of New York Rama-krishna Mission Center Allowed Entry." This is how it happened. Just two days before, Swami Nikhilananda, with whom we were traveling, requested certain high officials of Puri to ask the young Raja, custodian of the temple, to allow us to enter the temple. The Raja convened a meeting of *pandits* in the convocation hall of the temple to make a decision. A few of them argued that only someone born a Hindu could enter, not a convert from another faith. But the majority agreed that any-one who believed in Hinduism and followed its precepts was a Hindu, and the Raja supported this view. Though our dress was not prescribed, we decided to wear Indian dress. I cannot for-get the delighted smile on the face of the Hindu chauffeur of the Orissa state guest-house car when he learned of our good fortune.

With mingled feelings of hesitancy and anticipation I walked barefoot up the great flight of twenty-two steps leading from the square outside the temple into the temple precincts—steps made of huge gray slabs of stone laid between high walls.

Everything around us gave an impression of immense yet living antiquity. Twilight was slowly falling, and the great courtyard became a place of mystery. Wherever one looked were stately lines and sculptured figures that, had we not been intent on reaching the shrine, would have commanded rapt attention because of their artistry.

In the wake of several orange-robed swamis we circled the various subsidiary shrines ringing the main temple, above which loomed the tall central tower. At last we reached a wide flight of steps leading toward the great prayer hall. As we passed into the hall we had our first electrifying glimpse of the distant, round-eyed images—a sight made all the more impressive because of the utter starkness of the bare black stone that formed the walls. Since no worship was in progress, not many people were in the hall. Before proceeding toward the shrine, we turned to see the place where, four and a half centuries earlier, the saint Krishna Chaitanya had stood, day after day, contemplating the Lord Jagannath. He had preferred to look from this far corner, we were told, so as not to inconvenience other worshipers. "Be humbler and more modest than the grass. Show respect to others without expecting any in return," Chaitanya had told his disciples. Then we passed forward as far as we could, to a place in front of the shrine where a barrier kept worshipers from entering it. Here we gazed for some time at the images and made offerings of flowers. This visit, however, was only a foretaste of what was to come.

Much later that same evening, about ten o'clock, we again entered the temple precincts. This time we went straight to the barrier before the innermost shrine. There was now a large throng of worshipers, since the offering of food was still to be made. The thick darkness of the great unadorned prayer hall was relieved only by small flares of floating-wick lamps in niches high on the walls. In the shrine, priests were waving lights before the images. At intervals one heard the ringing of a small bell. Now and again the stillness was broken by loud cries of assisting priests warning worshipers not to obstruct the passage between the altar and the round platform, or *stamba,* at the far end of the hall, where the food offerings were made. (It is the belief of the faithful that a ray of light emanates from the eyes of the images and enables them to enjoy the offerings of food.)

The huge figures on the altar stood watching the whole scene, very much alive. At last, after the floor had been cleansed with water, a priest summoned us and we passed barefoot into the innermost shrine over the washed stone.

In their abstract, archaic simplicity, the three round-eyed images of Krishna, Subhadra, and Balarama, resting upon a broad, rectangular altar, pierce the beholder with an unforgettable sense of the all-seeingness of Deity. Reason steps aside and only awe remains. Here is how I expressed my reaction in my diary, which I reproduce unedited: "A feeling of primeval power. All the force of the unknown, the subterranean, the creative and destructive, the magic, the ultimately directing power behind the manifested world. The essence of mystery. The mover of the world, who could grant anything. The core of Hinduism. The core of the creation."

Part of the impressiveness of the three images lies, certainly, in their unrealistic, abstract quality. They have neither hands nor feet. The story is told that the famous artist commissioned to make the original images agreed to do so on condition that no one should observe him at work till they were completed. But the king who had commissioned him, impatient when the work took longer than expected and unable to control his curiosity, burst in upon the artist—whereupon he stopped work and left the images as they are.

To have received the gaze of the Lord Jagannath is to have understood the power of an inspired image to lift thought beyond the sphere of names and forms. One is in the presence of something that transcends this world, something to which the images bear imperfect—and yet startling—witness. In a poem I wrote afterward, I expressed some of the awe one feels when one bows before that fantastic, overwhelming presence and searches one's soul:

BEFORE THE LORD JAGANNATH

As I lift myself to your face, O unconquerable
Fire, the darkness and the dark stone that
Shelteringly surround me, and the high
Stillness of your inviolable home,
Melt into the one Presence that lives in your
Face, that is in your look, that is the
Light at the core of your imperious flaming.

And in the unsaid thankfulness that
Wraps me, holds me in my watchful place,
I know henceforth I shall be here always:

No matter where I am taken, still some hidden
Part of me will be standing in this corner,
Lifting myself up to the insatiable hunger
That haunts your great round inescapable eyes.

We bowed before the plain altar and in silence walked, from left to right, around the three awesome figures. As benediction we received a touch of the flame that had been ceremonially waved in front of the Lord Jagannath in the worship just concluded. When we made our individual offerings before leaving the shrine, the attending priest quietly spoke into my ear. "We are happy," he said.

Now we threaded our way out, bewildered, awed, satisfied, through the crowds of worshipers in the prayer hall, past the shrines of the gods and goddesses, to the tall, steep steps and the gate, and the now deserted square from which we had entered.

-10-

The three Puranic aspects of Deity, Brahma, Vishnu, and Shiva—Creator, Sustainer, and Dissolver of the universe—have been likened by certain Western scholars, not very aptly I think, to the Christian Trinity. In the first place, Brahma is no longer worshiped in India as Creator, except in one unimportant temple; Vishnu and Shiva have been accorded the title of Creator by their respective worshipers. More important, as we have seen, another satisfying parallel is to be found in the concept of Satchidananda. But one member of this triad, the Lord Vishnu, provides a second and far closer parallel with Christine doctrine. This similarity, perhaps the most striking of all between Hinduism and Christianity, has in the past created a certain disagreement between followers of the two religions, but in time it may become a source of mutual understanding.

We have more than once had occasion to refer, in passing, to the concept of the *avatara,* or descent of Vishnu, a term sometimes translated by Hindus as "incarnation of God." Vishnu is conceived, in some of the Puranas, to have embodied himself, in his function of Sustainer of the universe, in nine creaturely forms. They are listed in a strangely evolutionary series. About each of them is recorded an elaborate history. The series of *avataras* begins with a fish, a tortoise, a boar, a centaur-like man-lion, a pigmy-like dwarf, and a primitive warrior; it continues with the hero-king Rama, Balarama (or, sometimes, Krishna), and—in a stroke of religious diplomacy—the Lord Buddha. Krishna himself is often not included in this widely accepted listing. According to devout followers, as well as the Bhagavad Gita, he is Vishnu in his totality, the One who bodies himself forth as an *avatara* from age to age. The conception of the *avatara*, the descent of God on earth, has remained a living part of popular Hinduism to the present day.

The final *avatara* will be Kalki, who will come riding an apocalyptic white horse for the destruction of the world and its return to an age of purity. This concept, which in Vaishnavism takes the place of the idea in Shaivism of Shiva as Dissolver of the universe, finds a strange parallel in the vision of John in Revelation: "Then I saw heaven opened, and behold, a white horse! He who sat upon it is called Faithful and True, and in righteousness he judges and makes war. His eyes are like a flame of fire, and on his head are many diadems; and he has a name inscribed which no one knows but himself. . . . From his mouth issues a sharp sword with which to smite the nations, and he will rule them with a rod of iron; he will tread the wine press of the fury of the wrath of God the Almighty." It is to be noted that in the list of *avataras* Kalki is the tenth.

In Hindu tradition, the number ten is an indication of a number exceeding measure; hence in the very list itself is implicit a statement made by Chaitanya to the effect that there could be any number of *avataras*. This point, of which many Western Christian commentators are, I believe, not yet aware, allows for the possibility of a development in the concept of the *avatara* that the classical list of ten might appear to exclude. The *avataras* are generally held by Christian scholars in the West to be "appearances" of God, who only go through their human experiences in the sense of playing a role. These scholars would seem to tie the concept in with the early heresy of Docetism, which held that Jesus Christ had only an apparent body, that he had no true humanity, that he did not really suffer on the cross, and so on.

One might plausibly argue that the traditional human *avataras* of Vishnu were merely appearances of God and that as mythological figures they never were fully human. (The Buddha should be excluded from consideration because he removed himself from the argument by saying he was not God.) At the same time, in their lives as they are recorded, these same *avataras* seem to have suffered all the experiences men have to endure—excepting only the act of sinning. On the other hand, the human *avataras* who came later are indisputably historical beings. To a non-Christian the only real difference between the *avataras* after the Buddha and the Christian Incarnation of the Word appears to be the Christian claim of uniqueness for Jesus Christ. In modern India, in fact, Jesus himself is held to be an *avatara* of Vishnu.

For Christians the dogma of Jesus Christ's uniqueness carries with it further implications. In Christian belief, Jesus is not simply the appearance of a mythical God in human form. He possesses a true human nature that knows the meaning of love, fellow feeling, and grief, and that suffers and dies. At a critical moment in the history of God's people he enters into the world to authenticate human history and human nature. He is not in any sense the God of an ancient mythology, but is "the Creator of heaven and earth, the author of the moral law, the Judge of the living and the dead."

A believing Hindu will find difficulties with this Christian claim. It would be impossible for him to grant that whereas the Incarnation of the Word was the Creator of heaven and earth, the descents of Vishnu were not. And even were he willing to grant—which he is not—that the legendary descents of Vishnu in human form were merely appearances of a mythical God, he would certainly not be able to understand how the Judeo-Christian God, in his beginnings, was any less a "myth" than his own. For him the living God of his Hindu faith—who, he believes, answers prayer and bestows grace—is no less the Creator of the universe than the Christians' God. Indeed, the two conceptions refer to one and the same reality. Obviously, Christians have not convinced him there is any real difference between the Incarnation and his own *avataras*.

Hindus and Buddhists in general, being without a sense of the unique importance of human history as an unrepeatable phenomenon leading to a predetermined end, do not perhaps appreciate the historical aspect of the Christian argument in support of the Incarnation. Aside from revelation, it is the linear quality of the Christian view of history (which seems to have carried over, too, into the popular conception of heaven as an eternity in time) that makes only one Incarnation necessary. If history is unrepeatable, a Christian may argue, it is enough that God sacrifice himself only once for the redemption of mankind; and this being so, it is then up to men to take advantage of that sacrifice. If, however, history is cyclical, as Hindus and Buddhists believe, and the purpose of history itself is to afford means of liberation to all men, then a series of *avataras* to restore to men a sense of their true purpose is quite thinkable. Any argument from revelation hardly enters in here, since both parties can fall back on their own revelation.

One wonders sometimes whether Christians might come to see the mission of the Hindu *avataras* as somehow analogous to that of the great saints as understood in Roman Catholicism: channels through which the grace of Christ can flow to men. Though this interpretation would not satisfy many Hindus, it might prepare Christians to approach Eastern religions in a more receptive way. At all events, a lesson is to be learned, I believe, by Hindus and Christians alike through studying in conjunction the meaning of the word "unique" as applied to Jesus Christ's Sonship and the meaning of the word "God" (i.e., Vishnu) as used in the Hindu phrase "descent of God."

Here is what the Lord Krishna says about the subject in the Bhagavad Gita:

"Though I am unborn and eternal by nature, and though I am Lord of all beings, yet, subjugating my *Prakriti* [phenomenal aspect or lower nature], I accept birth through my own *maya* [delusive power]. Whenever there is a decline of righteousness and a rise of unrighteousness, I incarnate myself. For the protection of the good, for the destruction of the wicked, and for the establishment of righteousness, I am born in every age." In his commentary Swami Nikhilananda explains: "The Lord is free from ego. His embodiment as a human being is therefore unlike the embodiment of other men [whose past deeds, good and evil, have produced their present body and inclinations]. He assumes a human form, retaining his power over the inscrutable *maya* by which other souls are bound. This *maya* remains as a self-imposed limitation on the Lord as long as he chooses to dwell in a human body. On account of *maya*, he acts like a human being; but it does not affect his nature."

This passage, it is true, seems to substantiate the claim that the *avatara* merely appears like a man. I think further scrutiny of the statement as a whole may reveal that it is the "divine" nature that is spoken of here. The swami's interpretation seems reasonably close to St. Paul's declaration that Jesus Christ was "born in the likeness of men"—except, of course, for the capacity to commit sin. Aside from his being "free from ego" (and therefore being unable to commit sin), the *avatara's* self-imposed limitation—especially as we observe the more recent examples—may indeed make him "fully human." We shall do well to remember Ramakrishna's word on the subject: "God is born as man in every age." On another occasion he said, "No one knows the immensity of the sacrifice God makes in becoming man." He did not say "in becoming like man." If it involved only the semblance of humanity, where would be the sacrifice?

Swami Saradananda, the original biographer of Ramakrishna and one of his close disciples, adds this comment in his monumental work, *Sri Ramakrishna the Great Master*: "As soon as the body and mind of the incarnation [i.e., *avatara*] fully develop, the aim of his life is revealed to him. He then realizes that the sole purpose of his coming is to reestablish religion. . . . When such a want becomes overwhelmingly felt in every part of society, the infinite mercy of the Lord becomes, as it were, crystallized, and he appears as the spiritual teacher of the world."

Perhaps as good a test as any of whether a man may be called an "incarnation" in the Hindu sense is the vitality and persistence of the religious movement growing out of his life. Another, more direct, test is whether during his life on earth he had power to redeem those who seek his help by a mere look or word or touch.

It is entirely possible that, after sustained examination, no significant relation can be found between the Incarnation and the *avatara*. Nevertheless, this is a matter that requires devout and objective study. If Christians could find Christ's working in the *avatara*, a Hindu might ask, who would be the loser?

Whether or not there is anything more than a superficial similarity between these two concepts, there is in Hindu thought, as it happens, a fascinating hint of something closely related to the Incarnation: the doctrine of the Logos. The Hindu concept I refer to is that of the *Sphota*, the eternal Word, from which all sounds (and thus all names and forms) are derived. "I am the syllable *Om* in all the Vedas," says Krishna in the Bhagavad Gita. In his commentary on this sentence, Swami Nikhilananda states that the forms are the outer manifestation "of which the name or idea is the inner essence." Of the *Sphota* it can thus be said, "All things were made through [it]." The primal word that includes all sounds, according to Hindu belief, is the word *Om* (spelled in Sanskrit *Aum*). In the Vedanta philosophy there is an elaborate analysis of its significance. In itself it represents the wisdom contained in

the scriptures, which has existed always and through which
the Lord brings forth the universe. With St. John, Vedantist
Hindus can say, "In the beginning was the Word."

-11-

The parallels between devotional Hinduism and Christianity
are by no means exhausted with the Hindu devotional conceptions of God and "incarnations." In all the devotional schools,
as we have observed, the soul is a real entity, much as it is conceived in Christianity. Its nature is conceived as either similar
to and closely united with God, or as completely different from
and wholly dependent on God. As it performs good or evil
deeds, the pattern of its future life is determined. Its final goal
is to perfect itself, through God's grace, so that it will be able
to live with God eternally in heaven. (In the view of Nondualistic Vedantists of Shankara's school, this heaven comes to an
end at the completion of a "great cycle" of cosmic evolution,
and the soul realizes its identity with ultimate reality. In the
other schools, with the exception of Tantra, heaven appears to
be beyond the realm of cosmic cycles; once there, the soul enjoys
communion with God of a more or less intimate nature in a
timeless eternity.) But before attaining this goal of what
Christians call the beatific vision, the soul may have to pass
through various other experiences, its fate depending on the
degree of purity or egolessness it has achieved in the present
life. Communion with the personal God need not be considered
as something static, it may be added; since God's nature is infinite, there are an infinite number of ways in which he can put
perfected souls to use for the benefit of humanity.

Devotional Hinduism—like Buddhism in its later develop-
ments—includes parallels with the Christian heaven, hell, and
even purgatory. We have just seen that there are eternal
heavens where the soul, once purified of defect through spiritual
discipline and love of God, lives in God's presence in eternal
bliss. There are also lesser heavens where those who have done
"good works" (with a view to earning rewards) go to reap the
inevitable results of those deeds. On the exhaustion of their
merit, such souls return again to earth to continue their experience.

There are even hells to which evildoers must go to reap the inevitable fruit of their evil deeds. Though some strict dualists have affirmed the existence of an eternal hell, others hold that, as with the lesser heavens, no soul will remain indefinitely in hell. When their demerit is paid up, these souls too return to earth to continue their evolution. In this sense there is no specific Last Judgment, as in orthodox Christian belief, in which the soul is singled out to be eternally damned if it is not eternally blessed. In the general Hindu view, as no doubt in the Buddhist, a judgment is going on continuously during the soul's life on earth.

As for the Roman Catholic concept of purgatory, there is what seems to me a real parallel in the concept of *karma* itself. According to this doctrine, as we have seen, the soul suffers in a future life on earth (or in a temporary heaven or hell) according to the good and evil desires and deeds it entertained or performed during its earthly life. Viewed in this light, the temporary hells and heavens may be looked upon as places for purging; for even joys that are temporary are a kind of purgation. All souls, however, will one day realize their true relationship with God (or, in Mahayana Buddhism, their true Buddhahood). It may be noted that no merit or demerit is earned in any heaven or hell: the soul is simply paying up debts or reaping rewards.

The means in popular Hinduism through which the soul's life on earth is guided and brought in touch with God's grace are called "purifying rituals," or *samskaras*. The list includes parallels with the sacraments accepted by Protestant Christianity, and most of those practiced in Roman Catholicism. Among these *samskaras* or quasi-sacraments are birth ceremonies (roughly comparable to baptism), the naming ceremony, offerings to God when the child takes its first food, the "second birth" (comparable to confirmation) when the sacred thread is put on a young man and he is taught a sacred formula for daily repetition known as the Gayatri Mantra, rituals upon completion of school, the marriage ceremony, and the last rites. In addition to these purifying rituals there are prescribed forms of penance, the custom of taking consecrated food (roughly comparable to the Eucharist), and ceremonies on entrance into holy orders.

Though none of these rites corresponds exactly to any of the Christian sacraments, they are similar in spirit. They prompt one to ask whether their source is merely human necessity, or whether one is dealing with divine inspiration. Similar quasi-sacraments were in use in Judaism before the time of Jesus, and a number of comparable ones are today a part of popular Buddhism, both Theravada and Mahayana. Are the Christian sacraments alone instituted by Christ, and the others instituted by man?

The idea of divine grace presents a similar challenge. Here the decision should not be so difficult, since the concept is very much in evidence in all the theistic schools of Hinduism. It is sometimes implied even in the Upanishads, so often taken to be expressions of the voice of intuitive wisdom pure and simple. In the *Shvetashvatara Upanishad*, usually spoken of as the most theistic of these scriptures (though commented upon by Shankara in support of nondualism), it is not surprising to find the prayer: "O Rudra, thou who dwellest in the body and bestowest happiness! Look upon us with that most blessed form of thine, which is auspicious, unterrifying, and all good." (Rudra, the reader may recall, has been equated with Shiva, the austere and forbidding Dissolver of the universe.) But equally impressive appeals occur in earlier Upanishads. Expectation of grace is certainly indicated in the famous prayer in the *Brihadaranyaka Upanishad*: "Lead me from the unreal to the real. From darkness lead me to light. From death lead me to immortality." Even in an already quoted passage about Atman in the *Katha Upanished*, devotional philosophers find evidence of grace: "This Atman . . . is attained by him alone whom it chooses. To such a one Atman reveals its own form." For them the words "whom it chooses" mean (as Swami Nikhilananda has pointed out in his commentary on this verse) "whom the Supreme Lord chooses."

We noted in connection with our earlier discussion of this verse that these words seem to imply a doctrine of election. A believer in the personal God might hold that they are meant to show that divine grace cannot be purchased by mere human effort. Ramakrishna was fond of telling a story to illustrate this fact. Imagine a lovely young child, he would say, seated by a busy roadside. In his lap he is holding a small basket in which are visible a number of priceless gems. Those of the passers-by who are observant stop, from time to time, and beg the child to give them at least one of the gems. But to each of them he turns a deaf ear. Then, suddenly, he sees a man walking far off across the fields, who does not even know he is there. He calls to this man, who finally is attracted by his cries and comes to see what is the matter. The child says to him, "See, I have all these lovely gems. Take them. They are all for you." Such is the mystery, it seems to a saint, of God's grace; he knows he has done nothing to deserve the blessing he receives.

Perhaps the supreme example in all Hindu religious literature is the affirmation of his grace by the Lord Krishna near the end of the Bhagavad Gita: "Fix your heart on me, give your love to me, worship me, bow down before me; so shall you come to me. This is my pledge to you, for you are dear to me. Abandon all duties and come to me alone for shelter. I will deliver you from all sins." The waywardness of the child is only one aspect of God's grace. And even that may be largely an appearance. (The devotee may not think of his pious acts as a form of effort, or again, he may have earned the grace, in the Hindu way of thinking, through good deeds done in a previous life.) One should not try to equate the Christian and Hindu concepts of grace and its working. But their similarity is undeniable. "Take one step toward God, and he will take ten steps toward you," is a common saying in India.

Shaivites, the worshipers of Shiva, do not believe that the Lord "descends" to earth as an *avatara*, but rather that he directly shows his grace, from time to time, to help devotees in distress. A very simple example of this sort of intervention comes to mind. It represents the actual experience of a gentle and devout—and at the same time responsible and well-educated—worshiper of Shiva. The gentleman who told me the story is Mr. K. Ramalingam, of Madras, and he has given me leave to repeat it.

Mr. Ramalingam had made a pilgrimage to Thirupathy, a holy place of pilgrimage in southern India where the Deity is worshiped as Vishnu in an aspect named Venkatachalapathi. (It is further proof of the catholicity of many modern Hindus that this particular shrine was not a shrine of Shiva.) As was the custom at this particular place, before leaving the main temple Mr. Ramalingam made an offering of all the money he had in his pocket, keeping only what was necessary for his return train fare. On completing his visit he proceeded to the railway station and put the money for a ticket to Madras on the counter before the one open ticket window.

"Where are the two annas for pilgrim tax?" the man behind the window asked. Mr. Ramalingam was at a loss. "I didn't know there was a tax," he said. "I offered everything I had at the temple. Can't you give me a ticket anyway?'' ''I'm sorry,'' the man said. ''It's the rule that I cannot issue a ticket before the tax is paid.'' Mr. Ramalingam was quite distressed, since the train was scheduled to arrive in five minutes, and he knew no one in this small town.

While he was wondering what to do, a simple-looking man hurriedly entered the small waiting room. Approaching Mr. Ramalingam, he asked, ''Can you tell me the fare to Thirupathy?'' Mr. Ramalingam looked at him in astonishment. ''Why, *this* is Thirupathy,'' he said. ''How can there be a fare?'' ''Is that so?'' said the man. ''Can you show me on the list?'' Mr. Ramalingam took him over to a large sign hanging on the wall near another ticket window, which was closed. On the sign were listed all the station stops on the line, with the distances to or from Thirupathy and the fares marked opposite them. In the middle, opposite Thirupathy, was a blank space. Mr. Ramalingam pointed this out to the man. ''I see,'' he said. ''Thank you.'' Something on the counter before the closed window caught Mr. Ramalingam's eye. It was a two-anna piece. When he looked around the man was nowhere to be seen.

After telling me the story he said, ''Even if the coin was already there, how can you explain the man's suddenly appearing and asking that strange question?'' Mr. Ramalingam's life, one could see from his gentle appearance and mood of self-surrender, was centered in devotion to the Lord Shiva. It was for this reason, surely, that he could take this curious happening as a direct intervention of God to help a devotee in distress.

''Every smallest incident of life can be a help on the way, if you have an inner desire for spiritual achievement,'' Swami Vedavyasananda had said to my friend Krishna and me at his retreat in Rishikesh. Even those who would insist that this happening was nothing more than a coincidence must agree that it was Mr. Ramalingam's faith, his implicit desire for spiritual achievement, that made it possible for him to interpret it as he did.

All the similarities we have been considering in this chapter between Christianity and Hinduism are, in one way or another, bound up with the voice of devotional self-giving. Some of them may seem exaggerations of the voice or even aberrations from it. But unless Christians wish to say that every form of experience or doctrine or piety that differs from the mainstream of Christian experience or doctrine or piety is false, they will do well to reserve judgment here. Our first duty, in matters like these, is to make sure the meaning of the experiences described and the doctrines spoken of is faithfully conveyed to Westerners by the words that Hindus or others have used to express them. And until we are satisfied we can reject a doctrine or an experience out of hand, we may at least show Christian charity in our judging.

-12-

If I were asked to choose one man in Indian religious history who best represents the pure spirit of devotional self-giving, I would choose the Vaishnavite saint Chaitanya, whose full name in religion was Krishna Chaitanya, or "Krishna-consciousness." Of all the saints in recorded history, East or West, he seems to me the supreme example of a soul carried away on a tide of ecstatic love of God. This extraordinary man, who belongs to the rich period beginning with the end of the fourteenth century, represents the culmination of the devotional schools that grew up around Krishna.

Vishvambara Misra, born in 1486 A.D. in the town of Nadia, Bengal, was the sole remaining comfort of his parents, Jagannath Misra and Sachi Devi. Eight daughters born to them had died, one after another, in infancy, and his older brother, on the eve of marriage, had taken monastic vows and disappeared as a wandering monk. So the boy's mother, instead of sending him to school, kept him at home.

Nimai, as he was affectionately called in the family, had a bent for scholarship. His was a family famous for its learning, and Nadia was a university town. Hence he felt frustrated. The energy he might have devoted to study found expression in other ways. It is said he enjoyed nothing more than teasing pious brahmin scholars. While their eyes were closed in meditation, he sometimes ran away with their images, or he stole their clothes while they bathed in the river. With his friends he robbed mango orchards and played all sorts of mischief.

Though himself a brahmin, and brought up in strict orthodoxy, Nimai even at an early age completely disregarded caste prejudices. One day he took it into his head to sit on a pile of broken cooking pots considered "unclean" by everyone. When reproved by Sachi Devi, his mother, he said· "No impurity can remain in pots in which you have cooked offerings for the Lord Vishnu.'' But he showed his real purpose when he added, ''If you don't send me to school, I will never come down from these 'impure' pots.'' As a result, he was sent to a Sanskrit school in his sixth year.

Thus the Misras' young son entered on the first stage of an orthodox Hindu's life, that of studentship, or *brahmacharya*. Though he still retained his boyish vivacity, he was soon able to argue with learned *pandits* about difficult points in Sanskrit grammar and Hindu logic. While at school, he wrote his own commentary on a famous grammatical treatise. When his father died, however, he had somehow to support his mother and other members of the family, and took up a life of scholarship and teaching.

By the age of twenty Nimai had acquired a reputation as a scholar in his own right. He continued to excel in Sanskrit grammar and the Nyaya system of logic. When he founded an academy of his own, many pupils joined, drawn not only by his brilliant power of exposition but also by his lively nature and his wit. Like the other scholars of Nadia, though observing all the brahminical rites, he became a confirmed intellectual, perhaps even a skeptic. It was still customary for great scholars, as in former days, to travel about the country to establish their supremacy in logic, grammar, rhetoric, and kindred subjects. Several famous scholars from Banaras, following this tradition, visited Nadia for this purpose. Much to their discomfiture he defeated one and all.

At this time Nimai married. Rather contrary to the general custom, he and Lakshmi Devi themselves decided they were meant for each other. It had been a case of love at first sight. His mother, who normally would have initiated the proposal, at first refused to give her consent. But because of her son's entreaties and her own love for him she finally yielded. Thus Nimai entered the second stage of life, householdership, or *garhasthya*. As a result of generous daily entertaining of monks, however, his resources gave out, and he decided to visit East Bengal (now Bangladesh), where his father's family had originally come from. There his discussions with the *pandits* only increased his fame, and he returned with a considerable amount of money.

At last he came home. To his great dismay he found that his wife had died of the bite of a poisonous snake. His mother had wanted him to have a son to carry on the family traditions. Some time later, to please her, he married a second time. The girl's name was Vishnupriya Devi.

A short while after this marriage, Nimai started on foot on a pilgrimage to the holy town of Gaya, where pious Hindus offer oblations of food and drink for the welfare of their ancestors' souls. His visit was, of course, chiefly for the welfare of his father's soul. Here he met and came under the influence of a great Vaishnava teacher, Ishvara Puri, who initiated him into the path of devotion, or *bhakti.* Immediately on meeting the teacher, something moved him to say, "My pilgrimage to Gaya has become fruitful on seeing you." He then added, "Here and now I surrender to you my body and soul. Please grant me love of Lord Krishna." As a result of the initiation and Ishvara Puri's influence, Nimai became intoxicated with love of God. As the consummation of his surge of devotion, it is said, he had a vision of Krishna as a boy playing his flute.

On his return home, Nimai's students and friends found him completely changed. No longer was he the *pandit,* proud of his intellectual achievements, whose chief concern was to confound opponents in debate. In place of arguments about interpretation of texts, logic, and grammar, he began teaching them about spirituality. He spent hours chanting the names and glories of the Lord Krishna and discoursing on divine love. Humbler, now, than the humblest, his face was bathed in tears whenever he spoke of the Lord. "Be patient as a tree," he said, "which never complains even though men break its branches or cut it down. Even so, patiently serve others without expecting anything in return."

Practicing the sort of selfless service he preached, Nimai would go to a nearby river to help the old and infirm with their washing and would carry back their big bundles for them. Once, out of respect for his being a brahmin, someone hesitated to accept his service. "Please don't prevent me," he begged the man. "When I serve you I am serving Krishna. These deeds of service are holiness for me." It was about this time that Advaita Acharya and his group, who were worshipers of Vishnu, accepted him as an ideal type of Vaishnava. New disciples began to gather about him, and some of these he instructed in how to teach about divine love.

One day two notorious ruffians, Jagai and Madhai, waylaid two of Nimai's followers, Nityananda and the Muslim Haridasa. They beat them severely and sought to rob them. But the two devotees' utter freedom from anger and hatred shamed the men into repentance and they begged forgiveness. When Nityananda and Haridasa took the ruffians to their teacher his nature completely won them. They became disciples and adopted a new way of life.

Perhaps even from this time Nimai's followers began to note down his statements, which later grew into a profound system of philosophy centered around love of God. Nimai taught that human reason cannot approach the realm of the Divine Spirit. Only the religious sentiment in man, he said, has power to enter it. In spiritual matters, the Vedas and their explanatory commentary the Puranas are the only evidence. Reason may, however, be accepted as auxiliary evidence when applied to the Vedic revelation.

The Vedas, as Nimai interpreted them, teach the following truths: Hari, the Lord, is one and without a second. He is infinite in power within time and space (being the Creator of both of them); this power of his is not to be distinguished from his Person, and yet its manifestations are exhibited separately. He is an ocean of spiritual ecstasy and the source of man's spiritual feelings: the eternal play of Krishna is revealed when a man's eyes are opened by his grace. Man's soul is a separate part of the Lord, remaining at different degrees of distance from him. Certain souls, having abused their power of free will and forgotten they are servants of his, are caught up in matter. Others are released from matter through contact with a Vaishnava teacher, or *guru*. All phenomena, spiritual and material, are, like God's own power, related to God in an inconceivable simultaneous distinction and nondistinction (*achintya-bhedabedha-prakash*) from him. This last teaching, Vaishnavas hold, explains the seemingly opposed statements of the Upanishads about the identity and difference of the soul and God.

The only means of obtaining the goal of spiritual life, Nimai taught, is divine love. Its chief forms are hearing and chanting the name of the Lord, worship before an image, and serving devotees. The goal itself is *prema,* ecstatic love of Krishna, taking the form of various human relationships to the Lord and gradually leading up to the madness of the beloved for a secret lover. The devotee depends on the Lord Krishna's grace to grant him salvation. According to this school, virtue is not something to be acquired through stern moral discipline, but develops of itself as the soul dedicates itself more and more fully to God.

Nimai's followers held that their Master (who is also loosely

spoken of as an *avatara*) was Krishna himself, come for the completion of his divine sport on earth. There are said to be thirty-
two marks of the "superior person," or *mahapurusha*, recognized in secondary scripture—and derivatively in iconography
and sculpture—as applying to gods and great saints. All these
traits Nimai possessed. He had a long nose, long arms, long
cheeks, eyes, and knees. His skin was tight, not loose, and he
had short hair on the head, and short knuckles, teeth, and body
hair. The corners of his eyes, the soles of his feet, his palms,
palate, cheeks, lips, and nails were rosy. His chest, shoulders,
nails, nose, waist, and face were raised or expanded. He had
unusually short neck, thighs, and penis, and a very broad waist,
forehead, and chest. Finally his navel, voice, and mind were
deep. In addition he had many other bodily marks considered
auspicious.

Nimai wanted to share the truths of the Vaishnava religion
with as many people as possible. It was he who was responsible
for introducing a type of religious play, or *yatra*, among the
people of Bengal, in which the life and meaning of the youthful
Krishna were depicted. He may thus be said to be the father
of the Bengali theater. But besides this, he introduced another
element into contemporary religious life that was to have an
even wider effect. Instead of insisting that his followers observe the complex rituals of orthodox Hindu worship, he began
organizing singing parties in the houses of Vaishnavites. The
songs they sang were called *kirtans*. Stirred by the music, the
devotees would sing and dance to the accompaniment of drum,
cymbals, and the horn-like sound of the conch shell.

Owing to repressive policies of the government, which was at
that period in the control of Muslims, public observances by the
Vaishnavites had been forbidden. The brahmins of "respectable" society in Nadia, being distressed by the noise and excite-
ment created by the *kirtan* parties, and by the fact that even
low-caste persons were welcome to join them and sing with
them, further stirred up the disapproving authorities against
them. As a result, government officers broke up one such religious meeting. Nimai now showed himself to be an innovator in
another sphere, that of civil disobedience.

Spreading word among the whole Vaishnavite community of
the town, he urged every worshiper of Vishnu to have a light
burning at his house on a certain night. He then organized
thousands of demonstrators to go in four large parties to the
dwelling of the Muslim administrator who had been persecuting

them. Headed by himself and his chief disciple, Nityananda, these groups passed through the streets in procession, chanting the Lord's name. Reaching the administrator's house, some of the more ardent Vaishnavites, it is said, started to destroy his garden. But the administrator himself came out, welcomed Nimai civilly, and began to talk with him. Deeply stirred by the fervor that shone in Nimai's eyes and on his face, the Muslim official allowed the procession to proceed and forbade further persecution. He and many of the Muslims later became Nimai's followers. In a sense, at this period the Vaishnavite leader had entered on the third, or meditative, stage of Hindu life, *vanaprastha.*

Not long afterward, Nimai decided he should take the vows of monastic life, or *sannyasa,* the fourth and final stage. From his own words we learn that two considerations underlay the decision. In the first place, his feeling of separation from the Lord Krishna was intensified by family life. In the second, he wanted to teach his followers the need for asceticism in the life of a Vaishnava; for when a person adopts the extreme emotional approach to God there is danger of its degenerating into eroticism. Through a disciple he told his mother and a few others of his decision.

Sachi Devi was naturally distressed. As he was about to leave, however, Nimai clasped her feet with great tenderness and promised to be responsible for her spiritual and worldly welfare. He asked his wife, Vishnupriya, to accept Krishna as her eternal husband, and because she understood the depth of his renunciation she nobly agreed.

Going to the town of Katwa, Nimai received initiation into Vaishnavite monkhood from Keshava Bharati, who gave him the name Krishna Chaitanya, or "Krishna-consciousness." At this time he had planned to visit Vrindavan, the place where Krishna spent his childhood. But a disciple led him, unsuspecting, by another route to a place where his mother was waiting to see him. When he saw her he said, "Mother, I can never be indifferent to you. I shall live wherever you wish. But it is not becoming for a monk to live with his family." She then asked him to make his headquarters the holy town of Puri, in nearby Orissa, where the Temple of Jagannath was located. In that way, she said, she could have news of him and sometimes he could visit her at Nadia.

Krishna Chaitanya now set out on foot for Puri with some of his disciples. During the trip, which lasted a number of days, he visited many temples and fell into frequent spiritual ecstasies. On reaching Puri and seeing the image of Jagannath, he was overwhelmed with love and rushed forward to embrace the image. So deep was his ecstasy that no pulse could be felt and his breathing all but ceased; only at the end of the day did he return to normal consciousness.

After reaching Puri in February of the year 1510, and spending two months there, Chaitanya decided in April to make a long tour of the South—again on foot. The journey took a year and three months. During it he visited many places of pilgrimage and many temples, brought inspiration to thousands of spiritual seekers, and spread the doctrines of Vaishnavism by entering into discussions with Nondualistic Vedantists of Shankara's school and with Buddhists. In these scholarly discussions all his earlier skill in logic and debating were put to good use. The accounts state that he invariably defeated his opponents, who thereupon, as was still the custom, embraced Chaitanya's beliefs. One of his telling points against the Shankarites was the argument that when the Vedas spoke of the "attributeless" Brahman, they were referring to an absence of human qualities. He brought to their attention numerous passages where the reference, unless the texts were manipulated in a highhanded manner, could not be to anything but a personal God. Untold numbers of people received his blessing on this tour.

An interesting incident that took place shortly after Chaitanya's return to Puri was his acceptance of King Pratap Rudra as a disciple. The king had heard of Chaitanya's greatness from his chief scholar, a nondualist who had been converted to Vaishnavism, as well as from his chief minister. He was eager to meet the saint and be made a disciple. But Chaitanya kept him waiting a long time so as to test his sincerity, and also to let people understand he was not seeking the king as a disciple simply because of his position. Finally, after the urgent intervention of a few of his disciples, he agreed to initiate the king into the worship of Krishna.

A trip to Vrindavan proved one of the great satisfactions of Chaitanya's later years, and the pastoral scenes associated with the early life of Krishna constantly filled him with spiritual joy. He later visited Banaras, seat of the most renowned Nondualistic Vedantist philosophers and with great vigor put down their arguments.

When he debated with philosophers, Chaitanya could be as scholarly as the great teachers, or *acharyas,* of old—Shankara,

Ramanuja, and Madhva. We have already noted his conclusions about God and the soul. In his teaching of the path of devotion to the general public, however, he continued to stress utter devotion to the Lord. This devotion was to be developed through hearing and singing the name and glories of Krishna, meditating on his form and attributes and his life on earth, worshiping him in his temples, resigning oneself to his will, trying to do only what would please him, serving his devotees, and showing kindness to all beings.

Chaitanya aroused in his followers a flood of passionate love of God. As a result, a wave of religious fervor swept over Bengal and Orissa. Yet despite the emotionalism his teachings brought about, he himself was extremely strict. He closely watched the morals of those who were around him, sternly reproving any form of self-indulgence. Once he banished a favorite disciple for showing too much attention to a woman disciple. Though literally worshiped by thousands as Krishna himself, he led a simple and even austere life.

Chaitanya delighted intensely in nature. It is said that, like St. Francis of Assisi, he had a miraculous power over wild beasts. His life in the holy town of Puri is the story of a man in a state of almost continuous spiritual intoxication. Illuminating discourses, deep contemplation, moods of loving communion with God, were daily occurrences.

From about April 1516 to the end of his life Chaitanya spent most of his time at Puri. As a result of his extremely austere life, his body became reduced to little more than a skeleton. Now in the mood of the cowherd girl Radha, his feeling of pain at separation from Krishna sometimes became so intense that he was racked with anguish. At one time his disciples found him lying inert, his body so contorted that it seemed all his bones were dislocated. They finally succeeded in bringing him to normal consciousness by repeating the name of Krishna in his ear. "My Krishna disappears," he said, "giving me a glimpse brief as a flash of lightning." At another time, in a state of partial unawareness of the outer world, he plunged into the sea, thinking it to be the river Jamuna at Vrindavan, and was drawn to shore unconscious in a fisherman's net. Finally, one of his disciples was chosen to sleep always in his room to prevent him from doing further harm to himself in a state of spiritual ecstasy. By now his bodily strength was almost totally exhausted because of the energy expended in his spiritual moods.

In the year 1534, at the age of forty-eight, Chaitanya one day slipped away alone to the Temple of Gopinatha—dedicated to Krishna as Lord of the cowherd girls of Vrindavan. While he was inside, the temple doors were shut for the midday siesta. When they opened he was nowhere to be found. The pious have believed since then that Chaitanya was united with the Lord Gopinatha and disappeared into his image.

THE VOICE
OF CONSCIOUS
DISCIPLINE

As I LOOKED BACK on the trip to Gorakhpur, the third episode, our meeting with Bhagwan Dasji at his ashram and our brief glimpse of his white-clad novices sleeping in the dark, spoke to me of the disciplinary side of the spiritual life. In the East, because far more stress has been laid upon experience than upon faith, disciplines have always been recognized as of prime importance. Teachers of spirituality are available, even for laymen, to a degree unheard of in the West, but as they might have been, I imagine, in a society that could produce John the Baptist. Bhagwan Dasji was a man gifted with spiritual power —a power he made me feel with a touch. He had arrived at this state, I had no doubt, by consciously following some one aspect of spiritual discipline for many years. Now he was a teacher, a *guru*, whose instructions if loyally carried out should bear fruit in transformation of character. The very fact of his possessing a certain power was what had drawn his young disciples to him and persuaded them he could lead them to God.

In the chapter on devotional self-giving I quoted the Indian saying "Take one step toward God, and he will take ten steps toward you." I mentioned it there in terms of the ten steps God takes, and called these a symbol of God's grace. Here we shall look at the one step man takes, spiritual discipline, which usually—though not invariably—precedes the descent of grace. It is a subject unfamiliar to most modern Christians, but not less important for that reason. I myself have always tended to suspect that without a carefully chosen course of discipline the spiritual life in any religious tradition hardly deserves the name.

In purely Christian terms, the voice of conscious discipline tells a man that to be a thoroughgoing Christian he must not only hear, but follow, the first two voices. It sounds unmistakably in Jesus' hard teaching, ''Truly, truly, I say to you, unless a grain of wheat falls into the earth and dies, it remains alone; but if it dies, it bears much fruit. He who loves his life loses it, and he who hates his life in this world will keep it for eternal life.'' The passage, however special its application may be, is one that cannot be passed over lightly. Calling the Christian to empty himself through spiritual discipline of self-will and the narrow ego, it promises that he who manages to do so, disregarding the tug of his natural impulses, will live to enjoy the fruit of that emptying, that ''death,'' in this life as well as the life to come. Backing up and amplifying Jesus' statement is St. Paul's magnificent affirmation, ''I have been crucified with Christ; it is no longer I who live, but Christ who lives in me.'' This is the confident claim of a man who has passed through the fire of discipline.

It may be urged that repentance and self-denial are all that is needed, in addition to faith, in order to ''die to Christ.'' This may well be true in certain exceptional instances, where faith is complete, but I believe that generally something more is required. Hearing the voice of devotional self-giving and the voice of intuitive wisdom is, I venture to say, the substance of faith as it is commonly understood and experienced. A Christian may hope, through sincere faith in the message of these two voices, to win the beatific vision after death. But in the present instance Jesus is speaking of a dying in this very life. To this end, spiritual discipline is indicated, for only through calculated inattention to the concerns of the ego is it fully dissolved. To achieve sanctity here and now, a man must implement the message of one or both of the voices with the voice of conscious discipline. If the ''grain of wheat'' of ego is to perish beyond reviving, the Christian virtues must be accompanied by intense prayer, meditation, and (if it is granted) contemplation.

Those Christians who have spoken in terms of the voice of conscious discipline are relatively few. After St. Paul, we know that the Desert Fathers and other ascetics consciously sought to control their minds in prayer and meditation. The several examples best known to me from later times are St. Teresa of Avila, St. John of the Cross, and St. Ignatius Loyola. The writings of all three saints reveal the disciplines by which they curbed their minds and broke through to communion with God. These are naturally couched almost entirely in terms of the way of devotional self-giving; nevertheless the descriptions

of the state of union with God given by St. John of the Cross
(and, as we have seen, by St. Catherine of Genoa) possess overtones of the way of intuitive wisdom.

The core of spiritual discipline, as of any discipline, is training of the will. Its aim is to focus the mind on its objective—in
the present instance, God—to the exclusion of every other
thought. Subjection of the will is no easy task, of course, and
at the start it requires stern effort. Many obstacles, mostly
psychological, obstruct the progress of one practicing spiritual
discipline. It is said in an ancient Hindu scripture that the gods,
to whom men were enjoined to offer sustenance through sacrifices, tried to prevent a person from seeking union with ultimate
reality. For they feared that once he understood their own
subordinate nature, his sacrifices to them would cease! Undoubtedly the statement is an attempt to explain the eruption of
subconscious forces that so frequently discourages those who
embark on serious spiritual discipline.

A poem of mine—perhaps inspired by the tale of Jacob's
wrestling with an "angel," as well as by the Hindu scripture—
suggests the struggle in man between his upward aspiration
and such obstructing forces. (The gods were known in India
as the "shining ones," or *devas*.)

HEARD IN THE NIGHT

Who wrestled with a god on the dark stairs?
For was it not the desperate trample and scuff
Of feet on uneven stone, the lurch of hurled
Bodies and harsh gulp of breaths we caught
Half the night through? And whose was the form
That violently careered down an invisible
Turn and thumped hollow to sprawled silence?

Did the sure-eyed one burn there above,
Looking disdain upon his broken, slumped
Antagonist; or did the other, his beating
Flesh bared through rents in his stained shirt,
Loom unsteady in the exulting air
Over a wreck of pinions and huge limbs?

Once the will is subdued, however, and the mind has achieved
power to focus on its objective, the sense of effort is superseded
by a growing dedication to the goal. To put it differently, effort

becomes second nature. The Bhagavad Gita says there is a satisfaction to be attained through knowledge of truth, renunciation of transient pleasures and attachments, meditation, and absorption of mind. This state, won by the man of balance, it defines as "that in which a man comes to rejoice by practice . . . which is like poison at first but like nectar in the end." It is an apt description of the whole process. At the start the religious student perhaps decides to seek the goal since someone has told him about its worth and he feels he ought to seek it. Because of psychological obstacles or plain tedium, the effort does indeed for a long time seem like "poison." But as his self-control increases, so does his satisfaction. In the fullness of time, as his powers of concentration increase, the seeker's awareness of a perceiving subject and an object of perception is caught up and transfigured in the wholeness of his realization of the goal—just as happens, in everyday life, with all truly creative work or a duty accepted in any field of endeavor.

A twofold principle sums up the essence of conscious discipline: either make the goal the means or make the means the goal. There are some seekers who from the start can concentrate the mind so intently on the goal that all else is forgotten, and in a relatively short time the mind opens out to its full capacity and enjoys the experience of whatever goal is sought. Conversely, there are those who, once having learned of the goal and the means to attain it, forget everything but the means and concentrate on faithfully fulfilling them. The same opening out of the mind takes place in them. (We shall observe at the end of this chapter an example of both methods manifested in a single man.) Success depends not so much on the goal chosen or the means used as on the intensity of concentration.

The self-centeredness that many modern men and women see in spiritual practice is, I believe, only apparent. In the first place, if it is honestly undertaken by a qualified person—not as an escape from worldly obligations but out of a burning desire to know the truth about his relation to God—it requires tremendous courage. If self-centeredness is involved here, it is no more selfish than the intense concentration required of the scholar or the scientific researcher or the artist. And the fruit of successful spiritual practice is of no less benefit to society than these other "monkish" pursuits.

Nowhere in Christian practice, to the best of my knowledge, do we encounter the voice of conscious discipline in isolation. Once again it is to Hinduism that we must turn for an example.

After having studied this voice in its pure state, we shall be in a position to appreciate the special training in discrimination offered in Hinduism on the path of intuitive wisdom and the channeling of emotion in the way of devotional self-giving.

-2-

In religious literature in general we find two sources of instruction about spiritual discipline. The first is moral and spiritual teaching in primary, or canonical, scripture. The second is practical instruction contained in noncanonical scripture and in manuals written by those who had attained higher states of consciousness and wished to share what they knew—especially with those for whom the teaching in canonical scripture was not sufficiently detailed.

In early Buddhism, the sort of instruction usually found in manuals is contained in canonical scripture itself: the Tripitaka. In the second great collection of these teachings of the Buddha, the "collection of discourses," in addition to the intellectual and moral precepts taught in connection with the first five steps of the Noble Eightfold Path, concrete disciplines are laid down in connection with the last three steps: "correct effort," "correct mindfulness," and "correct concentration of mind." In Christianity, aside from some very general instruction in the Gospels about prayer, the only available teaching about spiritual discipline is found in manuals written by such authorities as the saints I have mentioned. No doubt in monasteries a tradition developed that was handed down from spirtual director to student.

In India, spiritual disciplines have been included in a seemingly haphazard manner in canonical scripture; they are found in more or less codified form in the Bhagavad Gita, but aside from this only in later works. It was the Hindu mystics who discovered more than two thousand years ago, no doubt through self-observation during times of intense prayer or thought, that one phenomenon invariably accompanied genuine spirtual illumination. This was what might be called one-pointedness of mind. They therefore assumed that they could obtain higher states of consciousness more easily if they could control their mental processes more efficiently. To control them, they set out to understand them. Thus there developed, gradually, a science of concentration.

The basic treatise in this field is the famous *Aphorisms on Yoga*, or *Yoga Sutras*, by Patanjali. Most of the treatise seems to have been in existence in the second century before Christ. There are also many references to the subject in the Bhagavad Gita. Indeed, there are very specific references to *yoga* in the sense of mental control in the Upanishads themselves. So the subject was familiar in India well before Patanjali's time.

But Patanjali's work is a model for all such treatises. It is, in fact, more detailed than many Indian works of a later period outlining the spiritual disciplines of the way of intuitive wisdom and of devotional self-giving. Its importance lies in the fact that what it recommends may be applied in some form in almost all types of spiritual practice. A study of the methods outlined by Patanjali should be of immense benefit to Christians of a mystical bent of mind and to other Christians who wish to understand, even if they do not practice, the mystical way.

The science of Yoga deals essentially with observation and control of the modifications of the mind, which are designated in the *Yoga Sutras* as *vrittis*. Swami Vivekananda, the well-known disciple of Ramakrishna, wrote a pioneering work, *Raja-Yoga*, based on the findings of Patanjali as corroborated by his own experience. In the introduction he states, "It is comparatively easy to observe facts in the external world, for many instruments have been invented for the purpose; but in the internal world we have no instrument to help us. . . . The science of *raja-yoga* proposes, in the first place, to give us such a means of observing the mental states. The instrument is the mind itself. . . . The same minute observation has to be directed to the internal world which the scientific man directs to the external; and this requires a great deal of practice." Later he adds, "In the study of *raja-yoga* no faith or belief is necessary. Believe nothing until you find it out for yourself— that is what it teaches you." The end result promised is religious faith based not upon the words of another, whether a scripture or a teacher, but upon personal experience.

Vivekananda points out that in undertaking Yogic practices one should observe certain preliminary rules. Only such food should be eaten as leads to a balanced and controlled state of mind: by this he appears to indicate a diet of fruits, nuts, vegetables, and milk products. In India it is thought that one direct result of such a diet is a lessening of sexual desire, which is held to impede perfect control of the mind. When the mind is strong enough, Vivekananda says, and the practice well advanced, one need not be so careful about one's food.

The yogi, the one who practices Yoga, must avoid the extremes of luxury and austerity. In this regard the Bhagavad Gita warns: "Yoga is not for him who eats too much nor for him who eats too little. It is not for him who sleeps too much nor for him who sleeps too little. For him who is temperate in his food and recreation, temperate in his exertion at work, temperate in sleep and waking, yoga puts an end to all sorrow." We are reminded of the Buddha's Middle Way. Extreme self-indulgence, like excessive self-denial, is as unfruitful in the meditative life as it is in the normal life of the world. Vivekananda has also noted that those who wish to seriously practice concentration of mind should be careful about the type of people they associate with.

I would like to stress here that it is not advisable to practice the disciplines of Yoga, or indeed any advanced spiritual disciplines, without the guidance of a qualified teacher. (The same may be said about the physical exercises that sometimes go under the name of Yoga, properly known as *hatha-yoga*. These were originally meant to strengthen the body so that the goal of Yoga could be realized in the course of one's present life.) It is easiest to center one's thought on a goal or a set of practices that is in harmony with one's individual temperament. The beginner, however, does not always understand what that goal or those practices may be. It is the experienced teacher who can fathom the student's character and so best determine what his spiritual goal is and suggest appropriate disciplines.

Spiritual counselors have been an integral part of the life of meditative orders of Christian monks and nuns. Again, among Roman Catholics, frequent confession has until recently been the rule; through this practice earnest laymen could also obtain instruction in prayer. Protestant ministers have always provided advice on such matters to those who have sought it. In the Hindu tradition, the *guru*, or spiritual teacher, has been of utmost importance from the earliest times. Aside from family *gurus*, who by accepted custom perform certain formal rites of initiation for the members of a particular family, monastic teachers are sought out by many laymen for private spiritual guidance. Monks, of course, all but invariably seek out a *guru* for initiation and claim membership in whatever sect he represents.

In the Hindu view, the ideal spiritual teacher is one who is well versed in scripture, leads an exemplary life, has realized what he teaches, and overflows with compassion for those seek-

ing shelter with him. An excellent example of such a teacher
we observed in Ramana Maharshi; and, in their own separate
ways, the *gurus* I have described—Bhagwan Dasji, Vedavyasananda, and Langa Baba—represent the same ideal. One
should put one's entire trust in such a teacher, who is a living
representative of God on earth. "Satchidananda is the *guru*,"
is a well-known saying in India. It is not always possible, however, to find a really qualified teacher. Much benefit is to be
gained from lesser teachers, but not every self-styled *guru*
is to be given unquestioning faith. The fact that a man is well
advertised is no guaranty that he is qualified. A student should
make certain there is no variance between teaching and
practice. Much that many well-advertised teachers from the
East speak about is unexceptionable, but a student should try
to make sure he comes from a tradition sufficiently living to in-
sure that the instruction will bear fruit in his own life.

-3-

Yoga, as Patanjali defines it at the beginning of the *Yoga
Sutras*, means "restraining the mind-stuff from taking various
forms." At the time of complete restraint of the mind, he says,
the seer, technically known as the *purusha*, "rests in his own
state." At other times the seer identifies himself mistakenly
with the various modifications of the mind. The goal of Yoga
practice is to enable the seer, the one who sees (i.e., experiences)
through the senses and mind, to rest in his own pure state. In
its first section the *Yoga Sutras* presents an overview of the
whole subject of mental concentration, including an analysis of
its final stages. The three succeeding sections describe the
means to attain such concentration, the results of some of the
practices, and finally the state of one who has attained the
goal, known as *samadhi*, or spiritual ecstasy.

For our purpose, the most important section is that dealing
with the eight steps, or "limbs," of Yoga. The first of these,
which consists of a group of five moral preparations, is called
yama. Without such moral preparations, in the Hindu view,
no real beginning can be made in spiritual life. They are
therefore called "universal great vows." These are: harmlessness (in thought, word, and deed), truthfulness, not stealing,

sexual continence, and not receiving gifts. About this last, Vivekananda says in his commentary, "The mind of the man who receives gifts is acted upon by the mind of the giver."

Two striking parallels with these five "universal great vows" for spiritual aspirants are to be found in Judaism and Buddhism. The last five of the Ten Commandments given by God to Moses are: "You shall not kill" (harmlessness), "You shall not commit adultery" (partial sexual continence), "You shall not steal" (not stealing), "You shall not bear false witness" (truthfulness), and "You shall not covet . . . anything that is your neighbor's" (prohibition of mental predisposition to receiving of gifts). Interestingly, these commandments are for all men, not just those who are seeking spiritual illumination.

The five rules of conduct binding on all who call themselves Buddhists, and voluntarily accepted by the individual Buddhist, are: "I undertake not to kill any living being," "I undertake not to take what is not given," "I undertake to abstain from sexual misconduct," "I undertake to abstain from false speech," and "I undertake to abstain from intoxicants and drugs causing heedlessness." Here is stressed, instead of the nonreceiving of gifts, abstention from agents that act upon the mind more powerfully than anything else one can receive. It is instructive to note that four great religions start out (for Christianity accepts the Jewish list, and Hinduism in general accepts Patanjali's list) with the same prescription for how to begin a meaningful spiritual life.

The second step of Yoga consists of external and internal cleanliness, contentment, mortification (i.e., conscious control of the body and senses), study, and worship of God. It is called *niyama*. Internal cleanliness is achieved by cultivating friendliness toward the happy, mercy toward the unhappy, gladness toward the good, and indifference toward those who would do one evil. If the first step is slanted toward social or objective morality, this second step is related to personal or subjective morality.

Without first becoming established in these preliminary disciplines, teachers of Yoga say, a man cannot reap any results from the more advanced practices. The once prevalent Christian charge that because (nondualist) Hindus affirmed that ultimate reality was beyond (relative) good and evil they had no moral sense is here revealed as meaningless. Moral disciplines are often considered so obviously necessary in the East that in many treatises they are not mentioned or are only hinted at. Even so, the warning in the *Katha Upanishad* is clear enough: "He who has not first turned away from wickedness, who is not tranquil and subdued, and whose mind is not at peace, cannot attain Atman." And the Bhagavad Gita, in chapter thirteen, lists twenty virtues, beginning with "humility, modesty, non-violence, forbearance, and uprightness," as means to attain insight into truth. Again, in chapter sixteen, it lists twenty-five more (with only six repeats) as "spiritual treasures" leading to liberation from ignorance.

The third step of Yoga is correct posture, *asana*. This term does not refer to the various complex postures practiced in *hatha-yoga*; it simply means learning to sit in a firm, erect position (usually with legs crossed). Buddhists often advocate sitting cross-legged in the "lotus posture," with the soles of the feet turned up. Not all Buddhists, however, follow this rule. And so competent an authority as Ramakrishna has said that one should take whatever position makes it possible to forget the body. The aphorism in the *Yoga Sutras* on *asana* says merely, "Posture is that which is firm and pleasant."

In the *Shvetashvatara Upanishad* it is written, "The wise man should hold his body steady, with the three parts [i.e., chest, neck, and head] erect; turn his senses, with the help of the mind, toward the heart; and by means of the raft of Brahman cross the fearful torrents of the world." (Shankara interprets "raft of Brahman" to mean repetition of Brahman's signifying name, or *Om*.) The Bhagavad Gita gives the following directions: "He should sit firm, holding his body, neck, and head erect and still, and gaze steadily at the tip of his nose, without looking around." As Swami Nikhilananda points out in his commentary, the instruction about the gaze should not be taken literally: "The gaze is directed, *as it were*, to the tip of the nose."

Vivekananda has written in *Raja-Yoga*, "During the study of these psychological matters a good deal of activity goes on in the body. . . . The whole constitution will be remodeled, as it were. But the main part of the activity will lie along the spinal column; so the one thing necessary for the posture is to hold the spinal column free."

Control of the vital force, or *prana*, is the fourth step. It is known as *pranayama*. This consists in getting hold of the vital force in the body through its most obvious manifestation, the breathing. In his introductory chapters in *Raja-Yoga*, Vivekananda explains the various types of regulation of breathing and discusses some of their effects. "*Pranayama* is not, as many think, concerned solely with the breath," he says; "breath indeed has very little to do with it." Control of the *prana* really means control of the omnipresent energy in the universe—first in the individual body, then beyond it. It is through this sort of control that so-called faith healings are caused; this is true, he claims, whether those who bring them about realize it or not. The physical sciences, too, are a form of *pranayama*, or control of energy—a form accomplished by external means. Yoga, however, is concerned with controlling thought, which is the "finest and highest manifestation of this *prana*." It is constantly stressed that no one should undertake any of the exercises without a teacher's guidance. Fitness to undertake the four final steps of Yoga follows on proficiency in *pranayama*.

The *Shvetashvatara Upanishad*, again, gives the following instruction: "The yogi of well-regulated endeavors should control the *prana* [i.e., the bodily nerve currents manifesting the *pranas*, or cosmic energy] ; when they are quieted he should breathe out through the nostrils. Then let him undistractedly restrain his mind, as a charioteer restrains vicious horses." As Swami Nikhilananda points out in his commentary on the Upanishad, Shankara gives the following advice concerning this verse: "First close the right nostril with a finger and breathe in through the left nostril as much as possible. Then breathe out by the right nostril, closing the left. Next breathe in by the right nostril and breathe out by the left. This process should be repeated three or five times." Nikhilananda adds, "Afterward the yogi should practice *pranayama*, which consists in the inhalation, exhalation, and retention of the breath, under the guidance of a qualified teacher."

The sort of rhythmic breathing prescribed in Buddhism of all schools as a preliminary exercise for calming the mind is undoubtedly related to this teaching. We may note in passing that Zen Buddhists and some others use the breathing not merely as a means of calming the mind, but as an object of meditation while ridding the mind of thoughts. In Christian or any other prayer the breathing gradually becomes calm, especially during the repetition of a sacred formula. It has not generally been employed, however, as a means of helping the mind grow calm or concentrated. In China, however, something of this discipline must have been known very early. "Can you govern your spirit so that it never strays away?'' asks Lao-tzu. ''Can you govern your breathing so that it is soft as a newborn child's? Can you purify yourself so that you become perfect? . . . Can you live content without women?''

The fifth step consists in learning to keep the centers in the brain from taking the forms of the objects perceived by the sense organs, and instead withdrawing them, as it were, into the mind-stuff. It is called *pratyahara*. Here Vivekananda advocates, at first, just sitting and letting the mind run on, while observing the various forms it takes. After a time, he says, the thoughts—good, bad, or indifferent—will grow fewer, and when some months have passed the mind will have become calm and under perfect control. The mind will no longer be attached even to thoughts that have resulted from earlier sense perceptions. Speaking of the man of ''steady wisdom,'' Krishna says in the Bhagavad Gita: ''When he completely withdraws the senses from their objects, as a tortoise draws in its limbs, then his wisdom is firmly fixed.''

In the chapter ''*Pratyahara* and *Dharana*,'' in *Raja-Yoga*, Vivekananda points out that until one knows what the mind contains and what it is capable of doing, one cannot control it. Many hideous thoughts may come into it during this practice thoughts one will be astonished to know the mind could harbor. Only after a patient, continuous struggle for years, the swami warns, can a man succeed.

The next step, which is the sixth, is the practice of holding the mind to certain objects, either inside or outside the body, and bringing it back again and again when it wanders. It is called *dharana*. As the *Yoga Sutras* indicates, the various modifications of the mind are to be brought under control by constant practice of concentration and by remaining unattached to the modifications and their effects. Obstacles are bound to arise, however. Patanjali carefully lists these: disease, mental laziness, doubt, lack of enthusiasm, physical lethargy, clinging to sense impressions, deluded ideas, failure to attain concentration, and falling away from concentration once it has been attained. As a result of the last obstacle other disturbances appear: grief, mental distress, trembling of the body, irregular breathing. To calm the mind, in addition to the moral and mental purifications and breathing exercises already mentioned, Patanjali suggests certain concentrations: fixing the mind on parts of the body (as described in part three of the *Yoga Sutras*) so as to produce extrasensory perceptions; on a light

in the heart; on the heart of a holy person; on a pleasant
dream; or on "anything that appeals to one as good."

When the individual has reached this stage, he should avoid
everything that can disturb the mind. Especially he should
avoid persons, places, foods, that unsettle him or repel him.
Avoidance of all company is necessary, it is said, for those who
wish to attain perfect concentration. It is for this reason that
certain spiritual aspirants for a time become hermits.

The seventh step is defined as an "unbroken flow of mind"
toward the object of meditation. It is called *dhyana*. (In China
this word became *Ch'an*, and in Japan *Zen*.) As Vivekananda
says, "When the mind has been trained to remain fixed on a
certain internal or external object, there comes to it the power
of flowing in an unbroken current, as it were, toward that object."

When one has intensified the power of *dhyana* to such an extent that one can "reject the external part of the perception and
meditate only on the internal part, the meaning," one has
reached the eighth and final step, *samadhi*, or, in Christian
terms, mystical union. There are various types of *samadhi*, of
increasing subtlety. First come meditations on external objects,
then on the mind itself. In all these there is still a consciousness
of perceiver and perceived, subject and object. They are called
"seed-bearing" *samadhis*, because they do not destroy the seeds
of past action, or *karma*.

Beyond these concentrations, Patanjali states, is a higher
concentration: "There is another *samadhi*, which is attained
by the constant practice of cessation of all mental activity, and
in which the mind-stuff retains only unmanifested impressions."
Swami Vivekananda's commentary on this aphorism is interesting: "The method is to meditate on the mind itself, and whenever any thought comes, to strike it down, allowing no thought
to come into the mind, thus making it an entire vacuum. When
we can really do this, that very moment we shall attain liberation. When persons without training and preparation try to
make their minds vacant, they are likely to succeed only in
covering themselves with *tamas* [dullness, inertia], the material
of ignorance, which . . . leads them to think that they are making a vacuum of the mind. To be able to really do that is to
manifest the greatest strength, the highest control."

Here we have come very nearly to the last of the concentrations discussed in the *Yoga Sutras*. But this concentration
must not be taken for the goal. One who has attained this
samadhi, unless he achieves at the same time a complete lack of

attachment even to it, is destined to become "merged in nature," and in a subsequent existence to become a higher being with power to control nature. Those who want to reach the final goal of Yoga, the "seedless *samadhi*," must abandon all desire to attain a higher position, such as that of a god or a ruler of a cycle. Persevering in the concentration in which there is a cessation of all mental activity, they attain their objective through "faith, energy, memory, concentration, and discrimination of the real from the unreal."

This same *samadhi* may also be attained, says the *Yoga Sutras*, through devotion to the Supreme Ruler, Ishvara. (Though not, according to the Yoga system of philosophy, the Creator, Ishvara is omniscient and not limited by time. We may assume that meditation on the personal God is a legitimate alternative.) Repetition of his "manifesting word," *Om*, is the way to achieve the *samadhi* that perfect meditation on Ishvara brings. It should be noted that by concentration on a single idea, all other ideas are excluded from the mind, and it progresses toward a state in which it can easily concentrate without distraction on the inner self.

We find here the same principle that is encountered in the Roman Catholic use of the rosary, in the exercise advocated by certain Orthodox Christians of repeating with concentration the prayer "Lord Jesus Christ, have mercy on me," and in the repetition of a sacred formula, or *mantra*, in devotional Hinduism and Mahayana Buddhism. Though such practices may sometimes become mechanical and thus fall into disfavor, the principle underlying them is not thereby refuted. Such repetition produces a deepened power of introspection and gradually destroys the obstacles that plague aspirants at every stage of meditative practice.

About the man who has attained this near-final *samadhi*, Patanjali states in the concluding section of his work: "For the discriminating the perception of the mind as Atman [or self] ceases." He is on the verge of illumination. After overcoming whatever obstructions remain as the result of impressions from the past, if the individual can give up the fruit of his discriminative knowledge he attains a *samadhi* called the "cloud of virtue." Knowledge for him becomes infinite. This state is known, in Yoga, as *kaivalya*, "isolation," which is "establishment of the power of knowledge in its own nature." Of this *samadhi* Vivekananda remarks, "When a man goes into *samadhi*, if he goes into it a fool, he comes out a saint."

Through practice of the three final steps of Yoga the yogi is said to attain supernormal powers, and these are also discussed in the *Yoga Sutras*, together with the meditations by which they may be attained. Of special interest to Christians should be the mention of exercises by which one "does not sink in water," becomes "surrounded by a blaze of light," and can "go through the skies." The various powers, says Patanjali, are attained through "birth, chemical means, the power of words, mortification, or concentration." Concentration of mind is not the only means to attain them. One may have acquired them in a previous life and may enjoy them in a succeeding one. One may take certain medicines (as was thought in Patanjali's time) to prolong life till the powers are attained, or even attain some of them by this means. (Patanjali does not refer to the sort of experience passively enjoyed by a person under the influence of mescalin, marijuana, heroin, or LSD.) One may acquire these powers through repetition of certain formulas, or *mantras*, or through the practice of extreme austerities. (It was such austerities that the Buddha denounced; apparently in his day certain yogis thought they could attain enlightenment through them, as well as the powers.)

But it must be remembered that all these disciplines are of secondary importance. If through practice of concentration one has acquired the supernormal powers and can reject them, one achieves the "seedless" *samadhi,* or perfect freedom.

In the *Shvetashvatara Upanishad* occurs the following description of some of the phenomena associated with this discipline: "When Yoga is practiced, the forms that appear first and that gradually manifest Brahman are those of snowflakes, smoke, sun, wind, fire, fireflies, lightning, crystal, and the moon. . . . The precursors of perfection in Yoga, they say, are lightness and healthiness of the body, absence of desire, clear complexion, pleasantness of voice, and slight excretions." Again, these phenomena are not to be mistaken for the goal.

The highest *samadhi* is called "seedless" because through it all the seeds of past action, or *karma*, embedded in the mind are destroyed; there is no cause for rebirth. It is to be attained by perseverance in the concentration in which there is cessation of of all mental activity. The impression, or wave, raised in the mind through the highest of the "seed-bearing" *samadhis* has to be suppressed before the "seedless" *samadhi,* the goal of Yoga, is manifested. Vivekananda thus sums up the central teaching of the *Yoga Sutras*: "The real nature of the soul is not perceived as long as there is one single wave in the lake of the mind stuff.

. . . So first Patanjali teaches us the meaning of these waves; secondly, the best way to repress them; and thirdly, how to make one wave so strong as to suppress all other waves. . . . When only one remains, it will be easy to suppress that also, and when that is done, the *samadhi* or concentration that follows is called 'seedless.' It leaves nothing, and the soul is manifested just as it is, in its own glory.''

About the yogi who has attained the goal, Krishna has this to say in the Bhagavad Gita: ''With the heart concentrated by Yoga, viewing all things with equal regard, he beholds himself in all beings and all beings in himself. He who sees me everywhere and sees everything in me, to him I am never lost, nor is he ever lost to me. He who, having been established in oneness, worships me dwelling in all beings—that yogi, in whatever way he leads his life, lives in me. Him I hold to be the supreme yogi, Arjuna, who looks on the pleasure and pain of all beings as he looks on them in himself.'' Most Christians will see in this passage a progress from identification with the Self (in the first sentence) to a recognition that there is something more than the Self. In the final sentence is a beautiful variant of the Golden Rule.

-4-

In the New Testament prayer is spoken of many times, but there is no explicit mention of the way of prayer and meditation as a conscious discipline in the Gospels or Epistles. Nevertheless, as we have seen, certain Christian mystics have strongly desired to reach, in this life, the goal that faith tells the Christian he will eventually attain after death. Many of them must have devised their own disciplines. In the writings of St. John of the Cross one finds an extraordinary parallel with the teachings of Patanjali. The correspondences have been detailed in masterly fashion by the late Swami Siddheswarananda in an article entitled ''The Raja-Yoga of St. John of the Cross.''

The swami points out that St. John's doctrine of the Dark Night is not a practice for everyone. It is reserved for those who have heard the call of the Lord: ''If any man would come after me, let him deny himself and take up his cross daily and follow me.'' In fact, in *The Ascent of Mount Carmel* he states that his method is addressed especially to certain members of

his own monastic order. In the swami's opinion, for St. John
the spiritual guide, or *guru*, is not any individual man, but the
Roman Catholic Church itself. (I rather think even St. John
would have advocated a spiritual director for all who undertook
his exercises.)

The first two steps of Patanjali's Yoga, which consist in the
practice of moral virtues and inner purity, *yama* and *niyama*,
are included, the swami says, in St. John's *via purgativa*, or
purgative way, the Night of the Senses. Here he urges the observance of absolute chastity. This stage consists of work that
the soul must do itself. As for the third step, correct posture, or
asana, he simply suggests a solitary place (and presumably
a kneeling position, which would incidentally keep the spine
straight). For the fourth, control of the breathing, or *pranayama*, he gives no direction; here, says the swami, we must turn
to the *Spiritual Exercises* of St. Ignatius Loyola (where there
is a suggestion to associate the words of the Lord's Prayer with
the breathing).

The fifth, sixth, and seventh steps of Patanjali's Yoga—
pratyahara, *dharana*, and *dhyana*—which consist in progres-
sively inward states of the soul, are included in St. John's *via
contemplativa*, or contemplative way. The first two of these
correspond to "discursive meditation." At the soul's arrival at
the seventh step, *dhyana*, it achieves "infused contemplation."
Before reaching this stage, there is a combination of the soul's
action and God's action in the soul. But at its farthest limit,
says St. John, it is impossible to distinguish between human
action and divine action infused in the soul. Here the soul
"gives up every initiative for its spiritual development."

The eighth and last step of Patanjali's Yoga, *samadhi*, which
corresponds, the swami states, to communion with God, is St.
John's *via unitiva*, or unitive way. Here God completely possesses the soul (as was the experience of St. Catherine of Genoa).
"The soul becomes God by participation," says St. John, speaking almost in terms of intuitive wisdom.

In describing systematically the processes of meditation and
contemplation—not discursive meditation, but what has been
called "vertical meditation"—Patanjali created the outstanding treatise on the subject in India that has come down to us.
Only rare individuals in modern India devote themselves solely
to this Hindu expression of conscious discipline. Nevertheless,
Patanjali's method provides invaluable help for implementing
the message of intuitive wisdom or of devotional self-giving. I

have presented it in some detail because I feel the voice of conscious discipline has not been sufficiently heard by the majority of serious Christians. Some of their distrust not only of non-Christian mystics but of their own mystics as well might be dispelled by a greater familiarity with the practices that saints have followed in Eastern traditions.

-5-

As we have read in the summary of the *Yoga Sutras*, supernormal powers and perceptions frequently come to a spiritual aspirant as a result of his spiritual exercises, whether he consciously seeks them or not. These phenomena are treated by responsible Hindu teachers, just as they are by Buddhists and Christians, as obstacles. Spiritual aspirants are warned against taking them seriously.

During my last visit to Calcutta I talked on a number of occasions with a man who has acquired extrasensory perception of a unique sort through concentration of mind. He is a learned Buddhist monk from Ceylon, engaged in important scholarly work. I met him by chance, having sought out the place where he stayed to learn more about Theravada Buddhism from someone who practiced it. I found this monk innately serious, highly intelligent, and liberal in regard to religions other than his own. He was also natural, very jolly, and altogether sympathetic; he kindly allowed me to visit him as often as his schedule allowed. After our first conversation I inquired how I should address him, and he told me I could call him "Bhante," a term, I found, customarily used to show respect.

I had seen Bhante several times when, in speaking of the Buddhist concentration on breathing in and breathing out, he mentioned the fact that sometimes, if the concentration is deep, one develops unusual capacities—the same supernormal powers and perceptions mentioned by Patanjali. No doubt because of his mentioning the powers, I began to tell him of several apparently supernormal phenomena I knew about; these, however, had nothing to do with any form of Yoga practice. "But perhaps you aren't interested," I said, hesitating to go on. "No, no," he said. "I, too, am a seeker." When I finished my story, Bhante said, "I have actually had a strange experience myself." Here is what he told me.

At the time his experience took place, the monk was living at Kalimpong, in the extreme north of India, in a house that stood on an isolated hill in sight of the magnificent range of the Himalaya mountains. He had been practicing the traditional concentration on his breathing for some years, and he found that his mind was becoming more and more easily controlled. While meditating one afternoon in his room, he suddenly heard an arresting sound. It was like a fragment of human speech. He heard it again; this time it lasted slightly longer. Still mechanically continuing the meditation, Bhante rose from his seat and went outside to see who was talking so near the house in this lonely place. No one was in sight. He began to walk up and down a footpath in view of the panorama of the snowy Himalayas. As he did so, he continued to concentrate on the breathing in and the breathing out.

Only a short while passed when he again heard the sound. Now he recognized it was a voice, and it was speaking in English about himself. "They say he's from Burma," it said, "but really he is from Ceylon." It was as if he was hearing half of a conversation. After a pause, the same voice said, "His two Sanskrit pupils did very well in their examination today." It mentioned a town at a distance of some hundreds of miles. Two of his students had indeed been scheduled to take an examination there that very day. The whole thing seemed incredible. Another voice now said, "He doesn't believe it. Why not send a telegram?" Then followed a longish pause. Bhante kept pacing up and down, still concentrating his mind on his breathing. The second voice finally spoke: "Yes, it says both pupils came out quite well. They received among the highest grades." The voices continued, but Bhante decided not to listen any longer and went into the house. Next day he received a telegram with the news that the two students had done very creditably in their examination. They had, in fact, obtained among the highest grades.

Thereafter, Bhante said, he could hear these voices whenever he concentrated his mind. He found he could get answers to perplexing problems or find out things otherwise difficult to know. Despite the fascination of the experience, he decided it was becoming a distraction, and he stopped paying attention to it. "Can you still hear the voices now, if you want to?" I asked. "Oh, yes, I can," he said. He had never seriously tried, I gathered, to find out if they belonged to any actual persons. Possibly they came from a deeper psychological level, he remarked. The experience appeared to him to be a sort of extension of sensory perception itself.

Though usually clairaudience is of words spoken at a distance, this seemed to be a sort of two-way or three-way phenomenon. The persons speaking appeared to be aware of what Bhante himself was thinking. They also appeared, though in Kalimpong, to be aware not only of what others were thinking but of what was going on in the town where the examination was being held. Perhaps, as Bhante hinted, the experience was completely subjective, but even then it was strangely involved, especially in view of the sending of the telegram. We talked of it only once, for there was not much time at our disposal. Bhante had generously taken it upon himself to give me as thorough a grounding as possible, in a few interviews, in the ideas and disciplines of Theravada Buddhism. Aside from illustrating dramatically the sort of powers that come to a man practicing spiritual discipline, it appeared to have no deep spiritual significance.

I could readily accept Bhante's claim of having no difficulty in stilling his mind. His thoughts, as he instructed me, were perfectly organized. Every phase of Theravada Buddhist belief seemed to be present to his mind at all times. Moreover, as with the Buddhist monk Shashanarasi at Sarnath, despite our conversing his attention never seemed to be deflected from an inner point of rest. Perhaps the impression was furthered by the quality of his eyes, which were without exaggeration the blackest and most penetrating I have ever seen.

Supernormal occurrences are not, as everyone knows, limited to the type we have just been considering. In the chapter on devotional self-giving we saw that believers in the personal God experience, according to their own testimony, the miraculous intervention of God in times of need or distress. God is also said to manifest his form to devotees who exhibit an intense spirit of faith. Though some of these happenings may be the result of pious imagination, there are too many from trustworthy sources in more than one religion—even within the preceding and the present century—to allow one to categorically deny that any of them are authentic. Again, as witnessed in both the Christian and the Hindu scriptures, miracles can take place by the will of a Savior or of a person in whom there is an unusual manifestation of God's presence. In India careful records have been kept of the lives of such persons—Ramanuja, Chaitanya, and Ramakrishna, to mention only a few—who are said to have caused happenings that went beyond the laws of nature. Here, too, though there is room for doubt whether all the accounts are accurate, there is no justification for dismissing all as fraudulent.

As commentators on the *Yoga Sutras* suggest, powers and experiences gained through control of the breathing and through concentration of the mind may be explained, where genuine, as being based on subtle physical laws yet to be fathomed by science. Here nature is being controlled, if we accept the word of Patanjali and other yogis, through its own subtler laws. (This would be the case whether the individual knew how he was controlling these forces or knew nothing about it.) Such happenings should not strictly be classed as miracles. It is entirely possible that many of the so-called miracles of saints, even of Jesus or of modern Hindu *avataras*, belong in this category. (The reader will recall mention of exercises permitting the yogi to walk on water, surround himself with a blaze of light, or pass through the skies.) But in instances of God's direct intervention, with or without a human intermediary, what occurs is simply an exercise of the divine will. The believing soul accepts these rightly as true miracles.

The Upanishads and the writings of St. John of the Cross and the Buddhists (including followers of Zen) alike mention supernormal phenomena as frequently accompanying spiritual practice. They are thus encountered not only in the way of pure conscious discipline, but in the ways of intuitive wisdom and devotional self-giving as well. To these latter disciplines as found in Hinduism we now turn, not indeed to continue a search for supernormal phenomena, but to investigate their special variations for possible evidences of the working of Christ.

-6-

We noted earlier that those who would effectively follow the voices of intuitive wisdom and devotional self-giving must implement them with some form of mental concentration. The disciplines in both these ways, like those of St. John of the Cross, in many instances approximate the exercises long ago outlined by Patanjali. So special are their needs, however, that they have developed their own unique approaches to God. I believe they too will be useful for Christian contemplatives.

In our discussion of the Yoga of St. John of the Cross, I stated that the discipline of intuitive wisdom was not explicitly elaborated in the New Testament. Seldom is clear instruction given about how a follower of Christ is to follow this hard road. The

underlying assumption is, no doubt, that since the four approaches are to be applied in combination, there is no need for
discussing them separately. Besides, through faith alone, it was
assumed, the average Christian could accomplish everything
that was needed. Yet the very fact that Christian mystics in
later centuries devised their own disciplines to supplement, as
it were, their faith points to a need on the part of men and
women of a contemplative temperament for greater explicitness.
There are in the New Testament, however, a number of symbolic
hints about what the discipline involves.

We read that Jesus allowed himself to be baptized by John
the Baptist—an action that suggests that ordinary men need a
spiritual director. His going into the wilderness for forty days
and being tempted by Satan may indicate not only that certain
souls require the discipline of solitude and meditation, but that
as a result of such discipline they may be faced with psychological upheavals that only stout hearts can pass through unscathed. We also know that Jesus retired from the multitudes at
night to pray and commune with his Father; and that in the
Garden of Gethsemane, at the very end of his earthly life, after
seeking out the Father in prayer he said, "Not my will, but
thine, be done." In other words, the man who would know God
must throw off even the most seemingly legitimate demands of
the ego. Finally, we recall that Jesus paid the ultimate price in
human suffering: that of being nailed to a cross and raised up to
die. He was acting out for all who had eyes to see his own instruction, "Unless a grain of wheat falls into the earth and dies,
it remains alone; but if it dies, it bears much fruit."

In the declaration of St. Paul, "We know that our old self
was crucified with him," there seems to be more than a hint that
conscious imitation of Jesus Christ is a means to receiving the
full grace of faith and ultimate communion with God. How this
is to be accomplished inwardly is suggested in Paul's exhortation
to "pray constantly." It was this statement that presumably
led to the advice by the author of *The Cloud of Unknowing*:
"And if you desire to have this intent lapped and folded in one
word . . . take but a little word of one syllable. . . . And such
a word is this word 'God' or this word 'love' . . . and fasten this
word to your heart." It certainly led to the Russian teacher's
advice in *The Way of a Pilgrim* to repeat unceasingly the prayer
"Lord Jesus Christ, have mercy on me." These injunctions are
involved also, of course, with the devotional attitude. But what
is primarily urged here is a use of the words to banish any other

thought from the mind, so as to dissolve the ego—not a use of them to serve the purposes of discursive meditation.

The discipline of devotional self-giving, on the other hand, is frequently and unequivocally referred to in the New Testament. In fact, the references to the discipline of intuitive wisdom are often so inextricably interrelated with it that the two may seem to be one. Illustrations used here for intuitive wisdom might sometimes be used equally well for the devotional approach. Indeed, the choices may often appear arbitrary. My purpose is simply to emphasize whatever differences there are, so as to draw parallels with similar divisions in Hindu practice that have been more clearly distinguished there—divisions that, while perhaps artificial from the Christian point of view, should help Christians better understand the various elements of their own faith.

I have already mentioned the first and great commandment, which Jesus took from the Old Testament, as being central to the voice of devotional self-giving: "Hear, O Israel: The Lord our God, the Lord is one; and you shall love the Lord your God with all your heart, and with all your soul, and with all your mind, and with all your strength." The commandment is, in a very real sense, central to all four voices of Christ.

But while this passage affirms that love of God includes all four approaches, we can find in the verse directly following, which contains the second commandment, how Jesus suggests we prepare for the discipline of devotional self-giving. "You shall love your neighbor as yourself," he says. This, too, is a borrowing from Jewish scripture. We understand how this verse relates to the question of discipline when we read St. John's comment: "He who does not love his brother whom he has seen, cannot love God whom he has not seen." Though the goal of Christian life is to love the Lord above all else, we must first learn to love those around us. Without possessing the ability to practice the most elementary form of love, it is useless to attempt love in its most refined form.

Once they really love their neighbor, however, Christians may legitimately take up a more direct approach to God. This the saints and mystics have never hesitated to do. And they have revealed their methods, as we have already seen, in various specialized works. Not all of these are intended, like those of St. John of the Cross, solely for contemplatives.

In the Christian tradition a number of practical aids have been developed that have given stability to those whose lives centered around devotional self-giving. Among these, the praying of the Divine Office (emphasizing the repetition of the Psalms) has been of prime importance for Roman Catholic monastics and priests. Reading of the Psalms has always been a source of inspiration and consolation for Protestants, too, both clerical and lay. Again, use of different types of prayer as described in some of the devotional treatises—the "prayer of quiet," the "prayer of simple regard," and so on—has been a central practice in many a Christian's life. The custom of making occasional retreats has helped many to reinvigorate their religious aspiration. Fasting (especially observance of the Lenten fast) and practice of the Way of the Cross, with its meditations on the various episodes during the Passion of Christ, have also been found useful, especially in the Roman Church. In addition, the needs of many a devotionally minded Christian have been satisfied by the saying of the rosary and other forms of piety.

There is a good reason why in Christianity, during its first nineteen hundred years, the manifestations of the way of intuitive wisdom and of devotional self-giving have been, except in very special instances, intimately related. The goal sought and achieved by those saintly Christians who tend toward intuitive wisdom and those who tend toward devotional self-giving is one and the same. Their experience is summed up in two sayings of Christ: "I am in my Father, and you in me, and I in you," and "He who abides in me, and I in him, he it is that bears much fruit, for apart from me you can do nothing."

-7-

As an introduction to the Hindu approaches to the disciplines of intuitive wisdom and of devotional self-giving, we go once more to the Bhagavad Gita, where the two disciplines are dealt with in juxtaposition, just as they are in Christian writings. We can perhaps get an idea of what spiritual discipline is all about if we listen to what the two voices, speaking as it were in dialogue, have to say on the subject.

After revealing to his friend and disciple Arjuna his universal form, the Lord Krishna says, "It is very hard to see this form of mine, which you have seen. Even the gods are ever eager to see this form. Neither by the Vedas, nor by penances, nor by almsgiving, nor yet by sacrifice, am I to be seen in the form in which you have now beheld me. But by devotion to me alone may I be known in this form, Arjuna, realized truly, and entered into. . . . He who does my work and looks on me as the Supreme Goal, who is devoted to me, who is without attachment and without hatred for any creature—he comes to me." There can be no question that the voice speaking here is that of devotional self-giving.

In the second chapter of the Bhagavad Gita, Krishna had laid emphasis on the suprapersonal aspect of God. Thereafter, in Shankara's view, occur a number of references to the attributeless Brahman (whose description is simply "Not this, not this"). But gradually—as seems clear from an unbiased reading of the text itself—Krishna brings the emphasis to bear upon his own person as ultimate reality. It is in the climactic eleventh chapter that the vision of Krishna's universal form is revealed to Arjuna. The verses quoted in the last paragraph conclude that chapter. In the next chapter Arjuna asks, "Those devotees who, ever steadfast, worship you after this fashion [as just described], and those others who worship the Imperishable and Unmanifest [as described in chapter two]—which of these have the greater knowledge of yoga?" (Here the word "yoga" refers simply to spiritual practice leading to union with God, or ultimate reality.)

Krishna replies, "Those who have fixed their minds on me, and who, ever steadfast, and endowed with supreme faith, worship me—them do I hold to be perfect in yoga. And those who have completely controlled their senses and are of even mind under all conditions and thus worship the Imperishable, the Ineffable, the Unmanifest, the Omnipresent, the Incomprehensible, the Immutable, the Unchanging, the Eternal—they, devoted to the welfare of all beings, attain me alone, and none else."

In this key passage, as Swami Nikhilananda points out in his commentary, no real contrast between the two is intended. My own opinion is that those who champion the second of these points of view as superior probably miss the full message of the Bhagavad Gita. The verse directly following the above quotation no doubt seems to justify them: "The task of those whose minds are set on the Unmanifest is more difficult; for the ideal of the Unmanifest is hard to attain for those who are embodied." The next verse, however, immediately restores the balance: "But those who consecrate all their actions to me, regarding me as the Supreme Goal, and who worship me, meditating on me with single-minded concentration—to them, whose minds are thus absorbed in me, verily I become ere long, Arjuna, the Savior from the death-fraught ocean of the world.''

Earlier, the Lord Krishna has said, ''The man endowed with wisdom I deem to be my very self.'' Followers of Shankara interpret this sentence to mean that *only they* are identified with the Lord's True Self. They do not, perhaps, give enough weight to Krishna's statement made directly after the revelation of his universal (and ''personal'') form: ''Those who . . . worship the Imperishable, the Ineffable, the Unmanifest . . . attain me alone.'' That word ''me'' makes all the difference. It is probable, in my opinion, that those who champion the voice of devotional self-giving as superior equally miss the point.

Here we may have reached the solution of the problem that troubles those who uphold the ''personal God'' as contrasted to the ''impersonal Absolute,'' and who see a ''tension'' between the two voices in Hinduism instead of that harmony we find in the teaching of Christ. Those who worship the Lord Krishna are ''perfect in yoga [union],'' and those who worship the ineffable Godhead attain none other than the Lord Krishna. These are Krishna's words in the key passage just quoted. There is no question of whether ''personal'' or ''impersonal'' is ultimate, because both are ways of speaking of the Lord himself.

Enthusiastic followers of Shankara and Ramanuja, I suspect, have made it difficult for Westerners to understand that what Shankara said about ultimate reality and what Ramanuja said about ultimate reality are two ways of saying one and the same thing. Chaitanya made it explicit when he defined the relation of the Godhead to souls and nature as an ''incomprehensible distinction and nondistinction.'' Ramakrishna, too, said something very similar in the last century, on the basis of his Vaishnavite and Tantric realizations alike: ''Brahman and Shakti [the suprapersonal Reality and the Creative Power] are identical. If you accept the one, you must accept the other. It is like fire and its power to burn. If you see fire, you must recognize its power to burn, also. You cannot think of fire without its power to burn, nor can you think of the power to burn without fire.'' Only practice of discipline, not philosophical or theological speculation, can clarify the problem.

There must be different emphases in discipline, however, depending on different temperaments and gifts. This is clear from a passage in the Bhagavad Gita that closely follows the ones we have been considering. In the chapter titled ''The Way of Divine Love,'' Krishna continues, ''Fix your mind on me alone, rest your thought on me alone, and in me alone you will live hereafter. Of this there is no doubt. If you are unable to fix your mind steadily on me, Arjuna, then seek to reach me by the yoga of constant practice [of concentration]. If you are incapable of constant practice, then devote yourself to my service. For even by rendering service to me you will attain perfection. If you are unable to do even this, then be self-controlled, surrender the fruit of all action, and take refuge in me.''

The Bhagavad Gita refers, in these passages, to the disciplines of all the voices we have studied so far. Let us now take up the more specific instructions for following the Hindu expressions of intuitive wisdom and devotional self-giving. These are the product, on the one hand, of the tradition stemming from the Upanishads and the Bhavagad Gita and Shankara's philosophy, and on the other, of that stemming from the Bhavagad Gita and the Puranas and Ramanuja's philosophy.

-8-

In ancient times, the prime requisites for attaining the goal of the way of intuitive wisdom were: hearing the truths enunciated in the Upanishads, reflection about their meaning, and meditation on them. The instruction could only be given to a qualified student by a qualified teacher. Earlier in this chapter we touched upon the characteristics of a worthy teacher. To be accepted as a qualified student by a qualified teacher, a young man had to have become proficient in various moral disciplines such as those that make up the first two of the ''eight limbs'' listed in the *Yoga Sutras*. (Even that most extreme of Nondualistic texts, the *Ashtavakra Samhita*, begins with a reminder about moral disciplines: ''Janaka asked, 'How can knowledge be acquired? How can liberation be attained? How is renunciation possible?' . . . Ashtavakra replied, 'If you aspire after liberation, my child, shun as poison the objects of the senses, and seek as nectar forgiveness, sincerity, kindness, contentment, and truth.' '') The student also had to have humility, and along with this, faith in the teacher and the words of scripture. Without all these, it was said, his attempt to lead the spiritual life would bear no fruit.

The truths taught in the Upanishads are many, but the four

"great statements," or *mahavakyas*, we read about in the chapter on intuitive wisdom embody their essence. They are these: "You are that [reality]," "I am Brahman," "Consciousness is Brahman," and "This Atman is Brahman." These statements, especially, the student was asked to hear, reflect about, and meditate upon.

The teacher, when he judged a student ready to receive the teaching, would first tell him, "You are that [reality]"—in other words, the reality underlying himself and the reality underlying the universe are one and the same. If the student was highly qualified, after simply hearing the scriptural revelation he at once realized its truth and exclaimed, "I am Brahman." (As we saw earlier, this does not mean that he is one with the Creator, but rather that what is the abiding reality of the Creator—that is to say, the Divine Ground, the "one nature" of the Father—is also the abiding reality in man.) For such a gifted student, the third and fourth "great statements" would be self-evident; they would serve to qualify the first two and make them more explicit.

If the student was slightly less gifted, after hearing the revelation embodied in the four great statements, he would have to reflect on them and spend long hours in meditation on them before realizing their truth. After having reflected on the meaning of one of the statements, he would then concentrate his mind on the words themselves, to the exclusion of all other mental images. The process would be the same as that described by Patanjali in the exercise of emptying the mind of thought. During the practice, should any distracting image arise, the student could make use of the Upanishadic formula "Not this, not this."

Even before St. John of the Cross, Christian practice included something very like this discipline. In *The Book of Divine Names*, the Pseudo-Dionysius speaks of certain souls who approach the Supereminent Unity "as far as it is possible for man . . . by the suspension of all intellectual operation." They speak of God, he says, "only through negations." In his *Mystical Theology* he enlarges on this theme: "We may venture to deny everything about God in order to penetrate into this sublime 'ignorance.'" Here we have something close to, if not identical with, the experience of the Upanishadic student.

A striking example in modern times of this sort of highly qualified student I have spoken of is Ramana Maharshi, whose life I have already described. The voice of intuitive wisdom spoke to him, as it were, directly—and immediately he realized the True Self. Thereafter he spent long periods of time in strengthening the experience, so that his mind might be established in it. Ramana knew instinctively that the mere attaining of such a realization is no guaranty of its permanence—a fact known to Nondualistic Vedantists for as long as their teachings have been transmitted from teacher to disciple. In his case, as it is said in India, "the mind itself became the *guru*."

Shankara, in his famous work *The Crest-Jewel of Discrimination*, based on the teachings of the Upanishads, describes in some detail the disciplines he judged indispensable for realizing the True Self, or Atman. These he gathers under four headings.

The aspirant, fully convinced of the truth of the voice of intuitive wisdom, must exercise, he says, constant discrimination: he must acquire the acuteness of mind to differentiate instantly between unchanging ultimate reality (his essential nature) and continuously changing objects and aspects of the phenomenal world. As a natural result, he attains to the second discipline: he renounces all possession of or concern for these changing objects and aspects of the world (which in Vedantic terminology are called "unreal," as opposed to the "real" or unchanging reality). If his discrimination is not perfect, his renunciation serves to bring his mind back to the first discipline.

The third discipline includes six mental virtues. In a sense, they, like the second discipline, manifest themselves as a result of practice of the preceding discipline; but they may also be practiced as a help toward strengthening the first two disciplines. They include calmness of mind, self-control, withdrawal of the senses from attachment to their objects, bearing of afflictions without seeking to redress them, faith in the existence of ultimate reality, and concern for nothing but the reality of the True Self. Most important of all is the discipline Shankara lists last: intense yearning for freedom from ignorance about reality. It is actually presupposed at the start, for without it no one would undertake the disciplines.

As a result of the student's practicing these disciplines, under a teacher's guidance, at last Atman, the True Self, reveals itself to him. Through long and continuous meditation on Atman, the man who has had a glimpse of reality comes to enjoy its uninterrupted vision.

It should be understood that disciplines that would amount to an unhealthy suppression of natural impulses in the man of the world are wholesome means of self-fulfillment in the man who is convinced of the impermanence of worldly enjoyments. Whether or not the goal he seeks represents the final goal of spirituality may be legitimately questioned. But that it is as valid a goal as that of the man who trusts entirely to the permanent reality of the world of the senses cannot be doubted.

Fortunate is he, says Shankara, who is in possession of these three gifts: a human body, intense desire for liberation from ignorance about the Self, and the help of a compassionate teacher. In the Hindu view, spiritual realization is to be obtained only in this world and in a human body. And it is the qualified teacher, as we have seen, who initiates one into spiritual life.

Aside from the many other disciplines of Yoga used in the way of intuitive wisdom (and in the way of devotional self-giving, as well), three deserve particular mention. We have considered all of them earlier. The first is repetition of a sacred formula, or *mantra*. In the discipline we are presently concerned with, repetition of the sacred word *Om* and meditation on its meaning (in this context, the undifferentiated Brahman, or reality) is sometimes prescribed. Also to be repeated is the formula "I am Brahman," or the other great statements, to the exclusion of every other thought.

The second discipline is control of the breathing. This exercise is employed in the disciplines of the three ways we have studied thus far, as a means of controlling the waves of the mind. As we noted, in the way of intuitive wisdom as represented by Buddhism it takes a special form. In the original or Theravada Buddhism a student is asked, among other disciplines, to watch the breathing and say to himself, "I breathe in, I breathe out." (This was the exercise that the monk I called Bhante was practicing when he heard the voices at Kalimpong that I told of earlier.) In Zen Buddhist practice the student merely watches the breathing in and breathing out without repeating any words. (The inhalation is performed by expanding the abdomen and the exhalation by contracting the abdomen.) In either form of the exercise, Buddhists make use of two techniques at one and the same time: that of calming the mind through controlling the vital energy and that of concentrating the mind.

A third Yogic discipline is almost universally insisted upon in Hinduism as indispensable for control of the mind. I refer to complete sexual continence. It has been stressed in Christian and early Buddhist monasticism, too. In Mahayana Buddhism the requirements for monks—as formerly in Tibet and presently in Japan—are not always so strict; sometimes marriage is tolerated. But in Theravada Buddhism the rule for monks includes both chastity and poverty. Chastity was, it will be recalled, one of the provisions of the first of the eight limbs of Yoga. So far as I am aware, all the Christian saints who have experienced profound mystical rapture were either under a vow of sexual continence or at least observing it.

Thus it has been generally recognized that those who desire to pierce through the ignorance or unbelief that veil the mind, and experience union with ultimate reality, must restrain the sexual impulse. Obviously advocating this discipline for mystical aspirants casts no aspersion on the "married chastity" of the majority of Christian or other laymen, whose aim is not, usually, to win through to direct experience of God in the present life. The two ways cannot be judged by the same standard. What is normal in the one would, in the other, call for a self-control that would inevitably lead to frustration and violent reaction. Neither way is to be considered in itself superior to the other.

Sexual restraint for the sake of mystical union would, at first glance, appear to have nothing to do with a question that has recently been troubling the Roman Church: celibacy for priests. In Hinduism, as in Judaism and Protestant and Orthodox Christianity, those carrying out priestly functions may marry. Nevertheless the agitation to release Roman Catholic priests from the vow of celibacy, from a certain point of view quite logical, may overlook one cardinal fact. As a result of his duties as confessor, the Roman Catholic priest is probably far closer to the Hindu monastic *guru* than other priests and ministers. At least in India, it is believed that conservation of sexual energy increases spiritual power and the capacity to transmit spirituality. Many priests today feel they can dispense with this gift; but perhaps, too, the special respect that many laymen, even those who are not Roman Catholics, feel for the priesthood stems from its requirement of chastity.

-9-

As we saw earlier, the disciplines of devotional self-giving are treated in the Bhagavad Gita in as great detail as those of intuitive wisdom. Indeed, in its second half they probably receive even greater stress, just as they do in the New Testament. Far more specific disciplines are outlined, however, in later devotional writings, and notably in the teachings of Chaitanya. Here, too, moral disciplines such as those outlined by Patanjali are held indispensable for receiving divine grace; but love of God is emphasized as the best guaranty of moral excellence. The grace of God cannot be purchased in this way, of course. But before it descends, the individual must usually make an effort. The saint Ramakrishna once put it in a colorful way: "The wind of God's grace is blowing night and day over your head. Unfurl the sails of your boat if you want to make rapid progress through the ocean of life."

According to Chaitanya, it is seldom that a soul develops the desire for love of God, or *bhakti*. This desire he obtains through the grace of the Lord Krishna and the compassion of a teacher. Once having obtained it, other desires fail to attract him. The mature fruit of love of God is supreme devotion, or *prema*. Chaitanya likens love to a vine that has to be sprinkled with the water of hearing and chanting the name of Krishna. To protect it from injury, one has to fence it round with general moral observances and religious regulations. During the process of growth, as a result of the watering various weeds may grow up around the vine; and secondary branches, too, may impede its further growth. Wrongdoing of different kinds, including unkindness to living beings, desire for wealth, fame, and success, as well as desire for the fruits of the way of intuitive wisdom (i.e., "liberation" from the world of relativity) and of Yoga (i.e., supernormal powers), and so on are the weeds and secondary branches. These must be uprooted or pruned so that the vine may produce the fruit of supreme devotion.

The negative aspect of love is to refrain from immorality, from the pursuit of intuitive wisdom, and from worship of gods other than Vishnu in the form of Krishna. The reason for this negative approach is, of course, that—as in any spiritual discipline—indulgence in what is known as immorality impedes the attaining of total concentration on the ideal. The positive aspect of love is to seek to serve the Lord through doing his will and using the senses as they should be used. Practice of this kind of love of God gives rise to five different "basic principles" of love, known as *ratis*, which represent attitudes by which a worshiper may approach God as a person. They are roles suited to the particular character of the devotee and are to be carried out where possible in painstaking detail (where circumstances require it, they may be enacted mentally). Only rarely does a devotee attain perfection in even one of the roles.

First comes the "peaceful" approach. This is a state of perpetual attachment to Krishna and renunciation of all other desires. Free from personal ties to the Lord, it does not possess the warmth of loving feeling. (Under this heading Ramakrishna included the Vedic sages; Vaishnavites give examples from the *Bhagavata Purana*.) It would appear to be concerned with a purely spiritual relationship with Krishna.

Next comes the approach of a servant. Here the worshiper takes Krishna as his Divine Master. (There are numerous examples in Vaishnavite mythology; Ramakrishna took as a classic example Rama's faithful servitor Hanuman.) In this attitude there is a more complete realization of the divine majesty of Krishna than in the peaceful approach, and a spirit of reverent and humble service to the Lord. (Many of the disciples of Jesus may be placed in this category, and the David of the Psalms.)

Third, and surpassing the approach of a servant in intensity, is the attitude of friendship. Krishna's boyhood friends in Vrindavan and the warrior Arjuna are examples of this type. Any thought of the divine majesty here causes confusion, as when Arjuna beheld Krishna's universal form. Something of the first two attitudes is found in this one, but here there is in addition a feeling of intimacy and trust without any sense of inferiority. The devotee feels that Krishna is his own. (Perhaps St. John the apostle may be thought of in this light.)

The last two approaches are characterized by more tender feelings toward the Lord. In the fourth type, that of a parent, no thought of Krishna's majesty intrudes—indeed, it only causes fear, as when his fostermother saw the universe in his mouth. It is characterized by feelings of loving protectiveness. (Christians will inevitably think of the attitude of Mary toward the Christ Child.)

Finally, and most intense of all, comes the attitude of passionate attachment to Krishna. The cowherd girls of Vrindavan, and especially Radha, are the principal examples of this approach. The love of bride for bridegroom would here seem most apposite for Christians, but though that approach belongs in this category, Hindus sometimes go beyond it and speak of the all-consuming love of a woman for her secret lover. There is no intention to condone this relationship in actual life; but in one sense it stands for utter devotion, for the woman is willing to sacrifice the good opinion of respectable society out of attachment to the one she loves.

The approach of passionate attachment includes five principles: the worshiper is constant in his devotion to Krishna, devotes himself completely to his service, feels no diffidence in his presence, cherishes an attitude of tender protectiveness toward him, and seeks to serve him in every way possible, as would a wife. Thus this attitude includes the elements of all the others.

In these relationships, if they are correctly practiced, the Lord responds in a manner befitting the role that is played. If the devotee assumes the role of a servant, for instance, the Lord may call him one day, as it were, and say to him, "Come, sit here beside me. You have served me long and faithfully. After all, there is really no difference between us." Similar mystical experiences would be granted in the other relationships. The point is that the devotee must throw himself into the role so completely that he forgets he is playing it at all and becomes what he is playing.

The tradition of the Japanese stage supplies a striking parallel to this sort of discipline. In a Noh play the actor is taught he is not to put his mask (representing the role he is to play) *on his face;* rather he must put his whole self, body and soul, *into the mask.* In exactly the same way (we shall observe an example in the last section of this chapter) the Vaishnava devotee must put himself into whatever devotional role his teacher prescribes as his proper discipline.

It goes without saying that when love of God ripens into supreme devotion, the concentration naturally attained becomes as complete as that arrived at through the disciplines prescribed by Patanjali or through those undertaken intellectually in the way of intuitive wisdom. We may draw the tentative conclusion that—whether or not its content is identical in every instance—what is needed for mystical experience is some sort of mental habit by which, through perfect attention, the mind is freed from discursive thought.

In addition to the basic Yoga discipline, we have briefly considered here two of the disciplines clearly related to the voices of intuitive wisdom and devotional self-giving. All the various denominations or cults have their particular disciplinary variations. As we saw in the previous chapter, Vaishnavism, Shaivism, and Tantra abound in elaborate rituals. These, too, can be used as disciplines for communing intimately with

God. The minute attention to detail required for their performance, along with the periods of prayer and meditation associated with worship, leads to the same sort of concentratedness
obtained through practice of the Yoga disciplines.

-10-

The life of one modern Indian saint has been aptly called a
"living laboratory of spiritual experimentation." I refer to
Ramakrishna Paramahamsa, who as a boy bore the name of
Gadadhar Chattopadhyaya. In a later chapter we shall see that
his life has further implications for our search for Christ beyond Christianity, but even the examples of discipline in his life
are so arresting that they are well worth considering for themselves. The lesson they convey is one that any spiritual—or
indeed other—aspirant may take to heart. It is simply this:
if you want to reach your goal, follow to the letter whatever
instruction you are given by your teacher and throw yourself
wholeheartedly into the quest.

Gadadhar Chattopadhyaya was born on February 18, 1836, in
Kamarpukur, a small village in the interior of West Bengal.
He was the fourth of five children. His father had died at the
age of sixty-six, when the boy was only seven years old. Because of the family's poverty, his eldest brother, Ramkumar,
left their village home in 1849 and went to Calcutta. There he
started a Sanskrit school; in addition, he performed priestly
duties each day for a number of Calcutta families. Three years
later, when his young brother was sixteen, he called Gadadhar
to help him.

Since the age of nine, when he was initiated into brahminhood and received the sacred thread, Gadadhar had regularly
performed ritualistic worship in the family shrine, where a
symbol of Rama represented the Deity. At the time of his
initiation he had received his first training in meditation. When,
on coming to Calcutta, Gadadhar showed no interest in learning
and teaching Sanskrit in order to enter upon the career of a
scholar, Ramkumar could think of only one solution. He had
him take over some of his priestly duties in the houses of the
families he was serving. Gadadhar's unusual sincerity and
fervor, and his utter simplicity, at once attracted everyone's
notice.

In the year 1855, a great temple of Mother Kali, the Divine Mother of the universe, was dedicated at Dakshineswar, on the outskirts of Calcutta. It stood on the bank of the Ganges, the center of a large complex including twelve shrines of Shiva in his various aspects and a temple of Krishna and Radha. Ramkumar had agreed to officiate at the dedication ceremonies as priest of Kali. When, at the urging of Rani Rasmani, the temple's owner, he accepted the permanent position of priest there, the two brothers gave up their work in Calcutta and remained at Dakshineswar. Shortly afterward Gadadhar was asked by the Rani's son-in-law, Mathurmohan Biswas, on her behalf, to assume the duties of priest in the Temple of Krishna and Radha. It is thought that it was Mathur Babu, as he was called, who gave the young priest the name of Ramakrishna.

Within the first year of their stay at the Temple of Kali, Ramkumar, perhaps sensing he would not live long, began to instruct Ramakrishna in the Tantric rituals of the worship of Mother Kali. Since worship of the Mother is not allowed without spiritual initiation, the older priest found a Tantric *guru* to initiate his brother. When the time came for the initiation, the teacher was taken aback by his pupil's behavior. No sooner had he uttered the sacred words of the *mantra*, or formula for repetition, into his ear than Ramakrishna, overwhelmed with spiritual ardor, gave a shout and entered into profound meditation. Before his brother Ramkumar's death in 1856, Ramakrishna became the priest of Mother Kali.

Now began one of the most poignant episodes in the history of Indian sainthood. Into his worship of the Mother, Ramakrishna day in and day out poured everything that was in him. The regular worship in the temple, where the Goddess was served three times a day—dawn, noon, and dusk—as Queen, awakened in him a hunger to know if she really existed. Most of the time outside what was needed for worship in the shrine, he spent in meditation. He almost forgot food and sleep. At length, much to the horror of the other temple officers, the young priest began to neglect the formalities of worship, acting as if the Mother was a living reality. He was heedless of everything but his passionate desire to see her. After somehow completing the worship, he would often spend hours singing devotional songs by poet-saints like Ramprasad. Separation from the Mother gripped him with anguish: it was as if, he later said, his heart was being wrung like a wet towel.

One day, overwhelmed by intense restlessness, he became

fearful he might not know Mother Kali in this life. He was seated in the shrine, and his eyes fell on a sword hanging on the wall. Leaping up, he thought to snatch it down and end his life—when suddenly the Mother revealed herself. In place of the objects of the outer world he saw a limitless, resplendent ocean of joy. Its dazzling waves extended as far as he could see, and they were rushing at him with a thunderous roar; caught up in their midst, he collapsed.

In after years Ramakrishna spoke to his disciples about the experience. ''What was going on in the world outside I did not know,'' he said, ''but inside me was a steady flow of pure bliss, altogether new. I felt the presence of the Mother.'' Without guidance, except for the sacred *mantra* he had received from the teacher for repetition, he attained communion with the Mother through sheer force of yearning, and through her grace.

But this one experience by no means satisfied him. He wanted to see Mother Kali uninterruptedly. And this desire, too, was granted. First he began to see her during meditation, and finally even while he was performing worship in the temple. His accounts of the phenomena he observed remind one of the passages from the *Shvetashvatara Upanishad* quoted earlier in connection with the phenomena experienced in the practice of Yoga.

Ramakrishna's was an imagination that illustrated everything to him with vivid visual or auditory images. Before sitting for meditation, he told his disciples, he would instruct his mind to be firm and motionless. Thereupon he would hear clattering sounds in the joints of his body, from the ankles upward, as if they were being locked with a key by someone within him. For as long as he had intended to meditate, he had no power to change his posture or abandon the meditation. Only when the clattering sounds were repeated at the end of the period determined on, this time from the neck downward, could he leave off the meditation. As he told his disciples, at first during meditation he would see particles of light like ''swarms of fireflies.'' Sometimes he saw a mist-like radiance that extended in all directions. At other times, all the objects around him were pervaded by waves of light, bright as molten silver. Not knowing whether such visions were to be regarded as helpful or harmful, he would pray, ''Mother, I don't understand what is happening to me. Please teach me how to realize thee.'' As he prayed he shed copious tears.

At first, when he was meditating during worship, he would see a hand or foot of the Divine Mother, delicate and luminous, or her exceedingly lovely black face, smiling on him. Finally he saw her full figure, even at times other than meditation. The Mother, he said, would go by his side. She would tell him how he should behave, saying, "Do this. Don't do that."

Twenty-five years later, one of his lay disciples heard him make an impassioned appeal to Mother Kali. It no doubt reproduces the sort of prayer he was using at this earlier time. "O Mother," he cried, "I throw myself on thy mercy. Keep me in constant thought of thee. I do not seek, Mother, the pleasures of the senses. I do not seek fame. Nor do I long for supernormal powers. What I pray for is pure love for thee, love untouched by desire, without alloy—love that does not seek the things of this world. Grant too, O Mother, that thy child, bewitched by the fascinations of the world, may never forget thee. Oh, grant that I may never feel the lure of sex or gold. Dost thou not see, Mother, that I have none else but thee? I do not know how to chant thy name. Utterly lacking am I in devotion, in knowledge, too, that leads to thee, in real love. Grant me that love, O Mother, out of thine infinite mercy."

Perhaps even before his first vision of the Mother, wanting to root out of his mind all desire for wealth, Ramakrishna had taken some coins in one hand and some earth in the other. Looking first at the coins and then at the earth, he reasoned that each of them was equally worthless in helping the mind to commune with God. "Rupee—earth, earth—rupee," he said again and again as he threw both into the Ganges. To destroy any sense of superiority at being born a brahmin, he went at night to the house of an untouchable and with his own hands carefully cleaned the latrine and other dirty places. He ate some of the leavings from the leaf-plates on which poor people had been fed at the temple, something no brahmin in his right mind would think of doing.

After his vision of the Mother, Ramakrishna had a strange experience. In a certain rite performed by brahmins, one has to think that what is called the Papa-Purusha, the embodiment of desire for worldly enjoyment, is being burned up. As a result of this exercise, he said, he began to have a sensation of burning all over the body. One day, as he was meditating, he saw a hideous jet-black figure come reeling out of his body, as if drunk. Almost immediately another person, with a calm face and dressed in the garb of a monk, emerged and with a trident killed the other. This figure of the monk began to accompany him and instruct him. At these times Ramakrishna was usually lost in a state of spiritual ecstasy. Interestingly, he stated that everything he later learned from the various teachers who came to him when he was practicing the different spiritual disciplines of various sects, had already been taught to him by this young and serene-faced monk. It seemed to him, as he thought about the situation, that his teachers had come to him simply so that the authority of the scriptures might be maintained by his following their commands.

Having obtained the vision of the Mother through his own unaided efforts, Ramakrishna decided also to know God through his own family ideal, Rama, whom he had worshiped in his village home. He therefore assumed the attitude of a servant to his master, as exemplified in the character of Hanuman, the monkey chieftain and staunch follower of Rama. In every way he tried to identify his actions and his thinking with those of Rama's servant. After a short time he had a vision—not, perhaps significantly, of Rama himself, but of his queen, Sita. He saw her, he said, in the normal state rather than in a state of spiritual ecstasy, and she was surpassingly lovely. Approaching him she entered his body. As she did so, she said, "To you I bequeath my smile." Sita, as we saw, was not a stranger to suffering. Perhaps this vision was prophetic of the suffering that was to come in Ramakrishna's own life. Often, after this experience, that smile was on his face. Of the several Vaishnavite relationships to be cultivated toward God, he now also took up the "peaceful" attitude and the attitude of friend toward intimate friend.

A cousin of Ramakrishna's named Haladhari had come to the temple during this first period of his spiritual practice. Because of his strenuous disciplines, Ramakrishna's health was none too good, so Mathurmohan Biswas, Rani Rasmani's son-in-law, appointed Haladhari priest of Kali. The latter had read various religious treatises and enjoyed arguing about the fine points of theology.

One day Haladhari thoroughly distressed his childlike and unscholarly cousin by stating that God is incomprehensible to the human mind. Because of his extraordinary spiritual experiences, Ramakrishna had already wondered sometimes if he was indeed going mad, as people had suggested. Now he was attacked by a terrible doubt. "How can you have the heart to deceive me like this," he complained to the Divine Mother, "just because I am a fool?" In a few moments a volume of mist rose from the floor of the room where he was seated and filled the space before him. Within it appeared the serene face of a sage with flowing beard. It was of fair complexion and profoundly expressive. Gazing at Ramakrishna steadily, the sage said solemnly, "Remain on the borderline between absolute and relative consciousness." Three times he repeated the command and then disappeared.

Ramakrishna heard the same words on two other occasions. In the light of his later life they are significant. Once he had completed his spiritual disciplines, that is exactly where his mind rested.

About this time Ramakrishna practiced with characteristic intensity the disciplines of *hatha-yoga,* which consist largely of physical exercises. One evening he felt a creeping sensation in his palate, and a quantity of dark, thickly clotted blood flowed from it and hung in ropes from his mouth. Everyone was alarmed. Despite various attempts to check the flow, it was only after some minutes that the bleeding stopped. A *sadhu,* or holy man, who happened to be staying at the temple, came and examined the color of the blood and the place it had escaped from in the palate. He told Gadadhar that, far from being a cause for alarm, the occurrence had been extremely fortunate. According to his explanation, as a result of Yoga practice blood was flowing toward Ramakrishna's head. Had it reached the brain he would have entered into a *samadhi* from which he could not have returned. The holy man felt that the Divine Mother was keeping his body for a special purpose.

In later years Ramakrishna would discourage people from practicing the disciplines of Yoga, saying that the minute attention to detail they required made them inadvisable for the modern age. Perhaps this experience also suggested that there was physical danger in practicing certain of the disciplines.

Reports of what appeared to almost everyone as the behavior of a madman filtered back to Ramakrishna's native village of Kamarpukur. His mother and his remaining older brother, naturally anxious, thought to cure him by arranging his marriage. Ramakrishna welcomed the proposal happily. As it turned out, the young girl chosen as his bride, Sarada Devi, became as great a saint as he. After the ceremony Ramakrishna stayed a year and a half with his mother. He was now somewhat restored in health. Because his wife had not yet reached maturity, she remained in her village home when he returned to Calcutta.

Hardly had the young priest of Kali reentered the temple precincts when the old "madness" seized him once more. Again the sensation of burning appeared in his body. Again sleep left him. Day and night one vision or another passed before his mind. Physicians were called in, but to no avail. Ramakrishna, however, having endured these symptoms before, was not overly concerned about them.

At this time Mathurmohan, the temple owner's wealthy son-in-law, had an extraordinary experience. As he was sitting in one of the rooms of the cottage reserved for the owner's family, he was watching Ramakrishna walking up and down along the veranda on the north side of the temple compound. To his astonishment, he suddenly noted that as the young priest walked toward the East it was the Divine Mother walking there, and when he turned around and walked toward the West, it was Shiva himself. Mathurmohan ran to the young priest, bowed before him, and seizing both his feet in his two hands, began weeping. He had seen Ramakrishna as what his final realization would show him to be, the embodiment of the indivisible Shiva-Shakti, the absolute Godhead and the divine Creative Power.

Ramakrishna now conceived a desire to practice the disciplines of as many of the recognized sects of India as he could. As it turned out, whenever he needed guidance, unaccountably an expert in the particular discipline he wished to follow appeared at the Temple of Kali. In answer to his need for instruction in the Tantra and Vaishnava practices, there came to Dakshineswar a remarkable woman *guru*, about forty years old, named Yogeshvari. Ramakrishna always referred to her as the Bhairavi Brahmani, the "brahmin-woman worshiper of the Goddess." Almost nothing is known about her background.

An adept in Tantric and Vaishnavite worship and discipline, Yogeshvari admirably fitted Ramakrishna's needs. She was self-assured in her convictions and commanded respect with her spirit of independence. She wore the traditional ocher-colored robe of a Hindu nun. To her Ramakrishna poured out the details of his previous experiences. After listening attentively to his accounts, Yogeshvari told him that what people took for ordinary madness was really an extraordinary madness for God. She assured him that the strange experiences he spoke of indicated he had known the highest stages of divine love, and she offered to teach him how to reach these same experiences through the disciplines taught in the scriptures.

Indeed, she was so filled with amazement at his account that she convened meetings of the most famous Bengali *pandits* of the day. On hearing directly from Ramakrishna about his experiences, all the scholars agreed with the Brahmani that he was that rarity, an *avatara*. Ramakrishna remained perfectly indifferent while the theological discussions went on, replying in a matter of fact way whenever the scholars asked him questions. At the conclusion of the discussions he said to Mathurmohan, like a boy, "Well, I'm glad to learn, after all, that it isn't a disease!"

Under the Bhairavi Brahmani's guidance, Ramakrishna now practiced the disciplines of the Tantra. She made him undergo, one by one, all the disciplines in the sixty-four principal scriptures. This undertaking involved an incredible amount of work on her part. During the day she would go about in search of the various articles necessary for the worship, and at night she would instruct her pupil and see that he went through the prescribed rituals. We have noted that Tantra does not prescribe outward renunciation, as Nondualistic Vedanta does. It seeks to turn the objects of the senses, which generally bind a man to the world, into means for his release. The rites it prescribes, if followed in the proper spirit, lead an aspirant to look on all women as embodiments of the Divine Mother. They are often perilous, and that is why a qualified *guru* is needed.

Ramakrishna, having already attained a high state of spiritual realization, passed through the most delicate of its rituals unscathed. One of these involved his sitting on the lap of a beautiful young woman whom the Bhairavi Brahmani brought to him in the dead of night. Though at first fearful, after praying to Mother Kali for assistance, he did as he was bidden. As he recited the prescribed *mantras*, a hitherto unknown power suddenly filled him. Seeing in the young woman an embodiment of the divine Shakti, his mind became absorbed in spiritual ecstasy and he became unaware of what was going on about him. As a result of his various practices, Ramakrishna's veneration for womanhood, already deep, became even more intense. At the conclusion of his period of spiritual discipline he would bear witness to this veneration in an impressive manner.

Ramakrishna's Tantric disciplines consumed from three to four years. During this period he had many unusual experiences. At one time, according to his account, he had a vision of a vast triangle of living light, symbol of the Creative Power in the form of the female organ. As he watched, he saw it was

giving birth to innumerable world systems. Again, he heard,
arising unceasingly throughout the universe, the sound of the
great *Pranava*, or *Om*, the Word of God, which combines all
the various sounds in creation. We have already discussed this
Word in the chapter on intuitive wisdom, where we saw that it
was conceived by the Vedantic seers as the *Sphota*.

Near the end of the period, Ramakrishna understood that he
possessed the "eight *siddhis*," the supernatural powers. These
include power to become small as an atom, to become weight-
less, to obtain whatever one asks for, to exercise irresistible
will, to increase to any desired size and weight, together with
the power of supreme lordship, of controlling all things, and of
suppressing desires. When he asked the Divine Mother whether
it was proper for him to use these powers, she bade him shun
them as if they were human dung. It is also said that at this
time the splendor of his features became so great that it attracted everyone's attention. Feeling troubled by this beauty,
and the attention it attracted, he prayed to the Divine Mother
to take away his outer beauty and give him instead inward
spiritual beauty. And his wish was granted.

After completing the disciplines of Tantra, Ramakrishna
followed, again with the Brahmani's assistance, the more advanced practices of Vaishnavism, or Vishnu worship. Even
before her coming, he had taken up, unaided, several of the
preliminary attitudes toward God. Now, having obtained a
small image of the boy Rama from a wandering holy man, he
cultivated the love of a mother for her child. Through this
discipline, he obtained a constant vision of Rama as a child.
Meditating on that form, he had two important realizations.
First, he understood that Rama exists as the individual soul
in each human being. Second, he saw that Rama, though entering into the universe and manifesting himself there, in his own
indescribable nature transcends the universe. Some years later
he had a vision of Rama and Sita together, the Godhead and
the Primal Power.

In the final Vaishnava discipline, as in the one just described,
a man must try to look on himself, in relation to God, as a
woman. To practice this discipline, the attitude of a passionate
lover, Gadadhar first meditated on the form of the purest of
Krishna's lovers, the cowherd girl Radha. His every action and
thought was in conformity with her mood of all-absorbing
devotion to her Lord. During this period he spent much of his
time with the ladies of Mathurmohan's household in Calcutta.

When at last he enjoyed a vision of Radha's enchantingly beautiful form, she, like all the other visions he had had, disappeared into his own body. Then, identified with Radha, Ramakrishna obtained a vision of Krishna, total embodiment of Satchidananda—absolute being, awareness, and joy. Lost in the thought of Krishna, he saw him manifested in all beings, "from the Creator down to a blade of grass" as it is said in scripture, and yet, at the same time, in himself the indescribable Satchidananda. Krishna and Radha, like Rama and Sita, symbolize the twofold mystery of the Godhead and the Power.

Ramakrishna had not yet completed his course of disciplines. It was necessary for him to experience, as well, the ineffable reality, the absolute Brahman-Atman, witnessed to in the Upanishads. At the end of 1864 there arrived at the temple a tall and sturdy wandering monk named Tota Puri, a member of the ascetical subsect of Nagas, who wear no clothes. (In the course of learning how to overcome the "eight fetters" that bind a man—hatred, shame, pride of lineage, pride of good conduct, fear, secretiveness, caste, and grief—the novices of this order are gradually taught, also, to remain naked without embarrassment.) Tota Puri was a Nondualistic Vedantist and had attained the stage of the *paramahamsa*, one who has transcended formal monastic rules.

For forty years Tota Puri, under his teacher's direction, had practiced discrimination between the permanent reality and the "unreal" or impermanent objects of the world. He had learned, painstakingly, to renounce everything impermanent. And he had acquired all the other qualities necessary for spiritual realization according to the teaching of Nondualistic Vedanta. At last he had succeeded in banishing every thought from his mind and achieved the goal of this discipline: direct knowledge of his identity with the True Self, or Atman. He was thus a *jivanmukta*, one who is "liberated in life." Such persons, after realizing the Self, continue to renew that experience from time to time in meditation. On the death of his teacher, Tota Puri had been elected as the abbot, or *mohant*, of his monastic community, which consisted of about seven hundred members. But like the other monks of his order, he sometimes took up a wandering life, visiting places of pilgrimage and living on such alms as people offered of their own accord.

When Tota Puri stopped at the Kali Temple in Dakshineswar, he at once noticed Ramakrishna's radiant face. Recognizing in him one eminently qualified for study and practice of the Non dualistic Vedanta philosophy and discipline, he proposed that the young priest should become his disciple. Immediately, like a child, Ramakrishna went to the shrine of Mother Kali and asked her permission. On returning, he told the monk it had been granted. Tota Puri was amused at what he thought to be the young man's superstition, but said nothing.

Since in order to receive the Vedantic instruction one must be initiated into monkhood, or *sannyasa*, Ramakrishna agreed to go through that ceremony. He asked only that it be performed in secret to spare the feelings of his old mother, now living in the temple precincts. After completing a long ritual which included making offerings into a sacred fire, symbolizing his complete renunciation of all desires, he uttered a *mantra*, or sacred formula, assuring all beings of freedom from fear on his account.

Tota Puri now took his disciple to a small meditation room and taught him the truths first announced in the Upanishads. Then he asked him to banish all thoughts from his mind and merge in meditation on the Self. Ramakrishna had no trouble in removing other ideas, but at first he found it impossible to rid his mind of the thought of Mother Kali, who when he meditated appeared before him as a vibrantly living reality. Disturbed, the teacher picked up a sliver of glass he found on the floor. "Fix the mind on this point," he commanded, piercing Ramakrishna's forehead between the eyebrows. Now, when the Mother appeared, the disciple pictured his power of discrimination as a sword and clove her form in two. His mind ceased functioning and he was lost in the ultimate *nirvikalpa samadhi*. In this state he remained for two days, after which the teacher brought his mind down to the normal plane by repeating the word *Om* in his ear again and again.

Tota Puri stayed with his pupil for eleven months, though he usually remained at a place no more than three days. There seems to have been a meaning in his breaking this custom. He had been an uncompromising nondualist; but before he left he finally came to understand that as long as one is identified with a human body one is under the jurisdiction of the personal God. After his departure, Ramakrishna remained for a half year in a state of continuous communion with Atman. Once in a while, to keep his body alive, a monk who was then staying at the temple and recognized his state forced a little food into his mouth.

Soon after this experience, Ramakrishna came to know a

devout Muslim, Govinda, who was much interested in Sufism. This gentleman read him passages from the Koran, and Ramakrishna became seized with a desire to know God through Islam. He was initiated by Govinda and under his guidance practiced its disciplines, regularly repeating the Islamic prayers and putting out of his mind all thought of his Hindu beliefs and customs. Here he was prompted, as so often before, by his insatiable desire to know God in as many ways as he could. At the end of this period of discipline he had a vision of an impressive person with shining features and a long beard, and he entered into communion with the all-pervading personal God and finally with the Godhead beyond thought. For him Islam thereafter was a valid way to attain experiential knowledge of God.

There are several reasons, Ramakrishna's followers say, why he had to undergo so many spiritual disciplines even after realizing God as Mother. In the first place, he himself could best be convinced of the validity of his own experiences if he could compare them with those of the sages and saints recorded in scripture. Such a conviction could only come to him if he practiced the disciplines laid down in those same scriptures, with the help of qualified teachers. He would then be in a position to understand how far the experiences he had gained through his own unaided efforts tallied with the scriptural accounts. (This explanation does not really conflict with his own estimate that his teachers had come to him so that the authority of the scriptures might be upheld by his obeying their commands.)

Moreover, according to his disciples, the purpose of his spiritual practice was not simply to win certainty and peace for himself. He was born for the good of mankind. In order to be a true spiritual guide he had to become acquainted—not merely through study but by practice—with the disciplines of every sort of spiritual path. Again, the spiritual states described in the various scriptures of the world would be shown to have meaning for the average person if they were reaffirmed through the person of an unlettered man of the day.

Believers in certain of the religions Ramakrishna is said to have practiced may not agree that he experienced them as an ordinary believer would. In view of what we have seen of his extraordinary spiritual sensitivity, we ought to withhold judgment about this man, whose every breath seems to have been drawn in union with God. (There is no record of his having practiced Buddhism or the Sikh religion, but he is known to have looked on both as paths leading to knowledge of ultimate reality.)

It was not till six years after his acquaintance with Islam that Ramakrishna undertook the last, and perhaps most significant, of his spiritual disciplines. When the monk Tota Puri had learned that his pupil was married, he had said, "What does it matter? That man alone is to be regarded as truly established in Brahman who can maintain his renunciation, nonattachment, discrimination, and wisdom even in the presence of a wife." Now Ramakrishna was to put himself to the test.

Sarada Devi, the saint's wife, had reached the age of eighteen. Distressed by continuing reports of her husband's madness and the mocking commiseration of her neighbors in her native village, she determined to visit Dakshineswar, clear up her doubts, and serve him as best she could. Four years earlier she had often been with him when he paid a visit to Kamarpukur, and at that time he had taught her many things, of both a worldly and a spiritual nature. She had been deeply impressed by his selfless love and concerned attention. She herself said after his visit, "Ever since that time I have felt as if a jar of bliss, full to overflowing, has been set in my heart." Was it possible that he had changed completely?

As soon as Sarada Devi appeared at the temple in Dakshineswar, she found all her fears were false. Ramakrishna immediately arranged for her to stay in his own room. The journey on foot from Kamarpukur (about sixty miles as the crow flies, but much longer by country roads) had tired her and she had become ill. Ramakrishna arranged for her treatment by a physician. Immediately on her recovery he shared his own bed with her each night. This would have been a severe test for an average husband and wife. But Sarada Devi had long before dedicated her heart to God, and she never demanded her conjugal rights. When Ramakrishna found that because of his frequent ecstasies during the night she became alarmed for him and had little rest, he told her to sleep in a nearby building with his mother.

After a year of close association, throughout which time no thought of his wife's body arose in his mind, Ramakrishna concluded that his spiritual practices had been completed. He thereupon made arrangements for a special worship of the Divine Mother according to the Tantra ritual, and placing Sarada Devi in the seat reserved for the Deity, worshiped her as the Goddess. Both husband and wife passed into a profound state of spiritual ecstasy and were united in communion with God. On returning to normal consciousness, Ramakrishna offered at his wife's feet, as to Mother Kali, the fruit of all his spiritual disciplines.

The saint was now ready to take up the task for which, knowingly or unknowingly, he had undergone all his disciplines— the task of bringing souls steeped in self-concern to a vision of the reality of God. It was only after this culmination of his spiritual practice that he began to make contact with the modern world. He had lived fully the life of ancient and medieval India. Now disciples gradually came to him : first, married lay devotees, and then, through them, the young men who were to become his monastic disciples and spread his message in India and the world outside.

THE VOICE
OF SERVICE AND
HUMAN COMMUNITY

THE LAST AND MOST immediately significant of the four episodes on our journey to Gorakhpur was that of the midnight
breakdown of the taxi. Far more precisely than the other three
it brings to mind the voice it represents. For it occasioned an
almost perfect example of effortless service, the ideal closest
to men's needs today. What is singularly revealing about the
episode is who among us were actively involved and who were
not. Those who could not by any stretch of the imagination have
rendered effective help—the two university men, professor and
student—finally went to sleep. A third member, myself, was
involved mostly by empathy, as interested observer and seeker
of meanings. It was our driver Atmaprasad Dubey, his helper
Pande, and the quiet brahmin schoolteacher-mechanic who
bore witness here to the voice of service and human community.

When one observes to what extent men in all parts of the
world, professing beliefs of widely varying kinds, are capable
of selflessness, one must ask oneself a few questions. How is it
that a substantial part of what Christians generally think of as
central to Christian behavior is already so well understood by
non-Christians? No matter if in some instances poverty or ill
health discourages its manifestation; still it is seen too frequently
to be denied. Is it merely because others are to that degree
Christian, or is that too easy an answer? Our study of this
particular aspect of the spiritual life seems specially useful
for our search for Christ's working outside the Church. Here
no differences of religious imagery or terminology make the
findings ambiguous. And in the reasons that motivate selfless
service, perhaps we have our best clue about where, ultimately,
to look for Christ beyond Christianity.

In Christian terms, the voice of service and human community bids a man worship God directly through his fellows,

seeing in them the living Christ. "You shall love your neighbor as yourself," expresses its message to perfection. How one is to practice this kind of love is made clear by the Golden Rule: "As you wish that men would do to you, do so to them"—an injunction that is to be found in one form or another in all the great religions. In the incident of the man waylaid by robbers on his way from Jerusalem to Jericho, Jesus sought to bring home this message of love of neighbor. Stripped, beaten, left half-dead, the man lay on the road. A priest going by, no doubt on some important mission, seeing him, went to the other side of the road. A Levite, one of those assigned to help priests take care of the temple, did the same thing. It was only a despised Samaritan, one upon whom society looked with scorn, who bound up the man's wounds and provided for his needs. It was he, Jesus made his listeners understand, who truly loved his neighbor.

Again, in that familiar but still awesome revelation that speaks of the Last Judgment, the message is amplified. As Jesus put it, "Then the King will say to those at his right hand, 'Come, O blessed of my Father, inherit the kingdom prepared for you from the foundation of the world; for I was hungry and you gave me food, I was thirsty and you gave me drink, I was naked and you clothed me, I was sick and you visited me, I was in prison and you came to me.' " And, he continued, when the righteous would ask the King when they had done all this, he would say, "Truly I say to you, as you did it to one of the least of these my brethren, you did it to me."

Jesus himself is for Christians the preeminent example of his own teaching. No one in the history of the West ever spent himself so continuously and unsparingly for others as he did. All the apostles, too, exemplify the true spirit of service and human community. Most of the saints of the Christian Church must likewise be included as examples. The active approach of Ignatius Loyola comes particularly to mind.

-2-

It is clear why men should be particularly conscious of the voice of service today. We are aware as never before of the poverty and hunger and disease and lack of education in today's developing and even developed world—afflictions due in no small part to a failure of Christian concern. But there

is another important reason, too: one that has always placed
a limit on the number of persons who could follow the other
voices. These latter, if they are to be heeded, require very
special conditions. And those conditions cannot be found
except in a monastic setting, or in such surroundings as money
or academic insulation (if such still exists) or perhaps the
atmosphere of a certain type of commune can provide. To very
many earnest Christians the practices to which intuitive wisdom
and devotional self-giving call men—whether as separate ways
or as ways conjoined—seem luxuries that few can afford. And
even were the proper conditions available, it is simply beyond
the capacity of most men to follow where these voices would
lead.

This is by no means to condemn the other three voices and
what they call for. When followed to their logical conclusion,
they constitute the backbone of the religious experience in
every religion. Without those who have in their own individual
fashion given expression to intuitive wisdom, without the
selfless lovers of God who have put into words and often poems
and hymns the spirit of devotional self-giving, without the
practicing mystics who by one or the other (or both) of these
ways have communed with God and often hit upon new disciplines to reach their goal, there would be far less basis for the
faith and hope and love that Christians and other religious believers cherish. But the voice of service and human community
gains special significance from the fact that the least of men can
follow it. It is one that even men who acknowledge no religion
are unknowingly heeding when they obey their most generous impulses. Indeed, without a man's heeding it, there is no
way to put into practice the command to love one's neighbor
as oneself, the second of Jesus' "great commandments," on
which, he said, "depend all the law and the prophets."

To really grasp the difference between this voice and the
others, we need only remind ourselves of the difference between
hearing the voices and heeding them. A large number of reli-
giously-minded people, perhaps a majority, are not thinking of
disciplines when they speak of their "religion." They are
referring to the set of beliefs that go with it and to certain
feelings those beliefs evoke in them. Many of these people
practice, from time to time, a little reflection or prayer. But
(to use the description of one modern Hindu saint) a sort of
"comfortable" faith appears to satisfy their religious needs.
This is a far cry from the wholehearted faith of which Jesus

spoke, one that immediately issues in a sense of the reality of God and in selfless works.

The sort of "popular devotional religion" we observed in the second episode of our trip to Gorakhpur can be, and often is, little more than emotionalism. But it is not the only type of popular faith. The Nondualistic Vedanta professed by many Hindus and some Westerners in the twentieth century, sometimes called "neo-Vedanta," can also take this form. It is wholly inspired by the voice of intuitive wisdom. "We are all one," such persons say, "and there is no 'sin,' only ignorance." Yet they stop with the words. Because their faith has an intellectual rather than an emotional cast, it is not any the less a popular faith. Both these aspects of religious persuasion consist in the acceptance by their adherents of a complex of ideas and sentiments. The same thing is true of comparable versions of these two approaches in Christianity. Neither of them in itself involves an all-out dedication that would inevitably result in discipline—the kind of dedication implied in Krishna's words to the warrior Arjuna: "Abandon all duties and come to me alone for shelter."

With those who hear the voice of service and human community, however, the position is reversed. Unlike the intellectual and devotional voices, it cannot become a means to cater merely to a "comfortable" faith. For the man who hears it there can be no distinction between belief and practice. Hearing *is* heeding. The voice *is* the way. Even in hearing it a man becomes a follower; for him morality and social service are almost automatic. Even if at first his personal behavior should not be irreproachable, something infectious in his own good works gradually forces inward goodness upon him, as well. His image of reality is mankind itself. Any action on his part that he recognizes as harmful to others—whether his own direct action or some form of inward persuasion that makes him a less useful and integral part of society—becomes repugnant to him. It weakens his sense of belonging to the human community.

The ideal that such a man strives to realize is a community that functions as a single healthy organism: first his own limited community, ultimately perhaps the total world community. For him immorality is simply what makes the social organism less healthy; an immoral man is a sick cell in the body of society and is, if possible, to be healed, not destroyed. The man I am thinking of is not one who seeks to force his "superior" ideas on other men for what he concludes is their own good, but one who desires only to serve according to the best norms the traditions of his race have evolved through the centuries. This man's salvation comes of the selflessness born of thinking only of others.

The voice of service and human community is thus that of an actually present world, a world that challenges men in society to meet its best demands or fall into meaninglessness and ultimate neglect. What is of prime importance to those who hear this voice is action: how to act to the best advantage of everyone. Theories will not suffice. It will not matter so much whether or not there is a God, whether or not there is a soul. True, belief in God and soul give many men an added incentive for developing the community sense and a desire to serve. But thousands of men and women—and not simply in countries that accept the Marxist interpretation of history and human destiny—are in no position to concern themselves with religious concepts. It is all they can do to stay alive, to find means to buy food and clothing and provide shelter for their own families, and keep on reasonably good terms with their fellow men.

Whether it is within reach of all men to achieve a deep and lasting sense of human community is not the point. What is important is that some men strive after it. Countless human experiences bear witness to the fact that, for a limited period of time, it *can* be realized on a large scale. During an unexpected emergency, such as an unplanned blackout in a great city or an earthquake or some other natural disaster, men for a moment forget *themselves* and unite to help each other combat the common danger. The very poor sometimes also achieve a high degree of community sense, at least among their own group. Soldiers have testified throughout history that they never felt such a sense of human community as when living with their comrades under enemy fire. The same thing is being accomplished in a more extended way for many people today by the current concern about ecology—born of a realization of how gravely pollution threatens the very life of mankind.

Citizens in democratic countries often wonder how people under the "iron rule" of Communist dictatorships in the Far East can display the endurance they do in defending their countries against non-Communist foes. Where the majority of the people have accepted the philosophy of dialectical materialism, the answer lies in the ideal held up before their society:

that each give according to his capacity and receive according
to his needs. The day before he died, Thomas Merton said in
Bangkok, in a meeting I attended, that this Communist ideal
for society was actually the definition of a monastic community and, he felt, could only be realized in such a community. In any case, in that goal, if one listens, can be heard
echoes of the voice of service and human community.

Cultivation and maintenance of the sense of community over
long periods of time is not beyond the capacity of men if the
ideals held up before society encourage forgetfulness of self.
Here is where the Western system is most open to criticism.
In assuming that each man is free to rise as high as he wants,
it fails to protect the less intellectually or inventively gifted
from those who, wittingly or unwittingly, would exploit them. It
also keeps these latter, the manipulators of society, from seeing
the extent to which tendencies toward colonialism still flourish—
especially in the United States and South Africa—in regard to
racial minorities (and to women). In these instances the sense
of human community has become atrophied despite the seem-
ing vitality of the general society.

It was toward forming a community sense that the ancient
Indian social system was devised after the Indo Aryan invasion
of the area that is now India and Pakistan. The human beings
to whose hands it was entrusted could not make the most of
it and finally allowed it to atrophy, but that is not the fault
of the system. True, the Indian lawgivers were also seeking
to provide a climate where a man who chose to could, in the
fullness of time, devote himself to the quest for ultimate
reality, and thus the individual's salvation was perhaps valued
over that of the whole society. Yet though a personal morality
may have been the overriding concern, a thoroughgoing social
morality was also evolved. Considering the state of human
nature, perhaps a democracy patterned on the *ideal* Indian
social system is, in the longer view, the only viable alternative
to the Marxist system.

There are two main Indian textual sources that comment
about developing the sense of community in society: the
Bhagavad Gita and certain secondary scriptures that deal with
social morality. They approach the problem from two different
points of view. The secondary scriptures concern themselves
with what men *ought* to do with regard to each other; they
speak purely "from authority." We shall briefly glance at
some of the provisions of one of these, the *Manava Dhar-*

mashastra, or *Code of Manu.* We shall then consider what the
Bhagavad Gita has to say—speaking less from above, and
more with the voice of reasonable persuasion—about how one
can develop the technique of selfless activity, what it calls
"skill in action," without which no social system can function
properly.

-3-

As I said before, the man who is an integral and active part
of society is in many cases so busy keeping alive that he cannot
afford to spend much time thinking about how to behave toward
others. When he does think about it, if he is a religious man,
he usually consults the code of laws enunciated by his civilization's original lawgiver or lawgivers. Though they may be
unaware of the fact, even those who profess no religion have
in large part derived their notions of good and bad, right and
wrong, from the teachings of such ancient lawgivers.

In India the *Code of Manu* is probably the most representative and influential code in existence. It dates from about the
fourth century B.C. Just as the laws governing the people of
Israel have been formulated in the Old Testament in Exodus
and Leviticus, so in the *Code of Manu* are gathered, in a systematic way, such rules as the Hindu lawgivers decided were
useful for the self-governing of a healthy people. (It is worth
noting that allowance is made in it for the role of conscience, in
contradistinction to the role of law, in determining a right
course of conduct for the individual.) Here was first set down
in ordered form the primeval Indo-Aryan concept of the
social hierarchy, of the goals of human life, and of the stages
of that life. The social system of ancient India was clearly an
attempt to devise a self-adjusting human community.

Indian society was divided into four basic groups. They had
been enunciated many centuries earlier in the "Hymn of the
Supreme Person," in the Rig-Veda, quoted in the third chapter of this book; but even there the poet is seeking to explain
the origin of something already long in existence. The divisions
recognized in the *Code of Manu* are found, in one form or
another, in every democratic and even classless society, though
they are not always given the same order of precedence.
Curiously enough, as Vivekananda has pointed out, each of

these four social divisions has, during the course of man's history, ruled in turn the destinies of human society—and in the Indian order.

The social divisions, which I have already mentioned in passing, were as follows: There were priests, known as *brahmins*, who conducted religious ceremonies thought to provide for the welfare of gods and men; they may be said to have been in charge of the spiritual and intellectual (i.e., cultural) welfare of society. There were nobles and warriors, known as *kshatriyas*, who protected the state from enemies within and without, and upheld the religious and cultural order; they concerned themselves with politics and statesmanship and wielded the military power. There were the farmers and merchants, known as *vaishyas*, who carried on business and provided food; it was they who upheld the economy. Finally, there were the manual workers, the *shudras*, who provided the physical effort needed for every sort of public and private undertaking in construction, for personal service, and for related occupations; as in all examples of social organization, it was they on whom depended, ultimately, the whole social fabric. This original system later became infinitely complicated in India as castes became divided into subcastes, each with its own rules.

Caste itself, as has been pointed out by scholars, was first based upon the color of the skin. In the beginning, as we shall see, there was a definite reason for this arrangement. Gradually it came to refer to the "color of one's character," and was no longer strictly hereditary.

According to a widely held theory in ancient India, the structure of every object and of every living being in nature is made up of three "qualities" or "strands" (*gunas*): activity, inertia, and balance (*rajas, tamas*, and *sattva*). They are sometimes interpreted, according to their manifestation, as "passion," "dullness or viciousness," and "purity." *Sattva* represents a balance between *rajas* and *tamas*; it is something like an expression of the Golden Mean of Aristotle.

We are told in the Bhagavad Gita that the work expected of a true *brahmin*, in whom balance or purity (*sattva*) prevails, is control of the mind and senses, austerity of life, cleanliness, forbearance, uprightness, knowledge, realization, and faith. The behavior expected of a *kshatriya*, in whom activity or passion (*rajas*) predominates over balance (*sattva*), is heroism, high spirit, firmness, resourcefulness, dauntlessness in battle, generosity, and sovereignty. The pursuits of a true *vaishya*, in whom activity or passion predominates over dullness (*tamas*), are agriculture, cattle rearing, and trade. And the duty of a *shudra*, in whom dullness is said to predominate over activity or passion, is service.

It is stated in various scriptures, including the *Code of Manu*, that if the action of a certain caste member corresponds to that of another caste, whether higher or lower, the man is really a member of that caste. Even in one of the early Upanishads, a would-be student is asked by a teacher what caste he belongs to. The young man replies that his mother has served in a house where she had to take care of a number of guests; she does not know who his father was. The teacher at once decides he must be a *brahmin*, because he has told the truth, even though it is damaging to himself.

A strict system of hereditary caste returned many centuries later, when the question of the color of a man's skin was no longer a vital consideration. In the system at its best, each caste was supposed to recognize its dependence on the others; and the punishment for a particular transgression of the law was stricter in the case of a member of a ''superior'' caste. Not only the rituals of the three upper castes, but also very many social regulations, are meticulously formulated in the *Code of Manu* on the basis of immemorial practice.

It is said that originally the members of the fourth, or *shudra*, caste included the dark-skinned race that the Indo-Aryans found inhabiting India. The invaders sought to dominate them by refusing them access to their special wisdom. (These people actually had a highly developed culture of their own, which, according to certain scholars, though at first suppressed, later asserted itself and was assimilated into the total Indian culture.) On occasion the *shudras* were accepted into higher castes, as were members of certain invading tribes in later centuries, when they manifested the Indo-Aryan qualities required of members of such castes.

From the most ancient times, it would appear from references in the Vedas, there was also a group of unfortunates called ''untouchables'' (very much like the members of certain minority groups in the Western world), with whom people of respectable society did not eat or intermarry. Among the inhabitants of the newly conquered country encountered by the Indo-Aryans were persons who differed from the *shudras*. These, it is conjectured, were the aboriginal inhabitants of India. They observed no rules of health, were willing to perform the most menial tasks, such as removal of human dung and offal, and even ate the flesh of dead animals. Contact with them was found to produce disease. They were therefore, as a health precaution, declared "untouchable." In time, members of the ruling classes who had transgressed caste laws, as for instance by marrying into a lower caste, were as a punishment demoted to the level of untouchables.

Though the voice of human community has through ages been stifled by this sort of practice—whether frankly acknowledged, as in India, or largely unacknowledged, as in the West —there are few if any countries where as eloquent and effective opposition to the practice has been launched as in India. Following the lead of Ramakrishna and his disciple Vivekananda, yeoman service was performed not only for India but for the world by Mahatma Gandhi in his heroic opposition to this abuse.

Along with their discussion of caste duties, the ancient Hindu thinkers formulated what they considered the prime goals of human life on earth. These, like the castes, were four in number, and were related to four stages through which the normal man was ideally supposed to pass. The four goals of human life are these: righteousness, or *dharma*; economic security, or *artha*; sensuous and aesthetic enjoyment, or *kama*; and liberation from delusion, or *moksha*.

The four successive stages of life through which members of the three upper castes were ideally supposed to pass were celibate studenthood, or *brahmacharya*; householder's life, or *garhasthya*; the life of a recluse, or *vanaprastha*; and monkhood, or *sannyasa*. We observed in the second chapter that in the first of these stages a young man learned, in one of the forest retreats, how to achieve the goal of righteousness (especially the truths taught in the Vedas), together with the precise *dharma*, or inner law, of a man in his own particular division and stage of society. In the second stage, as a man of the world, he learned by experience (and through consulting treatises on the subject) about the second and third goals: how to obtain economic security (or, if he was of noble birth, how to rule) and how to enjoy, in a controlled way, the life of the senses. Both these goals of life, if they were to bear fruit, had to be pursued in accordance with the ideal of righteousness, already learned in the stage of studenthood. Their correct pursuit would naturally lead him, once his sons had reached maturity, to the understanding necessary for pursuing in the

third and fourth stages the fourth goal of life, namely, liberation from the ignorance or unbelief that hinders him from
communing with ultimate reality.

If a man felt a sufficiently strong urge, it was said, he could
renounce the worldly life and enter the fourth stage, that of
monkhood, or *sannyasa*, at any time—though in general it was
held to be more psychologically sound to have experienced the
three preliminary stages before embracing the fourth. Shankara
in the ninth century and Ramana Maharshi in the twentieth
renounced the world from the first stage. The Buddha in the
last decade of the sixth century B.C. and Chaitanya in the first
decade of the sixteenth century of the modern era renounced
it from the second stage. Ramakrishna, whose marriage remained unconsummated, also technically renounced it from
the second stage. Jesus, who in his own words had "nowhere to
lay his head," was in Hindu eyes a *sannyasi* as much as these
others.

The practice in modern Thailand of urging a young man to
undergo at least a short period of monastic training before
becoming a husband and active member of society is an interesting variant. Possibly this custom is equivalent only to a prolong-
ing of the student period; possibly it represents a holdover from
the teaching of early Buddhism that only a monk or nun can
attain Nirvana. Both in India (except among very orthodox
Hindus) and in Buddhist countries more men renounce the
world while still young than the original Indian scheme would
seem to have advocated. The ancient scheme of the four stages
still makes sense to most lay members of Hindu society who are
religiously inclined. It is a scheme well suited to encourage a
true spirit of human community.

Along with the four divisions of caste, the four goals of
human life, and the four stages of that life as set forth in the
secondary scriptures, we must not overlook another important
contribution in Hindu culture to the sense of human community. I refer to the great epics, the *Ramayana* and *Mahabharata,* also of course a form of secondary scripture. These,
thanks to the understanding of their authors, presented the
spiritual and moral truths of the canonical scriptures in understandable form to the members of the lowest caste, to whom
reading or hearing of the Vedas had been prohibited by the
original Indo-Aryans. It may well be that the cultural unity of
the whole Indian peninsula is due to their foresight.

- 4 -

An impressive extension of the sense of community is to be found in certain Hindu scriptural teachings about men's obligations to other living beings. These obligations, mentioned, like most of the social duties we have been considering, in the *Code of Manu*, are given the name "sacrifice." The "sacrifice for men" consists in feeding the poor and the homeless and in receiving guests as God. (Service proffered to one's fellow beings was clearly recognized as worship long before the Christian era.) Even in the Upanishads the same thought occurs: "Let [a man] not deny lodgings to anyone: this is the vow. Therefore he should procure much food by any means whatsoever. [To guests] he should say, 'This food has been prepared for you.'" In addition to this there is a "sacrifice for creatures"; it consists in taking care of domestic animals. Buddhists, too, have been influential in encouraging the feeling of compassion for all living beings. (The Jainas even have a custom of feeding ants and other insects whatever food is pleasing to them.)

Men also have obligations to those who are no longer living. The "sacrifice for ancestors" consists in performing ceremonies intended for the welfare of the dead. These are to be carried out by an oldest son for his father or mother a year after their death, and for all his ancestors as well. Before being initiated into monkhood, or *sannyasa*, a man must perform not only these ceremonies but also his own funeral rites, because he is now dead to the things of this world.

In Thai Buddhism, certain acts of service bring merit to the doer, and that merit can be transferred to others. For instance, the merit derived from feeding a monk may be destined in thought for the welfare of a departed relative. Again, monks are always fed at the funeral services for a parent, as I observed at a ceremony for the father of a friend in Bangkok. This sort of concern for the departed is widespread throughout the East. In the Noh plays of Japan, for instance, characters on many occasions offer prayers for a dead person, and gratitude is expressed by that person's spirit after they have been offered. Prayers for the souls in purgatory by Roman Catholics, and visits to the graves of family members by all Christians, similarly serve to strengthen the sense of community. Whether one believes in an afterlife or not, a feeling of gratitude to one's forebears—as also to those great writers or artists or scientists or philosophers or statesmen or saints of the past who have enriched the present life of humanity—must inevitably deepen one's community sense.

It is among the living, however, that this sense demands fullest cultivation. Westerners like to think they excel in a sense of fellow feeling. They are not alone. As many have affirmed, and as Malcolm X recorded in his *Autobiography*, the sense of brotherhood experienced among Muslims on pilgrimage to Mecca is hard to match elsewhere. Though this latter is perhaps a religious phenomenon, there are in the East purely social manifestations as well.

In India, especially up to the time of the First World War, one custom has contributed notably to the development of such a community sense. It is what is known as the joint-family system. (Even now it has not completely disappeared.) The custom was that sons should bring their wives home to live as daughters in one large family community, while daughters should go to their husbands' homes to live there as family members. Through a friend, I knew of such a family, consisting of forty-odd members, which had lived in what is now Bangladesh. The single earning member was a lawyer. My friend, one of his sons, told me that when he asked his father for a new pair of shoes, he was told, "Yes, you can have a new pair. But only when there is enough for all the boys to have a pair." In such families, older persons who for some reason could earn no money performed various functions. They helped with the household chores, or with the farm work if the family lived in a rural village. Sometimes, too, distant relatives were brought into the family. Never was an older member sent away to die in an old people's home—there were none, not only because of India's poverty but because the idea was unthinkable. When the father in the particular family I have spoken of suddenly died at the age of forty, all the members were absorbed into other relatives' households.

The sense of community thus engendered was so strong that on occasion it could result in the most exquisite expressions of charity. In this large joint family in East Bengal, before each meal the Hindu mother would stand outside their compound and call out, "Is there anyone who is without food?" If such a person appeared, he would first be fed. Then the family would sit down for their meal. In a joint-family the burden on a few earning members was sometimes heavy. But the lessons in communal sharing and adjusting were profound.

I have also visited, on several occasions, with an only slightly smaller family in the heart of Calcutta, that of my friend Shibdas Bhattacharyya. There, despite the drawbacks that living in close quarters inevitably gives rise to, I found a spirit of natural cooperation that is hard to come by in modern-style establishments. Thirty members are housed within a small enclosure in which are a number of very simply furnished rooms, eleven in all, clustered around the family shrine. On one side of the shrine is the kitchen and dining space; on the other is a small plot, open to the sky, with flowering trees that provide some of the special flower offerings needed for daily worship. The wives of the various sons all mix on terms of equality. The children are like brothers and sisters. Several orphans have been taken in and live as family members.

Shibdas, who is the largest contributor to the family exchequer, has been known to me for perhaps a dozen years. I met him in New York when he first came there as a seaman in the Indian merchant marine. Each time his ship touched at New York he came to see me, and on his last visit he urged me, when next I visited Calcutta, to stay at his place. Several years ago I was planning to pass through India, and I wrote him I was coming. As poor luck would have it, Shibdas had to sail with his freighter the very day I arrived. Though he was absent, the family insisted I use the room he and his wife Sulata usually occupied. (It was actually a separate tiny cottage of one room, mostly occupied by a big double bed, on the far side of the "garden.")

When I carried my things there, I found Shibdas' old father, Nishikanta Bhattacharyya, sitting on a chair at the door, waiting to greet me. He beamed with good will and showed me a sandalwood cane I had given Shibdas several years before, which he had in turn given his father. Though only three or four of the thirty family members spoke English, such was their kindliness that I never for a moment felt ill at ease. A bright twelve-year-old lad, who spoke English so fast he was constantly stumbling over his words, immediately attached himself to me. He took me on several errands I had to attend to—calling me "Uncle" with every other sentence. In the late afternoon Shibdas' wife, a Sanskrit scholar, returned from the school where she taught. She and her sisters-in-law went out of their way to make me comfortable. In the evening came my friend's "cousin brother," Abhayapada, who had excused himself from his job for the next day so he could accompany me wherever I needed to go.

This young man—one of the most truly simple and artless persons I have met—told me he had decided not to marry, but to devote himself to others' welfare. He had therefore accepted an accountant's position with the municipality of Calcutta, which paid just enough to let him contribute his share to the family, and each night put himself at the disposal of the people of the neighborhood. Having taken instruction in practical nursing, he gave hypodermic injections to those who needed them, bandaged cuts and bruises, took people to the hospital, and so on. When he came, he said he would sleep in the same bed with me so that in case I needed to go to the toilet at night he could lead me there, around the various small buildings, with a flashlight.

A special atmosphere was created by the fact that Shibdas' father, a brahmin priest, conducted ritualistic worship of the Deity regularly every day. I was told the old gentleman began his preparations about three in the morning and continued till nine o'clock. Again at midday there was worship, and finally at sundown. One late afternoon I sat at the door of the shrine while he performed the beautiful ritual of waving of lights—to the accompaniment of a bell vigorously rung by my young "nephew"—before the image of the Lord Krishna. The family also worshiped the Divine Mother and some symbol of her may have been on the altar, too. To show my respect I had brought a small garland of jasmine flowers, and this was included among the offerings made during the ceremony.

The sheer goodness of this orthodox priest suffused the whole establishment with a tranquillity one noticed even more in retrospect. Contributing to this atmosphere, certainly, was the untiring and ever watchful service of his retiring and dignified wife. Because I was their son's friend, nothing was too good for me.

On my next visit to Calcutta, Shibdas was present. He was about to take his examination to become a sea captain—a very difficult examination for a very responsible job. The same unfailing kindness was lavished on me. I was touched, as on the previous visit, by the loving solicitude with which the women of the family fed me and stood around while I ate, to see that everything was right. No doubt the fact that I had come from a far-off land just to see them made them eager to make me happy. Yet the size of the establishment, too, I felt, had much to do with it, in some inexplicable way making my reception the unforced act of worship it seemed to be. The guest, in ancient India, was worshiped almost as if he were a messenger from God. With his dying words, a Hindu king who had just been stabbed by someone posing as a holy man, ordered his followers to give the person he had received as an honored guest safe conduct to the border.

The institution of the joint family is disappearing in Bengal —indeed it has almost completely disappeared—under the impact of modern thinking. Many young people, as in the West, wish to lead independent lives. Yet I am not persuaded the drawbacks outweigh the benefits. In large families, such as the ones I have been telling about, friction there must always be. Whenever people live in crowded conditions, the occasions for misunderstanding are multiplied. Nevertheless, the presence of two such selfless persons as the father and mother in my friend Shibdas' family would seem to ensure a great measure of understanding and compromise. Since in India there still seems to be much less need of privacy than in the West, the institution may, where it survives, work better than in the United States or in Europe. But a study of the joint-family system in India would no doubt yield lessons for those interested in the experiment of the commune.

Because of this tradition, Hindus—and people in the East, generally—seem able to form intimate relationships with those unrelated to them by blood, and even with foreigners. Very many men in India have learned to look on women other than their wives as they would on their mother. Older men are often addressed as Father or Uncle. In the course of my trips in the East I have acquired at least four "sons," half a dozen "brothers," and several "sisters."

Perhaps I am particularly aware of this capacity because of one unforgettable relationship I formed with a retired professor of chemistry, Chandicharan Palit, in Allahabad. Dr. Palit came to look on me as his son. In our correspondence during the ten years between our first meeting, in 1949, and our second, in Banaras in 1959, he never failed to include copious information about the state of his own health and about doings in the family. On one occasion he even asked my opinion about the marriage of one of his grandchildren. When we met the second time, the old man was sobbing for joy. Fortunately I saw him again in 1968. Recently, when I learned of his death from my two brothers, his sons—who wrote me immediately on their arrival for the funeral—I felt an emptiness that one would expect to feel only for a real father. Such relationships, especially when they are genuinely acted upon, as in Chandicharan Palit's case, add a dimension of human warmth lacking in modern life in the West.

From the purely spiritual point of view, the ultimate in the sense of human community is probably found in the Christian concept of the Mystical Body of Christ—especially if it is interpreted as potentially including all humanity, and not simply all Christians (or all one's own sect of Christians). A graphically similar conception is implicit in the description of the universal form of the Lord Krishna, as found in the Bhagavad Gita, in which all created things are included. Even in the Vedas the four castes were seen as forming various parts of the Supreme Person. But the implications of this idea have yet to be worked out by Indians as they have been by Christians. (Perhaps to them this would seem superfluous.) Possibly nearest to the Christian concept, and influenced by it, is an idea found among certain members of the Ramakrishna Order, for whom the brotherhood and the lay disciples, together with the physical manifestations of the organization (schools, hospitals, monasteries, and so on), constitute the "body of Ramakrishna." A sense of human community is also embodied in the concept of the United Nations and in the idea—found in democratic and, more explicitly, in Marxist countries—of citizens' being vital members of one body politic.

- 5 -

The *Code of Manu,* like almost all the Hindu scriptures, presents its recommendations about moral conduct in society in an authoritarian manner. All these recommendations presuppose the acceptance of a certain way of behavior, but only in the Bhagavad Gita are they offered from the standpoint of reasonable persuasion. A large proportion of its verses deal with how to develop what it calls "skill" in action. All men, it reminds us, perform some sort of action. "No one can remain even for an instant without doing work," says Krishna. But how are we to act effectively? Without such a technique, all the good will in the world will be of no avail, and the works of service demanded by the voice of human community will fail of their intention. To this scripture, then, to which we have so often referred for illustrations, we turn once more.

In chapter two, the first chapter of instruction, the Bhagavad Gita gives a succinct summary of its later teachings on this "yoga," or way, of selfless activity. Krishna is concerned with the spirit in which a man performs his work as a discipline for liberation. First he gives a few hints about the technique of selfless work. "To [your] work, alone, you are entitled, never to its fruit," he says. Though the teaching applies to men in all walks of life, he speaks here, of course, to the man preeminently fitted for life in society. "Neither let your motive be the fruit of action," Krishna continues, "nor let your attachment be to nonaction. Being established in [this] yoga, Arjuna, perform your actions, casting off attachment and remaining even-minded both in success and in failure." Giving his reason for this injunction, he says, "Wretched are they who work for results. Endued with evenness of mind, one casts off, in this very life, both good deeds and evil deeds. Therefore strive for [this] yoga. Yoga is skill in action."

This same truth was known to Lao tzu in China. "The really wise man," he said, "acts without asserting himself, achieves without looking behind to claim any credit. He has no desire for empty praise." A man's time is best spent on the work necessary to attain the goal he works for, not on thinking of the satisfaction success will bring. Though this advice has its own message for nonbelievers, for the religious man it means he should remain an instrument in the hand of God. Krishna's teaching is, in effect, a commentary on Jesus' saying "But when you give alms, do not let your left hand know what your right hand is doing, so that your alms may be in secret." The fruit of the action will take care of itself, so long as a man does not seek merely his own satisfaction or the approbation of others. The words that follow—"and your Father who sees in secret will reward you"—may be understood to express this same thought.

The whole of chapter three of the Bhagavad Gita is also devoted to the "way of action." Lest an active man should think his way inferior to that of the all-renouncing monk, Krishna points out the danger of self-deception in the monastic life: "Not by merely abstaining from action does a man reach the state of actionlessness, nor by renunciation does he arrive at perfection. . . . He who restrains his organs of action [hands, feet, etc.], but continues to dwell in his mind on the objects of the senses, deludes himself and is called a hypocrite. But he who restrains his senses with his mind and directs his organs of action to work, with no feeling of attachment—he, Arjuna, is indeed superior. Do your allotted action; for action is superior to inaction. And even the bare maintenance of your body will not be possible if you remain inactive. The world becomes bound by action, unless it be done for the sake of sacrifice. Therefore give up attachment and do your work for the sake of the Lord.''

Here Krishna introduces the term ''sacrifice,'' which, as we have seen, includes service to living beings. Since he is also teaching Arjuna that self-surrender to himself, the Lord, is his final duty, he introduces a devotional note as well.

By way of contrast, Krishna next mentions the ''knower of the Self,'' the man who has heeded the voice of intuitive wisdom. Such a man, he says, has no object to gain nor anything to lose and depends on no one. Nevertheless the man of enlightenment also works. Arjuna, though not yet enlightened, should imitate him. But there is more than a personal reason for such an approach: ''By action alone men like Janaka attained perfection. Further, you should perform work with a view to guiding people along the right path. Whatever a great man does, that others follow. . . . I have, Arjuna, no duty; there is nothing . . . that I have not gained and nothing that I have to gain. Yet I continue to work. For should I not ever engage, unwearied, in action, men would in every way follow in my wake.'' Arjuna is a man of the warrior, or *kshatriya*, caste; his position is not that of the common man. Hence Krishna brings in his own example as something to emulate.

''Action does not defile me,'' Krishna continues in the next chapter, ''nor do I long for its fruit. He who knows me thus is not bound by his action. Men of old who sought liberation knew this and did their work. Therefore do your work as the ancients did in former times.'' As Swami Nikhilananda states in his commentary, ''Everyone conscious of his body must work. If he is ignorant [of truth], he should work for self-purification, and if he is wise and a knower of truth, he should work to set an example to others.''

Krishna now utters one of his subtlest and most profound intuitive insights concerning action. It is this: ''He who sees inaction in action, and action in inaction—he is wise among men, he is a yogi, he has performed all action.'' In Shankara's interpretation this means that such a man understands it is not the Self that acts, but the body, senses, and mind; the Self is beyond action. He thus sees inaction in what is commonly held to be the Self's "action." Again, he understands that though the ignorant man looks upon the body, senses, and mind as inactive and the Self as the real doer, just the opposite is true. He sees action in what is commonly called "inaction." (Or, in an alternative interpretation, he understands that though an ignorant man may strive to remain inactive in order to attain wisdom, such a person, though apparently inactive, is really active since his mind is full of ideas.)

In the fifth chapter Krishna has this to say, as it were in explanation of the verse just quoted: " 'I do nothing at all,' thinks the yogi, the knower of truth. For in seeing, hearing, touching, smelling, and tasting; in walking, breathing, and sleeping; in speaking, emitting, and seizing; in opening and closing the eyes, he is assured that it is only the senses busied with their objects."

Finally, in the eighteenth and last chapter, the Lord Krishna defines action in terms of the three "qualities," or *gunas*, which I mentioned in connection with the four divisions of caste. The concept of the *gunas* was first evolved in the Sankhya school of Hindu philosophy; later both the Yoga and Vedanta systems adopted the same classification of the components of nature. Krishna says: "The action that is obligatory and is done without love or hate by one who desires no fruit and who is free from attachment—that action is characterized by *sattva* [ballance]." In this verse is practically a summary of his whole teaching about correct action. It is an ideal achieved only by the saint, as can be seen by comparing it with the passage that directly follows: "But the action that is performed with much effort by one who seeks to gratify his desires or who is prompted by a feeling of 'I'—that action is declared to be of the nature of *rajas* [passion]. Whereas the action that is undertaken through ignorance, without regard to consequences or loss or injury, and without regard to one's ability—that action is said to be of the nature of *tamas* [dullness]."

The doer of action in the proper spirit, says Krishna, is free from "attachment and egoism"; he is endowed with "fortitude and zeal" and "unaffected by success and failure." It is not the kind of work we do, but the spirit in which we do it, that counts: "One ought not to give up the work to which one is born, though it has its imperfections; for all undertakings are beset with imperfections, as fire with smoke." But action for action's

sake, like wisdom for wisdom's sake, is perhaps a forbidding
ideal for the average man. In the end Krishna joins the doing
of action with devotion to himself: "Surrendering, in thought,
all actions to me, regarding me as the Supreme Goal, and
practicing steadiness of mind, fix your heart, Arjuna, constantly
on me."

In discussing action from more than one point of view,
Krishna seems, in the Bhagavad Gita, to hint not only that there
are several valid approaches to ultimate reality that may be used
in conjunction with the way of service and human community,
but that all these approaches can be used by one and the same
person to correct and fulfill each other.

Vivekananda, in his series of published lectures entitled
Karma-Yoga, has distilled from the Bhagavad Gita the essentials
of the technique of selfless action, in the light of his own
experience. He states in the first chapter: "*Karma-yoga,* the
Bhagavad Gita says, is doing work with cleverness and as a
science. . . . Man works with various motives; there cannot be
work without motive. Some people want to get fame and they
work for fame. Others want money and they work for money.
Some want to have power and they work for power. Others want
to go to heaven and they work for that. . . . There are some who
are really the salt of the earth, who work for work's sake, who
do not care for name or fame or even to go to heaven. They
work just because good will come of it. There are others who
do good to the poor and help mankind from still higher motives,
because they believe in doing good and love the good. . . . A
man who can work for five days, or even five minutes, without
any selfish motive whatever, without thinking of the future, of
heaven, of punishment, or anything of the kind, has in him
the capacity to become a powerful moral giant."

This may sound like an impossible, even a one-sided, ideal.
Vivekananda continues: "There arises a difficult question in
this ideal of work. Intense activity is necessary; we must always work. We cannot live a minute without work. What then
becomes of rest? Here is one side of life: struggle and work by
which we are whirled rapidly round. And here is the other:
calm, retiring renunciation. . . . The ideal man is he who in
the midst of the greatest silence and solitude finds the intensest
activity, and in the midst of the intensest activity the silence
and solitude of the desert. He has learned the secret of restraint; he has controlled himself. . . . That is the ideal of
karma-yoga; and if you have attained to that, you have really

learned the secret of work.'' Vivekananda here gives his own practical interpretation of Krishna's words ''inaction in action, and action in inaction.'' It is an interpretation that transcends the voice of intuitive wisdom and the voice of devotional self-giving alike and speaks in terms of personal experience.

-6-

The man who wishes to serve humanity, but also leans toward one of the other approaches to some degree, can have further dimensions added to his thinking. Such a man may have at first only a vague sense of the interrelatedness of all life. Thinking in terms of another approach than that of service can make that sense more explicit. If he is inclined to the view of the Nondualistic Vedantist, who thinks in terms of intuitive wisdom, his sense of human community—in fact, of the community of all living beings—is heightened through the concept of seeing ''himself in all beings and all beings in himself.'' The sense of human community itself carries with it a sense of unity. For the man of intuitive wisdom, the ultimate truth is the unity (or, more technically, the ''nonduality'') of all existence. Anything that denies this ultimate fact experienced by intuitive mystics is a denial of truth. The active man who leans toward this view comes to see immorality as anything that divides. What is generally called ''sin'' is simply the thinking or saying or doing of something that asserts the separateness of the individual and thus denies the basic truth, the nonduality of all existence.

Again, if by faith the active man inclines to the view of the lover of a personal God, who thinks in terms of devotional self-giving, his sense of community with all living beings—and particularly with human beings—is heightened through the concept of ''seeing the Lord everywhere and everything in the Lord.'' All men, as children or friends or lovers of God, are members as it were of one family. For such a man, immorality becomes anything that thwarts the will of God for all his sons and daughters, or friends or lovers. What is called sin is the thinking or saying or doing of something that asserts the self-rule of the individual and thus denies the basic truth, the dependence of all existence on God.

The voice of conscious discipline would seem to have no

place in this scheme. The practicing mystic appears not to think in terms of service and human community at all. Such a man, hearing the voice of discipline and following in earnest the way of intuition or devotion, or (as in Yoga proper or Zen Buddhism) seeking to rid his mind of discursive thought, has to all intents and purposes withdrawn from the community. Two points should be noted, however, in this connection. First, before embarking on his apparently self-centered practice, the man who would devote all his energies to meditation or prayer must, at least in the traditional Hindu view, have satisfied to a high degree the demands of personal and social morality. He sets a twofold example: through his moral preparation he reminds men of the value of conventional morality, and through his spiritual striving he bears witness to those higher values that, as all religions teach, must one day claim a man's allegiance. Secondly, through the power of his meditation or prayer, it is said, the Hindu or Buddhist mystic —like Christian contemplatives in "enclosed" orders—bestows intangible blessings upon mankind.

A certain amount of confusion was caused in India, at the very beginning of the twentieth century, by criticism leveled by orthodox monks at those more modern monks who heard the voice of service and human community. The former expressed strong disapproval of the works of service initiated by Ramakrishna's disciples at the instance of their leader, Vivekananda.

As a result of a thousand years of rule by foreigners, very many average Indians had lost the sense of responsibility that a generous number of ordinary citizens take for granted in countries where they have been born "free." The great swami had therefore asked his monks to set an example by organizing relief work in times of flood, famine, earthquake, or epidemics; by providing food and clothes for the poor; by tending the sick. Some observers have seen in the orthodox monks' criticism only the expression of inflexible custom. But where it represented something more than this, one can derive a positive lesson.

The point of view behind such thinking, when it was sincere, reflected a conviction that no real, lasting help can be given to others on the physical, moral, or intellectual plane. The only truly efficacious help is the kind that radically transforms character: spiritual help, the power of example and the power to uplift souls. Other kinds of help—giving money to the poor, feeding the hungry, clothing the naked, ministering to the sick —are at best palliatives and of temporary usefulness. Let householders help to the best of their ability, but let monks confine themselves, outside of meditation, to giving lectures or personal instruction on religion and morality, or improving people's education. They ought not, however, to forget their vocation. For the real help cannot be given till the would-be helper has acquired spiritual stature sufficient to enable him to *transmit* spirituality—that is, till the man has become a saint. And since in general a man can only attain some degree of sanctity through spiritual discipline, this should be the monk's total concern. Let works of mercy wait. True, the "Saviors" of mankind men like Gautama Buddha, Shankara, Ramanuja, Chaitanya—spent all their time serving others. But they devoted themselves to service only *after* having been established in selflessness through discipline.

In Ramakrishna's own teachings is a Hindu answer to this Hindu challenge. It is not the obvious answer he usually gave his disciples: that the worship of God through service to men was a logical necessity for all those not completely taken up with spiritual practice, because he himself saw God in his fellow men. Although this was a truth that had been taught by Krishna and other Hindu teachers, just as it had been taught by Jesus Christ, it would not really have met the orthodox monks' objections. What Ramakrishna taught that has special relevance, at least in the Hindu situation, was that service of others can itself be a spiritual discipline. In contributing to the individual's own development it brings him nearer the point where he can bestow the highest kind of help. Meanwhile, even though a monk cannot help spiritually, let him help materially, for, as Vivekananda and others before and after him have said, "You cannot teach religion to empty stomachs."

For Hindus this answer welds the voices of intuitive wisdom and devotional self-giving into a harmony with the voice of service and human community, enabling Hinduism to realize its integral truth as perhaps never before. It presupposes, however, that all such work of social welfare be done sincerely as a discipline. When it becomes merely routine, or a substitute for what others can do as well, it is better for monks to return to the life of meditation. And now that the government and the general public have taken up this sort of work, that is the challenge that faces education-centered and welfare-oriented monastic organizations. The positive lesson to be drawn from the orthodox monks' disapproval is perhaps also of some value for priests and monks in the West.

The goal of the way of service and human community, pure and simple, is work for work's sake. It is the ideal of concentration on the task in hand, on the present moment's demands, without any intervening thought—especially thought of rewards to come. The satisfaction of the work is its own reward, and if the work is properly done the result will take care of itself. This attitude is unknowingly exhibited by many simple people in India, such as the schoolteacher-mechanic who helped our driver repair the broken part of the motor.

-7-

Three types of social leaders respond to the voice of service and human community. The first is the man of spiritual religion, who by his inspired example persuades those who believe in him to go and do likewise. The second is the secular man, the agnostic or atheist; he, too, by the force of logic, influences those who think in his way to act as he urges. The third is the ethical man, the man of principle; by his passionate allegiance to what he sees to be just, he persuades other men through the sheer force of his moral conviction. The leader of the first or third type may combine with his own inborn tendency something of the other's, but one of the two tendencies clearly predominates. The leader of the second type of necessity combines this tendency only with that of the third.

Vivekananda, the disciple of Ramakrishna, born January 12, 1863, was predominantly a man of the first type. A complex personality, he has often been misunderstood; but his influence on the social awakening of India was immense. His feeling for the downtrodden masses makes him, in addition to whatever else he was, a true servant of the people. In a letter written in July 1897 to his American "sister," Mary Hale, he expressed that feeling forcefully: "May I be born again and again, and suffer thousands of miseries, so that I may worship the only God that exists, the only God I believe in, the sum total of all souls. And above all, my God the wicked, my God the miserable, my God the poor of all races, of all species, is the especial object of my worship."

How Vivekananda came to feel so strongly is described by Swami Nikhilananda in his life of the swami, entitled *Vivekananda*. When in 1891, at the age of twenty-eight, Vivekananda had completed a journey, mostly on foot, from the Himalayas to Cape Comorin, the southernmost point of India, he swam to a large rock offshore—now known as Vivekananda Rock—and thought about his experiences. His biographer writes: "He recalled what he had seen with his own eyes: the pitiable condition of the Indian masses, victims of the unscrupulous whims of their rulers, landlords, and priests. . . . Now he asked himself what his duty was. . . . He remembered that, as a *sannyasi*, a monk, he had taken the vow to dedicate himself to the service of God; but this God, he was convinced, was revealed through humanity. And his own service to this God must begin, therefore, with the humanity of India."

Vivekananda's personal realization of God in the poor and the unfortunate was heightened by the earlier realizations of his Master. Once, during a pilgrimage with Mathurmohan Biswas, Ramakrishna visited one of the villages on the large estates whose revenues supported the temple. Seeing the villagers' abject poverty, the saint was overcome with sorrow. He sat down among them and said to Mathurmohan that he would not leave till Mathur promised to give each of the villagers a new wearing cloth and a full meal. Despite his protector's remonstrances that they would not have enough funds to continue their pilgrimage, the saint was unyielding. And Mathurmohan was forced to grant his request.

Many years later, after talking with his disciples about the Vaishnava doctrine of showing compassion to all beings, Ramakrishna entered into spiritual ecstasy. When shortly he regained normal consciousness, he exclaimed, "Compassion for beings! Will you, you insignificant creatures, bestow compassion? Who are you to show it? No, no! Not compassion for beings, but service to them as the Lord." Commenting on these words, Vivekananda said, "Until an aspirant sees God in all beings, he hasn't the remotest chance of realizing true transcendental devotion."

These two examples from his Master's life were sufficient to persuade Vivekananda's mystically inclined nature, yet naturally warm heart, to a tremendous expenditure of energy in behalf of mankind, and especially the poor and afflicted. It brought his life to an end at the age of thirty-nine. As he once wrote, try as he might to run off to a cave in the Himalayas, some force always drove him out to work among his fellow men. Fired by the example of Ramakrishna, Vivekananda founded the Ramakrishna Math and Mission. (The word *math* here means "monastic order.") The order, which at present includes about seven hundred monks and novices and claims the allegiance of thousands of lay followers, is dedicated to the two-fold ideal of realizing God and serving man. It has established monasteries in all the principal cities of India and numerous smaller towns and villages. Through colleges, schools, hospitals, and other organizations, it serves all of India. Before India won independence it was perhaps the principal initiator of large-scale relief work in times of flood, famine, epidemic, or other disaster. It has also established teaching centers outside India, not only in Asia, but in Europe and the Americas. A women's order is loosely affiliated with the Ramakrishna Order.

No less than Vivekananda, the man who founded the People's Republic of China has been intensely aware of the need for uplifting the depressed masses. Mao Tse-tung, who was born on December 26, 1893, is a leader of the second type: the secular man, in this case an atheist. It would not be appropriate, even if it were feasible, to trace in detail the story of his early life, his maneuverings in the Chinese Communist movement, the hardships he endured during the famous "Long March" of the Red Armies in 1934-35, or his final emergence as leader of the People's Republic. Still, his social thinking should not be neglected. Disagree as completely as one will with Mao's philosophical or political ideas, or with his methods of enforcing compliance, there is still no reason to ignore the positive lessons to be learned from his nonpolemical statements. That he, too, had heard and followed the voice of service and human community is nowhere so plainly shown as in his discussions of how to help the masses. It may be argued that he had to speak in this reasonable way before he and his party had seized control of the government. But it should be remembered that the quotations that follow are all included in the little red book, *Quotations From Chairman Mao Tse-tung*, which the Chinese people have been required to read almost as if it were a scripture.

In March-April of 1941, Mao said, "The masses are the real heroes, while we ourselves are often childish and ignorant, and without this understanding it is impossible to acquire even the most rudimentary knowledge." There must, of course, be a leading group to properly organize the activities of the masses.

But though most elements of the masses need guidance, the leaders must not seek to indoctrinate them with ideas that are not their own. On June 1, 1943, Mao said, "In all the practical work of our party, all correct leadership is necessarily 'from the masses to the masses.' This means: take the ideas of the masses (scattered and unsystematic ideas) and concentrate them (through study turn them into concentrated and systematic ideas), then go to the masses and propagate and explain these ideas until the masses embrace them as their own, hold fast to them and translate them into action, and test the correctness of these ideas in such action. Then once again concentrate ideas from the masses and once again go to the masses so that the ideas are persevered in and carried through. And so on, over and over again in an endless spiral, with the ideas becoming more correct, more vital, and richer each time." Unceasing dedication is called for in those who would educate the masses in their own ideas.

This approach is central to Mao's thinking, for he returns to it more than once. On October 30, 1944, he said, "To link oneself with the masses, one must act in accordance with the needs and wishes of the masses. All work done for the masses must start from their needs and not from the desire of any individual, however well-intentioned."

Even in the previous decade, before the revolutionary movement had gained decisive momentum, Mao had expressed himself eloquently on the needs of the masses. On January 27, 1934, he reminded his followers, "We should pay close attention to the well-being of the masses, from the problems of land and labor to those of fuel, rice, cooking oil, and salt. . . . We should help the masses to realize that we represent their interests, that our lives are intimately bound up with theirs." Again, in a tribute to the Canadian Norman Bethune, delivered on December 21, 1939, after his death, he said, "Comrade Bethune's spirit, his utter devotion to others without any thought of self, was shown in his boundless warmheartedness toward all comrades and the people. . . . We must all learn the spirit of absolute selflessness from him. With this spirit everyone can be useful to the people. A man's ability may be great or small, but if he has this spirit, he is already noble-minded and pure, a man of moral integrity and above vulgar interests, a man who is of value to the people."

Finally, on September 8, 1944, in "Serve the People," Mao summed up his feelings: "Wherever there is struggle there is sacrifice, and death is a common occurrence. But we have the interests of the people and the sufferings of the great majority at heart, and when we die for the people it is a worthy death." The resonance of such statements (especially their implications for the Third World) is self-evident. It should not be forgotten that Mao, like the original Communist leaders in Russia, was fired from the start with a desire for the advancement of those whom a crushing feudal system had for centuries exploited as a matter of course. His method for lifting the masses deserves respectful attention, not automatic revulsion.

Philippe Devillers has written of Mao that whatever one's opinion of his character, his ideological choice, and his methods, one can only conclude after an honest study of his thought and works that Mao is "a man who has given his entire life to China and the restoration of her dignity and independence, to the Chinese people, to the peasants of China, and especially to the poorest of them."

During the period we have been dealing with, the years between 1891 and 1949, another man was heeding the voice of service and human community in such a way as to claim the special attention of the Christian world. That man was Mahatma Gandhi.

Mao Tse-tung's response to the voice, of which the outside world knew little at the time, was that of a nonreligious man devoted to "work for work's sake"—or rather, work for the people's sake. From what we know of him, I believe we can say that Mao, like Gandhi, has lived up to the Bhagavad Gita's requirements for a follower of the way of action: he has been even-minded in success and failure, his action has been performed as a sacrifice (for the people), and what he has done was not prompted by desire for self-aggrandizement. But, as Vivekananda said, there are also those who "do good to the poor and help mankind" simply because they "believe in doing good and love the good." Gandhi's insistence on truth and nonviolence puts him in the third class of leaders we have spoken of, that of the ethical reformers.

Gandhi and Mao sought with equal passion to weld the masses into a healthy organization by raising them, after centuries of oppression, to an awareness of their own dignity and strength. It seems likely that the Indian leader would have agreed in principle with Mao's prescription for leading the masses forward with the help of their own best thinking—though in working toward that end he did not, like Mao, reject the insights of religion. Gandhi also believed, like Mao, in using force against the ruling power and the ruling class to advance the cause of the masses. The force he used, however, was not physical force. He sought to bring about a change of heart by appealing to their inherent moral instincts through suffering imposed upon himself.

Effective as were Gandhi's civil disobedience campaigns against the British government, quite as effective with Indians of all classes were his fasts of protest or self-purification. Mao did not hesitate to employ for the sake of the masses "corrective" methods against government or the upper levels of society that to Christians appear harsh and repressive—methods that in bourgeois society, as he himself wryly pointed out, are characterized as "going too far." Whether Mao's ruthlessness proves, in the end, more successful from a purely practical, materialistic point of view than Gandhi's, remains for history to decide.

And yet the moral ruthlessness of Gandhi provides a needed corrective for the practical ruthlessness of Mao by preserving those moral and spiritual values that most Christians hold to be the best legacy of the Christian centuries. Gandhi, it should be remembered, was no less uncompromising in his demands upon himself than in his demands upon others. Even in Marxist countries a need may one day be felt for something more than merely practical moral values. This remains true, of course, whether finally the Christian religion as now practiced by the majority of its adherents proves worthy of the high charge it has been given, or whether Jesus Christ's own ruthlessness shall demand that this "Christianity" itself be driven out of the temple. It seems appropriate to end this chapter with a brief sketch of Gandhi's work for the masses.

While wrestling with the problem of how to write about a man so complex as the Mahatma, a particular incident about him came to my mind. It was related to me by one who became an especially close associate of his for a short period in his last, difficult years, Professor Nirmal Kumar Bose. In 1939 Professor Bose had published a collection of his sayings on key subjects entitled *Selections from Gandhi*. One day, as he told me in 1970 when I was in New Delhi, Gandhi called him and said, "Look here, you haven't presented the real Gandhi in your book. You have presented my aspirations rather than my actual attainments." The professor was equal to the occasion. In his semihumorous, laconic way, he said, borrowing a thought from Rabindranath Tagore, "Sometimes I think a man's aspirations are the realest part of him."

Recalling this incident, I decided I might justifiably concentrate on the Gandhi that best represents what we are occupied with in this chapter, the passionate follower of the way of service and human community—disregarding for the most part the many other, sometimes contradictory, facets of his character. Surely this Gandhi represents the quintessence of his aspirations. My decision seemed all the more justifiable in this instance because where it is a question of direct action for the masses, his aspirations and actual attainments are all of a piece.

The Mahatma's career as a political leader, after his nonviolent campaigns against the British government in India had made him a world figure, need not be rehearsed once more. I shall concentrate on five nonviolent campaigns of his that appear central to his mission—all of them directed against various types of what today we should call violence. In addition, I shall try to indicate why I include him among ethical reformers rather than among spiritual leaders.

-8-

Mohandas Karamchand Gandhi was born on October 2, 1869. His childhood and even his young manhood give scarcely a hint of the man he was to become. As a young husband he was still afraid of "thieves, ghosts, and serpents." Indeed, up till his twenty-fourth year, when he was sent on a legal assignment to help a firm of Muslim merchants in Natal and the Transvaal, in South Africa, his life had been strikingly unimpressive. His law practice after his return from studies in England in 1891 seemed headed for disaster, for he never rose to speak without being covered with confusion. Moreover, by his own estimate he was sexually aggressive and demanded more than his due of his young wife. (Whether he was indeed unusual in this respect remains open to question, since when he wrote his autobiography, *The Story of My Experiments With Truth,* he was plagued with the title "Mahatma," meaning "great soul," and perhaps wished to show he was no saint.) From the records available we find nothing to indicate that he was anything more than the lackluster son of the chief minister, or *dewan,* in a very small Indian "native state."

In trying to explain how Gandhi became the mentally, morally, and physically fearless man he later was, one may cite the example of his politically influential father's incorruptibility and spirit of religious tolerance. and of his mother's deep piety and extraordinary power of will. But other men have had parents as gifted as these and made no mark upon history. Granting they had an influence, I nevertheless feel it was out of his own life experience that Gandhi slowly forged himself— profiting by many mistakes along the way—into the giant he became. As much as most more specifically religious leaders, he should be given full credit for gaining the victory over himself that he achieved. His life of service was his spiritual discipline.

What sets Gandhi apart from the great majority of outstanding men in modern times is his spontaneous moral outrage at the plight of the poor. This feeling of outrage was directed not toward those who kept the poor in their state of appalling ignorance, but toward the system that had reduced them almost to the condition of dumb brutes. Gandhi's sense of community with those whom Franz Fanon has called the "wretched of the earth," coupled with the spirit of nonviolence for which he is famous, grew out of a dedication to truth that early took possession of his soul—truth that was, at first, a moral truth and later became identified in his mind with the Deity. In him these three virtues were so interrelated as to be almost one. Along with them there developed in him, as a natural consequence, a love of man so intense that eventually it became contagious. This combination of characteristics is what makes him, despite his minor contradictions, the commanding figure he is.

It was in 1893 that Gandhi went to Natal, in South Africa— the same year, by coincidence, in which Vivekananda awakened many people in the United States to the fact of Indian spirituality and Mao Tse-tung was born. Here, at the very outset of his stay in Africa, Gandhi personally came up against the oppression suffered there not only by simple Indian farmers (who had originally gone there as indentured workers from India) but by Muslim merchants or anyone with a skin darker than that of the British and Dutch. On his first trip from Natal to the Transvaal, Gandhi was ousted from his first-class seat and spent a night shivering in a railway waiting room. Instead of submitting to the insult as a Muslim merchant would have done, he immediately telegraphed complaints to the railroad company. The following day, on a stagecoach ride, he was refused entry into the coach for which he had a ticket and had to ride near the driver. He was actually beaten when the man in charge tried to take his place and make him sit on the floor in front of him. Later he was to trace the beginning of his public career to these first experiences in South Africa. His mission, he realized, was to root out the "disease" of color prejudice.

During the next fifteen years, though Gandhi returned twice to India and made contacts with Indian leaders and the Indian public, he found that his services were needed in South Africa. Early he organized a Natal Indian Congress to call the government's attention to the grievances of the Indian community. These ranged all the way from excessive taxes and ordinances against Indians' working in any but menial occupations, to a 9 P.M. curfew and prohibition from walking on the sidewalks. But the Indians, too, he saw, must mend their ways. Upon the Muslim merchants he urged the need for strict honesty in business transactions, better sanitation in their district, and a disregarding of religious distinctions.

Very soon he overcame his previous timidity and became a forceful public speaker. Noting a lack of facilities for the sick poor, he encouraged the start of a free hospital and even took up nursing. (Gradually, however, he lost faith in the methods of modern medicine and began advocating various "nature cure" remedies.) Because he still believed in supporting the British government, during the Boer War and later during the Zulu rebellion he organized an ambulance corps of Indians. On several occasions, when outbreaks of plague occurred, at great personal risk he sought to improve the sanitary conditions in Indian homes. Somehow, because of his innate gift for evoking enthusiastic support, there were always volunteers to carry out his sometimes difficult demands. During all this activity he somehow managed to carry on a busy law practice.

In 1904 Gandhi read Ruskin's book of social criticism, *Unto This Last*, and by it was inspired to buy a farm at Phoenix, in Natal, later known as the Phoenix Settlement, where Ruskin's ideas could be put into practice. Ruskin had argued that employer and employed must be bound together in genuine fellow feeling and that the wealthy should look upon themselves as trustees of their wealth, which should be put at the disposal of the community. From *Unto This Last* Gandhi derived the idea of the dignity of all types of labor. *Indian Opinion*, a newspaper he had founded to disseminate news of the grievances of the Indians in South Africa, was now shifted to Phoenix, where willing helpers built a plant to house the presses.

Finally, in 1906, came the first decisive crisis for Indians with the publication of the provisions of a proposed law in the Transvaal, under which Indians were to be treated little better than criminals. All above the age of eight years were to be fingerprinted and forced to carry registration cards under pain of fine, imprisonment, or deportation. Gandhi foresaw that if the draft law was passed by the legislature, similar laws would eventually be passed in the other South African colonies. He called a mass meeting, attended by three thousand Indians, where it was unanimously agreed that if the proposed law was passed they would go to jail rather than obey. Abdul Gani, a prominent Muslim businessman, was the first to pledge his refusal to obey. Perhaps we find here a partial explanation of Gandhi's consistent championing of the rights of the Muslim community in India—a cause for which he literally gave his life.

It was at this time, also, that the strategy was adopted with which the Mahatma's name would henceforth be associated: the use of nonviolent disobedience to unjust legislation. Although the idea did not originate with him, it was used here in a novel way. The plan was to nullify racist thinking by refusing to cooperate with it and to disobey unjust laws imposed by the government that were inspired by such thinking. Gandhi defined the aim of his method—which he came to call *satyagraha,* or "firmness in truth"—as "conversion, not coercion" of the opponent. It was, in fact, a sort of moral coercion *through* conversion to principles to which the opponent had always given lip service. The sources of his idea are fairly clear. Very early in his stay in South Africa he had met Christians of varying types and had read at least parts of the New Testament. He already knew the Sermon on the Mount, and it had no doubt awakened him to the rightness and value of nonresistance of evil. He also knew something of the Bhagavad Gita, which, in its praise of noninjury, or *ahimsa,* corroborated the conviction that was growing in his mind. He read Thoreau on civil disobedience several years later. Perhaps through him he learned to join nonviolence with resistance.

Within a short time the protested bill became law as the

Aliens Registration Act. Carefully organized demonstrations postponed its enforcement for several months. When, out of the approximately thirteen thousand Indian citizens of the Transvaal, only a few more than five hundred had registered by the final deadline, Gandhi was sent to jail. Here he at once complained to the director of prisons about the diet imposed on Indian prisoners, and a slight improvement was made. After consultations with the Transvaal Prime Minister, General Smuts, a compromise was reached. Gandhi was released. The law would be ''repealed.'' Gandhi agreed that the registration should be made voluntary. Extremists among the Indians understandably regarded this as a betrayal. As a result, when he himself went to register and voluntarily give his fingerprints, he was almost killed by one of these men he had earlier incited to resist the law.

Gradually it became clear, however, that the government was about to impose even more stringent regulations. As a result Gandhi now encouraged the Indians to provoke arrest by disobeying the new laws. Later, when the government refused his petition to stop passage of the Asiatic Act in revised form, he organized a mass meeting at which about thirteen hundred Indians burned their registration cards. As a result of his agitation, he was sent to jail a second, and then a third time. But the struggle went on.

Under the influence of Tolstoy, whose *The Kingdom of Heaven Is Within You* he had admired for many years, Gandhi now began to extend his criticism to the basic assumptions of modern industrial civilization. He founded another settlement, Tolstoy Farm, this time in the Transvaal, where the families of Indians imprisoned for nonviolent resistance of the new law could remain and support themselves. All were supposed to live in utmost simplicity, work for the common good, eat the same vegetarian meals, and devote their minds to God. (Gandhi, like other members of his Vaishnava family, was a vegetarian; as a law student in London he became an enthusiastic advocate of vegetarianism.) Despite a certain moral severity in the regime at the Farm, its founder's natural sense of good humor won the enthusiastic cooperation of the whole community.

As a result of a Transvaal Supreme Court decision, more demonstrations had to be organized. The court decreed that all marriages except those performed according to the Christian ritual were invalid. Women marchers crossed, against the law, from the Phoenix Settlement in Natal into the Transvaal. They were arrested. Others, not arrested, marched from Tolstoy Farm into Natal, where they persuaded Indian miners to strike. These, together with workers in sugar plantations, now marched to the Transvaal border under Gandhi's personal leadership, being supplied with food by Indian merchants along the way. Though arrested by the authorities, Gandhi was unexpectedly released because of the sudden intervention of the British Governor of Bombay and the Viceroy of India. (It was on the arrival of the delegation from India that Gandhi met the Christian missionary Charlie Andrews, who became his lifelong friend.) As a result of the negotiations, General Smuts agreed in 1914 to abolish the hated taxes exacted from Indians, recognize the legality of Indian marriages, and remove the restrictive statutes on registration and immigration. The *satyagraha* campaign was abandoned.

Gandhi was now forty-five years old. His fame had long since spread over the whole of India. When in 1915 he returned to his motherland he was received as a national hero. After a period of observing conditions in India, during which time he became the virtual leader of the Indian National Congress Party, he entered upon a struggle for justice for Indians in their own country. Throughout his long career of thirty-three years in India, he continued to heed, despite the other more secular claims that inevitably forced themselves upon him, the same call of service and human community he had followed for the past twenty-two years in South Africa. Here his struggle was directed against violence not only on the part of the government, but violence in all sectors of society.

The British, who had taken power in India after about eight centuries of Muslim rule, had persuaded themselves they were there not for any mere reason of commercial gain but because of an almost divinely ordained obligation to civilize the disadvantaged peoples of the East. On returning to India, Gandhi gradually came to realize that the government he once looked upon as a blessing to India was not really a true servant of the people. Here again, because of existing conditions as well as his own personal preferences, he chose to oppose the government by nonviolent means.

In South Africa Gandhi had seen what could be accomplished when a small and more or less homogeneous group of people thought as one and acted upon that thought with one will. Now his problem would be different: to persuade a whole people to one way of thinking. Here it was no matter of a few Muslim merchants and a large number of indentured farm workers. In India his problem was to weld the minority of educated members of an ancient culture and the dumb millions of the neglected poor into an instrument for their own liberation. Among the educated were to be found not only those who were violently restive under the repressive foreign rule, but also those who though dissatisfied believed in discretion, and some who, for their own gain, wished to collaborate with the government.

How Gandhi dealt with those young intellectuals in favor of drastic action may be illustrated by a story told me by Swami Nikhilananda. Before becoming a monk, the swami had joined, during his college days, a small group of young Bengalis who had conceived their own strategy for ousting the British. Not long after Gandhi returned to India, Nikhilananda and several of his group went to see the hero of the Indians in South Africa. "What is your plan?" Gandhi asked them. "We plan to drive the British out," the future swami said, "by killing one British official every day. This will intimidate them and they will be forced to leave." Gandhi looked at the young anarchists and smiled. "I should be with you if your plan would work. But it won't," he said. "You don't understand the English character. For every Englishman you kill, ten will come." The young men were dissuaded.

The first problem forced upon Gandhi's attention was one not of government violence, as in South Africa, but of violence on the part of private ownership. Government violence he was to deal with during almost his entire Indian career. In opposing it, he largely refined upon methods already devised in South Africa. Since these anti-government campaigns are so well known, I shall refer to them only in passing or as they bear on the others. Ownership violence he had dealt with there only briefly, in the case of some striking mine workers. Now, at the instance of one Ramkumar Shukla, a persistent agitator from the district of Champaran, in Bihar state, he turned his full attention to this equally vicious type of injustice.

It was a question of the maltreatment of helpless indigo farmers by habitually greedy landowners. Wages were extremely low, and the farmers were in perpetual debt to the "planters." During the First World War the price of indigo, which had temporarily dropped when German-made aniline dyes had been introduced, once again soared. The planters made huge profits, but the farmers remained as poor as ever. As an added grievance, the owners imposed extra taxes at will. Agitation was quelled by imprisoning or killing those who organized it.

Gandhi's methods in the successful fight in 1916 to redress the indigo farmers' grievances reveal the same unemotional, devoted zeal he had shown in his South African campaigns. Aided by past experience, he organized the work with masterly skill. Ramkumar Shukla introduced him to some of the lawyers and teachers of his district in Bihar, and Gandhi persuaded them to collect thousands of reports from peasants. The reports were to be collected openly, so that those who collected them could be arrested by the police. There was to be no agitation, not the slightest hint of violence. The government of the district of Champaran ordered Gandhi's expulsion on the grounds that his object was more likely agitation than a search for genuine knowledge of conditions; but at his trial on his refusal to leave, the local magistrate was persuaded to delay a verdict—partly because several thousand farmers had gathered and there might be riots or resentment if he was imprisoned.

To Gandhi's surprise, with the help of friends close to the government the Lieutenant Governor of Bihar and Orissa was induced to order the local authorities to help instead of hinder his mission. The people had now become aware that Gandhi was their liberator, and wherever he went crowds gathered to welcome him, seeking merely to catch a glimpse of him as if he were a saint. They began to believe he had superhuman power. Gandhi's feelings about the reaction of the farmers are revealed in his autobiography. There he wrote that in this meeting with the peasants he had been face to face with "God, *ahimsa* (nonviolence), and Truth."

In all, the lawyers and teachers collected about twenty-five thousand affidavits of highhandedness on the part of owners. They made up a staggering record of services demanded and frequently not paid for; beatings, imprisonings, starvation; threats of court suits; exclusion from use of village wells; and so on. From time to time Gandhi submitted factual reports. His rule for reformers like himself was to keep from being "overzealous, indiscreet, or indolent and ignorant." His advice to the government with regard to reformers was to be neither impatient with them nor overconfident that it could do without them. He explained to a government officer at this time that success was to be had, in his view, ''not by cooperation with government . . . but by pressure on it,'' to compel it in deference to expediency to take the course of action he pointed out.

At last the Governor appointed him as a member of a commission of inquiry. As a result of Gandhi's ceaseless efforts from April to August 1916, culminating in the findings of the commission, the farmers' cause was won. Gandhi suggested only a twenty-five percent refund of the owners' illegal exactions, saying that this was enough to destroy their prestige.

The following year, having founded an ashram at Sarbamati, near Ahmedabad, Gandhi started his movement for making homespun, or *khadi*, to replace foreign-made cloth. He himself took up spinning with an old-fashioned spinning wheel. At the same time he learned that the mill hands in the textile mills in Ahmedabad were demanding a 50 percent increase in wages. The owners refused to arbitrate and the workers were locked out. It was another case of owner violence. Knowing they were really too poor to strike, he nevertheless urged the men not to return to work without a wage increase. Meetings were held every day. Here was a test of *satyagraha* far more valuable than at Champaran; for all depended in this case on the will of the workers to suffer for their cause.

When, after an inconclusive month, many of the workers began to waver, Gandhi made a new departure. He suddenly announced that unless the workers rallied and held out for higher wages, he would not touch food. The action, the first of its kind in his public life, electrified the workers, and they rallied to the cause. Two days later Gandhi suggested that they accept a 35 percent increase instead of the 20 percent the owners had offered. The workers agreed. At once the fast and the strike ended, amid general rejoicing. What made the situation extremely delicate in this instance was the fact that here, in contrast to Champaran, he was on friendly terms with the owners, who had supported his nearby ashram when it was in financial straits. Curiously, a woman member of the same family had first organized the mill hands' union.

Aside from the fact of the fast, this episode—important though it was—did not have any seminal influence on Gandhi's methods. It was a means of testing out methods of *satyagraha* that Gandhi had already devised in South Africa. The fast was the first of fifteen he would use in support of one cause or another during the remainder of his public life.

From 1919 onward there were many occasions for the use of *satyagraha* against the government. In that year the Anarchical and Revolutionary Crimes Act, known popularly as the Rowlatt Act, was passed by the government of India. This act provided that anyone engaged in or suspected of terrorist activity could be secretly tried without right of appeal, and the possession of any seditious document was punishable by two years' imprisonment and two subsequent years in work solely of a kind allowed by the government. The nationwide noncooperation struggle called for in protest against the act was enthusiastic; when it led to violence, Gandhi called it off. But a barbaric reprisal, the Amritsar Massacre, violently inflamed an already aroused public.

On this occasion a crowd of thousands of Sikhs, peaceably assembled for a festival, was shot into for ten minutes by Indian soldiers under the command of a Britisher. They had gathered in a square from which there were very inadequate means of escape, and between three hundred and fifty and four hundred people died. The wounded were left unattended where they lay. (The British commander had mistakenly taken the gathering as defiance of a not very well publicized order forbidding public meetings.) Soon after this tragedy, an English schoolmistress was brutally treated by rowdy elements of the population, and thereafter any Indian walking by the spot was forced on pain of flogging to crawl past it.

The complex events following upon full revelation of the details of the massacre (covered up for two months) cannot be included here in their entirety. By 1920 Gandhi, with the Congress party's backing, was demanding self-rule for India. Indians were called upon not to cooperate in any way with the ruling power. Leaders were to surrender titles and honorary offices, and seats in local councils, and not to attend government functions. The people were asked to withdraw children from government-aided schools and establish national schools, to boycott the British courts of law and establish private arbitration courts, to boycott foreign goods and use only homespun, and so on. Though only comparatively few leaders answered the call, the people in general responded well, and those who had taken a special *satyagrahi* pledge were allowed to court arrest by disobeying government orders. As a result, about thirty thousand persons were jailed.

Following a Congress call for a general strike to protest the arrival of the Prince of Wales in Bombay, there were

riots and some killings throughout India. The situation in
Bombay itself was especially violent, and Gandhi sorrowfully
realized that the Indian people were not sufficiently disciplined
to practice nonviolent resistance. Even so, since the government
showed no signs of relaxing its oppression, Gandhi announced,
on February 1, 1922, that he would resort to the final step
planned by Congress for attaining of self-rule: refusal to pay
taxes.

The Mahatma placed great hope in the cooperation of the
masses in the final stages of noncooperation with the government. As he wrote in *Young India*, one of his publications, the
party had been trying to act on the masses from the start. It
regarded them as its mainstay, for they were the ones who had
to attain self-rule—not simply the monied or educated class.
As soon as the masses should attain sufficient self-control to
be able to practice nonviolence even when their possessions were
being sold, Gandhi said, he would not hesitate to ask them to
suspend payment of taxes. This he finally did, choosing the
peasants of Bardoli Taluka in the Bombay Presidency for the
first demonstration.

Before the action could take place, however, Gandhi suddenly
called off the whole civil disobedience movement. He had
learned that certain members of the Congress party had taken
part in a riot at Chauri Chaura, in Gorakhpur district, a
thousand miles away. A police station in which twenty-two
members of the police force had taken refuge from a mob was
burned down and the men were hacked to pieces as they tried to
escape. No matter that the incident had begun when the police
taunted a few stragglers in an orderly procession of Gandhi's
men; for Congress members were implicated. It was not just
any outbreak of violence, but violence on the part of those who
had taken the pledge of nonviolence, that could not be tolerated.

The vows of a civil resister bound him to harbor no anger
against his oppressor, but rather to suffer the oppressor's
anger; never to retaliate, but never to submit to any order
given in anger; to voluntarily submit to arrest and even to
seizure of one's property, but to refuse to surrender, even at
the cost of life, property left in his possession as a trustee;
and to protect any government official who was assaulted by
anyone else in the struggle. There were many other equally
demanding requirements, but these governed the *satyagrahi*'s
behavior in public struggle, and their spirit had been violated
at Chauri Chaura.

Here, then, began a third campaign against violence: violence on the part of professed *satyagrahis*, nonviolent resisters. Gandhi himself was arrested soon after the withdrawal of civil disobedience. He insisted that Congress members should now undertake a program of constructive activities for the entire nation until the people as a whole could learn to practice nonviolent noncooperation. He asked Congressmen, as a preparation for true nonviolent struggle, to go to the villages, encourage the production of homespun, try to wipe out unemployment, improve sanitary conditions, blot out communal strife between Hindus and Muslims, destroy untouchability, and encourage a great variety of similar projects. Only a minority of the Congressmen showed real enthusiasm for this "constructive program."

Gandhi was not a man to become emotional about the oppressed. He was one of those who, as Vivekananda had said in speaking of the ideal *karma-yogi*, "believe in doing good and love the good." His singleminded pursuit of justice allowed no waste of energy on mere sentiment: something had to be done—and he was the one to do it. It was not that he had no emotions (he certainly reacted strongly when people failed to live up to the ideal of nonviolence), but he kept his feelings for the masses under control. In his famous trial for sedition, which took place in 1922, shortly after the events I have just described, he reveals the depth of distress he was capable of. "Before the British advent," he declared in his statement to the court, "India spun and wove in her millions of cottages, just the supplement she needed for adding to her meager agricultural resources. This cottage industry, so vital for India's existence, has been ruined by incredibly heartless and inhuman processes as described by English witnesses. Little do town dwellers know how the semistarved masses of India are slowly sinking into lifelessness. Little do they know that their miserable comfort represents the brokerage they get for the work they do for the foreign exploiter, that the profits and brokerage are sucked from the masses. Little do they realize that the government established by law in British India is carried on for this exploitation of the masses. No sophistry, no jugglery in figures, can explain away the evidence that the skeletons in many villages present to the naked eye." As a result of the trial he was sent to Yeravda Jail in March 1922.

The Mahatma's pursuit of the goals of service and human community was strengthened by his personal devotion to God. This devotion did not begin to develop, by his own account, till after he reached South Africa. In childhood and youth the only writing of a religious nature that had impressed Gandhi was the sixteenth-century poet Tulsidas' version of the *Ramayana*. He had learned something of Christianity in England, and later in South Africa, but though he respected much that it taught, it did not deeply persuade him. On his return from England to India, a colorful Bombay jeweler and poet, Rajchandra Mehta, had exerted a profound influence upon his religious thinking, sending letters of advice in reply to his queries from South Africa till his untimely death ten years later. Yet Gandhi had had no real spiritual instruction from a qualified *guru*. He had first found the Bhagavad Gita in Edwin Arnold's verse translation, *The Song Celestial*, while he was a student in London, and from the year 1908 he had read the original regularly. From the time of the founding of the Phoenix Farm in 1904 he had held daily prayer meetings.

During the two years from 1922 to 1924 that he served in Yeravda Jail, Gandhi undertook a study of the epic *Mahabharata*. Though he read many other books during this time, he spent over one hundred and sixty-three days on that one work. A third of the time was devoted to the famous Shanti Parva, or "Section on Peace," in which the sage Bhishma discourses on the laws and duties of life. Gandhi in his search for truth seized upon this great work. Though he perhaps learned little from it about the subject of truth that he had not already learned from experience, it cannot have failed to corroborate his own conclusions. "That alone is truth which is wholly beneficial to others," he read there. The epic's lack of dogmatism may have helped to temper some of his own strongly held opinions. Its lofty conception of duty, or *dharma*, finds expression in his own conception of "truth and nonviolence." In fact, Gandhi is reported to have said after his first release from Yeravda Jail that he had plunged into politics simply in search of truth; he wanted to "show how to epitomize the *Mahabharata*." He had said much the same thing a few years earlier in his *Autobiography*.

The earnestness of this period of study would in itself be compelling evidence of Gandhi's deep concern for religious values. Yet the difference between Gandhi and even a man like Vivekananda (not to mention Ramakrishna) is perfectly clear. He was in no sense a mystic. As time went on, his faith noticeably matured—possibly because of the increasingly strict demands he made upon himself in the way of giving up possessions and enjoyments, not to mention the vow of continence he had been faithfully observing since 1906. Even so, his was not a faith in God based on indubitable experience. "I have not seen him, neither have I known him," Gandhi wrote in his *Autobiography*. "I have made the world's faith in God my own, and as my faith is ineffaceable, I regard that faith as amounting to experience. However, as it may be said that to describe faith as experience is to tamper with truth, it may perhaps be more correct to say that I have no word for characterizing my belief in God." All his life he cherished a deep yearning for something more than this sort of faith. Nevertheless he appears to have mistrusted the purely spiritual disciplines that might have brought him mystical experience. An innate compunction against what looked like a refined self-indulgence may have warred against the very desire he said he cherished most.

In the Introduction to his *Autobiography* he had written, "What I want to achieve—what I have been striving and pining to achieve these thirty years—is self-realization, to see God face to face, to attain *moksha* [liberation]. I live and move and have my being in pursuit of this goal." All his speaking and writing, he went on, all his ventures in the political field, had been directed to that same end. He had carried on his experiments with truth in the open, instead of in private, however, because he believed that what was possible for one was possible for all. Certain things known only to oneself and one's Maker, he said, were of course incommunicable. Then he added, revealingly, "The experiments I am about to relate are not such. But they are spiritual, or rather moral; for the essence of religion is morality." He clearly differed here with the majority of saints and mystics in all parts of the world, who would have seen true morality as the fruit of union with God. He could never have brought himself to declare, as Vivekananda once did, fully aware of what he was saying, "The idea of duty is the midday sun of misery scorching the soul."

In the *Autobiography* Gandhi also wrote, however, "I believe in the Hindu theory of the *guru* and his importance in spiritual realization. I think there is a great deal in the doctrine that true knowledge is impossible without a *guru*." Such a teacher he never found. It seems highly probable that, unknown to himself, he carried about with him an unresolved conflict of the soul.

Once during this politically troubled period, sometime before 1931, Swami Nikhilananda, in talking with Gandhi,
brought up the subject of religious experience. The swami had
seen him on a number of occasions before this and was fairly
well known to him. "Have you realized anything of God,
Gandhiji?" the younger man asked him somewhat boldly. "I am
knocking at the door," was the reply. It was just after Gandhi
had submitted a controversial program of his to the Congress
Party Working Committee. The swami, saying that the Mahatma
owed it to himself to take a rest, extended an invitation to visit
the Ramakrishna Order's monastery at Mayavati, in the foothills of the Himalayas. "Oh, Swamiji," said Gandhi, "pray I
may not win the vote. Then I will come and lose myself in meditation at your monastery." For a moment, it seems, the rigor-
ously suppressed side of the conflict surfaced. But the Committee
accepted his program, and the strength of his urge toward
complete renunciation never came to the test.

There can be little doubt that faith in God as consistent as
Gandhi's must be accounted a kind of experience. In later
years Gandhi actually came to rely, for his decisions, on an
inner voice that spoke to him in times of crisis and that seemed
to him the voice of God. Once Rajendra Prasad, who became
the first President of India, visited Ramana Maharshi at the
Mahatma's request. When he asked what message he could
take back, the Maharshi replied, "What message is needed
when heart speaks to heart?" He added, "The same Shakti
[Power] that is working here is working there." In response
to a question asked earlier that day, as to whether the desire
for self-rule was right, Ramana Maharshi had replied in the
affirmative. "Prolonged practical work for the goal," he said,
"gradually widens the outlook so that the individual becomes
gradually merged in the country. Such merging of the individual is desirable, and the *karma* [work] becomes *nishkama
karma* [motiveless work]." These words seem to express precisely what happened in Gandhi's case. What he aimed at and
what he succeeded in accomplishing for others, especially the
poor, mark him out as an unparalleled witness to the voice
of service and human community.

As a person, Gandhi is more difficult to understand than
many great men. To the moral fervor of the reformer he
joined the candor of the true saint. So much of his private life
became public knowledge that in comparing him with other
well-known reformers we seize upon baffling and often ir-

relevant details that, though frequently present in a normal man, would ordinarilly have remained private knowledge. Eagerness to tell the whole truth may also have led him to give more importance to certain "weaknesses" of his than was fair to himself. And his distress at the cult of Mahatmahood on occasion led him to try, as perhaps in the instance of reporting his sexual excesses, to cut himself down to human size. ("The woes of Mahatmas," he once said, "are known only to Mahatmas.") What is essential in him, his complete dedication to the voice of service and human community as the voice of God, is what really matters in estimating his character. What he wanted of others was not that they should put him on a pedestal, but that they should themselves carry out in their lives the search for truth and nonviolence he had pursued.

The fourth of Gandhi's campaigns against violence was turned in another direction: against the violence of established society toward the untouchables. Though he had been preaching from the beginning of his career the importance of erasing this blot on Hindu society, it first became the subject of his undivided attention when he was confined to Yeravda Jail in 1932.

Prior to this several more national convulsions had occurred, resulting in another period of imprisonment for Gandhi and severe repression of the public. On January 26, 1930, Gandhi had proclaimed India's independence. Two months later after leading the symbolic Salt March against the government tax on salt, he was jailed but released in about nine months. After a strike throughout India came the signing of the Irwin-Gandhi Pact and his attendance at the fruitless Round Table Conference in London. Shortly after his return, as a result of further threats of civil disobedience he was again jailed. Now, in 1932, while Gandhi was at Yeravda Jail, he received news of a decision by Prime Minister MacDonald that the untouchables (euphemistically called the "depressed classes") were to be recognized by the government as a separate minority with separate rights. A year before, at the Round Table Conference, Gandhi had warned the Foreign Secretary for India that in the event of such a decision he would fast unto death; for he feared that this policy would lead to dismemberment of the Hindu community. He began his fast on September 20, 1932.

The struggle here was not really with the government, but with Hindu society. The government's decision was only a pretext for beginning it. "What I want, what I am living for, and what I should delight in dying for," Gandhi declared, "is the eradication of untouchability root and branch." He felt that by his fast he was fasting for all the underprivileged classes in the world. There was general apprehension about his health. Conferences of Indian leaders of different groups were held at the jail and, as a result, temples began to open their doors to those who had hitherto been excluded. The British agreed to substitute for their own arrangement the new agreement forged by the leaders condemning untouchability. The fast ended six days after it had begun. Very soon the temple priests and the public reverted to their former practices.

Gandhi now started a newspaper called the *Harijan* to push the fight against untouchability. (The word *Harijan* means "the Lord's people.") But, as he realized, this was not enough. People's hearts change painfully slowly. He had been considering a penitential sacrifice on his part for the untouchables when suddenly, in the middle of the night, he awoke to hear a voice commanding him to undertake a twenty-one day fast. It began May 8, 1933. He was over sixty years old, and if the previous fast had caused concern, one more than three times as long aroused consternation. The government freed him from jail, and though he became dangerously weak, he survived.

But the problem of untouchability remained. Gandhi disbanded his Sarbamati ashram, donating it for work for untouchables. Shortly thereafter he courted arrest by organizing a freedom march. Soon again imprisoned, he began a third fast on August 16, 1933, when he was not allowed to continue his work for the untouchables while in jail. This time he nearly died and was removed to a hospital.

In November of the same year, having recovered his health, he set out on a pilgrimage in behalf of the untouchables that was to extend to the southernmost part of India and to the extreme north, as well. From town to town he traveled for nine months, holding meetings, opening temples, collecting funds. He begged for a change of heart on the part of the Indian people. Certain orthodox Hindus sought to thwart him, even threatening his life. When, in a struggle, one of these men was hit with a club, Gandhi vowed to undertake another penitential fast. This he began after completing his pilgrimage of one hundred and twenty-five thousand miles and raising over a half-million rupees for his *Harijan* Fund. (Though he was not immediately successful in his endeavors, one of the first laws passed in newly free India, thirteen years later, abolished untouchability.)

Gandhi's fifth campaign was waged against mass communal violence—the result of animosity between the Muslim and Hindu communities. We have already seen him upholding the rights of Muslim merchants in South Africa and lecturing them to put aside religious differences. Years later, in 1920, to show his support of the Muslims in India, he had made common cause with them in their concern over the treatment of the Sultan of Turkey after the First World War. What was known as the "Khilafat question" became one of his chief grievances against the government, along with the outrage of the Amritsar Massacre. And in 1924, when violent rioting broke out in the Northwest Frontier Province between Muslims and Hindus, Gandhi had felt he must do personal penance. The Muslims had started the trouble by killing Hindus and setting fire to their houses. Gandhi undertook a fast of twenty-one days, which temporarily lessened the hard feelings. Again, interestingly, he decided about 1931 to change his chief article of faith, "God is Truth," to the more universal sounding "Truth is God." Whether or not he knew it, he had given first place to that one of the Koran's ninety-nine names of Allah preferred by the Muslim Sufis.

Finally, in September 1944, Gandhi met with the Muslim leader, Mohammed Ali Jinnah, for a series of talks. It was a desperate attempt to find terms for a common agreement with Jinnah, who was pushing his demand for a separate state of Pakistan. The talks were foredoomed to failure; Jinnah showed even less appreciation for Gandhi's method and what he stood for than the Hindu extremists who accused him of betraying them. The Muslim leader had no intention of making any agreement that did not accept his full demands for partition of the country. He feared for the Muslims in a free India dominated by Hindus. As time went by the situation only worsened.

Jinnah had come to hate the Hindus, and inaugurated his long-threatened "Direct Action" against them in Calcutta on August 16, 1946. Muslim ruffians butchered Hindus indiscriminately. For two days the Hindu population was stunned; though the majority, they did nothing. But then they reacted, their own ruffians retaliating as brutally as the Muslims had attacked before. The carnage only came to an end after four days. On October 10, violence began again in East Bengal, where the Muslims were in the majority. From this time Gandhi's energies were for the most part directed to quelling communal fury; even when the cause of an undivided India was lost, he continued his struggle for communal peace.

Gandhi's lifelong campaign against communal violence had reached its climax. In his eyes it was now a matter of life and death for India. But it seemed as if he expected more of the Hindus than of the Muslims. He had not gone to Calcutta at the time of Jinnah's Direct Action; yet several years later, when the Hindus started violence there and had the upper hand, Gandhi visited the city long enough to work a change in men's hearts. Many Hindu extremists came to see him as an enemy.

Long before, in the conversation with Nirmal Bose about his book of selections, Gandhi had made an unexpected request of the professor. "I would like you to come and work with me. Will you?" he asked. Professor Bose paused a moment. "You know," he said at last, "the university is my first love. You are only my second love!" Gandhi laughed. "Well then, will you promise me that when I badly need you, you will come?" "That I can promise," Nirmal Bose replied. The day of need had now arrived. Gandhi had made up his mind to go to Noakhali, in East Bengal, the scene of some of the worst rioting and killing, to see if he could restore calm. With him he would take his secretary, his doctor, and an interpreter. The only language spoken in East Bengal was Bengali, and he thought of Professor Bose. So he called him to his side and told of his plan. "You know it may mean your death," he said. "Are you ready to face that?" "I won't answer the personal question," the professor replied. "But I will come." For four months their small party toured the villages. Everywhere violence was in the air. Gandhi sought to instill courage into the hearts of bereaved Hindu women. He did not commiserate with them; he asked them to be strong.

At the end of four months, a massacre of Muslims by some of the Hindus in Bihar called Gandhi to that state. Violence had flared when Hindu women refugees reached Bihar, their necks torn and bleeding where Muslims in East Bengal had snatched off their only wealth, their gold necklaces. Meanwhile final deliberations were being held to determine India's fate once it became independent of British rule on August 15, 1947. Desperately trying to stave off partition, Gandhi even suggested that Jinnah should form a Muslim government for India, with a Muslim Prime Minister. (This proposal incensed Hindu extremists even further.) But his own chief associates in the Congress party did not agree, and partition became inevitable.

After touring several parts of the North, where rioting was taking place with increasing frequency, Gandhi paused in Calcutta on his way back to Noakhali, where he feared would be the greatest bloodshed on Independence Day. Hindu and Muslim leaders begged him to remain in the city a few days, for the people were in an ugly mood. During that short time, showing utmost unconcern for his own personal safety, he lived in a house abandoned by its Muslim owners. With him, at his request, was Shaheed Suhrawardy, the Muslim police chief who a year before had been responsible for not stopping the bloody anti-Hindu rioting there. Somehow, by exposing himself at a window to a crowd of infuriated Hindu youths and bringing Suhrawardy out beside him (where the Muslim was unexpectedly moved to acknowledge his guilt), Gandhi managed to turn the tide.

Independence Day he spent in the desolate house, unmoved by the festivities, plying his spinning wheel. Outside crowds were jubilantly celebrating independence, and Hindus and Muslims fraternized. Soon again, however, rioting broke out, and finally Gandhi undertook another fast unto death. At last even a group of hardened ruffians came to him in a body and asked his forgiveness. Again he abandoned his fast.

But in many parts of India Muslims were no longer safe. Gandhi, in Delhi, decided that his only recourse was still another fast. This he would not break till leaders of all sections of the people swore they would put an end to communal rioting and that Hindus and Muslims would live like brothers. The fast lasted six days. Only when Gandhi was growing delirious and had become nearly too weak to survive was the necessary agreement obtained and signed. Since that day, with only minor exceptions, Hindus and Muslims within India have forgotten their animosities. But the victory was bought dearly.

During their tour in East Bengal, Nirmal Bose had asked Gandhi if he really believed in God. "The depth of my faith," Gandhi said, "will be shown by the manner of my death." At the fateful prayer meeting on January 30, 1948, only twelve days after he had ended his last fast, Gandhi stepped up to the platform, leaning on his grandniece Manubehn for support. His palms were joined in a gesture of salutation. Suddenly a Hindu extremist pushed his way through the crowd, and after bending low in salute, shot him, at pointblank range, in the abdomen and chest. Twice, softly, the great friend of the helpless, bondslave of the voice of service and human community, took the name of the ideal ruler, Rama, the *avatara* he had revered all his life. As he fell, his hands were still joined in the gesture of reverence. It was as if, at last, he was seeing God face to face.

TOWARD THE
SOURCE OF THE
VOICES

Because of an unusual set of circumstances, as I said in the introduction, a meeting of Hindu and Christian beliefs has taken place in my mind, slowly transforming my own religious outlook. In these pages I have tried to share with the reader something of the experience I have passed through.

Our study of the Hindu expressions of what, for Christians, I have called the four voices of Christ has led to a rather extended confrontation with many of the insights of Hinduism— Vedic, medieval, and modern—and especially with those that show similarities with those of Christianity. As a matter of fact, in looking for evidences of Christ's working beyond Christianity we have in a certain sense by-passed what could strictly be called confrontation. That would require a study of dissimilarities, as well. But ours is a journey of exploration rather than a campaign of conquest. In another sense, though, it may be even more ambitious than a strict confrontation.

What, after all, is implied in a search for Christ beyond the Church if not the possibility of learning something new about him? Our aim, it should be obvious by this time, is not to affirm a Christ already known in experience, but to find a further Christ as yet not clearly known. Through the search we may reach nothing more than a few tentative conclusions, intimations of possibilities that may never be realized. Yet instinct tells me there is promise of something more definite than that—if only we know how to pursue it. For a hint of where my own explorations have been taking me, I turn once more to the journey to Gorakhpur.

In my diary entry about the night-long trip in the taxi, I failed to note down what the final episode stood for. It was a natural omission; at the time I had no way of knowing how I

would see it later. Our arrival, early in the morning, at the
house of my friend B. B. Singh; our heartwarming welcome
there; and, after a few hours' sleep, our complete absorption
into the household—all this had been a reaffirmation of the
quiet acceptance so natural to most Indians I have met and so
fully exemplified on the journey. I had recognized anew the
spirit of India, and my own relationship with India.

Ten years before, I celebrated that spirit in a poem:

SPIRIT OF THE LAND

Out of unaging earth,
Out of a dark, soft, immemorial
Womb—not the thick paddies only,
Not the slim herons, not the buffalo
And the calm milch cow,
The lifted palm and sturdy deodar;
Not the thatched hut, the naked boy
On the road's edge, the grain winnowed
And piled on the road; not the flowing
Woman, the jolly hawker, the clasped hands
Of brothers joined in artless affection,
The spare, orange-clad monk striding alone;
Not the close bazars, the cozy
Lamps dotting the twilight,
The straining coolie, the round brass pot
Poised on the lithe peasant woman's
Head; not the soiled white saris
Stretched in the sun to dry:
Not all these only, but above and beyond
And through all these, the veiled
Shape, the infinite Mother brooding,
The much affronted, the reviled, the secretly
Serene—long-suffering and forgiving:
She, rising out of this earth,
Above and beyond them all—it is she,
Mysterious and benign,
Whose presence, as you thread the crowded lanes,
Stills you, holds you,
Cheers you like a healing wind.

The journey to Gorakhpur had reminded me, subtly, of
what Indian spirituality and the Indian culture in general

meant for me, and what it might mean for others.

But that was not all. I was in a position, now, to do more than ponder the meaning of a journey that by this time had assumed the proportions of a dream. What I had experienced was in fact a reflex of my own slowly awakening sense of a surer spiritual identity. I was no longer as one apart. I was being prepared to see my own meaning, my own religion, in a new light. Though I was as yet unaware of it, this was for me the beginning of a fresh beginning.

Once Father Robert Antoine in Calcutta gave me the hint, I could see that in the awakening in my friend's house at Gorakhpur I had arrived at a new Emmaus. Not that earlier I had not been intellectually and even emotionally aware of something analogous to the Christ I was now finding. Though I had not known how to name him, during my years as a Hindu I had written more than one poem around this aspect of him   an aspect 1 would one day feel was indispensable for realizing the total Christ. But after our journey to Emmaus via Gorakhpur he began to come home to me, as a Christian, more vividly than before. I was finding for myself, indistinctly as yet, a Christ who had been waiting to be recognized as long as I had drawn breath.

I thought of the end of the story of the two disciples of Jesus who walked with the stranger on that puzzling day of the resurrection: "So they drew near to the village to which they were going. He appeared to be going further, but they constrained him, saying, 'Stay with us, for it is toward evening and the day is now far spent.' So he went in to stay with them. When he was at table with them, he took the bread and blessed, and broke it, and gave it to them. And their eyes were opened and they recognized him; and he vanished out of their sight. They said to each other, 'Did not our hearts burn within us while he talked to us on the road, while he opened to us the scriptures?' "

Now I knew why my own heart burned within me all during that unforgettable ride to Gorakhpur. Who it was I had recognized, I was to learn by slow degrees. It was not when Christ was opening the scriptures to them, but when he gave them the actual bread, that the disciples knew him. I received the bread only in Calcutta.

Before we reach the end of this chapter the reader, I hope, whether he agrees with me or not, will have some idea of the promise my own journey of discovery holds before me.

-2-

In the central chapters of this book I have tried to convey something of the four voices of Christ as they are expressed in Hinduism. It was, of course, the four episodes of our trip through northern India that prompted me to think in terms of them in the first place. I said at the start that the presence of these approaches to God in Hinduism did not make them any the less truly Christian. A Hindu, to be sure, might understandably ask why I did not write a book about the four voices of Krishna as found outside Hinduism. After all, they were clearly enunciated in the Bhagavad Gita probably several centuries before the time of Jesus. Here, I must frankly say, my reply may not fully satisfy our Hindu questioner. In any study of religious truth, it seems to me, people have to begin with the position of their own faith. Those who have been taught to believe that theirs is a complete revelation of God's purpose for men will necessarily try to interpret others' beliefs in terms of their own. (Even Hindus have been known to do this, on occasion, with regard to Christianity.) The conclusion they reach, however, as a result of their honest facing of other religions is another matter.

From our study of the voice of intuitive wisdom as manifested in Hinduism, we have noted that it bears witness to the nonduality of the Godhead—to the oneness of God's nature, to put it in Christian terms—and to the soul's nondifference from the Godhead. (Though this experience is hinted at by not a few Christian mystics, when taken in isolation it appears to differ radically from the usual Christian interpretation.) Through the words of seers who have actually penetrated beyond the subject-object relationship to the True Self, we have learned that suprapersonal reality is something to be *seen*, that is to say, participated in, through the sheer power of reason purified of egoistic prejudice—aided, so to speak, by the grace of the Self. Shankara's grand system, we saw, was based on this voice. The modern seer Ramana Maharshi provided an instructive example of a man in whom there was a preponderance of intuitive wisdom.

Again, we noted that the voice of devotional self-giving bears witness to a mysterious differentiation of attributes within the

one Godhead—a difference of Persons, Christians might say
—and of a subtle but real distinction between the Godhead
and the soul. (Here the experience of many Hindu mystics corresponds rather closely to the witness of Christian mystics.)
Through the recorded experiences of saints, we could see
that by devotional commitment the soul can lose its selfwardness and bring to birth within itself, as it were, an incarnation
of the personal God. Ramanuja's system and the various
devotional schools all express this voice. Krishna Chaitanya,
in the sixteenth century, offered a vivid example of one in
whom there was a preponderance of devotional self-giving.

We saw, further, that the voice of conscious discipline has
a unique function. While an easy acceptance of the witness of
either of the first two voices satisfies many so-called religious
persons, this third approach reminds us that to achieve here
and now the goal promised by the first two, stern personal
effort is needed. As we learned from Patanjali, the mind must
be bent inward upon itself, past all distraction, through
exercise of its innate power to concentrate. Both Ramana
Maharshi and Krishna Chaitanya heard this voice as well as
their own characteristic one. (There is little essential difference
here between Christian and Hindu practice, though Christians
will question whether the full vision of God may be had in this
life.) Ramakrishna Paramahamsa's period of spiritual practice
provided a most impressive illustration of conscious discipline
because of the great variety of ways he explored—and because
he showed, as well, that the goal may be won by untutored
spiritual yearning, if only it is strong enough.

Finally we noted that the voice of service and human community provides the average man with a joining of end and
means: God is, as it were, present here and now to one who
worships him through humanity. Quite as much as the other
approaches, it too offers an effective way to dissolve the limited
ego. Moreover, by putting into practice the moral ideals that
flow from realization of the goals of the other approaches, it
becomes a living sign of their truth. The idealized Hindu social
system and certain aspects of modern Hindu society express
this voice very effectively. (I personally find little real difference between its Christian and Hindu expressions.) It is the
voice of service and human community that sounds most
urgently to men today—religious and irreligious alike—in
both East and West. Mahatma Gandhi provided the best
example of the man in whom there is a preponderance of this

voice. His public life, which spanned fifty-five years, shows him to have been as untiring in his obedience to its call as any man in the world's history. The four central voices of the Christian message are present in some degree, I suspect, in any complete religious message. Because Hinduism has allowed an experimental separation of the voices, in many instances their expression has seemed unfamiliar or strange. Christianity requires, by its very nature, an imitation of Christ. In Christ the four voices are wedded in an unforced synthesis—a synthesis not of words only, but of deeds. Those who have lived Christianity most richly, the saints, have mirrored the example of their Master. This is not to say that the man of simple devotional faith and good works is not a proper Christian. But in following all the voices to the utmost of his capacity, the saint allows Christ to become incarnate in him more abundantly than in others.

It is especially in the experimental separation by mystics of the disciplines of the first two approaches that Hindu practice has contrasted sharply with Christian. The lack of any central "teaching authority" in India such as was found in the early Christian Church may in part account for the tendency. For religious philosophers were able to interpret the scriptures in terms of their own preferred approach and thus make it appear that it alone represented ultimate truth. But the situation is not perhaps as confused as it seems. In one sense, the Hindu method may be more scientific. In treating the voices as if they could be validly separated, as if God could be attained through one alone, Hindus may have obtained a firm grasp on the practical elements of the mystical life. I have proceeded in our present study on the assumption that Christians have something to learn about their own religion through examining the voices as if they could be validly isolated.

Actually, this comparison between Christian and Hindu practice is not quite fair to Hindu mystics and philosophers. In their daily lives, at the conclusion of their periods of discipline, both types of men have usually combined the voices in a fusion quite comparable to that found in Christian mystics and philosophers. Their words and deeds bear witness to a breadth and depth of character that closely approximates those of Christian saints. Moreover, they have not always separated the various approaches even in their teaching.

We are not at all certain, for instance, about what the Upanishadic seers sought to teach. There is no doubt that they experienced the oneness (nonduality) of the Godhead, which would imply a following of the voice of intuitive wisdom. Shankara, though he gave a place to the concerns of the ordinary world, in the last analysis interpreted the Upanishadic record in the light of intuitive wisdom. Ramanuja nevertheless interpreted these same teachings as expressing the voice of devotional self-giving. The Vedic seers may thus have transcended the merely intuitive realization. The Upanishadic texts "All this is, indeed, Brahman" and "That is full; this is full" strongly suggest that at least some of the seers proceeded from the experience of oneness to recognizing the importance of the world of diversity and becoming.

In any event, it seems quite clear that the teaching of Krishna in the Bhagavad Gita transcends the purely intuitive approach and recognizes the supreme importance of the personal God and thus the meaningfulness of the creation. Throughout this scripture the four voices are explained as if they go hand in hand. Again, in the vision of Mahayana Buddhism (also a product of India) and of the Tantra philosophy, it was understood that somehow the world was as real as, and a necessary complement to, the ultimate reality known by intuitive mystics. Indeed, for them, realization of that reality involved devotional means. In modern times the same vision has been reaffirmed in the definitive experiences of Ramakrishna as a result of his following a great number of separate disciplines. In fact, in his example we find a perfect reconciliation of the two tendencies. As a result the meaning of each has become illuminated.

There is no doubt, however, that many more philosophers than Shankara and Ramanuja have asserted in their theorizing —and sometimes through their practice—that one approach, and one alone, was true. The question therefore remains: granting the several approaches as expressed in Hinduism are at least in large part true expressions of the voice of Christ, are they any the less real and true when found in isolation? In other words, does the mystical goal their adherents attain bring them to the fullness of the beatific vision?

Perhaps we can liken the voices taken in isolation to the colors of the spectrum. Light, as we know, is in itself white. When it is refracted by a prism into various colors, none of these has any being except in the original light. Each of these, if pursued to its source, will be found to resolve itself into that light. Is this the case with the four separate voices, too?

Though the fact has not been given particular attention by Christians, it is clear that in certain Christian saints and mystics there has been, along with the others, a preponderance of one particular approach. Where the separate Hindu expressions do not contradict the teaching of Jesus, may we consider them to be as valid for Hindus as they are for Christians when found, say, in a Pseudo-Dionysius or a Meister Eckhart, who are predominantly intuitive? Or in a Francis of Assisi or Catherine of Genoa, who are predominantly devotional? Or in a Brother Lawrence or Thérèse of Lisieux, who (in their implications for the average man) are predominantly active? And what are we to say of those many earnest modern Christians who are abandoning all concern with intuitive wisdom or devotional self-giving in favor of an almost complete dedication to the way of service and human community?

-3-

The reader who has come thus far with me on our voyage of exploration and discovery will decide for himself whether, and to what degree, the voices outside Christianity represent authentic voices of Christ. This is perhaps not as difficult a task as it at first appears.

What various non-Christians, and especially Hindus, have said about the authority of scripture, the nature of God and the soul, the meaning and goal of life, the approaches of the soul to God through spiritual and moral disciplines, and many other matters, shows a striking similarity to what Christian authorities have said. Their words offer persuasive evidence of a common source of inspiration at work in the great religions. But similarities may be of two kinds. Some of the observable similarities, it would appear, are true similarities; some of them, superficial or false. Even what we at first take to be false similarities may, upon close examination, prove to be teachings or customs complementary to those of the Christian Churches. Though seemingly at variance with accepted Anglican, Orthodox, Protestant, or Roman Catholic teachings or customs, they may in no way contradict their spirit and may even at times serve to illuminate the Christian revelation.

Our business in the present discussion is to concentrate on the true similarities—the evidences of Christ's working in

other religions—and to explore the possible meaning for ourselves of his presence there. But this much may be said about
the undoubted dissimilarities to be noted between the myths
and symbols, rituals and customs, teachings and disciplines of
non-Christian religions and those of Christianity: some of these
too are true dissimilarities; others, again, may be superficial or
false. Many of the teachings and customs proper to Hinduism
may be found to represent truths that, while they do not contradict Christian truth, are not for Christians—the belief in
reincarnation, for instance, or the custom of spiritual initiation,
or specific temple rituals. Some of the apparent dissimilarities,
again, may turn out to be valid matters that Christians have
either forgotten or might even learn from—methods of medita
tion and prayer, for instance.

While rejecting whatever is for them palpably false in other
religions, Christians need not assume that all that differs from
their own beliefs and practices is for that reason untrue.
Christ may well speak in different tongues to different cultures. I think a general rule for determining which are true
and which false similarities or dissimilarities is to judge them
by their fruits.

But if, after honest self-searching, a Christian concludes
that the Hindu expressions of the voices of intuitive wisdom
and devotional self-giving and conscious discipline, and of the
voice of service and human community—as they speak through
the Upanishadic seers, the Krishna of the Bhagavad Gita, and
the later Hindu saints and philosophers—are largely authentic,
another legitimate question arises. Is the gospel message for
non-Christians not being sufficiently preached to them already
through the four voices? Are the dogmas and rites of the
organized Christian Churches, centered around the Fatherhood
of God and his intervention in history for the salvation of
men, really a part of that message? Is explicit acceptance of the
historical Jesus as unique Savior required for salvation by
those who do not profess the Christian faith? In a word, does
God intend all men in the East—in the world, for that matter
—to become professing Christians?

This is a radical question. I do not know the answer. But
in view of what we have observed thus far, I am in all honesty
compelled to ask it. I do not suggest that the complete Christian gospel message should not be preached and lived by
Christian missionaries. In fact, I think it is most important
that it should be. I ask only whether we should any longer

expect conversions on a large scale in Hindu and Buddhist
lands. Provided, of course, the voices that speak to the faithful
in other religions do not contradict the truth of Christ, are
we doing violence to people when we ask those already committed to a spiritual and cultural tradition other than our
own to adapt themselves to our historically determined theological scheme and our theory of what happens after death?
Are these considerations essential for their salvation? What
of those, for instance, who sincerely worship God as Mother
instead of Father?

I am led to ask myself these questions especially in view of
what is to be observed in the life of one of the greatest of
India's spiritual geniuses, about whose spiritual practices we
have already read. If we are to come at all close to an understanding of Christ's working outside Christianity, we must, I
believe, honestly face certain arresting incidents in the life
of Ramakrishna Paramahamsa. Let us try to determine, by
looking at these incidents, and at a few of his teachings, whether
in some way Christ is speaking directly through him.

-4-

Gadadhar Chattopadhyaya, as we saw, was born in the year
1836, in a very small village, Kamarpukur, in the interior of
West Bengal. His father, Khudiram, and his mother, Chandra
Devi, were persons of the utmost rectitude and piety. Too
honest to bear false witness, at the behest of his all-powerful
landlord, against another tenant, Khudiram found himself in
late middle age ousted from his ancestral property. He never
lost faith, however, in God's mercy. Through the generosity of a
friendly landowner who lived quite a distance away he obtained
a gift of a small portion of land, on which he could live and
grow enough rice and vegetables to support his family. The
form of the Deity worshiped in the family shrine was Raghuvir,
an aspect of Rama.

Early in 1835, Khudiram set out on foot on a long pilgrimage
to Gaya to fulfill his obligations to his ancestors by making
offerings for their welfare in the temple of Vishnu. He reached
Gaya in the middle of March and stayed about a month. While
there he had a dream in which the Lord Vishnu appeared to
him, surrounded with a divine radiance, and said, "Khudiram,

I am well pleased with your extraordinary devotion. I bless you, and I will be born as your son and accept your loving protection.'' Filled with gratitude at this sign of the Lord's grace, which he implicitly believed to be true, Khudiram left Gaya and returned, again on foot, to Kamarpukur in the summer.

When Khudiram reached home he found that Chandra Devi was pregnant. She told him a strange story. One night while she was asleep in their small mud-walled cottage, with only her three children there, she dreamed a luminous being was at her side. Waking up, she rose, frightened to think someone had entered. But the form had disappeared. After trying the lock and finding it fast, she went back to bed. But in the morning she told her low-caste friend Dhani and another woman of the incident. Dhani knew that Chandra Devi was so simplehearted that she never thought of keeping anything secret. She also knew how things can become distorted by village gossip. So she reassured her friend it was only a dream and told her to speak of it to no one. Another day, as Chandra Devi was standing before a small shrine of Shiva not fifty yards from the house, she saw waves of light begin to flow toward her from the image. The light seemed to enter her womb, and she dropped to the ground, unconscious. Afterward she felt that the light was still within her and that she had conceived.

Being forewarned by his dream at Gaya, Khudiram was not at all surprised. He told his wife of his own experience, and together they awaited the birth of a son. Meanwhile a transformation had come over Chandra Devi. Filled with an all-embracing love, she seemed more concerned about her neighbors' welfare than about her own. Secretly she would take articles of food from her own meager supply and give them to the poor of the village. She began, also, to experience many transcendental visions. Whenever she told her husband about them he explained that such experiences were to be expected. In due course a son was born. As the child grew, the parents gradually forgot the visions they had had and began to think of him just as they did of their other children.

On account of the dream, Khudiram had given his son the name Gadadhar, a title of Vishnu. The boy was very lively and strikingly handsome. All the village loved him. Many are the stories, charming or strange, told about him. Most of these, if not heard from his own lips in later life, were gathered from close associates after his death by a disciple, Swami Saradananda, who took it upon himself to verify them in preparation for writing his definitive biography, *Sri Ramakrishna the Great Master.*

One of the tales told about Gadadhar's youth, of special interest for Christians, concerns an elderly maker of shell bracelets by the name of Srinivas. Finding the boy alone, he said to him, weeping, "I have become old and feel that my death is approaching. I shall not have the good fortune to see the many wonderful things you will do on earth." Asking the boy to sit down in a secluded spot, he brought flowers and other articles for offering and performed ritualistic worship before him as the priest would before the Deity in the temple. Is one not reminded of the aged Simeon blessing the youthful Jesus?

At the time of Gadadhar's being invested with the sacred thread on the assumption of brahminhood, a ritual something like Christian confirmation, he was to receive his first alms of food, according to custom, from a brahmin. But long before, at Dhani's earnest request, he had promised her this privilege. That she was a low-caste woman made no difference. Much to his family's distress he insisted on keeping his promise. Even at the age of eight, Gadadhar valued truth more highly than inherited social distinctions.

On another occasion, a little later, some *pandits* were having a lively discussion on certain abstruse theological points. They were sitting in a shed-like building with roof but no walls, near the center of the village, which was used as a school for young children. Gradually the discussion turned into a heated argument. Others gathered to watch the scholars. Happening by, Gadadhar stood and listened. In a short while, calling one of the *pandits* aside, he asked if such-and-such was not the solution. When the scholar repeated the boy's words, all were dumbfounded. They accepted what he said as the only possible solution. The incident recalls Jesus sitting among the teachers in the temple.

Throughout his youth, Gadadhar showed an indifference toward his schoolwork. Mathematics he found particularly uncongenial. But anything having to do with religion claimed his attention. When a dramatic troupe was formed to give popular religious plays, he joined it and spent many hours learning and playing the roles of various gods or goddesses. During the performances he would sometimes become so fully identified with the divine personage he was portraying that he lost outward consciousness. Seeing him usefully engaged, his family did not insist that he should complete his formal education. Later, when he went to Calcutta, he exhibited the same lack of interest in secular learning. To his brother Ramkumar, who wished him to continue his studies, he said, ''Brother, what shall I do with a breadwinning education? I would rather learn the secret of how to know God.''

This willingness to learn about God never left him. Even after he had been declared an *avatara,* a manifestation of Vishnu, by leading Vaishnava *pandits* of Bengal, there was no change in his attitude. As we observed in a previous chapter, whenever he undertook a particular discipline, he continued to seek initiation from various teachers and submit to their direction about how to reach its spiritual goal. It will be recalled that Jesus, too, allowed John the Baptist to baptize him—a ritual in some ways corresponding to initiation.

During the period of his spiritual disciplines, Gadadhar, by now known as Ramakrishna, was one day walking in the garden that stretched along the steep bank between the temples and the Ganges. A well-dressed visitor from Calcutta, seeing him, called down from the footpath at the top of the bank, ''Hey there, gardener! Pick me a gardenia.'' Ramakrishna, whose childlike simplicity stayed with him to the end of his life, obediently plucked a flower and handed it to the gentleman without a word.

As we observed earlier, Mathurmohan grew more and more devoted to Ramakrishna as a result of his contact with him. When the young priest was practicing his Vaishnava disciplines, he spent much time at Mathurmohan's house in Calcutta. There the priestly services were performed by a family priest from the Kalighat Temple named Chandra Haldar. Seeing his master's growing devotion to Ramakrishna, he became uneasy. Once, finding Ramakrishna alone in a room in Mathurmohan's house, Haldar asked him mockingly, ''Tell me, priest, how have you managed to cast a spell over Mathur?'' Ramakrishna, who happened to be in a state of partial spiritual ecstasy, was lying on the floor and could not reply. (Like Chaitanya, sometimes in this state the saint was unable to speak or move.) Taking it for effrontery, the priest gave him three hard kicks in the side and left the room. Ramakrishna said nothing to Mathurmohan about the priest's behavior. One day, as a result of some misdeed, Haldar was dismissed. Only then did Ramakrishna tell his protector what he had done.

Another time when he had passed into a mood of spiritual semiconsciousness—something that occurred very often throughout his life he saw two boatmen arguing in one of the long and narrow country boats tied up at the landing place before the temple. Suddenly one of them gave the other a violent blow on the back. "Look! Look!" Gadadhar cried to someone who was there, as soon as he could speak. To his amazement the man saw the mark of the blow imprinted as a huge welt on Ramakrishna's back. On another occasion when he was in such a mood, he was looking at some tender new grass that had grown on the lawn near his room at the temple. As he was enjoying the sight, a man walked across the lawn. Ramakrishna cried out in pain: on his chest were printed bruises as if someone had walked across it.

This capacity for vicarious suffering we noted earlier, in the story of how, on observing the plight of certain villagers on the temple estates, he sat with them and refused to move till all were given clothes and a meal. Much later, he was to tell his disciples to worship God through service of the poor.

The naked monk Tota Puri initiated Ramakrishna into the austere discipline of Nondualistic Vedanta. After his teacher's departure, Ramakrishna decided to remain uninterruptedly in communion with the True Self, or Atman. He continued thus for a period of six months. Such an experience, it is said, would completely devastate an ordinary man's mind and body. Even at the end of this period, when his mind returned to the sphere of ordinary consciousness, it would plunge into *samadhi*, ecstasy, at the slightest suggestion. At this time, we are told, he heard for the third time a voice in his heart that said, "Remain on the borderline between absolute and relative consciousness."

It was only after a severe and long-drawn-out attack of dysentery that his mind returned more continuously to normal consciousness of the body and the outside world. According to Ramakrishna's explanation, the dysentery resulted from his taking on the serious illness of Mathurmohan's wife.

Near the end of Ramakrishna's life, the great Bengali dramatist Girish Ghosh, a man of notoriously free morals, began to visit him. Finally Girish asked Ramakrishna for spiritual help. When the dramatist confessed he could not, on account of his extremely disorganized life as manager of a theater, be responsible for carrying out even the simple instructions Ramakrishna gave him, the latter said, "All right, then give me your power of attorney." He took on all responsibility for Girish. There is a tradition in India that the true spiritual guide takes on the *karma*, the results of the past actions, of his disciples. The dramatist became a disciple whose devotion was second to none.

Ramakrishna's physical body early became so finely attuned that he could not touch money, or even a newspaper, without recoiling in pain. Once Narendranath Dutt, his chief disciple, after he had been coming to him for some time, wanted to make sure he was telling the truth when he said he could not touch money. When Ramakrishna was absent from his room, the disciple hid a coin under the mattress of his bed, where he usually sat. On returning, the saint sat down but at once jumped up with a cry of pain. Narendra (the future Vivekananda) was ashamed. But Ramakrishna was pleased, for he often asked his young disciples to test him as a moneychanger tests coins. Similarly, his feet would burn when people who led morally indifferent lives bowed before him and touched his feet. And yet he allowed drunkards and prostitutes to come to him for solace, as publicans and sinners came to Jesus. He shared with one and all the wisdom that was his to impart—and to the extent the individual could receive.

According to the biographical accounts, the saint not only took on others' sufferings or sins; he also shared his own mental states with others. In his later years, Ramakrishna was taking a trip on the Ganges in a country boat with a woman disciple and two young men. It was a fairly long journey, and somehow the young men had forgotten to bring any food. The sun was very hot. All began to feel extremely hungry. They had the boatman draw up at a landing place, and one of the young men went to buy some refreshments. When he returned, to their disappointment they found that all he could purchase was a handful of fried peas. At once Ramakrishna asked for them, and the boy poured them into his hand. All expected he would give each of them a share. To their amazement, without offering any to them, he ate them all. "Ah! I am satisfied," he said. Immediately the others felt that their stomachs had been filled. One glimpses here another possible explanation of the feeding of the multitude with five loaves and two fishes. As we shall see later, the saint could share spiritual experiences as well.

An amusing and tender incident is related in *The Gospel of Sri Ramakrishna,* again toward the end of his life. Two brahmin sisters, both of them widows, were expecting Ramakrishna's arrival for the first time at their very unpretentious house. The saint had been detained. One of the sisters kept running out to see if he was coming. She talked about what drastic things she would do if, after all, he failed to come: she would throw all the food they had prepared for him into the Ganges, and when Ramakrishna went anywhere to visit the devotees, she would stand at the door and look on, but never again say a word to him. Finally she ran to another devotee's house to see if he was there.

On returning, she found to her great joy that he had come with a group of disciples. Then, while the other sister went on arranging the delicacies they would entertain their Master with, the first sister simply sat at his feet. Later the other sister complained about how little help she had received. But the first sister was overwhelmed. She could not take her eyes away from Ramakrishna. Even at the time, one of the disciples was reminded of Mary and Martha.

Another day, Ramakrishna returned to normal consciousness from a deep ecstasy. He was sitting in the midst of a group of devotees. "Do you know what I just saw?" he asked them. "I saw I had gone to a far-off country where the people had white skins, and I was being worshiped there." In this connection we recall Jesus' words, "And I have other sheep."

Ramakrishna spent almost all his time, during his teaching years, talking with those who came to him for enlightenment. Feeling compassion for men in their preoccupation with the world, he gave his love to all. And they returned the love. Even many who could not accept his views were bound to him inexplicably by his love. His disciple Vivekananda was bound to him with an especially strong bond. And his Master loved him perhaps even more. Yet he said to the disciple one day, "The moment I fail to feel the Lord's presence in you, that moment I shall not even look at your face."

About the month of June, in the year 1885, the saint developed a sore throat. The strain of so much teaching had caused an inflammation; finally it was diagnosed as cancer. The physician forbade Ramakrishna to speak unrestrainedly to people and asked him to control his spiritual moods. Remaining as he did on the "borderline between absolute and relative consciousness," he still passed frequently into *samadhis* of varying profundity—even at the mention of some inspiring thought. As a result of spiritual ecstasy there is a rush of blood toward the head, and this, the physician told him, would aggravate the inflammation in the throat. But the advice was of no use. He taught whoever came, and he continued to experience the ecstasies.

Now, however, it had become impossible for him to swallow anything but liquid food. He was removed from the Temple of Kali at Dakshineswar to a house in Calcutta. There the young disciples organized themselves to nurse him round the clock, while Sarada Devi, his wife, prepared his food.

His conversations during these final days, as recorded in *The Gospel of Sri Ramakrishna*, are suffused with a poignancy and a peace that can only be experienced by reading them. As we have seen, long years before, during his practice of the Tantra disciplines, he had realized he was in possession of the supernormal powers. Though he avoided using them, so far as he could, someone now suggested that he had power to heal his throat. He refused to entertain the thought. At the importunity of some of his disciples, however, he prayed to the Mother. "Do you know what she said to me?" he asked them afterward. "I was covered with shame. I said to her, 'Mother, on account of the pain I can hardly eat. Make it possible for me to eat a little.' She said to me, pointing to all of you, 'What! Aren't you eating through all these mouths?' I couldn't say a word."

On January 1, 1886, Ramakrishna was strong enough to walk into the garden of the house where he was being tended by his young disciples. On that day many of his lay disciples had come to see him. At his touch, all received a powerful infusion of spiritual insight—each receiving an experience in keeping with his own spiritual ideal. The younger, unmarried disciples who were present that day took the opportunity to air his bed and clean his room. They had had the blessing of his touch on many occasions. To a number of these young men he one day gave the orange robe of monkhood, and he asked them to beg food from door to door in token of their renunciation.

It has been claimed by some that Ramakrishna's last illness was purely the result of his taking on Girish Ghosh's sins. But according to Ramakrishna's own testimony he alone was not the cause. It is reported that near the end of his life his disciple Vivekananda once said, in his hearing, "How can the Master suffer, since he is an incarnation of the Divine Mother?" At once Ramakrishna prayed to the Mother for enlightenment. He then had a vision of another Ramakrishna, bathed in celestial light, and healthy and vigorous. To his feet were coming a long line of disciples. One after another he touched them all as they bowed before him. One after another, he saw, each was delivered of his sins and attained perfect enlightenment. At the same time, as the sins of the disciples were transferred to the other Ramakrishna's body, ulcers appeared upon it. These finally gathered at his throat and caused the cancer from which he was suffering. Thus it was revealed to him that his suffering was the result not of his individual *karma*, his own past deeds, but of those of his disciples.

"Greater love has no man than this, that a man should lay down his life for his friends," said Jesus. After many months of virtual crucifixion from cancer of the throat, Ramakrishna said to his devotees, "I have gone on suffering so much for fear of making you all weep. If you all say, 'Oh, there is so much suffering! Let the body die,' then I may give up the body." The disciples did not know what to reply. It was as if he was saying to them, "Greater love has no man than this, that a man should *keep* his life for his friends." The one statement seems to complement the other.

Knowing that Vivekananda would have much preaching to do, near the end Ramakrishna transferred to him his spiritual powers. He put him in charge of the young disciples. Despite all these experiences, just two days before his Master's death a lurking doubt reappeared in the disciple's mind. "If he affirms now, in the midst of all this pain," he said to himself, "that he is really God, I will believe him. Only then." Almost at once Ramakrishna, raising himself with difficulty from a lying position, said in a clear voice, "He who was Rama and Krishna is now, here in this body, Ramakrishna—but not in your Vedantic sense."

About this time Sarada Devi, Ramakrishna's wife, had a dream in which she saw the Divine Mother Kali with her throat afflicted like her husband's. Since she had always looked upon him as the Divine Mother herself, she realized that his illness was beyond curing. When she told him about the dream, he said to her, "I am going through all this suffering. You have escaped it. I have taken upon myself the suffering of the world." This is the *avatara*'s affirmation of his complete humanity. Immediately Sarada Devi was filled with a boundless compassion for mankind.

During his last few days Ramakrishna spent many hours closeted with his chief disciple, instructing him in the things he was to teach to men. Later Vivekananda was to say to an Indian audience, "If I have told you one word of truth, it was his and his alone, and if I have told you many things that were not true, that were not correct, that were not beneficial to the human race, they were all mine, and on me is the responsibility."

On the last night the disciples gathered around Ramakrishna's bed. About sundown he passed into a deep ecstasy, but after midnight he returned to normal consciousness. He

sat up and took some gruel. He was leaning against five or six
pillows held in place by one of the two young disciples he had
said were, in a former life, disciples of Christ. Vivekananda
began to rub his feet. "Take care of these boys," he said to him
again and again. Three times, in a clear voice, he took the
name of Kali. Then the child of the Divine Mother lay back. At
two minutes past one o'clock, Ramakrishna's head fell to the
side and there was a low sound in his throat. Almost immediately a thrill passed through his body and all its hair stood on
end. A smile came over his face and his eyes were fixed on the
tip of his nose. He had entered into the great and final ecstasy.

After his death Ramakrishna, like Jesus, appeared to his
disciples. In the evening, on the following day, Sarada Devi
was about to remove her bracelets and put on the white *sari*
of a widow in place of the red-bordered one she usually wore.
Ramakrishna's body had been cremated, and this was the immemorial custom. Before she could take the bracelets off, he
appeared in front of her. He looked just as he had before he had
become ill. Taking one of her hands in his, he said, "Am I dead,
that you are behaving like a widow? I have just moved from one
room to another." For the rest of her life, like one whose
husband was living, his wife kept the bracelets on and did not
hesitate to wear a *sari* with a border.

Before a week had passed, Vivekananda was walking with a
brother disciple in the garden of the house where their Master
had died. Suddenly he saw a shining figure ahead of him. He
recognized it as the form of Ramakrishna, but said nothing,
thinking it was a figment of his mind. But his brother disciple
cried out, "Look, Naren! Look!" As Vivekananda called the
other brothers from the house the figure vanished.

-5-

The parallels between Ramakrishna's life and that of Jesus
are numerous enough to arrest the attention. Many more could
be found. What they mean is not for me to determine. I cannot
help wondering, however, whether their presence in the life of
a saint who worshiped God as Mother does not strongly suggest
that we are being given a lesson in how actively Christ can work
outside the context of Christianity.

Certainly the most significant of all Ramakrishna's experiences in connection with Jesus is one that occurred shortly after

his offering up of the fruit of his spiritual practices at the feet of his wife. That it took place after his period of discipline seems to give it a special meaning.

Ramakrishna had met, some time earlier, a gentleman who had read to him parts of the Bible. In this way he had come to know of the life of Jesus and of the marvelous faith and works of the first apostles. One day, as he was sitting alone in the house of a friend not far from the temple at Dakshineswar, he began to look intently at a picture of the Virgin and Child on the wall opposite him. He was reflecting on Jesus' extraordinary life, when suddenly the picture came alive. Rays of light issuing from the Mother and Child entered his heart. Immediately his mind underwent a change. All his innate Hindu feelings and tendencies disappeared, and in their place arose ideas totally unfamiliar.

Seeking to control his mind, he prayed to his Mother Kali, "What strange changes are you bringing about in me, Mother?" But it was to no avail. The love he bore the Hindu gods and goddesses vanished, and in their stead arose a new faith in Jesus and reverence for him and his religion. His mind showed him Christian priests waving incense before the altars of Christ and burning candles. He saw the earnestness with which they prayed and felt the fervor in their hearts.

When Ramakrishna returned to the temple precincts, he forgot to salute the Mother in her shrine. For three days he was absorbed in meditation on what he had seen. At length, on the third day, toward evening, as he was walking near the scene of many of his spiritual disciplines, he saw a man of fair complexion approaching him. Just as when he had had his vision of Sita, he was in the normal state of consciousness. At once he saw the figure was not merely human. Looking at Ramakrishna steadfastly, the man, obviously not an Indian, kept coming toward him. The saint described him, at a much later time, to his disciples: his long eyes added an unusual beauty to his face, and the end of the nose seemed slightly flat.

As he was wondering who this person could be, in his heart rang out the words: "Jesus! Jesus the Christ, the great Yogi, the loving Son of God, one with the Father, who gave his heart's blood and endured endless torture to deliver men from sorrow and misery!" The figure then embraced Ramakrishna and disappeared within his body. Ramakrishna, losing normal consciousness, entered into spiritual ecstasy and remained for some time in communion with the omnipresent personal God with attributes, the Saguna Brahman. He thus had no doubt that Jesus was the Son of God—though for him Jesus was not the only Son.

A monk of the Ramakrishna Order, the late Swami Siddheswarananda, has commented on Ramakrishna's vision of Christ: "The Christian scriptures insist on the point that no one can come to God except through Jesus Christ. But I do not believe they say anywhere that it is impossible for those who have not received Christian baptism to be in contact with Christ. Saul, when he had a vision of Christ, experienced him though he had not yet been baptized: the experience of Christ came first."

In Ramakrishna's case, however, it was not the vision of Jesus Christ that brought out his Christlike qualities. The whole spirit of his life had been in conformity with the spirit of Christ. "Unless you turn and become like children, you will never enter the kingdom of heaven," said Jesus. Ramakrishna, as all who knew him testified, was nothing if not a child.

"Ask, and it will be given you; seek, and you will find; knock, and it will be opened to you," said Jesus. "Cry to your Mother Shyama with a real cry, O Mind, and how can she hold herself from you?" said Ramakrishna, who was fond of quoting from the beautiful song of Ramprasad.

We read earlier the fervent prayer that Ramakrishna taught his disciples—a prayer overflowing with the same spirit of reverence, adoration, and confident dependence that we find in the Lord's Prayer.

"The words that I say to you I do not speak on my own authority," said Jesus. "I am the machine, O Mother, and you are the operator," said Ramakrishna. Often he sang a song, "O Mother, all is done after thine own sweet will." In it occur the words:

> Thou art the moving force, and I the mere machine;
> The house am I, and thou the Spirit dwelling there;
> I am the chariot, and thou the Charioteer:
> I move alone as thou, O Mother, movest me.

Jesus worked miracles. But often he asked people not to speak of them. "An evil and adulterous generation seeks for a sign," he said. Though Ramakrishna had power to work miracles, and did work them on occasion, he sought to avoid doing so.

Jesus taught in simple words and homely parables. Ramakrishna did the same. Here are a few of his characteristic teachings:

"So long as the child remains engrossed with its toys, the mother looks after her cooking and other household duties. But when the child no longer relishes the toys, it throws them aside and yells for its mother. Then the mother takes the rice pot down from the hearth, runs in haste, and takes the child in her arms."

"People shed a whole jug of tears for wife and children. They swim in tears for money. But who weeps for God? Cry to him with a real cry."

"Longing is like the rosy dawn. After the dawn out comes the sun. Longing is followed by the vision of God."

"One need not fear anything if one has received the grace of God. It is rather easy for a child to stumble if he holds his father's hand; but there can be no such fear if the father holds the child's hand."

"God dwells, no doubt, in all beings, but he especially manifests himself in the heart of the devotee. A landlord may at one time or another visit all parts of his estate, but people say he is generally to be found in a particular drawing-room. The heart of the devotee is the drawing-room of God."

"Entangled souls repeat those very actions that make them suffer so much. They are like the camel, which eats thorny bushes till the blood streams from its mouth, but still will not give them up."

"The feeling of 'thee and thine' is the outcome of knowledge; 'I and mine' comes from ignorance. Knowledge makes one feel, 'O God, thou art the doer and I am thy instrument. O God, to thee belongs all—body, mind, house, family, living beings, and the universe. All these are thine. Nothing belongs to me."

"Live in the world like a maidservant in a rich man's house. She performs all the household duties, brings up her master's child, and speaks of him as 'my Hari.' But in her heart she knows quite well that neither the house nor the child belongs to her. She performs all her duties, but just the same her mind dwells on her native place."

"Some ordinary men attain *samadhi* [ecstasy] through spiritual discipline. But when God himself is born as a man, holding in his hand the key to others' liberation, then for the welfare of humanity the incarnation returns [i.e., *avatara*] from *samadhi* to consciousness of the world."

"There are signs by which you can know whether a man has

truly seen God. One of these is joy; there is no hesitancy in him. He is like the ocean: the waves and sounds are on the surface; below are the profound depths. The man who has seen God behaves sometimes like a madman; sometimes like a ghoul, without any feeling of purity or impurity; sometimes like an inert thing, remaining speechless because he sees God within and without; sometimes like a child, without any attachment."

"All things in the world—the Vedas, the Puranas, the Tan-tras, the six systems of philosophy—have been defiled, like food that has been touched by the tongue, for they have been read or uttered by the tongue. Only one thing has not been defiled in this way, and that is Brahman. No one has ever been able to say what Brahman is."

Even very subtle concepts Ramakrishna made comprehensible. One of his most illuminating teachings is about what he called *vijnana*. Here are his words: "What is *vijnana?* It is knowing God in a special way. The awareness and conviction that fire exists in wood is *jnana,* knowledge. But to cook rice on that fire, eat the rice, and get nourishment from it is *vijnana.* To know by one's inner experience that God exists is *jnana.* But to talk to him as Child, as Friend, as Master, as Beloved, is *vijnana.*" Again, he said, *"Jnana* [intuitive wisdom] is the realization of the Self through the process of *'Neti, neti,'* 'Not this, not this.' One goes into *samadhi* through this process of elimination and realizes Atman. . . . You want to climb to the roof; then you must eliminate and leave behind all the steps, one by one. The steps are by no means the roof. But after reaching the roof, you find that the steps are made of the same materials—brick, lime, and brick-dust—as the roof."

"A *vijnani,*" Ramakrishna said, "isn't afraid of anything. He has realized both aspects of God: Personal and Impersonal. He has talked with God. He has enjoyed the bliss of God. It is a joy to merge the mind in the Indivisible Brahman through contemplation. And it is also a joy to keep the mind on the *Lila,* the Relative, without dissolving it in the Absolute."

Ramakrishna's biographer states that at the end of the period of his spiritual disciplines, while dwelling constantly in the Divine Mother on the borderline between absolute and relative consciousness, he received certain revelations about himself and about spirituality in general. He had come to know all his past lives. It was thus revealed to him that he was a special *avatara* of God, ever free, ever pure, and ever awakened. For him there was no question of "liberation" or "salvation" as with an ordinary soul. As long as God's work of helping souls on their way continued, he would continue to be born from age to age. It was so that he might teach men that he had received the command to remain on the borderline between absolute and relative consciousness. He also came to know when he would die.

Through his spiritual disciplines, as well as by force of logic, Ramakrishna was convinced that the various religions are so many paths to the experience of God. He also commended the Hindu schools of Dualism, Modal Nondualism, and Pure Nondualism, says his biographer, as suited to men in various stages of development. This is a point of view that has often been misunderstood. As I see it, there was no desire on Ramakrishna's part to belittle the value of one or another school, or magnify any one in particular. One and the same state is achieved, he said, by knowers of God, followers of the path of intuitive wisdom, and lovers of God, followers of the path of devotional self-giving. Assuredly, he never suggested that those who chose to follow one path were in some way superior to those who followed another.

Ramakrishna's harmonizing of the three classical schools of Hindu philosophy is something very subtle; one cannot be sure one has fully grasped it. Vivekananda once asked him, near the end of his life, the boon of being able to remain continuously absorbed in the highest *samadhi* for three or four days, coming down to the plane of ordinary consciousness only now and then to take some food. (The disciple was then in great distress about his family's impoverished state.) His Master berated him for being so smallminded. ''There is a state higher even than that,'' he said. '' 'All that exists art thou'—it is you yourself who sing that song. Settle your family affairs first and then come to me. You will know a state higher than *samadhi*.'' This incident sheds light on another teaching of his: that *samadhi* is only the beginning of the spiritual life.

As we saw in Ramakrishna's discussion of the *vijnani*, the man of special wisdom, one returns to the world of relativity after attaining the experience of the Absolute, the Atman, and sees the same reality in the steps to the goal that one saw in the goal itself. This is a state, however, attained only by those who have a special mission in the world. Others must accept its implications as a matter of faith. The experience appears to parallel very closely the Mahayana Buddhist ideal of the *Bodhisattva*, who refuses Nirvana for himself till all beings in the universe have attained enlightenment. May one hazard a guess that something of this vision may be attained by ordinary men through intensity of faith—and that that is what inspired the utterances of, for instance, the Sufi poets?

Ramakrishna adjusted his guidance to his hearer's temperament and his stage of development. To a lover of God he never taught what he taught a follower of the path of intuitive wisdom. His method was not limited to matters of doctrine. Girish Ghosh, the dramatist, on one of his first visits to Ramakrishna came in a state of drunkenness. As soon as he saw him, the saint asked, "Where have you left your bottle?" "Why, in the carriage," Girish said. "Go and fetch it," Ramakrishna bade him. "The driver may steal it." Later, when some of his more proper devotees asked whether it did not reflect on his teacher that the dramatist kept on drinking and even visiting prostitutes, Ramakrishna said sharply, "That is none of your business. He who has taken charge of him will look after him." Gradually all the dramatist's questionable habits dropped away. No wonder Girish once said to his Master, "Sir, God made everyone else, as it were, by machine. But you he made with his own hands!"

Ramakrishna's final message to mankind—men and women alike—is perhaps to be found in his virgin wife Sarada Devi. No one could be conceived of more in harmony with the Christian ideal. Even from childhood she had been drawn to God. One night, looking at the full moon, she prayed, "O Lord, there are a few stains even in the moon. But make my heart stainless." Born in a poor family, in another small village in Bengal, she was unlettered as her husband. As we have seen, she had been married to Ramakrishna when very young. Later she joined him and served him at the Temple of Kali at Dakshineswar. Both through the influence of her husband and through her own inborn genius, she developed the qualities of love, service, self-forgetfulness, understanding, and compassion to such a degree that she became a living symbol of motherliness to all who knew her. In fact, those who became her disciples— and they numbered in the thousands—called her Sri Ma, "Holy Mother."

Whether in her native home in the country, or at her small room in the precincts of the Kali Temple near Calcutta, this simple but profound woman, wife and nun in one, spent much of her day in the usual tasks of a Hindu mother: preparing and cooking food and tending to other household duties. Yet so deep was her spiritual understanding that when, in the years after Ramakrishna's death, she was sought out by spiritual aspirants for advice and comfort, she was able to satisfy one and all—the most intellectual as well as the most simple. Somehow she could communicate even with those whose language she could not speak.

A few days before her death, a woman devotee stood at the door of her room. She did not dare go in, for it was against the doctor's orders that any but authorized persons should enter. But Sarada Devi, though suffering from fever, saw her and called her in. In a low voice she said to the sorrowing woman, "Let me tell you something. My child, if you want peace, then do not look into anybody's faults. Look into your own faults. Learn to make the world your own. No one is a stranger, my child. The whole world is your own."

-6-

Of Ramakrishna, the modern Hindu mystic and philosopher Aurobindo Ghose has said, in discussing his ideas for a synthesis of Yoga, "In a recent and unique example, in the life of Ramakrishna Paramahamsa, we see a colossal spiritual capacity first driving straight to the divine realization, taking, as it were, the kingdom of heaven by violence, and then seizing upon one Yogic method after another and extracting the substance out of it with incredible rapidity, always to return to the heart of the whole matter, the realization and possession of God by the power of love, by the extension of inborn spirituality into various experience, and by the spontaneous play of an intuitive knowledge. Such an example cannot be generalized. Its object also was special and temporal, to exemplify in the great and decisive experience of a master soul the truth, now most necessary to humanity, toward which a world long divided into jarring sects and schools is with difficulty laboring, that all sects are forms and fragments of a single integral truth and all disciplines labor in their different ways toward one supreme experience."

And Mahatma Gandhi has said, "The story of Ramakrishna Paramahamsa's life is a story of religion in practice. His life enables us to see God face to face. . . . His sayings are not those of a mere learned man, but they are pages from the Book of Life.''

As we have noted, Christian scholars speak of the *avatara* as the appearance of a ''mythical god,'' in contrast to the Incarnation, who is fully man and fully God. They seem not to be aware of what may be taken as a development in the concept of the *avatara*, from the time of Chaitanya, through which the *avatara* concept (if indeed it ever was what Western scholars claimed) has as it were fused with something very like the concept of the Incarnation—not as to its uniqueness, but in so far as the *avatara* is now seen to be fully human as well as fully divine. And we have noted also that Ramakrishna has been called an *avatara*.

In the light of what we have seen of his life and teachings, we may justifiably ask ourselves whether in him the concept of the *avatara* and that of the Incarnation have in this sense fused. There is no doubt that in him we have found expressions of all the voices of Christ, wedded in a luminous harmony. It is not for me to draw conclusions. All I can do is call attention to facts.

A further and very interesting comment on this whole matter requires mention here. I received a letter unexpectedly, as I was writing this book, from one who has thought deeply and without bias about the relation between Christianity and Hinduism—Dom Bede Griffiths. I visited him at his ashram in southern India and observed the work he is doing to try to bring Indian Christians in closer touch with the culture from which their ancestors sprang. After returning to the United States, I wrote him about my book, saying, among other things, that it would be interesting if Ramakrishna's realization of God as Mother turned out to be complementary to Jesus' realization of God as Father. Here is his reply:

''I put it to myself in this way: that there is one absolute, infinite, eternal mystery of Being, which is in itself beyond our comprehension and can only be described as '*Neti, neti.*' But this one infinite and eternal mystery is manifested in the whole order of nature and in all human consciousness. Each religion—from primitive tribal religion to the most developed forms of religion in Hinduism, Buddhism, Christianity, and Islam—has its own unique insight into this transcendent mystery and 'names' it in its own way. Brahman, Atman, Nirvana, Sunya, Tao, the Kingdom of Heaven, Yahweh, Allah, God—we have to recognize the validity of all these insights and approaches to the truth, but at the same time we cannot simply equate them with one another. They are complementary, and each is necessary to a perfect understanding of the divine mystery.

"An integral Catholicism would be one that had integrated all these insights into a comprehensive vision of the total Christ. Likewise, a fully achieved Vedanta would be one that had integrated the knowledge of Christ and of the Sufis in its vision. Probably this final integration will only take place at the Parousia, when we shall 'see him as he is' and shall fully realize God. Meanwhile we have to be open to every aspect of truth, which means every experience of God or of the divine mystery, so that our knowledge of Christ, who is the Word in which the whole truth is expressed, grows continually and embraces the truth in all its dimensions.

"To apply this to the example that you give: I would say that Ramakrishna 'realized God' (or experienced the mystery) in his own way as Mother, and Jesus realized God in his way in the mystery of the Trinity (i.e., of his living relation as Son to the Father and his experience of the gift of the Spirit). These two 'realizations' are complementary—how precisely they are related is our task to discover. They are not the same, but neither, I think, are they opposed. Could the Mother, or the Shakti [Power] of God, be one with the Spirit, whom some of the Fathers spoke of as feminine? Certainly I see no reason why one should not address God as Mother."

This statement could have been written, almost word for word (except for the reference to the Parousia, or coming of the risen Christ for judgment) by a follower of Ramakrishna. It reflects a growing tendency among those who have been studying interreligious relations in India, one that was well expressed to me by a Roman Catholic priest there: "Formerly I used to think of men's coming to Christ *through* the Vedanta. Now I think of Christ *in* the Vedanta."

A few months earlier than Dom Bede Griffiths' letter, this same tendency was forcibly expressed by George Khodr, a Greek Orthodox metropolitan from Lebanon. His remarks were made in a major address before a meeting of the World Council of Churches held in January 1971 at Addis Ababa, Ethiopia. Bishop Khodr declared that Christianity's encounter with other religions might well turn out to be an epiphany in which the Christian would recognize Christ's presence. If he could overcome his subtle spiritual imperialism, "de-Westernize'' himself, he might come to a new understanding. He could then see the spiritual values in the religions of others and name him "whom others have recognized as the Beloved" and "show them Christ as their own possession." Moreover, he added, it might appear to the Christian that since the Holy Spirit has his own proper function, so to speak, the non-Christian religions could be looked upon as "places where his inspiration is at work."

If what Bishop Khodr says is acceptable, it would appear that it will be the work of the Holy Spirit to help Christians understand the evidences of Christ's working outside the Church, and to help non-Christians understand that what, under different names, they call the Beloved, is what Christians worship as Christ. We come here very close to what Ramakrishna himself was trying to say. In his conversation of August 13, 1882, the following statement is recorded: "You may say that there are many errors and superstitions in another religion. I should reply: Suppose there are. Every religion has errors. Everyone thinks that his watch alone gives the right time. It is enough to have yearning for God. It is enough to love him and feel attracted to him. Don't you know that God is the Inner Guide? He sees the longing of our heart and the yearning of our soul. Suppose a man has several sons. The older boys address him distinctly as 'Baba' or 'Papa,' but the babies can at best call him 'Ba' or 'Pa.' Now, will the father be angry with those who address him in this indistinct way? The father knows that they, too, are calling him, only they cannot pronounce his name well. All the children are the same to the father. Likewise, the devotees call on God alone, though by different names. They call on one Person only. God is one, but his names are many."

Something of the same idea is expressed in a few words in this true story I heard from a great Hindu scholar in Calcutta, Suniti Chatterji. There was an elderly Indian woman who had become a Christian because in that way she could obtain sufficient food—a "rice Christian," Hindus would call her. She became ill. On her deathbed, becoming aware that her end was approaching, she cried out, "Mother Kali! Mother Kali!" Her Christian friends were horrified. "What are you saying!" one of them exclaimed. But a priest who was there to administer the last rites put up his hand for silence. "God understands," he said.

Not long after receiving the letter from Dom Bede in which

he spoke of looking on God as Mother, I came upon a statement that sheds an entirely new light on the question. It made me realize, even more than Dom Bede's remarks, that in Christian tradition itself we have striking evidence of the concept of God as Mother. Ellen Weaver, of Princeton University, thus writes about a not too well-known contemplative nun:

"Lady Julian of Norwich is often referred to as a 'simple and unlearned' medieval anchoress. I believe her to be one of the most subtle and profound of medieval theologians. In the *Revelations of Divine Love* she develops the concept of the 'Motherhood of God' in a long and interesting passage. She begins quietly enough: 'I saw the blessed Trinity working. I saw that there were these three attributes: Fatherhood, Motherhood, and Lordship—all in one God.' As she continues, her attribution of the 'Motherhood' to Jesus appears to be original. Yet in this Lady Julian is following orthodox directions traced out by those early Fathers who recognized the Second Person of the Trinity in the figure of Wisdom in the Old Testament. Lady Julian stands firmly in this tradition when she says, 'The great power of the Trinity is our Father, the deep Wisdom our Mother, and great Love our Lord.'

"Her treatment becomes boldly original when she works out the details of her understanding of Jesus as our Mother: 'What does Jesus, our true Mother, do? Why, he, All-love, bears us to joy and eternal life! . . . Our beloved Mother, Jesus, feeds us with himself. . . . In the matter of our spiritual birth, he preserves us with infinitely greater tenderness. . . . He allows some of us to fall. . . . A Mother may allow her child sometimes to fall, and to learn the hard way. But because she loves the child she will never allow the situation to become dangerous. Admittedly, earthly mothers have been known to let their children die, but our heavenly Mother, Jesus, will never let us, his children, die. . . . He wants us to copy the child who always and naturally trusts mother's love.'

"Again, Lady Julian is simply working out logically the scriptural image of Isaiah: 'As one whom his mother comforts, so I will comfort you'; or, indeed, the image offered by Jesus himself in the Gospels: 'O Jerusalem! How often would I have gathered your children together as a hen gathers her brood under her wings.' But she proceeds with a bold freedom found in none of her contemporaries. From her mystical (i.e., symbolic, allegorical, and contemplative) understanding of God as Mother, Lady Julian develops an overwhelming trust in

God. It is a trust that flies in the very face of sin and human failing, in a style that anticipates a 'simple and unlearned' modern nun, Thérèse of Lisieux.''

Immediately there comes to mind Ramakrishna's parable about God's motherly love. The mother in a family, he said, prepares different types of food for her different children according to their power of digestion—for one, simple fish soup; for another, fish stew; for another, fried fish; and for still another, rich pilau of fish. Or again, one thinks of his fervent prayer to the Mother that we read in an earlier chapter, "O Mother, I throw myself upon thy mercy. Keep me in constant thought of thee. . . .'' But most vividly one recalls that beautiful song of Ramprasad's that Ramakrishna was so fond of singing. This, because of its utter simplicity, reflects perhaps better than anything else the "overwhelming trust in God" that Ellen Weaver finds in Lady Julian of Norwich. It is about Mother Kali, whom the poet here calls Shyama, "the Dark One.''

> Cry to your Mother Shyama with a real cry, O Mind!
> And how can she hold herself from you?
> How can Shyama stay away?
> How can your Mother Kali hold herself away?
>
> O Mind, if you are in earnest, bring her an offering
> Of bel leaves and hibiscus flowers;
> Lay at her feet your offering
> And with it mingle the fragrant sandal paste of love.

Sarada Devi, the virgin wife of Ramakrishna, looked on her Master and husband as the Divine Mother. Julian of Norwich, the virgin anchoress, looked on her Master and Bridegroom as the Divine Mother. Though we have forgotten the Motherhood of God in our Western tradition, should we not ask ourselves what this parallelism indicates? Surely it is more than co-incidental. Are then the two concepts of the Fatherhood and Motherhood of God indeed complementary? Jesus himself looked upon God as the Father. Can Jesus, as Christ, be looked upon as Mother? If so, are we justified in seeing his working in a Ramakrishna?

Questions like these may trouble the orthodox Christian. Are we faced here, he may ask, with something that Jesus himself prophesied to his disciples? This would not be the first time

the subject had been raised. Romain Rolland's monumental
Life of Ramakrishna was published in France in 1929. On a
Sunday after the book appeared, from not a few pulpits were
delivered sermons with an identical title: "Beware the False
Christ." Though such a happening might be impossible today,
the fact of its occurrence forty-odd years ago bears lively witness to the impact of the book. Was it so great a threat? No one,
so far as I know, has advanced the claim that Jesus Christ has
come again. Even Romain Rolland called Ramakrishna merely
the "younger brother" of Jesus Christ. Today his life spurs
us to find out, in Dom Bede Griffiths' words, how precisely their
realizations are related.

-7-

I suggested near the start of this chapter that the very search
for a Christ beyond Christianity implies a belief that there is
something still to be learned about Christ. If, after reflection,
the reader agrees with me that a great proportion of what we
have observed in the foregoing chapters is truly Christ's working, he owes it to himself to accompany me a little farther on
my journey of exploration. Just who, we must now ask, is this
Christ who speaks and works outside the Church?

It is obvious that Christians must be able to associate the
four voices we have been studying in some way with the Jesus
of history. After all, it was through Jesus' words and example
that the voices were first made known to Christian men and
women. But these same voices appear to have been manifested
to some degree, in all ages, in parts of the world having no
connection with the Judeo-Christian tradition. And the origin
of the voices would in many cases have to be a Christ in existence *prior* to the time of the historical Jesus. Is this an impossibility? We have it on the authority of St. Augustine that
it is not. "What is now called the Christian religion," he wrote,
"existed even among the ancients and was not lacking from the
beginning of the human race until 'Christ came in the flesh.'
From that time, true religion, which already existed, began to
be called Christian." (A Hindu reading these lines might
emend the last sentence to read: "From that time, true religion,
which already existed, began to be called Christian—by the
followers of Christ.")

From the New Testament we obtain more than a hint of the Christ we seek. Jesus himself, through his statements, showed he was possessed of an absolutely unique awareness that marked him off from those around him—a self-understanding that no one in the history of his race had possessed before him. It was this self-understanding that allowed him to affirm, "Truly, truly, I say unto you, before Abraham was, I am." And again, "Lo, I am with you always, to the close of the age." It had been revealed to him that his "I" was not merely a human personality but something that transcended time past and time future. There is never any indication that he thought it came into being with his advent on earth.

After his resurrection, Jesus Christ commissioned the eleven disciples who remained faithful to him, "Go therefore and make disciples of all nations, baptizing them in the name of the Father and of the Son and of the Holy Spirit, teaching them to observe all I have commanded you." Here he spoke in terms that refer quite as much to a timeless and nonhistorical reality as to a historical person.

The awareness on the part of Jesus of his timeless nature was only gradually understood by his disciples—and especially after his death and resurrection. St. John, of course, gave it clearest expression in that often repeated but still deeply impressive passage: "In the beginning was the Word, and the Word was with God, and the Word was God. . . . In him was life, and the life was the light of men. . . . And the Word became flesh and dwelt among us." St. Paul (or one of his school of thought) seems to have shared John's understanding of Christ when he wrote in the Epistle to the Hebrews that God "in these last days" had spoken to men by a Son who "reflects the glory of God and bears the very stamp of his nature, upholding the universe by his word of power."

This timeless or nonhistorical Christ is, in the view of certain modern theologians, not only the divinity of Christ the Word; he is also the body of the risen Christ, which is in some way present to the entire universe.

Must followers of non-Christian religions be asked to recognize Jesus Christ as bodily present to the universe? And in what sense? If the timeless Christ may be said to have worked through the Upanishadic seers, and through Buddha and Krishna, may he not be allowed to work in the same fashion _after_ the birth of Jesus? It is held by many Christian theologians that those non-Christians who receive the grace of God are saved through an "implicit faith" in Christ, which unites them at least "invisibly" to his Church. And, as Cipriano Vagaggini of Rome has assured me, there is no reason to believe that such persons of sincere faith do not obtain salvation equally after the time of Jesus as before. If that is so, does this fact not suggest that the nonhistorical Christ may continue to speak to and work through men of other religions to this day? A Hindu or other non-Christian might ask whether the statement about Jesus Christ's being present to the entire universe is just a human way of saying that through the historical Jesus we now *understand* the Word that was from the beginning as it really is and always has been. This is the same as asking whether, if Jesus is God's self-giving to mankind, anything has been added to the Word by his death.

I have gone to some length to draw attention to the divine aspect of Jesus Christ, which though manifested in time is itself beyond time, for a definite reason. I have long suspected that one of the reasons for Christian lack of success in "making disciples" in India and the Buddhist Far East has been an overstressing on their part of the historical Jesus at the expense of the nonhistorical Christ. Perhaps St. Paul is responsible. He hammers at the point when he says, "The times of ignorance God overlooked, but now he commands all men everywhere to repent, because he has fixed a day on which he will judge the world in righteousness by a man whom he has appointed." These words do not speak to most men born outside the Judeo-Christian tradition. Yet they express something integral to Christian belief from Paul's time onward, and as such have influenced the preaching of the gospel in all the nations.

It is fundamental, of course, to Christian belief that the man Jesus of Nazareth and he who, calling himself the Son, identified himself with the Godhead are one. In him is a mysterious union of natures that makes him at once fully human (except for the capacity to commit sin) and fully divine. I nevertheless ask if it is not in the nonhistorical Christ, with whom Jesus of Nazareth identified himself in the words "Before Abraham was, I am," that we find the Christ beyond Christianity. For here is a Christ who can speak to Buddhists, Hindus, Jews, Muslims, even Marxists of whatever hue—one in whom, if rightly presented, they can recognize their own truth. Could this conceivably be the Christ that Jesus actually intended the disciples to preach to the Eastern nations—the Christ that John seems to have indicated: a God who manifests himself daily, hourly, in the motions of wisdom, love, and service?

Assuming this hypothesis to be substantially correct, we may then come to a tentative conclusion: The Christ we have sought and found outside Christianity is not simply the historical Jesus, not even the risen and glorified Lord. Both these images, whether taken separately or together, tend in average men's thinking—and more especially in the thinking of those who are not Christians—to become mythological figures, ideal forms dwelling in a realm of their own. For the majority of us they remain objects of thought. But the reality of Christ, whether within Christianity or without, is an immediate presence. It is the Word who was from the beginning that adds the dimension endowing these figures with their actuality, supplying a fourth dimension, as it were, to their three-dimensional abstractness. This Christ of the living moment is the timeless reality incarnated in time.

We get a new insight into the timeless Christ, I believe, from Ramakrishna's life story. From it we learn that for this Hindu saint—as for all saints—the presence was a constant experience, just as it was for Jesus. And we, too, in a much less intense and vivid way, can share in that experience if we will. The very existence of saints and mystics, and indeed of the Savior, has no meaning if that is not so.

"Here is the whole of sanctity," wrote Jean Pierre de Caussade. "Here is the grain of mustard seed of which the fruits, because we do not recognize it on account of its tiny size, are lost. Here is the penny of the Gospel parable, the treasure which we cannot find because we imagine it to be too far off to be discovered.

"Do not ask the secret of its discovery. There is no such secret. The treasure is everywhere. It is offered to us at every moment, in every place. Our fellow creatures, friendly or hostile, pour it forth freely and make it penetrate through all the powers of our bodies and souls, right into the depths of our hearts. We have but to open our mouths: they will be filled. God's action inundates the universe; it penetrates all creatures; it transcends them all; it is to be found wherever they are; it precedes, accompanies, and follows them; we have but to allow ourselves to be carried forward on its waves."

Whatever else we may say about Christ, then, this much we can assuredly say: Christ is now. Now, not merely in the sense of the ever enriching fruit of an ever increasing store of pasts,

Now, not merely in the sense of the seed of an infinite series of promised futures. Now, not simply in the sense of that right and proper social awareness that urges young men and women today to think first of their neighbor, of the poor of God, and to fight against war and race prejudice and pollution of the environment. Now not simply, either, in the sense of the Abyss of the Godhead, of that inexpressible light sought ceaselessly through history by saints and mystics, scientists and lovers, philosophers and theologians. But along with these, now as the indivisible immediate presence outside time; now in that deceptively simple sense of Christ's ceaseless working in us and through us day and night, without which we could not be or know or love.

It is that timeless now—whether we see him as the only-begotten Son of the Father (which he surely is) or as the Son begotten only of the Mother (which he may well be)—whom we daily crucify by our inattention. "See, see, where Christ's blood streams in the firmament!"—Dr. Faustus' agonized cry in Marlowe's play—we can take for our own condemnation. It is that timeless now who is not only the locus of our salvation, but the very life of our person (and, at least in the Hindu view, of the personal God in the form of both Father and Mother). It is that timeless now with whom we die when we are emptied of narrow selfhood, and with whom we are resurrected when we touch it in intuitive wisdom or devotional self-giving, or receive it in simple Christian faith.

This sort of terminology is terminology proper to Christian use. Yet if Christians are to practice Christian charity toward members of other faiths—intellectually and spiritually, as well as physically and morally—we may have to alter our terms slightly. We may have to allow that it is this very same Christ of the living moment that endows with actuality Yahweh for Jews, Krishna or Chaitanya or Ramakrishna for Hindus, Amida Buddha for Mahayana Buddhists—even perhaps the dialectical process for Marxists. This Christ cannot simply be equated with Yahweh, with Krishna and the Hindu saints, with Amida Buddha, or with dialectical process. But, if our hypothesis is correct, he it is that gives them life. Could we arrive, some day, at the point where we grant that he is whatever in their natures partakes of the divine or the true?

"In him was life, and the life was the light of men," said St. John. Is it not this Christ, therefore, that gives urgency to the four voices, so that all men—even those who do not believe in a personal God—know they must one day follow at least one of them? Is it not this Christ that through the Holy Spirit is vividly present to the Hindu, the Buddhist, the Muslim, the Christian, not as an ideal but as a living, palpitating reality, when he achieves the miracle of faith in his own reading of reality? Here is the Word become flesh in a new sense, which dwells among us, "full of grace and truth," and from whose fullness we have "all received, grace upon grace."

Jesus said that all sins, even sins against himself, can be forgiven, but not the sin against the Holy Spirit. Could this sin be to deny the Holy Spirit's working everywhere, since such a denial stands self-condemned of self-contradiction?

-8-

A word of caution is in order here. The timeless Christ, who is the way and the truth and the life, may indeed—whether we know it or not—be born anew each instant in the soul. But orthodox believers and responsible scholars alike have scoffed, and rightly, at those who celebrate the idea in words without making the slightest effort to live it. The concept of such a Christ can, like every other concept, become no more than an abstraction if it is not rightly used. Our best warning against such carelessness comes from one who, though an unbeliever, is an outstanding example of selfless service. Here is what Mao Tse-tung has to say: "Idealism and metaphysics are the easiest things in the world, because people can talk as much nonsense as they like without basing it on objective reality. Materialism and dialectics, on the other hand, need effort. They must be based on and tested by reality. Unless one makes the effort, one is liable to slip into idealism and metaphysics."

The warning is one that the mystically inclined should take to heart. The intoxication that comes of merely ruminating about lofty spiritual ideas and ideals, while not translating them into action, can indeed become the "opiate" of a certain type of person. The idea of the Christ of the living moment, if not rightly used, brings about the same stillbirth of Christ that comes of the use of the hallucinogens and even of the most "harmless" and least habitforming drugs. The devotees of "materialism and dialectics" may have no conception (indeed, who really has?) of a reality that is neither objective nor subjective, but stands between these two—more real than either, because it is the source of the reality of subject and object alike. But their reasoning applies here; for to *know* the timeless Christ takes quite as much effort as any "correct" Marxist thinking based on "objective reality." That is what the voice of conscious discipline tells us about the voices of intuitive wisdom and devotional self-giving: to follow them one must not only hear them but heed them. It is what the voice of service and human community takes for granted in its welding of hearing and heeding into one.

Assuming that in this timeless Christ we have found both the source of the voices and the source of faith, does not the earnest Christian have, then, a further obligation: to ask himself what that Christ means to him personally—not as an object of belief only, but as daily experience—and how he is letting that Christ live through him? I do not refer here merely to how well he follows the four voices or how fervently he believes in the truth that Christ has revealed through the Christian scriptures. I refer also to how generously he is recognizing the Christ that speaks to non-Christians through their own revelations. This recognition, I believe, must of necessity come to one who truly knows the Christ of the living moment.

The treasure is indeed everywhere, as Jean Pierre de Caussade assures us. But how are we to seize it? As things stand today, Christians who wish to intensify their participation in the living moment might do well to learn certain methods of Zen meditation.

During my visit to Kyoto in the fall of 1970 I met a scholar named Masao Abe, who allowed me to converse with him for an entire afternoon. His interest in the spiritual life, and especially Zen, is something more than academic. Professor Abe impressed on me very forcefully that Zen wants one to plunge into the stream of life, as it passes from moment to moment, instead of standing on the bank and detachedly watching it. Zen Buddhists, he said, aim at breaking through our lifelong habits of thinking *about* ideas and things so as to get to the vibrant heart of the "here-and-now experience." He used the word "experience" advisedly, because the here-and-now is still within time and place.

Many descriptions have been written of the various exercises a Zen monk must put himself through—the prolonged sitting in the meditation hall, the attention to the breathing so as to empty the mind of discursive thought, the concentration on an undecipherable saying, or *koan*, of a master—before he achieves the Zen experience. The discipline involved in reaching *satori*, or enlightenment, is a rigorous one. Those who are not prepared to undergo it may derive considerable benefit from a conscientious study of the sayings of Japanese and Chinese Zen masters who have unquestionably succeeded. As a living Zen master, Abbot Zenkei Shibayama, has pointed out, only a handful of "religiously endowed people under favorable conditions" are able to attain enlightenment. "There has to be another way of Zen open for ordinary people to follow," he says. This way is to make the "religious living attitudes" of the old Zen masters into the guiding principles of their lives. Here we would have a "Zen life based on faith." By following such a method, day in and day out, to the best of one's ability—together with one's inherited or chosen Christian practices—a man would prepare himself, I believe, for the death of ego without which the timeless Christ cannot be incarnated in the soul. I suggest the approach of faith because I believe it may prove greatly useful for many ordinary Christians, especially in implementing the way of service and human community.

"Zen and Christianity are the future"—these words, spoken to me by Thomas Merton at Bangkok in December 1968, the night before he died, have stayed with me ever since. At first I could not accept them, because I had seen so many parallels between Hinduism and Christianity that I should have said something like "Vedanta and Christianity are the future." But as time passed—and as I was writing this book—I came to see his words in a new light.

Christianity and Hinduism are two complementary streams, involving not only faith in the voices of intuitive wisdom, devotional self-giving, and service and human community, but also conscious disciplines by which to follow those voices—to the ultimate vision of God and, in the interim, it is to be hoped, to an intimate knowledge of the total Christ through the Christ who is outside time. Yet both religions are so richly endowed with metaphysical and mystical concepts that the believer is often in danger of taking the concepts for the actuality, the "here-and-now experience" that I have called the timeless Christ. Zen, on the other hand, provides a corrective. Avoiding any conceptualized picture of reality, intellectual or devotional, it provides in the sayings of its masters a constant reminder of where to be looking. (And it enforces this search, for those who are capable, with strict discipline.) In these sayings it seems to be close to the way of service and human community, a way unhampered by distracting theory.

"How wondrously supernatural and how miraculous this! I draw water and I carry fuel!" exclaims the ancient Zen master Hokoji. "Tao [ultimate truth] is your everyday mind," another master says. Which means that "when tired you sleep; when hungry you eat." "Die while alive," says a third, "and be completely dead; then do whatever you will—all is good." In the enlightened Zen master, statements like these come out of an identification with the living moment. But they can become, for others, the basis for an "imitation of Zen"—the "Zen life based on faith" that I have already referred to.

If the Zen approach to reality is too foreign to Western ways of thinking and feeling for a Christian to be comfortable with it, a relaxed use of Ramana Maharshi's discipline, as described previously, in the chapter on intuitive wisdom, may serve equally well. Here are some practical instructions of his to a Western woman who visited him at his ashram. "What are the hindrances to the realization of the True Self?" she asked him. "Memory chiefly, habits of thought, accumulated tendencies," he replied. "How does one get rid of these tendencies?" "Seek for the Self through meditation in this manner: trace every thought back to its origin, which is only the mind. Never allow thought to run on. If you do, it will be unending. Take it back to its starting place—the mind—again and again, and it and the mind will both die of inaction. The mind only exists by reason of thought. Stop that and there is no mind. As each doubt and depression arises, ask yourself, 'Who is it that doubts? What is it that is depressed?' Go back constantly to the question, 'Who is the "I"'? Where is it?' Tear everything away until there is nothing left but the Source of all. And then—live always in the present and *only in it*. There is no past or future save in the mind." These are, of course, directions for one who wishes to meditate, but they can be used too, I believe, as a basis for faith and the forming of right habits of thought.

For any Christian who can accept them, there are still the numerous writings of Christian mystics, study of which has been unfashionable for a long time. Patanjali's advice to make use of "anything that appeals to one as good" seems the best advice to follow. The goal is simply to arrive, by the best means available, at a faith in the Christ of the living moment that one can feel is, in Gandhi's phrase, something "amounting to experience.'' There is a commendable humility in recognizing one's limitations, in being willing to practice what Thérèse of Lisieux called a ''little way.'' Out of that humility the spirit of Christ is born. And that is really what religion is all about.

When I was in Calcutta in 1970, I visited several times a dedicated worshiper of the Lord Krishna. His name is Pran Kishore Goswami. Everything about him was quiet: his gestures, his face, his presence. When he spoke, his words seemed to rise from a deep inner stillness. Pran Kishore is a direct descendant of Nityananda, an intimate companion of the saint Chaitanya. When I told him about the book I had been asked to write, he said, ''Your book will be about love.'' He was right, of course. For what essentially is the timeless Christ who grows out of the death of ego, and who embraces in himself the voices of wisdom and devotion and discipline and service, and the way of faith, but pure love? What else manifests itself in the lives of all those who have known him? But this is a special, ripe sort of love—not a love of demanding or of yearning, but a love of accepting and bestowing. It comes, finally, of belief: it is the justification of belief. For love is truth. And truth is God.

In his last words of instruction to his disciples, which St. John places during the Last Supper, Jesus prayed, ''O righteous Father, the world has not known thee, but I have known thee; and these know that thou hast sent me. I made known to them thy name, and I will make it known, that the love with which thou hast loved me may be in them, and I in them.'' When we have begun to know his presence in unforced communion, the nonentity we called our narrow self, our ego, falls apart. Nothing but the love that is God, is Christ, remains to grow and bear fruit. And this love is a love so unflawed that it really cannot be named: ''I AM WHO I AM.''

-9-

I have offered here a number of suggestions for self-questioning, thoughts that have come to me in the course of my own journey of discovery. The answers I must leave to the reader himself—Christian or non-Christian. As I pointed out at the start, this is a book for inquiring and open-minded people, written by one who is himself no trained theologian, yet who, by a strange quirk of fate, has been asked to deal with a subject that theologians would usually be expected to handle. Just possibly, like the composer my teacher in musical composition spoke of—who, not recognizing the limitations of the instrument he was writing for, created living music that professional musicians at first thought impossible to execute—I have come up with a few suggestions that may not prove unworkable. Perhaps one or two of them may encourage individual readers to consider as probabilities what they might otherwise have held to be impossibilities. And among these suggestions perhaps there are even some that will help non-Christians look upon Christianity with a more understanding eye.

Many years back, in writing about efforts by Protestants and Catholics toward achieving a united Church through ecumenical dialogue, the Protestant leader Robert McAfee Brown set forth an arresting idea. In carrying on the dialogue, he said, both parties would be "engaging in a risk—the risk of prayer—which is that God might choose to answer their prayers in ways quite different from those that any of his children contemplate." His words apply equally, it seems to me, to the meeting between Christianity and other religions.

All Christians, whether well or illinformed about the theological niceties their particular tradition entertains about Jesus Christ, must one day have their Master ask them, "But who do you say that I am?" When it broke upon Peter who his Master really was, he cried out, "You are the Christ, the Son of the living God." In those few words lay the seed of centuries of Christian growth. Such may be the result, in an equally potent way, with today's Christian when it breaks upon him who his Master really is: a Christ of the living moment, of the unnamable truth which is love—not only within but beyond Christianity. Only through such a Christ, I firmly believe, can a loving and humble meeting be achieved with men of other faiths.

"Among you stands one whom you do not know," said John the Baptist when Jesus came to him at the Jordan river. His words remain to haunt us. After all these years of Christian faith, too many of us have yet to know the total Christ. For some few that knowledge, if they come to it, may truly mark the beginning of a fresh beginning.

As a last, paradoxical solution to the whole matter, I suggest that if indeed there is no Christ beyond the Church, it may well be because there is no place where true Christianity—

like true Hinduism, true Buddhism, true Islam—is not already. Should we be able to embrace this solution, possibly we should then understand a little better how a Japanese can be at once a Buddhist and a Shintoist or a Taoist; how a Chinese may be both a Confucian and a Buddhist. Possibly it would explain how I myself could say, so unexpectedly, to my priest friend in Toyko, "I am a Christian, but I can no longer say I am *not* a Hindu or a Buddhist."

A faint echo of what this Christ of the living moment can mean for non-Christians may be found in a poem I wrote just a few years before I returned to the Christian Church. It might have some meaning for Christians, too.

PRESENCE

Between me and the moving world's
Variable play of light and sound
You interpose, not less revealed
Because too instant to be known.

Between me and my clearest thought,
My fiercest love, my closest prayer,
Still you contrive to penetrate:
The crux of now, the core of here.

Though I could cross creation out,
Dissolve all elements in one,
Your presence would unvarying wait
Where, from forever, it has been

The silent mover of the play,
The focus of its myriad parts—
Fashioning, for the world and me,
A wholeness from our opposites.

The call is still as urgent as it ever was: "Behold, I stand at the door and knock."

REFERENCE NOTES

The references are to direct quotations on the pages indicated or, when marked with a ¶ sign, to material within the paragraph beginning with the words following it. Books marked with an asterisk are especially recommended for further study.

INTRODUCTION

xii ¶ *For the past*   The two papers were published in *Theological Studies* vol. 27, No. 1 (March 1966), p. 58, and vol. 30, No. 2 (June 1969), p. 207. The second appeared, in abridged form, in *A New Charter for Monasticism* (Notre Dame: University of Notre Dame Press, 1970), p. 322.

EPIGRAPH

xv *Behold, I stand*   Revelation 3.20. The Scripture quotations in this publication are from the Revised Standard Version of the Bible, copyright 1946 and 1952 by the Division of Christian Education of the National Council of the Churches of Christ in the U.S.A., and are used by permission.

JOURNEY TO GORAKHPUR

1 ¶ *It was shortly*   For a description of the Ramakrishna Order, see John Moffitt (ed.), *A New Charter for Monasticism* (reference note for p. xiv above), p. 153ff.
4 ¶ *Many Westerners*   For certain details of the Buddha's life and teachings I am indebted to Nyanatiloka (trans., ed.), *The Word of the Buddha* (Kandy: Buddhist Publication Society, 1968); Narada Thera, *Buddhism in a Nutshell* (Kandy: Buddhist Publication Society, 1966); Joseph Campbell (ed.), Heinrich Zimmer, *Philosophies of India* (New York: Pantheon Books, 1951); Étienne Lamotte, *Towards the Meeting With Buddhism* (Rome: Secretariat for Non-Christians, Ancora, 1970).
     Did you sigh   *Adam's Choice* (Francestown, N.H.: The Golden Quill Press, 1967), p. 39; used by permission.
6 *base, common, vulgar*   *Samyutta Nikaya* 56.11; from *The Word of the Buddha* (ref. note for p. 4 above), p. 26
     Did you smile   *Adam's Choice* (ref. note for p. 4 above), p. 42.

7 *Go forth now* Vinaya Pitaka, *Mahavagga* 1.11; compare
Sutta Pitaka, *Samyutta Nikaya* 5.420; quoted in Piyadassi Thera,
Buddhism: A Living Message (Kandy: Buddhist Publication Society,
no date), p. 16.

¶ *When the Buddha* See *Buddhism: A Living Message*, p. 34.

All things in this Sutta Pitaka, *Digha Nikaya*, Parinibbana
Sutta, 16; quoted in *Buddhism: A Living Message*, p. 18.

And so, as I lay *Adam's Choice* (ref. note for p. 4 above),
p. 46.

11 *for the welfare* See reference note for p. 7 above ("Go
forth now.")

Never does hatred *Dhammapada 5-6, 252, 81, 146, 153-4,
36, 33, 383, 421-2. The quotations of pp. 11-12 are from Buddha,
The Dhammapada, translated by Irving Babbitt, copyright 1936 by
Edward S. Babbitt and Esther B. Howe and are reprinted by permission of New Directions Publishing Corporation.

16 *Whenever there is* *Bhagavad Gita 4.7-8. All quotations
from this scripture are from Swami Nikhilananda (trans.), *The
Bhagavad Gita* (New York: Ramakrishna-Vivekananda Center, 1944),
and are used by permission, with occasional slight adaptations.

Of warriors I am Bhagavad Gita 10.31

¶ *The story of Rama's* For a more detailed account of the
story of the *Ramayana*, see Sister Nivedita and Ananda Coomara-
swamy, **Myths of the Hindus and Buddhists* (London: George G.
Harrap, 1913); also P. Thomas, *Epics, Myths & Legends of India*
(Bombay: D. B. Taraporevala Sons & Co., Ltd., no date), to which
I am indebted for a few incidents.

THE VOICE OF INTUITIVE WISDOM

31 *Then God said* Genesis 1.26.

32 *I and the Father* John 10.30

Yet he is not far Acts 17.27

For behold, the kingdom Luke 17.21

Sometimes peradventure Justin McCann (ed.), **The Cloud
of Unknowing* (London: Burns and Oates Ltd., 1943), chap. 26. For
further information about this book, see William Johnston, *The Still
Point* (New York: Fordham University Press, 1970), pp. 25–30.

¶ *Early echoes of* For information about Origen, St. Gregory
of Nyssa, Eckhart, Ruysbroeck, and *Theologia Germanica*, see Evelyn
Underhill, *Mysticism* (London: Methuen and Co., Ltd. 1952); "Mysticism," in *Sacramentum Mundi* (New York: Herder and Herder, 1969),
Vol. 4, pp. 140-41, 142-8). For George Fox, see Ronald Knox,
Enthusiasm (New York: Oxford University Press, 1961), pp. 152-
156.

35 *To the enlightened* Bhagavad Gita 2.46

37 *This Atman is Brahman* *Mandukya Upanishad* 2; *Brihadaranyaka Upanishad* 4.4.5. All quotations from the Upanishads are
from Swami Nikhilananda (trans.), *The Upanishads, Abridged Edition (New York: Harper & Row, 1964), and are used by permission.

You are that *Chhandogya Upanishad* 6.8.7 (slightly adapted)

I am Brahman *Brihadaranyaka Upanishad* 1.4.10

Consciousness is Brahman *Aitareya Upanishad* 3.1.3

37 continued
      That is full   Brihadaranyaka Upanishad, Invocation; also 5.1.1
   38 Now, therefore   Brihadaranyaka Upanishad 2.3.6
      Nothing, nothing   From *The Dark Night of the Soul;* see Benedict Zimmerman (ed.), *St. John of the Cross* (New York: Sheed & Ward, 1957); also William Johnston, *The Still Point* (ref. note for p. 32 above), pp. 132-4.
      The Tao that is   Tao Teh Ching 1. All quotations from this scripture have been newly translated by Shu-Jen Tao and are used with his permission; they are hitherto unpublished.
      It is the form   Tao Teh Ching 14
      Now the designation   Brihadaranyaka Upanishad 2.3.6
   39 Then Moses went up   Exodus 24.15-16
      I AM WHO I AM   *Exodus* 3.14, 15
      It is truth   Rig-Veda 10.85.1a; quoted in T. K. Mahadevan, "An Approach to the Study of Gandhi," *Gandhi Marg* 49, vol. 13, No. 1 (New Delhi, January 1969), p. 39.
      The Satya [*the True*]   *Taittiriya Upanishad* 2.6.1
      God is Truth   See Nirmal Kumar Bose, *Studies in Gandhism* (Calcutta: Indian Associated Publishing Co., 1947), p. 269.
   40 eternally begotten   From the Nicene Creed.
      proceeds from   From the Nicene Creed.
   42 Venerable Sir, if even   Brihadaranyaka Upanishad 2.4.1-4 (shortened and slightly adapted)
      Truly . . . not for   Brihadaranyaka Upanishad 2.4.5
      the true light   John 1.9
      The brahmin rejects   Brihadaranyaka Upanishad 2.4.6
      Truly, I say to you   Matthew 25.40
      When there is   Brihadaranyaka Upanishad 2.4.14
   43 [It is] not this   Brihadaranyaka Upanishad 2.3.6
      Grasping without hands   Shvetashvatara Upanishad 3.19
      I see without eyes   *Life and Works of St. Catherine of Genoa,* chap. 9; quoted in Paul Garvin (trans., ed.), *The Life and Sayings of St. Catherine of Genoa* (New York: Alba House, 1964), p. 83; used by permission.
      Though the reality   *The Upanishads,* Abridged Edition (ref. note for p. 37 above), p. 186.
   44 This Atman cannot   *Katha Upanishad* 1.2.23
      Election is true   *Vivekananda: The Yogas and Other Works* (New York: Ramakrishna-Vivekananda Center, 1953), p. 541. All quotations from Vivekananda are from this volume, based on *The Complete Works of Swami Vivekananda,* in 8 vols. (Mayavati: Advaita Ashrama, 1907 and after), and are used by permission.
      Transmission outside   Zenkei Shibayama, *A Flower Does Not Talk* (Tokyo, Japan and Rutland, Vt.: Charles E. Tuttle Co., 1970), p. 19, used by permission.
      He who has not   *Katha Upanishad* 1.2.24
      When the creature   See quotation on p. 43 of text and reference note for p. 43 above ("I see without eyes").
      Both self-effort   *The Upanishads,* Abridged Edition (ref. note for p. 37 above), p. 74, n. 17.
      When all the desires   *Katha Upanishad* 2.3.14

45 By the mind alone   Katha Upanishad 2.1.11
    The radiant Brahman   Mundaka Upanishad 2.2.1
    It is pure   Mundaka Upanishad 2.2.9-10
    And the city has   Revelation 21.23-5
    He came for testimony   John 1.7-8
    The true light   John 1.9-10
46 Do not give dogs   Matthew 7.6
47 The unreal never   Bhagavad Gita 2.16-17, 20
    Weapons cut it not   Bhagavad Gita 2.23
    This is my lower   Bhagavad Gita 7.5-7
    By me, in my   Bhagavad Gita 9.4-5
48 You are the one   Ashtavakra Samhita 1.7. All quotations from
this work are from Swami Nityaswarupananda (trans.), *Ashtavakra
Samhita* (Mayavati: Advaita Ashrama, 1940), and are used by permission.
    As I alone   Ashtavakra Samhita 2.2
    Wonderful am I   Ashtavakra Samhita 2.11-14
49 Rare is the man   Ashtavakra Samhita 6.4
    Thinking about   Ashtavakra Samhita 12.7
    The tranquillity   Ashtavakra Samhita 13.1
    He who has seen   Ashtavakra Samhita 18.16
    What is existence   Ashtavakra Samhita 20.14
50 Every valley   Isaiah 40.4
    When everything has   Brihadaranyaka Upanishad 2.4.14
57 All this is Brahman   Chhandogya Upanishad 3.14.1
58 ¶ A great deal   For some of the details of Shankara's life I
am indebted to Swami Prabhavananda and Christopher Isherwood
(trans.), Shankara, *Crest-Jewel of Discrimination* (Hollywood: The
Vedanta Society, 1947), p. 1ff.
62 creation out of nothing   The sole Biblical reference to this
early Christian doctrine is found in the Apocrypha: 2 Maccabees 7.28.
    qualified mode   For the reference to Ruysbroeck I am in-
debted to Thomas Merton, *Zen and the Birds of Appetite* (New Directions Publishing Corporation, 1968), p. 135.
    Not this, not this   Brihadaranyaka Upanishad 2.3.6
63 ¶ The Hindu scriptures   A fuller treatment of cosmic cycles
is given in John Moffitt, "A Christian Approach to Hindu Beliefs,"
in *Theological Studies* vol. 27, No. 1 (March 1966), p. 63; see also
The Bhagavad Gita (ref. note for p. 16 above), pp. 204-6.
64 ¶ According to a   See *Taittiriya Upanishad* 2.2.1-2; 2.3.1-2;
2.4.1-2; 2.5.1-2; 2.6.1; and the commentary in *The Upanishads*,
Abridged Edition (ref. note for p. 37 above), p. 266, n.33, n.34, n.39,
n.40, n.43.
    What is sown   1 Corinthians 15.42, 44
    Whatever a man   Galatians 6.7
    Even as a person   Bhagavad Gita 2.22
    An eternal portion   Bhagavad Gita 15.7-8
66 themselves in all   Bhagavad Gita 6.29
67 ¶ In the present   A brief summary of Sri Aurobindo's thought
is given in T. M. P. Mahadevan, *Outlines of Hinduism* (Bombay:
Chetana, Ltd., 1966), p. 232ff.
    the glorious liberty   Romans 8.21
68 true light that   John 1.9

68 continued
    God is my being   *Life and Works,* chap. 14; from *The Life and Sayings of St. Catherine of Genoa* (ref. note for p. 43 above), p. 81.
    Inside me I can   *Life and Works,* chap. 14; from *The Life and Sayings of St. Catherine of Genoa,* p. 81.
    When the soul   *Life and Works,* chap. 31; from *The Life and Sayings of St. Catherine of Genoa,* p. 122.
70 Watching the weaver   *This Narrow World* (New York: Dodd, Mead & Co., 1958), p. 60; used by permission.
71 ¶ The man now known   I am indebted for the facts and quotations in this section to *Sri Maharshi: A Short Life Sketch* (Tiruvannamalai: Sri Ramanasramam, 1965); they are used by permission.
74 ¶ During the more   *Self-Enquiry* and *Who Am I?* are published by Sri Ramanasramam, Tiruvannamalai (no date).
76 ¶ Ganapathi and his   *Sri Ramana Gita* is also published by Sri Ramanasramam.

THE VOICE OF DEVOTIONAL SELF-GIVING

79 You shall love   Mark 12.30; see also Deuteronomy 6.5
80 God so loved   John 3.16
    As the Father   John 15.9-10
    Greater love has no   John 15.13
    A new commandment   John 13.34
    ¶ Perhaps, if this   For the reference to St. John, see J. Edgar Bruns, *The Christian Buddhism of St. John* (New York: Paulist Press, 1971), p. 24ff.
82 Thousands of heads   A new rendering of Rig-Veda 10.90; for the complete text see R. T. H. Griffith (trans.), *The Hymns of the Rig-Veda* (Varanasi: Chowkhmaba Sanskrit Series Office, 1963).
83 Rudra, the Lord   *Shvetashvatara Upanishad* 3.2-4 (slightly adapted). Hiranyagarbha, mentioned at the end of this passage, is the same as the Creator God, Brahma, first manifestation of ultimate reality, or Brahman.
84 ¶ The Golden Egg   See *The Upanishads,* Abridged Edition (ref. note for p. 37 above), Glossary, p. 370.
    The Spirit of God   Genesis 1.2
    Unless one is born   John 3.5
86 In whatsoever way   Bhagavad Gita 4.11
    Those persons who   Bhagavad Gita 9.22-24
    Whoever offers me   Bhagavad Gita 9.26-27
    On those who are   Bhagavad Gita 10.10; the commentary is from *The Bhagavad Gita* (ref. note for p. 16 above), p. 240.
87 Behold here today   Bhagavad Gita 11.7
    In an ineffable   *The Bhagavad Gita* (ref. note for p. 16 above), p. 268.
    Thou art the first   Bhagavad Gita 11.38-9 (slightly adapted)
    Neither by the Vedas   Bhagavad Gita 11.53-4
88 He who never hates   Bhagavad Gita 12.13-14, 20
    Again listen   Bhagavad Gita 18.64-6
    Come to me   Matthew 11.28

89 ¶ The child who was   The story of Krishna is adapted from the version in the introductory chapter, "The Story of the Mahabharata," in Swami Nikhilananda (trans.), *The Bhagavad Gita* (ref. note for p. 16 above); I am also indebted for a few incidents to P. Thomas, *Epics, Myths & Legends of India* (ref. note for p. 16 above).

91 Dance! Dance!   *The Living Seed* (New York: Harcourt Brace Jovanich, 1962), p. 74; used by permission.

96 ¶ The poetic tradition   The list of Indian poet saints of this period includes: Kabir (A.D. 1380-1460), Guru Nanak (1469-1539), Chaitanya (1486-1534), Tulsidas (1532-1623), Mirabai (1547-1614), Tukaram (1598-1649), Ramdas (1608-1680). Except for the Bengali songs of Chaitanya, the songs of these poets were written in Hindi.

The longer I live   *Life and Works*, chap. 18; from *The Life and Sayings of St. Catherine of Genoa* (ref. note for p. 43 above), p. 66.

I will have nothing   *Life and Works*, chap. 28; from *The Life and Sayings of St. Catherine of Genoa*, p. 81.

O friend, I am mad   For a complete version of the song, see Bankey Bihari, *Bhakta Mira* (Bombay: Bharatiya Vidya Bhavan, 1961), p. 53.

97 Whom shall I   For the complete song, see *Bhakta Mira*, p. 125.

Listen! The flute   Swami Nikhilananda (trans.), Mahendranath Gupta, *The Gospel of Sri Ramakrishna* (New York: Ramaakrishna-Vivekananda Center, 1942), p. 140; used by permission.

O that he would   Song of Solomon 1.2, 2.10, 3.2, 3.3-4, 5.4, 6, 5.8, 6.3, 8.13-14. In 1.2 I have retained the Hebrew "he" and "his" in place of "you" and "your."

99 As I listen   This saying, not recorded to my knowledge in any of the works on Ramakrishna, was reported by Swami Gnaneswarananda, of the Ramakrishna Order, an accomplished musician and disciple of one of Ramakrishna's disciples. The quotation conveys the gist of Ramakrishna's statement; it is not reproduced word for word.

Beloved, love me   *Tajalliat* 81; translated from a French version in *L'Echo du Sikkhim* (no date).

100 ¶ Tiruppanalvar used   The complete story is given in Swami Ramakrishnananda, *Life of Sri Ramanuja* (Madras: Sri Ramakrishna Math, 1959), p. 29ff.; used by permission.

102 ¶ The caliber of   See *Life of Sri Ramanuja*, p. 149ff.

Om, namo Narayanaya   The word *Om*, a symbol of ultimate reality, is often used at the beginning of a prayer or sacred text as a solemn affirmation, somewhat like "Amen."

¶ Another story   See *Life of Sri Ramanuja* (ref. note for p. 100 above), p. 170.

105 ¶ In his great commentary   For some of the information in this and the following two paragraphs I am indebted to the short article "Vishishtadvaita, the Philosophy of Sri Ramanuja," by Swami Adidevananda, in *Life of Sri Ramanuja* (ref. note for p. 100 above), Appendix C-II, p. 251.

He who inhabits   *Brihadaranyaka Upanishad* 3.7.22,23

106 Beyond this unmanifested   Bhagavad Gita 8.20-21

108 The nature of divine   A new rendering of *Bhakti Sutras* 2-6, 16-21, 25-6, 33, 34-8, 51-2, 58-9, 65, 72-3, 78-9, 82, 84; for the complete text from which these quotations are adapted, see E. T. Sturdy (trans., ed.), *Narada Sutra: An Inquiry Into Love* (London:

108 continued
Longmans, Green & Co., 1896), p. 19ff., used by permission of
Longman's Group Limited, Harlow, England.
109 ¶ In the Puranas For the complete story see *Epics, Myths &
Legends of India* (ref. note for p. 16 above), to which I am indebted
for some of the details.
110 ¶ In many ways For much of the information in this and
the two following paragraphs I am indebted to Swami Nikhilananda,
*The Gospel of Sri Ramakrishna, Abridged Edition (New York:
Ramakrishna-Vivekananda Center, 1958), Appendix, p. 573. Further
details of the system of Tantra are given in Pramathanath Mukho-
padhyaya, "Tantra as a Way of Realization," **Cultural Heritage of
India* (Calcutta: Sri Ramakrishna Centenary Committee, 1937), vol. 2.
111 I have put duality Quoted in James Kritzeck, *Sons of
Abraham* (Baltimore: Helicon Press, Inc., 1965), p. 73; see also James
Kritzeck, *Anthology of Islamic Literature* (New York: Holt, Rinehart
and Winston, 1964), p. 239.
112 In dense darkness The Gospel of Sri Ramakrishna (ref. note
for p. 97 above), p. 692.
 dazzling halo Sambidananda Das, **Sri Chaitanya Mahaprabhu* (Madras: Sri Gaudiya Math, 1961), p. 219.
113 Truth is one Rig-Veda 1.164.46
116 RIGID TRADITION Amrita Bazar Patrika (Calcutta), dateline
of Puri, February 7, 1959.
117 Be humbler and Sri Chaitanya Mahaprabhu (ref. note for
p. 112 above), p. 33.
118 As I lift myself Unpublished poem.
120 Then I saw heaven Revelation 19.11-12, 15
121 ¶ For Christians See Bede Griffiths, "Indian Spirituality and
the Eucharist," *India and the Eucharist* (Bombay, 1964).
122 Though I am unborn Bhagavad Gita 4.6-7
 The Lord is free The Bhagavad Gita (ref. note for p. 16
above), commentary p. 125.
 born in the likeness Philippians 2.7
123 God is born as man The Gospel of Sri Ramakrishna (ref. note
for p. 97 above), p. 186.
 No one knows Teachings of Sri Ramakrishna (Mayavati:
Advaita Ashrama, 1934), p. 59; used by permission.
 As soon as the body Swami Jagadananda (trans.), Swami
Saradananda, *Sri Ramakrishna the Great Master* (Madras: Sri Ramakrishna Math, 1952), p. 9; used by permission.
 I am the syllable Bhagavad Gita 7.8
 of which the name Swami Nikhilananda (trans.), *The Bhagavad Gita* (ref. note for p. 16 above), commentary p. 183.
 All things were made John 1.3
124 In the beginning John 1.1
126 O Rudra, thou who Shvetashvatara Upanishad 3.5
 Lead me from Brihadaranyaka Upanishad 1.3.28
 This Atman . . . is Katha Upanishad 1.2.23
 whom the Supreme Lord The Upanishads, Abridged Edition
(ref. note for p. 37 above), p. 74, n.17.
127 Fix your heart Bhagavad Gita 18.65-6
129 ¶ If I were asked For the facts and quotations in this outline

129 continued
of Chaitanya's life I am indebted to *Sri Chaitanya Mahaprabhu* (ref. note for p. 112 above), and to *The Gospel of Sri Ramakrishna*, Abridged Edition (ref. note for p. 110 above), Appendix p. 567.
132 ¶ *Perhaps even from this*   I am indebted for much of the information in this and the following paragraph to *Sri Chaitanya Mahaprabhu*.
¶ *Nimai's followers*   The list of thirty-two marks is found in *Sri Chaitanya Mahaprabhu*, p. 4; in the third category the word "cheeks" has there been omitted.

THE VOICE OF CONSCIOUS DISCIPLINE

139   Truly, truly, I say   John 12. 24-5
I have been crucified   Galatians 2.20
140 ¶ *The core of spiritual*   For the reference to the gods, compare *Brihadaranyaka Upanishad* 1.4.10; see also *The Upanishads*, Abridged Edition, (ref. note for p. 37 above), p. 192; nn. 10-14.
¶ *A poem I*   Compare Genesis 32.24-8
Who wrestled with   The Living Seed (ref. note for p. 91 above), p. 78; quoted by permission.
141   that in which a man   Bhagavad Gita 18.36-7
142 ¶ *In early Buddhism*   The Theravada Buddhist disciplines are systematically listed in Bhikku Nyanatiloka, *The Word of the Buddha* (ref. note for p. 4 above), p. 26ff.
143 ¶ *The basic treatise*   For the early availability of the Yoga doctrines, see Heinrich Zimmer, *Philosophies of India* (ref. note for p. 4 above), p. 282.
It is comparatively   Vivekananda: The Yogas and Other Works (ref. note for p. 44 above), *Raja-Yoga*, p. 581.
In the study   Vivekananda: The Yogas and Other Works, p. 582.
144   Yoga is not for him   Bhagavad Gita 6.16-17
145   restraining the mind-stuff, etc.   Yoga Sutras 1.2,3; from *Vivekananda: The Yogas and Other Works* (ref. note for p. 44 above), *Raja-Yoga*, pp. 625, 627.
¶ *For our purpose   Yoga Sutras* 2.30; from *Vivekananda: The Yogas and Other Works*, p. 660.
146   The mind of the man   Vivekananda: The Yogas and Other Works, commentary p. 660.
You shall not kill, etc.   Exodus 20.13-17
I undertake not to, etc.   See Paul Dahlke and others, *The Five Precepts* (Kandy: Buddhist Publication Society, 1963), pp. iii, 1-3.
¶ *The second step   Yoga Sutras* 2.32; from *Vivekananda: The Yogas and Other Works*, *Raja-Yoga*, p. 661.
147   He who has not first   Katha Upanishad 1.2.24
humility, modesty   Bhagavad Gita 13.7-11
spiritual treasures   Bhagavad Gita 16.1-3
Posture is that   Yoga Sutras 2.46; from *Vivekananda: The Yogas and Other Works* (ref. note for p. 44 above), p. 664.
The wise man should   Shvetashvatara Upanishad 2.8
He should sit firm   Bhagavad Gita 6.13
The gaze is directed   Swami Nikhilananda (trans.), *The Bha-*

147 *continued*
gavad Gita (ref. note for p. 16 above), commentary p. 166.
During the study Vivekananda: *The Yogas and Other Works,*
(ref. note for p. 44 above), *Raja-Yoga,* p. 586.
¶ *Control of the vital* Yoga Sutras 2.51; from *Vivekananda:
The Yogas and Other Works,* p. 665.
148 Pranayama *is not* Vivekananda: *The Yogas and Other Works,*
p. 592.
finest and highest Vivekananda: *The Yogas and Other Works,*
p. 593.
The yogi of Shvetashvatara Upanishad 2.9
First close the right The Upanishads, Abridged Edition
(ref. note for p. 37 above), p. 130, n.33.
Can you govern Tao Teh Ching 10; translation by Shu-Jen
Tao (hitherto unpublished)
149 ¶ *The fifth step* Yoga Sutras 2.54; from *Vivekananda: The
Yogas and Other Works* (ref. note for p. 44 above), p. 665.
When he completely Bhagavad Gita 2.58
¶ *In the chapter* Vivekananda: *The Yogas and Other Works,*
p. 609.
¶ *The next step* Yoga Sutras 3.1; for control of modifica-
tions of mind, see *Vivekananda: The Yogas and Other Works,* com-
mentary on 1.12-14, pp. 629-630, and on 1.30-38, p. 637.
150 *anything that appeals* Yoga Sutras 1.39
unbroken flow Yoga Sutras 3.2
When the mind has Vivekananda: *The Yogas and Other
Works,* p. 616.
reject the external part Vivekananda: *The Yogas and Other
Works,* p. 616; see also *Yoga Sutras* 3.3.
There is another Yoga Sutras 1.18
The method is to Vivekananda: *The Yogas and Other Works,*
commentary on 1.18 p. 632.
151 *faith, energy, memory* Yoga Sutras 1.20
¶ *We find here* For details about the "Jesus prayer" see
R. M. French (trans.), *The Way of a Pilgrim* (London: Society for
Promoting Christian Knowledge, 1941), pp. 19-21, 23, etc.
For the discriminating Yoga Sutras 4.24; from *Vivekananda:
The Yogas and Other Works,* p. 686.
cloud of virtue Yoga Sutras 4.28
establishment of the Yoga Sutras 4.33
When a man goes Vivekananda: *The Yogas and Other
Works,* p. 613.
152 *does not sink, etc.* Yoga Sutras 3.40, 41, 43
birth, chemical means Yoga Sutras 4.1
When Yoga is practiced Shvetashvatara Upanishad 2. 11,
13
The real nature Vivekananda: *The Yogas and Other Works,*
(ref. note for p. 44 above), p. 645.
153 *With the heart* Bhagavad Gita 6. 29-32
¶ *The swami points out* The details in this and the next
three paragraphs are derived from Swami Siddheswarananda, "Le
Raja-Yoga de St.-Jean de la Croix" (Gretz: Centre Védantique Ramakrichna).
If any man would Luke 9. 23

159 *Not my will*   Luke 22.42
   Unless a grain   John 12.24
   We know that our   Romans 6.6
   pray constantly   1 Thessalonians 5.17
   And if you desire   *The Cloud of Unknowing* (ref. note for
p. 32 above), chap. 7.
   Lord Jesus Christ   Compare Psalm 123.3; Matthew 15.22
160 *Hear, O Israel*   Mark 12.29-30; compare Deuteronomy 6.4-5
   You shall love your   Leviticus 19.18; Mark 12.31
   He who does not love   1 John 4.20
161 *I am in my Father*   John 14.20
   He who abides   John 15.5
   It is very hard   Bhagavad Gita, 11. 52-5
162 *Not this, not this*   *Brihadaranyaka Upanishad* 2.3.6
   Those devotees who   Bhagavad Gita 12.1
   Those who have fixed   Bhagavad Gita 12.2-4
   ¶ *In this key passage*   *The Bhagavad Gita* (ref. note for p.
16 above), commentary p. 274.
   The task of those   Bhagavad Gita 12.5
   But those who   Bhagavad Gita 12.6-7
163 *The man endowed*   Bhagavad Gita 7.18
   Those who . . . worship   Bhagavad Gita 12.3-4
   perfect in yoga   Bhagavad Gita 12.2
   Brahman and Shakti   *The Gospel of Sri Ramakrishna* (ref.
note for p. 97 above), p. 134.
164 *Fix your mind*   Bhagavad Gita 12.8-11
   Janaka asked   *Ashtavakra Samhita* 1.1-2 (ref. note for p. 48
above).
165 *You are that*   *Chhandogya Upanishad* 6.8.7; 6.9.4; 6.10.3;
6.11.3; 6.12.3; 6.13.3; 6.14.3; 6.15.3; 6.16.3 (slightly adapted)
   I am Brahman   *Brihadaranyaka Upanishad* 1.4.10
   Consciousness is Brahman   *Aitareya Upanishad* 3.1.3.
   This Atman is Brahman   *Mandukya Upanishad* 2; *Brihadaranyaka Upanishad* 4.4.5
   Not this, not this   *Brihadaranyaka Upanishad* 2.3.6
   as far as it is   *The Book of Divine Names* 1.5; from John
Parker (trans.), *The Works of St. Denis the Areopagite* (1897),
quoted in Romain Rolland, *Prophets of the New India* (New York:
Albert & Charles Boni, 1930), Appendix pp. 666-7.
   We may venture   *Mystical Theology* 2; from *The Works of
St. Denis the Areopagite,* quoted in *Prophets of the New India.*
166 ¶ *Shankara, in his famous*   The disciplines listed in the following paragraphs are from *Vivekachudamani* 17-30; see Swami Mad-
havananda (trans.), *Vivekachudamani* (Mayavati: Advaita Ashrama,
1952), pp. 7-11.
167 *I am Brahman*   *Brihadaranyaka Upanishad* 1.4.10
   ¶ *A third Yogic discipline*   For the Theravada rule, see *The
Word of the Buddha* (ref. note for p. 4 above), pp. 83-5.
169 *The wind of God's grace*   *Teachings of Sri Ramakrishna* (ref.
note for p. 123 above), p. 275.
   basic principles   For a fuller discussion of the disciplines in
the five following paragraphs see *Sri Chaitanya Mahaprabhu* (ref.
note for p. 112 above), pp. 260-66.

171 ¶ *The tradition*   See Daiji Maruoka and Tatsuo Yoshikoshi, *Noh* (Osaka: Hoikuhsa, 1969), p. 118.
¶ *In addition to the basic*   For more detailed discussions of Tantra ritual and discipline, see T. M. P. Mahadevan, *Outlines of Hinduism* (ref. note for p. 67 above), pp. 206-15; also Heinrich Zimmer, *Philosophies of India* (ref. note for p. 4 above), pp. 581-8.
172 ¶ *The life of one*   For most of the incidents and quotations in this section I am indebted to the Introduction of *The Gospel of Sri Ramakrishna*, (ref. note for p. 97 above), to *Sri Ramakrishna the Great Master* (ref. note for p. 123 above), and *Life of Sri Ramakrishna* (Mayavati: Advaita Ashrama, 1929); they are used by permission.
174 ¶ *But this one*   See p. 152; the reference is to *Shvetashvatara Upanishad* 2. 11,13.
175 *O Mother . . . I throw*   *Life of Sri Ramakrishna* (ref. note for p. 172 above), p. 423.
184 ¶ *It was not till*   For further details of the episode discussed in this and the three following paragraphs see *Sri Ramakrishna The Great Master* (ref. note for p. 123 above), pp. 290-93, and *The Gospel of Sri Ramakrishna* (ref. note for p. 97 above), Introduction, p. 37.

THE VOICE OF SERVICE AND HUMAN COMMUNITY

187 *You shall love*   Mark 12.31
As you wish that   Luke 6.31; for the story of the Good Samaritan, see Luke 10.30-37.
Then the King will   Matthew 25.34-6
Truly, I say   Matthew 25.40
188 *depend all the law*   Matthew 22.40
189 *Abandon all duties*   Bhagavad Gita 18.66
190 ¶ *Citizens in democratic*   Thomas Merton's statement occurs in his paper "Marxism and Monastic Perspectives," *A New Charter for Monasticism* (ref. note for p. xii above), pp. 74-5.
192 ¶ *In India the*   For the parenthetical reference to conscience, see *Manava Dharmashastra* 2.1; mentioned in T. M. P. Mahadevan, *Outlines of Hinduism* (ref. note for p. 67 above), p. 33, n.3.
¶ *Indian society*   See reference note for p. 82 above.
193 *color of one's*   *Outlines of Hinduism* (ref. note for p. 67 above), p. 71.
¶ *We are told*   Bhagavad Gita 18.42,43,44; the analysis of the castes in terms of the *gunas* is given in Swami Nikhilananda's commentary on 18.41, *The Bhagavad Gita* (ref. note for p. 16 above), p. 359.
194 ¶ *A strict system*   For the reference to the *Code of Manu*, see *Philosophies of India* (ref. note for p. 4 above), p. 40.
196 *nowhere to lay*   Matthew 8.20.
197 ¶ *An impressive*   For further discussion of sacrifice, see Swami Nikhilananda's commentary on Bhagavad Gita 3.11-13, *The Bhagavad Gita* (ref. note for p. 16 above), pp. 108-9; also *Outlines of Hinduism* (ref. note for p. 67 above), p. 77. There are two other sacrifices, with which we are not concerned here: the "sacrifice to the gods" (i.e., propitiation through worship) and the "sacrifice to Brahman" (i.e., teaching and reciting the scriptures).
Let [*a man*] *not*   *Taittiriya Upanishad* 3.10.1

198 ¶ It is among   See *The Autobiography of Malcolm X* (New York: Grove Press, 1966), pp. 339-42.
202 No one can remain   Bhagavad Gita 3.5
203 To [your] work, alone   Bhagavad Gita 2.47-8
     Wretched are they   Bhagavad Gita 2.49-50
     The really wise   Tao Teh Ching 77; translation by Shu-Jen Tao (hitherto unpublished).
     But when you give   Matthew 6.3-4
     Not by merely   Bhagavad Gita 3.4, 6-9
204 By action alone   Bhagavad Gita 3.20-23
     Action does not   Bhagavad Gita 4.14-15
     Everyone conscious of   *The Bhagavad Gita* (ref. note for p. 16 above), commentary on 4.15, p. 131.
     He who sees inaction   Bhagavad Gita 4.18
205 I do nothing   Bhagavad Gita 5.8-9
     The action that is   Bhagavad Gita 18.23
     But the action that   Bhagavad Gita 18.24-5
     ¶ The doer of action   Bhagavad Gita 18.26
     One ought not to   Bhagavad Gita 18.48
206 Surrendering, in thought   Bhagavad Gita 18.57
     Karma-yoga, *the*   *Vivekananda: The Yogas and Other Works* (ref. note for p. 44 above), *Karma-Yoga*, p. 459-60
     There arises a   *Vivekananda: The Yogas and Other Works*, p. 461.
207 inaction in action   Bhagavad Gita 4.18
     himself in all beings   Bhagavad Gita 6.29
     seeing the Lord   Bhagavad Gita 6.30
210 May I be born   *Vivekananda: The Yogas and Other Works* (ref. note for p. 44 above), Letters, p. 929.
211 ¶ How Vivekananda   Vivekananda's biography, by Swami Nikhilananda, published in New York by the Ramakrishna-Vivekananda Center in 1953, also forms the opening section of *Vivekananda: The Yogas and Other Works*.
     He recalled what   *Vivekananda: The Yogas and Other Works*, p. 50.
     Compassion for beings   *Sri Ramakrishna the Great Master* (ref. note for p. 123 above), p. 817.
     Until an aspirant   *Sri Ramakrishna the Great Master*, p. 818.
212 ¶ Fired by the example   For further details about the work of the order founded by Vivekananda, see *A New Charter for Monasticism* (ref. note for p. xii above), p. 153ff.
     The masses are   Mao Tse-tung, *Selected Works*, vol. 3, p. 12; from *Quotations From Chairman Mao Tse-tung* (Peking: Foreign Languages Press, 1967), "The Mass Line," p. 118.
213 In all the practical   *Selected Works*, vol. 3, p. 119; from *Quotations From Chairman Mao Tse-tung*, pp. 128-9.
     To link oneself   *Selected Works*, vol. 3, pp. 236-7; from *Quotations From Mao Tse-tung*, p. 124.
     We should pay close   *Selected Works*, vol. 1, p. 149; from *Quotations From Chairman Mao Tse-tung*, p. 132.
     Comrade Bethune's   *Selected Works*, vol. 2, pp. 337-8; from *Quotations From Chairman Mao Tse-tung*, "Serving the People," p. 171.

213 continued

    Wherever there is   *Selected Works,* vol. 3, p. 228; from *Quotations From Chairman Mao Tse-tung,* p. 173.

214 a man who has   Tony White (tians.), Philippe Devillers, *Mao* New York: Schocken, 1969), p. 292; used by permission.

    do good to the poor   See quotation on p. 206 of text, and reference note (*"Karma-yoga,* the") for p. 206 above.

215 ¶ *And yet the moral*   The reference in the next to last sentence of this paragraph is to Mark 11.15-17.

216 ¶ *Mohandas Karamchand*   For the incidents in this section I am indebted to Mahadev Desai (trans.), **Gandhi's Autobiography* (Washington: Public Affairs Press, 1948); Nirmal Kumar Bose, **Studies in Gandhism* (ref. note for p. 39 above); and Robert Payne, **The Life and Death of Mahatma Gandhi* (New York: E. P. Dutton, 1969).

223 ¶ *To Gandhi's surprise*   The statement referred to in the last sentence occurs in *Gandhi's Autobiography,* p. 504; quoted in *The Life and Death of Mahatma Gandhi,* p. 315.

    ¶ *In all, the lawyers*   For Gandhi's remarks about reformers and the government's attitude, see *The Collected Works of Mahatma Gandhi* (New Delhi: Government of India, 1958 and after), vol. 12, p. 405; quoted in *The Life and Death of Mahatma Gandhi,* p. 317. For his formula for success, see D. G. Tendulkar, *Gandhi in Champaran* (Delhi: Government of India, 1957), p. 60; quoted in *The Life and Death of Mahatma Gandhi,* p. 317.

226 ¶ *The vows of a*   See B. P. Sitaramayya, *Gandhi and Gandhism* (Allahabad: Kitabistan, 1943), pp. 178-80; quoted in *The Life and Death of Mahatma Gandhi,* p. 479. For a documented treatment of nonviolent resistance, see *Studies in Gandhism* (ref. note for p. 39 above), "Satyagraha: Its Meaning and Method," pp. 119-76.

227 believe in doing good   See quotation on p. 206 of text, and reference note (*"Karma-yoga,* the") for p. 206 above.

    Before the British   For the full statement see *The Collected Works of Mahatma Gandhi* (ref. note for p. 223 above), vol. 23, p. 115-18; quoted in *The Life and Death of Mahatma Gandhi* (ref. note for p. 216 above), p. 366. Direct quotations from the works of Gandhi are reprinted by permission of the Navajivan Trust, Ahmedabad, India.

228 ¶ *During the two years*   For the details in this paragraph I am indebted to K. T. Mahadevan, "An Approach to the Study of Gandhi," *Gandhi Marg* 49 (ref. note for p. 39 above), pp. 34-5.

    That alone is truth   *Mahabharata* 12.276.19; quoted in "An Approach to the Study of Gandhi," *Gandhi Marg* 49, p. 41.

    show how to epitomize   From "An Approach to the Study of Gandhi," *Gandhi Marg* 49, p. 34.

229 I have not seen him   *Gandhi's Autobiography* (ref. note for p. 216 above), p. 341; used by permission.

    What I want to achieve   *Gandhi's Autobiography,* Introduction, pp. 4-5; used by permission.

    The idea of duty   *Vivekananda: The Yogas and Other Works* (ref. note for p. 44), *Inspired Talks,* Saturday, July 13, 1895, p. 539.

    I believe in the   *Gandhi's Autobiography* (ref. note for p. 216 above), p. 113; used by permission.

230 What message is needed   Sri Maharshi (ref. note for p. 71 above), p. 37.
    Prolonged practical   Sri Maharshi, p. 36.
232 What I want, what I   Pyarelal, *The Epic Fast* (Ahmedabad: Mohanlal Bhatt, 1932), p. 120; quoted in *The Life and Death of Mahatma Gandhi* (ref. note for p. 216 above), p. 442.
233 Truth is God   *Studies in Gandhism* (ref. note for p. 39 above), p. 269. For the reference immediately following the ninety-nine names of Allah, I am indebted to A. Vail and E. McC. Vail, *Transforming Light* (New York: Harper & Row, 1970), p. 305.

TOWARD THE SOURCE OF THE VOICES

238 Out of unaging earth   *The Living Seed* (ref. note for p. 91 above), p. 72; used by permission.
239 So they drew near   Luke 24.28-32
243 All this is   *Mandukya Upanishad* 2; compare also *Chhandogya Upanishad* 3.14.1.
    That is full   *Brihadaranyaka Upanishad,* Invocation; also 5.1.1
246 ¶ Gadadhar Chattopadhyaya   For most of the incidents and quotations in this and the following section I am indebted to *Life of Sri Ramakrishna* (ref. note for p. 172 above), *The Gospel of Sri Ramakrishna* (ref. note for p. 97 above), and *Sri Ramakrishna the Great Master* (ref. note for p. 123 above); they are used by permission.
    Khudiram, I am well   Compare Matthew 1.20-21.
248 I have become old   Compare Luke 2.25-32.
    ¶ On another occasion   Compare Luke 2.46-7.
249 ¶ This willingness   With regard to Ramakrishna's accepting initiation, compare Matthew 3.15.
    ¶ During the period   Compare Philippians 2.7.
    ¶ As we observed   Compare Matthew 5. 39, 44.
    ¶ Another time when   Compare Isaiah 53.5.
250 ¶ This capacity   See p. 211 of text; compare Matthew 10.42 and Luke 10.30-37.
    ¶ It was only   Compare Isaiah 53.4 (nn. *x, y*).
    ¶ Near the end   Compare Isaiah 53.4 (nn. *x, y*).
251 ¶ Ramakrishna's physical   For the reference to drunkards etc., compare Matthew 9.10-13.
    ¶ According to the   Compare Matthew 14.13-20.
    ¶ An amusing and   Compare Luke 10.38-42; also John 12.2-3. For the complete story, see *The Gospel of Sri Ramakrishna* (ref. note for p. 97 above), pp. 822-5.
252 ¶ Another day   Compare John 10.16.
253 ¶ It has been claimed   For the complete story, see Swami Siddheswarananda, "Le Yoga de St.-Jean de la Croix" (Gretz: Centre Védantique Ramakrichna, 1949), p. 15; compare Isaiah 53.3 (nn. *v, w*), 4-5.
254 Greater love has   John 15.13
    I have gone on suffering   *The Gospel of Sri Ramakrishna* (ref. note for p. 97 above), p. 941.
    I am going through   Swami Nikhilananda, *Holy Mother* (New York: Ramakrishna-Vivekananda Center, 1962), p. 92; compare Isaiah 53.4-5.

254 continued
    If I have told you   "The Sages of India," *The Complete Works of Swami Vivekananda* (ref. note for p. 44 above), vol. 3, p. 268.
257   *The Christian scriptures*   "Le Yoga de St.-Jean de la Croix" (ref. note for p. 253 above), p. 14.
    Unless you turn   Matthew 18.3; compare same 11.25; Mark 10.15; Luke 18.17.
    Ask, and it will   Matthew 7.7-8
    Cry to your Mother   For the full song, see p. 267 of text.
    ¶ *We read earlier*   For Ramakrishna's prayer see p. 175 of text; for the Lord's Prayer see Matthew 6.9-13.
    The words that I say   John 14.10
    O Mother, all is   *The Gospel of Sri Ramakrishna* (ref. note for p. 97 above), p. 818.
    An evil and adulterous   Compare Matthew 16.1, 4.
258   *So long as the child, etc.*   The quotations on pp. 258-9 are from *The Gospel of Sri Ramakrishna* (ref. note for p. 97 above, "Listen! The flute"), pp. 149, 83, 83, 116, 133, 631, 265, 561, 237, 678, 102, 288, 417, 479.
259   ¶ *Ramakrishna's biographer*   *Sri Ramakrishna the Great Master* (ref. note for p. 123 above), p. 298; also the same, p. 256.
260   *There is a state*   *The Gospel of Sri Ramakrishna* (ref. note for p. 97 above), pp. 935-936.
262   *Let me tell you*   *Holy Mother* (ref. note for p. 254 above), p. 319. The details in the two preceding paragraphs are also from this work.
    In a recent and   Sri Aurobindo, *The Synthesis of Yoga* (Pondicherry: Sri Aurobindo International University Centre of Education, 1957), p. 45; quoted in Romain Rolland, *Prophets of the New India* (ref. note for p. 165 above), p. 268; used by permission.
    The story of Ramakrishna   *Life of Sri Ramakrishna* (ref. note for p. 172 above), Foreword.
263   *I put it to myself*   From a letter to the author dated March 18, 1971; used by permission of the writer.
264   ¶ *A few months*   A report of the World Council of Churches meeting, "From Proclamation to Dialogue," by John C. Haughey, was published in *America,* vol. 124, No. 18 (May 8, 1971), p. 483; the quotations are used by permission.
265   *You may say that*   *The Gospel of Sri Ramakrishna* (ref. note for p. 97 above), p. 112.
266   *Lady Julian of Norwich*   *America,* vol. 124, No. 13 (April 3, 1971), p. 329; reprinted by permission of publisher and writer, and revised by the latter.
    As one whom his mother   Isaiah 66.13
    O Jerusalem   Matthew 23.37
267   *O Mother, I throw*   *Life of Sri Ramakrishna* (ref. note p. 172 above), p. 423; for the full prayer, see p. 175 of text.
    Cry to your Mother   *The Gospel of Sri Ramakrishna* (ref. note for p. 97 above), p. 83.
268   *What is now called*   *The Retractations* 1.12.3; from *The Fathers of the Church* (Washington: Catholic University of America Press, 1968), vol. 60, p. 52.

269   *Truly, truly, I say*   John 8:58
        Lo, I am with you   Matthew 28.20
        Go therefore and make   Matthew 28.19-20
        In the beginning   John 1.1,4,14
        in these last days, etc.   Hebrews 1.2,3
270   *The times of ignorance*   Acts 17.30-31
        Before Abraham was   John 8.58
271   *Here is the whole*   Algar Thorold (trans.), J. P. de Caussade,
Self-Abandonment to Divine Providence (Burns and Oates Ltd., 1952),
p. 9.
272   *See, see, where*   Christopher Marlowe, *The Tragical History*
of Dr. Faustus, Act 5, scene 4.
        In him was life   John 1.4
273   *full of grace, etc.*   John 1.14, 16
        Idealism and metaphysics   *Quotations From Chairman Mao*
Tse-tung (ref. note for p. 212 above), "Methods of Thinking and
Methods of Work," p. 212; introductory note to "Material on the
Hu Feng Counter-Revolutionary Clique" (May 1955).
275   *religiously endowed, etc.*   *A Flower Does Not Talk* (ref. note
for p. 44 above), p. 48.
        Those who have not   *A Flower Does Not Talk*, p. 34.
        Zen and Christianity   *A New Charter for Monasticism* (ref.
note p. xii), Narrative Introduction, p. 6.
276   *How wondrously*   Quoted in Daisetz T. Suzuki, *Essays in*
Zen Buddhism, First Series (New York: Grove Press, 1961), p. 319.
        Tao [ultimate truth]   D. T. Suzuki in Thomas Merton, *Zen*
and the Birds of Appetite (ref. note for p. 62 above), p. 134.
        Die while alive   *A Flower Does Not Talk* (ref. note for p. 44
above), p. 46.
        What are the hindrances   Maud Piggott, "My Reminiscences
of Ramana Maharshi," *The Mountain Path* (Tiruvannamalai: Sri
Ramanasramam); quoted in *Vedanta and the West*, November-
December 1970 (Hollywood: The Vedanta Center), p. 43; used by
permission of Sri Ramanasramam.
        anything that appeals   *Yoga Sutras* 1.39; see also *Vivekan-*
anda: The Yogas and Other Works (ref. note for p. 44 above), commentary in *Raja-Yoga*, p. 641.
277   *O righteous Father*   John 17.25-26
        I AM WHO I AM   Exodus 3.14
278   *engaging in a risk*   Robert McAfee Brown and Gustav Weigel,
S.J., *An American Dialogue* (Garden City: Doubleday & Co., 1960),
p. 112.
        But who do you say   Matthew 16.15, 16
        Among you stands one   John 1.26
279   *Between me and the*   *The Living Seed* (ref. note for p. 91
above), p. 92.
        Behold, I stand   Revelation 3.20

INDEX